Being Here...Too

Short Stories of
Modern Day Enlightenment

ARIEL & SHYA KANE

Copyright ASK Productions, Inc. © 2018.
All Rights Reserved

Library of Congress Cataloging-in-Publication Data

Kane, Ariel.
    Being here...too, short stories of modern day
    enlightenment / by Ariel & Shya Kane.
    ISBN-13: 978-1-888043-20-4

    1. Self-help 2. Spirituality 3. Happiness.
    I. Kane, Shya. II. Title

The publisher gratefully acknowledges the many individuals who
granted ASK Productions, Inc. permission to reprint their essays.

Library of Congress Control Number: 2018956936

Cover Design – Wendy Madhusudan
Layout Design – Stefanie Lück
Photo of Kanes – Terri Diamond
Editor – Andrea Cagan

Instantaneous Transformation® is a registered trademark of
ASK Productions, Inc.

To all of our ancestors:

Thank you for enduring life's privations

so that we all can be here

and make transformation available to the world.

CONTENTS

FOREWORD

Like all of the contributors in this book, I have experienced Instantaneous Transformation: a way of accessing a deep sense of well-being developed by seminar leaders and authors Ariel and Shya Kane. I like to call it the "lazy person's way to enlightenment" because it's so easy. I remember walking out of my first transformational seminar with the Kanes in 2006 and strolling up 8th Avenue in Manhattan. Everything seemed bright, clear, and three-dimensional in a way it never had before. It was so…quiet, even in the heart of New York City.

I suddenly realized that for the first time in my life, my mind was quiet. I was simply experiencing what was around me, rather than listening to the incessant internal chatter that picked on me, picked on others, and worried. It was as if I had "shed a skin" during that course and found the person I truly was, hidden behind all that mind chatter.

Before long, life got busy and I drifted away from attending seminars. I missed the Kanes, the transformational community, and the feelings I remembered from that post-seminar walk up 8th Avenue – but I told myself I didn't need it anymore and could find it somewhere else. While I wasn't particularly happy, I was productive and successful during that time. Although my relationship broke down, I moved up in my career from being a New York City public school teacher to an assistant principal, and then eventually I became the founding principal of my own public high school.

One day, six years later, I was feeling stressed and tired and I realized that I wanted things to be easy again. When I searched on Google for the Kanes, I found they had a new book, *How to Have A Match Made in Heaven.* I ordered a copy and when it came, I took the book to Central Park, sat on the grass and started to read. Soon I felt a weight lifting off my shoulders, a weight I didn't even know I'd been carrying.

I saw that I had been resisting all authority figures: my parents, my boss, other school principals, and even educational consultants that I had chosen and hired. It was so obvious, and yet I felt no remorse or regret. I just saw it as the truth, neither bad nor good. In fact, I was able to see the humor in it. Even though I was a high school principal, I was being as bratty and resistant as some of my students.

Over the next several weeks, I continued to see more examples of how I was resisting the life I had chosen and was currently living. I subsequently shared my experience with the Kanes in an email. Then one evening, I gathered the courage to come back to one of their Monday Night Alive seminars. My heart was pounding as the elevator doors opened in the New Yorker Hotel where the event was taking place.

"Hi," Shya said. "We know you!"

And that was it. They welcomed me back as if no time had passed. That evening, I stood on the stage and said, "Hi, I'm Julie and I'm a brat."

Ariel looked at me thoughtfully. "You know," she said, "you wrote us the loveliest email about all these epiphanies you're having, and thanked us for writing our last book. Maybe you were acting like a brat in the past, but you're not a brat now."

It was true. Ariel's words opened up a space of non-judgment for me to realize that I had transformed. All it took was for me to see my behavior and it dissolved, no work or pain involved.

From that day on, I became a full participant in the Kanes' courses and their transformational community. Life has gotten simpler and far more fulfilling. I'm now in a loving relationship that is a true partnership. My job feels easy and satisfying. Whether I'm filling out paperwork, leading a meeting with teachers, organizing a fire drill, or coaching a student, each interaction becomes all-encompassing and satisfying, the only thing I want to be doing in that moment.

Of course, unexpected situations arise that don't fit into my "plan" of how my day should go. But I'm quickly able to recognize that what I have planned and what I prefer doesn't matter. Taking care of what's happening in the moment does. So I drop my preference and handle each unplanned situation as it arises as if it's my idea. All it takes is being here and engaging in what's actually happening rather than investing in a complaint that things aren't going the way I want.

The following chapters are written by ordinary people from all walks of life who are living extraordinary lives. Their stories are about discovering they are exactly where they want to be, whether it's studying for an exam, going through childbirth, or being with a cousin on her deathbed.

I invite you to immerse yourself in *Being Here...Too*. That's enough to bring you into the current moment where you, too, can effortlessly access your own brilliance and experience the extraordinary nature of life.

Julie – Bronx, New York

PREFACE

It was early in 1987 when a chance meeting on the streets of Manhattan led us to our careers as seminar leaders, coaches, authors and radio show hosts. On that fateful day, we ran into an old friend of ours. He'd known that we'd been seeking to improve the quality of our lives for years, trying every self-help technique under the sun – from affirmations and goal-setting to a two-year stint in a meditation center. Staring at us, wide-eyed, he suddenly said, "What are you doing now? You are so different. I've never seen you so…peaceful, so relaxed, looking so well."

We assured him that we weren't doing anything special, that we were just living. He thought for a moment, then asked, "Can you come talk with my friends and my company? You're clearly on to something real."

As we sat down with folks for the first time, we didn't want to tell anybody how to live their lives. Rather, we wanted to do our best to describe how we were approaching *our* lives.

It was quite a challenge back then to articulate how our lives had instantaneously transformed. It was hard to explain because it was so simple. It often felt as if we were speaking a foreign language that people were struggling to understand. We saw that no matter how good our explanation, people translated what we said through what they already knew, which simply reinforced what they already believed. We recognized that we needed to create the experience of transformation, not explain it as a concept. It quickly became clear that one of the most effective ways to illustrate the ideas we were talking about was to offer real examples from our own lives. Perhaps we were calling upon humanity's rich tradition of storytelling – harkening back to simpler times where important life lessons were passed on from one generation to the next through an oral tradition.

So we began to relate anecdotes about our experiences – funny stories, poignant encounters, and the ordinary moments that made our lives extraordinary. People listened and asked questions. We saw tension fall away as individuals dropped into the moment and spontaneously experienced well-being. Watching their faces light up we realized that transformation was a communicable "ease." In that moment, our seminars came into being.

As we write this more than thirty years later, we feel fortunate to have touched the lives of so many people who now have experienced the possibility of Instantaneous Transformation for themselves.

Our approach is simple. It's all about being here in the current moment – a rare thing for most of us since we've been taught to rehash the past and to strive for future accomplishments. The two of us have discovered that a new possibility exists to access and actually live in the experience of the current moment – that you can slow down enough to be here for your life as it unfolds. By merely being where you are in current time, rather than worrying about a future that hasn't gotten here or fretting about things from the past, your life becomes an effortless expression of yourself. As this happens, your day-to-day experience of living literally transforms so that accomplishments come naturally and things you have strived to change dissolve on their own, like ice on a warm summer's day.

The majority of the stories in *Being Here... Too* have been written by the people who have participated with us in this radical, yet gentle form of self-discovery. Each of the anecdotes is a roadmap to Instantaneous Transformation. In the following pages, we share with you the possibility that life can be easy and life will support you if you let it.

We've been deeply moved by the courage and magnificence of our contributors. As you read their words and absorb their experiences, we imagine you will be spontaneously touched by your own magnificence as well.

~ Ariel & Shya Kane

PART ONE:

THE MAGIC OF BEING BOLDLY YOU

1

ANDY'S PERFECT EARS

By Ariel and Shya – Milford, New Jersey

*O*ne day, on an antiquated subway car, Andy discovered that his ears were perfect. Oh, but there had been a time when they were not. Kids can be cruel after all.

Growing up in St. Joseph, Missouri, Andy was a normal boy except for one thing – his exceptionally large, stick-out-from-his-head ears. For as long as he could remember his big ears had been a source of embarrassment. His parents loved him and his mom thought he was cute but she was his mother after all and Andy knew she was biased. He was certain that she was mistaken about how he looked and he had proof.

Once, when Andy was about ten, he waited with several other kids at the bus stop for "Ol' Yeller," the old yellow school bus. Wearing a red t-shirt, blue jeans and high tops, Andy was self-conscious. He kept looking down at his feet, which had started to outgrow the rest of his body, and he was upset when his friends began to taunt him. But they didn't razz him about his feet. It seems that his ears had caught the early morning sun as it rose above a neighboring rooftop.

"Look, it's Dumbo!" one of the boys said.

"Yeah, just like that elephant. Hey Andy, you could fly with those things!" another boy yelled. Everybody

3

laughed. Andy was dumbstruck. He couldn't think of anything to say in return. Ears aflame, Andy tried to hide them, which only made things worse.

Within the next couple of years, Andy began to dream about being an actor and he confided in a teacher about his ambitions.

"You better get your ears pinned back then," his teacher said. "Yours are just too much."

In middle school, Jake Pressman, a popular boy, said Andy looked like a taxicab with both back doors thrown open and that convinced him that he would never have a girlfriend.

In high school, Andy grew his hair as long as his parents would allow. When they made him get a haircut, he wore a stocking cap pulled down low to disguise his ears and he eventually began wearing that cap all the time, even in the summer. When he started to grow facial hair, Andy discovered that big, long sideburns drew a person's eye and his ready smile was great camouflage for those unwanted "flaps" on the side of his head.

When Andy turned nineteen, he took a breath, took a leap and moved to New York City to pursue his dream of acting. He became a pizza server by night and an aspiring actor by day. He didn't like his headshots and his auditions and casting calls didn't go well. But Andy was talented – he knew he was. Something must be wrong! Could it be his ears?

One day, a fellow actor invited him to a Monday Night Alive event in Manhattan. Intrigued, he asked what it was about.

"It's about living in the moment," his friend said, "and accessing your hidden genius."

That sounded interesting so he decided to give it a try. Little did Andy know that part of his genius lay hidden behind shaggy hair, long sideburns and a killer smile.

One evening, after he had attended the Monday

seminars for a while, Shya suggested to Andy that he would be more hirable if he trimmed his hair and shaved the sideburns. Andy barely suppressed a laugh. His girlfriend, Leah, had been telling him the same thing. She said she found him cute and sexy but she was his girlfriend after all and Andy knew she was biased. But Shya looked so sincere and had never steered him wrong before. This time he had to take notice.

"OK," he said. "I'll do it."

Standing in front of the mirror the next morning, Andy took a breath, took a leap and applied razor to face. Later that same day, he got a great haircut. It felt like he had come out of hiding. The sun no longer seemed to shine through his ears. Rather he saw that it lit up his face. It was the beginning of a new Andy. It was perfection.

Fast forward a couple of years and Andy's manager called. "You just got offered a job in a new Steven Spielberg project. They specifically asked for you because they love your look, especially your ears! I told you they would make you money."

The following day Andy spoke with Mr. Spielberg's assistant. "Your call time will be at seven thirty," he'd said, "but come early if you want and look around."

Who wouldn't want to come early? Andy thought.

That morning, nerves all a jumble, Andy kissed his wife Leah goodbye and stepped out of his Brooklyn apartment. He headed to the Brooklyn Transit Museum where he was scheduled to shoot that morning. The movie was a period piece and they were doing the scene in one of the vintage cars.

The lights, the set, the cables, the costumes, and the crew – it was all very exciting. But nowhere near as exciting as playing a role with a famous actor he had admired his whole life – Tom Hanks. And *that* was nothing compared to hearing Mr. Spielberg's heartfelt comment, "Andy, if Norman Rockwell were alive today, he would surely paint you."

That day, they shot scene after scene including several close ups of Andy and his exceptionally large, stick-out-from-his head, absolutely perfect ears.

2

BEING COMPLETELY, UNAPOLOGETICALLY ME!

By Tracy – Manhattan, New York

I remember attending my first Monday Night Alive seminar in New York City. Midway through the evening, we took a break and the room was buzzing with excited energy from all the attendees. I'd never been among so many happy people before and I felt like I didn't fit in. I hid, standing at the back of the room and pretending to look at the books displayed on a table. Then I picked up a copy of *Working on Yourself Doesn't Work*.

I thought, *Wow! Catchy title.*

The subtitle read: The 3 Simple Ideas That Will Instantaneously Transform Your Life.

Intrigued, I turned to the back cover to discover the Three Principles of Instantaneous Transformation:

The First Principle: What you resist persists and grows stronger.

This made sense and made me laugh to myself as I thought of all the things I resisted that didn't seem to go away.

The Second Principle: You can only be exactly as you are in the moment.

Yes, I thought. *That makes sense, too.*

And the Third Principle: Anything you allow to be

exactly as it is completes itself.

Huh? That one stumped me.

Until that night, I was used to relying on my mind to try to figure out everything in a logical manner. Logic is something I've always liked. It led me to study engineering and eventually work as an engineer, designing and implementing heating and cooling systems for large buildings in New York City.

In the small town where I grew up, working on yourself was part of the culture. You weren't considered normal if you weren't being critical towards yourself or someone else. This was the culture I absorbed as a child and, at the same time, I sensed there might be another possibility.

Growing up, I had watched *Oprah* during dinner and a new world opened as I got a sense of *something* that I couldn't learn at university. When I went to a bookstore, looking for that something, I began skimming the self-help sections. I checked to see if anyone I knew was around and then I casually and coolly slid over to the self-help section as if I had it all together, as if I was there because my sister or friend needed the book, not me. I was worried back then about what other people thought.

When I moved to New York, I was less hesitant in approaching the self-help section, but only because I didn't know anyone who might be judging me. I still carried around a sense of embarrassment and concern about what other people thought, not only at the bookstore but in all aspects of my life. I was hard on myself, working on all my flaws as if I needed to change my life and be a better version of me. I thought I should be further along in my life financially, I should be less shy, I should be an artist, and I should be in a relationship. I felt I needed to improve. I needed to change. I knew it would be hard work and require focus to get from where I was to where I needed to be. I made a lot of lists of what I needed to do to meet my goals and I analyzed them repeatedly. But when I finally found the book *Working on Yourself Doesn't Work*, it made me smile. It went against everything I believed, and at the same time I hoped it might be true.

A few months after I moved to New York, I saw a postcard for a series of Monday Night Alive seminars led by Ariel and Shya Kane. I thought they looked interesting but I didn't end up going. I hesitated. I second-guessed myself. I postponed the moment, which was how I lived my life back then. Life moved on. I worked at my job as an engineer. And then, two years later, a coworker introduced me to an architect named Karen. She invited me via email to meet her at one of those very same Monday Night Alive events. This time I said, "Yes." I couldn't turn away from serendipity like that.

On that first night, after hovering around the book display table during the break, I purchased *Working on Yourself Doesn't Work* and started reading it as soon as I got home. It intrigued me and I was inspired to come back for more.

After attending my second or third Monday night event, I signed up for one of the Kanes' weekend seminars: The Freedom to Breathe and Art of Being a Healer. The weekend was an incredible experience for me, and what I remember most was the Freedom to Breathe day, which happened on Saturday. We each had the opportunity to do a breathing technique while a partner sat with us. It was amazing to have someone there to support me in being myself, exactly as I was, doing nothing, just breathing. It was emotional, it was moving, it was peaceful, it was happy, and it was challenging at times. When it was over, I felt I'd gone to a spa for my body, mind, and soul. I felt perfect. I felt I was perfect.

That was a first! My mind was clear. It wasn't questioning or picking on me. I felt more awake yet more relaxed and more like me. There was nowhere to get to, nothing to improve, no moment more perfect than being exactly where I was. I had a spontaneous experience of being in the moment, something up until that point, I had only heard or read about. I had bypassed my mind and found the moment – or the moment had found me. The experience was simple. It was so extraordinary and profound, I've taken every Freedom to Breathe and Art of Being a Healer seminar Ariel and Shya have held in New York since. The experience is always new and refreshing.

I still visit the self-help section at the bookstore sometimes, but now I walk with confidence and ease, no longer looking for a book for my fictitious sister. I don't worry who might be watching or what they might be thinking. In fact, I walk with more ease in every area of my life now, which has been one of my biggest transformations. My mind still picks on me from time-to-time, but my critical thoughts have softened and are not nearly so hard on me anymore. I'm comfortable in myself. I smile more often and notice the little miracles in life. I sit on a subway and proudly display the cover of *Working on Yourself Doesn't Work* or any other book that I am reading. As I write this piece, I'm not worrying that someone may see what I'm writing. Most of all, I feel that it's okay to be completely, unapologetically me.

3

THE TOURIST

By Paul – Brooklyn, New York

*T*oday I did something bold. I spontaneously let go of my identity as a "Native New Yorker" and gave myself permission to be a tourist. Here's what happened:

Recently I started a job in close proximity to Rockefeller Center in New York City. When I got off work early, instead of immediately getting on the subway as usual, I suddenly thought, *I've got a couple hours to kill before yoga. Maybe I'll go to the Top of the Rock.* That's the observation deck of 30 Rockefeller Plaza, a seventy-story skyscraper.

Feeling adventurous and hungry, I crossed the street and fired up the Maps application on my phone. *Pizza,* I typed in. A few local "slice" establishments came up, but the closest one with a decent rating was somewhere in 30 Rockefeller Plaza. I'd gone around the block twice when I realized the pizza place was inside the building. I walked through two big brass-lined doors into the iconic landmark for the first time in my life.

Wow. Everything about the inside of this building was immaculate: the polished stone floors trimmed with gold, the retro floor numbers that designated which sets of elevators went where, and the guards who stood by the shiny gold turnstiles.

I walked past a couple of shops, but still no sign

of pizza. I punched in the phone number of the Italian Pizza Kitchen. "Hi," I said, "where are you located?"
"Inside 30 Rockefeller Plaza."
"I'm there, but where exactly?"
"On the concourse level."
"Okay, great. Where is that exactly? Downstairs?"
"Yes."
When I walked in from the street, I didn't realize that an entire shopping mall lived beneath this building. It's like a little city of its own, lined with shops and restaurants. I descended a flight of stairs and made my way to the pizza place. There, I joined other travelers at the counter who were eager to experience a real New York slice.

When I finished my favorite, pepperoni with extra cheese, I was ready for the "real" purpose of my little personal outing. The sign was pretty easy for us newcomers to find:
TOP OF THE ROCK – TICKETS
"How much to go up?" I asked the concierge.
"It's thirty-two dollars for adults."
Whoa boy. Thirty-two dollars to ride up an elevator? I thought it was going to be free. I wasn't sure I still wanted to go up. I checked my phone. *Hmm, still ninety minutes 'til yoga.*

The ticket machine didn't accept my credit card at first but eventually I got a screen with big green letters that said, "Purchase Tickets." *What the hell.* I hit the button.

When you buy a ticket for the Top of the Rock, you get assigned a time to arrive at the elevator to keep everything moving smoothly. When it was time for my ride, I gave my ticket to one of the nicest ticket-takers I'd ever met. I got on the elevator with a family and an older couple. As it ascended, we couldn't wait to see what was on the other side of the door. The doors opened and there it was – a longer line, to the main elevator.

At this point, I had to go through security like it was an airport. The doors opened, we all stepped in and the elevator operator announced with enthusiasm, "Okay, ladies and gentlemen, you're on your way up tooo theeee SIXTY-seventh floor of 30 Rockefeller Plaza...arriving in approximately thirty seconds. Enjoooy theeee ride!!!"

The lights dimmed and the ride up felt like a 90's music video, or a middle school birthday party at an arcade. What happened next I only half expected, but man-oh-man. I'd never been up that high in New York City. I followed the crowd to the observation deck on the sixty-seventh floor and the first thing I saw was the Empire State Building. I'd seen it before, of course, but this was the first time it wasn't towering over me. It wasn't a megalith in the distance, a symbol of modern engineering and architectural discovery. I saw it as my peer. I was walking slower than some of the others who rushed past to get to the last escalator to the observation deck. "Ohhh myyy Gawd" came out of my mouth. The woman next to me seemed pleased by my exhilaration. I smiled at her and got on the escalator that took me up a little further to another observation deck.

I spent a good twenty minutes there, standing in the same spot, staring at my city in astonishment. This triumph of humanity struck me as a natural wonder, like seeing the Rocky Mountains for the first time or flying over the Grand Canyon.

Suddenly I realized that my life had quietly transformed. I don't know how old I was when I decided that being a tourist was something to look down upon but that internalized idea had prevented me from enjoying many things. It occurred to me then that people from out of town had seen many of the wonders of my city that I had been denying myself because I thought that being a tourist wasn't "cool."

Going to the Top of the Rock wasn't something I thought a New Yorker did on a weekday afternoon, if at all. But now, the experience was vibrant and full of childlike discovery. Even walking through the catacombs beneath the tower had filled me with a sense of wonder I hadn't often felt in my adult life.

With the tool of transformation in my pocket, so to speak, I didn't spend a lot of time second-guessing myself. Though initially I thought about just getting on the subway, skipping yoga class and heading home, I didn't. Then when I stood at the ticket machine hesitating to spend thirty-two dollars on myself to "use an elevator," I went ahead and purchased my ticket because that's what I really wanted. I'll let you know if I ever feel the thirty-two dollar deficit in my bank account.

I'd lived in the New York City area for most of my life, judging tourists. I'd believed that tourists got in the way, they walked too slowly, they looked silly, and didn't know what the *real* New York City was about and never would. In the past, those judgments kept me from being a tourist myself. Now I've noticed a newfound willingness to drop stories like this. If I hadn't, I would have missed this amazing afternoon. I feel like I have a life of possibilities that didn't exist before.

I left 30 Rockefeller Plaza giddy and full of energy. I got on the subway, took out my phone right then and there and started writing about my trip.

So here's the tourist reporting back: New York City is a great place to visit! And, don't be afraid – being a tourist is cool.

4

THREE BIG "SCREW IT" MOMENTS THAT LED ME TO ENLIGHTENMENT

By Aaron – Boulder, Colorado

I've always had an impulsive personality. For many decisions in my life, I haven't tended to think long and hard. I just went for it and lived with the consequences. This especially pertained to things I thought of as "cool" or things I wanted. As a result, this trait has been alternately beneficial and detrimental to my life and well-being.

Traditionally, I've been hard on myself about my impulsiveness. For the most part, I thought I was irresponsible and a bit reckless with my body and my choices. I still falter at times, but I've learned that this trait has also been one of my greatest assets.

"Screw it" Moment Number 1

A few years ago, I was in a relationship that wasn't going anywhere, I dreaded going to my job every morning, and I constantly wondered why I wasn't happy. I had the things I thought I needed to be well in myself, but I wasn't at ease. It was time for a change and I had the idea to just move and start over. I thought that a new environment and location would be the key to solving all my "problems." From as far back as I can remember, I had the desire to move away to a new city, so now was the perfect opportunity.

It wasn't an easy decision to make. I'd never lived more than thirty minutes away from my family and I would be all alone in a new city. But my desire to change my current circumstances was greater than my fear of leaving my old life behind. I said, "Screw it," and in the course of three months, I had moved from the suburbs of Kansas City to my new home in Denver, Colorado.

I got settled, took on a new job and made new friends. I found it thrilling and exciting, but each night when I was alone I felt empty. This move was supposed to make me happy, but I was feeling bewildered and frustrated.

"Screw it" Moment Number 2

I'd been living in Denver for about six months and I was struggling. Getting settled into a new city and a new job had its challenges. My main challenge was dealing with the lingering effects of a nasty breakup that coincided with my move. The repercussions from the fallout of the relationship were all-consuming and affected every area of my life. It was a huge drain for both my ex-girlfriend and me. I didn't know what to do or to whom I could turn.

A couple of years prior, I'd stumbled across a podcast on the internet that featured an interview with Ariel and Shya Kane. I enjoyed listening to them, their approach, and how they interacted with the show guests and each other. They were so easy to relate to, truly genuine, and they seemed to have a wonderful relationship. Afterwards, I looked them up online and bought their book *Working on Yourself Doesn't Work*. On occasion, I also listened to podcasts of their internet radio show, *Being Here*. In my despair, they were the ones who came to mind to get advice about my relationship woes.

I reached out to Ariel and Shya and had an hour-long phone consultation with them. I gained so much clarity. They didn't judge me or my circumstances. I felt truly heard, which was somewhat of a first for me. Near the end of the call, the Kanes invited me to come to New York City for one of their weekend seminars. They talked about all the brilliant and amazing people who attended them. I felt that I wasn't brilliant or amazing, but I wanted to be. I had seen these courses offered on their website, but it had never crossed my mind that I would actually attend one. I thought that I knew enough and I didn't need anyone's help. But the call went so well, I considered their invitation.

A few weeks later, I said, "Screw it, I'm going to New York City."

"Screw it" Moment Number 3

Being in New York City was an amazing experience. I had never been there before, so I planned to stay a few extra days to explore. It was surreal for me being in such a big and beautiful city.

Initially, the seminar was confronting. I had taken a leap of faith and jumped on a plane to take a seminar about creativity and intuition with people I'd never met. The first night of the seminar, I went to the Penthouse Ballroom of the Skyline Hotel where the event was taking place. I stepped out of the elevator and heard loud conversation and laughter. I thought, *What am I getting myself into?* Ariel and Shya greeted me warmly and while I waited for start time, I chatted with some attendees. I thought, *Wow, how can these people be so damn happy?*

The seminar was amazing! It was an eye-opening experience for me about what was possible in my life. I saw firsthand how genuine and amazing the Kanes and all the people who attended were. I also discovered that I, too, was amazing, just for being myself.

Fast forward about a year. I had attended a few more weekend seminars. I was ingraining the habit of living in the moment. My experience of happiness and well-being was becoming an everyday, moment-to-moment reality rather than a pipe dream. I was strengthening my ability to say "yes" to how my life was showing up, even when the circumstances weren't what I preferred. I felt more in tune with myself and was able to find joy in things I once despised, especially my work.

I've learned that enlightenment is not a destination or something that's achieved, but rather, it's a moment-to-moment lifestyle. Enlightenment is possible right here, right now, in each moment. As I practiced being present, I began to decode my impulsive behavior. I'd always thought that only women possessed intuition, but I discovered that I have it, too. I realized that my choice to move to a new city and to meet the Kanes was an example of acting on my intuition and not just a random impulse.

Around this time, I felt the urge to make another change. I wanted to leave my current job and start a new career in the health and fitness industry. For years, I had wanted to make this transition, but I was always too scared to do it. I was in a safe job that paid really well and I had a great future with the company. This time, though, while I still had some fear and anxiety around changing my career, I felt comfortable enough in myself that I could just go for it and trust that things would work out.

I said, "Screw it. Let's do this!"

I've since started my own health and fitness business. There are still challenges, but I'm happy. My happiness is not due to the fact that I changed my physical location and career, but rather it's my willingness to listen to my heart, my truth and my intuition, even if it seems frightening or unreasonable. I've discovered that everything, including me, is perfect.

Life is short and there are no guarantees. If you have the desire to do something, you may just want to say, "Screw it!" and go for it. It worked for me.

5

THE TUNA SANDWICH

By Karen – Sunnyside, New York

It was a lovely evening in early spring and the air felt crisp and refreshing. I'd just come out of the building where I'd attended Ariel and Shya's Monday Night Alive evening seminar, along with a group of almost one hundred other people. Going to these seminars on Mondays has become my favorite weekly routine. Afterwards, I always feel open, receptive and energized from absorbing so much inspiration, which rekindles my own well-being.

I picked up my pace as I headed toward the subway station, passing a delicatessen on the street corner. All of a sudden, I heard a voice. Without looking, I could tell it came from someone standing next to the door of the deli. At first, I didn't pay much attention and kept walking, but then she spoke up again.

"Could you order me a tuna sandwich, please?"

This unusual question stopped me in my tracks, although it wasn't a totally surprising request given the large homeless population in New York City. I looked to see who was speaking to me. She was short with cropped brown hair and a big brown-eyed stare. Maybe it was the way she stood in front of the deli, but she blended in.

As a New Yorker, I'm no stranger to interacting with people on the street less fortunate than I am. Sometimes

I give them pocket change or some food but I rarely go out of my way to help. From time-to-time I find myself wondering whether or not I should lend a helping hand, or whether the act of giving is truly helping or not. But this was not one of those days. After my immersion into being in the moment that night, my mind was pleasantly silent and so, instead of talking to myself, I listened to her.

"Could you order me a tuna sandwich, please?" she asked one more time.

"You want a tuna sandwich?" I repeated.

"Yes," she said. "I'd like a tuna sandwich on toasted wheat bread, with mayo, lettuce and tomato. No onion."

I was surprised by the specificity of the request. She was being clear and direct, asking for help without reciting the usual script that I'd heard before in a scenario like this, such as, "I'm hungry, I haven't had any food for two days..."

On any other day I probably would have walked straight past, intent upon my destination, not even hearing her. But tonight was different. I'd just attended a seminar about listening and being present to life's requests and the usual thoughts weren't clouding my head. I saw her. I heard her. Instead of dipping into my internal dialogue about what to do next, I stood in the clarity of the moment. In that moment, I could help her, or not. It was just that simple.

Before I knew it, my feet were leading me to the deli counter where I ordered a tuna sandwich on toasted wheat bread, with mayo, lettuce and tomato, no onion, exactly like she had described. I waited while the chef prepared and wrapped it. I paid, walked out of the deli, and handed it to her.

As she held the sandwich in her hands, she suddenly seemed a bit unsure. Pausing, she looked at me for a moment with surprise showing in those big brown eyes, and then said, "Thank you."

"You're welcome," I replied. "Enjoy!"

That was the end of the conversation and I went on my way. It had all happened within a few minutes. I felt humbled and enriched by the experience, though it was so seemingly ordinary.

I've always admired people who act quickly without questioning or analyzing a situation, without second-guessing themselves. But I've never considered myself to be that type of person. And yet, on this evening, I was such a person. I didn't need to figure anything out. I didn't need to think about it. It was simple. I could say "yes" or "no." And, in that moment, my feet had chosen for me.

It was so freeing to feel like I didn't need to make up rules to be a "better me" or berate myself or create standards to live by in order to become a "better" person. I simply saw what was wanted and needed in that moment and made a choice. I experienced the perfection of the moment and how it contains everything I need to live my life. I found myself smiling as I continued my walk toward the subway, feeling like I was the person who had just been well fed.

6

FEAR NOT, JUST DANCE

By Simon – Overland Park, Kansas

After eight years of seeing the horrors of combat during my military service in Iraq, I was inspired to change my career path and enter the healthcare field. I became a nurse and spent several years in critical care and emergency departments. Then I applied for my dream job as a healthcare information systems consultant and trainer. This was a role that intrigued me because it drew on my military experience, computer science skills, and strong clinical background to improve health outcomes in patient care.

A few weeks after I applied for the position, I successfully navigated through a gauntlet of phone interviews, written tests, and a three-hour hands-on skills assessment to reach the all-important in-person interview stage. The afternoon before the in-person interview, I was teaching some nurses a block of instruction on arterial blood gas analysis. It's not generally considered to be a favorite subject among the nurses at my institution, but the feedback I received after class was positive. A couple of the nurses told me that while they expected the class to be super boring, they'd actually enjoyed it and learned quite a bit.

"What did you enjoy about the class?" I asked.

"Your enthusiasm," they told me. "It was fun and you

turned this ordinary and mundane topic into something compelling and memorable."

"Right on," I said, giving them both fist bumps.

When I was ready to go home for the day, I checked my phone and heard a voicemail message requesting my attendance the next morning at a panel interview with the directors and managers. They instructed me to bring my laptop computer and be prepared to deliver a ten-minute instructional presentation on a topic of my choice.

On the drive home, I brainstormed ideas for presentation topics. As an experienced nurse and educator, the logical choice would be something that demonstrated my medical knowledge and work skills. *Easy peasy,* I said to myself, *I can do this in my sleep.* Ideas popped into my head such as how to reset an MRI machine or how to interpret a twelve-lead EKG.

But the more I thought about it, the more I realized my interviewers were all experienced healthcare professionals and I had already passed the written tests and hands-on skills assessment. The instructions were to teach on a topic of *my* choice and my intuition told me to do something different – to pick a topic that resonated with me outside the realm of healthcare. I reasoned that if I was passionate about it, then at the very least, it wouldn't be boring.

Later that night, I still hadn't settled on a topic, so I went to the gym to lift weights, blow off some steam and clear my head. During a break between sets of pull-ups, I heard MC Hammer's song "U Can't Touch This" blaring from the speakers overhead. My body began to move to the rhythm as if it was on autopilot. I was not in my head. I was completely in my body, allowing myself to feel the sensations of pleasure through movement.

I was there in the moment and time seemed to slow down. A lady walked by and smiled at me. I looked around and people were bobbing their heads, tapping their feet, doing the shoulder shimmy and generally having a good time. It was a sign. *Maybe I could teach my interviewers the finer points of MC Hammer's "Running Man" dance*, I thought. This idea stuck with me throughout the rest of the workout.

I grew up dancing to the music of Michael Jackson, Billy Ocean, and MC Hammer, but as an adult, I hadn't sought out opportunities to "bust a move." When I left the gym and entertained this Running Man dance idea, there was this big wall of "NO" that I encountered. I was bombarded by thoughts like, *This will be the stupidest thing ever*, and *You don't even like to dance in front of other people*. I smiled and allowed the thoughts to be there. I told myself that my thoughts were not me. Besides, the interview went both ways. It was not just about their evaluation of me. It was also about whether or not I wanted to work with them.

How can I make this fun? I asked myself. I recalled the nurses who had reminded me that my enthusiasm had transformed the mundane into something fun and memorable. *They're going to get a full dose of Hammer time!* I laughed as I got my presentation together.

When I arrived at the interview the next morning, there was a very serious, all-business vibe in the room. The interviewers chose me to deliver the presentation first. It was go-time. I had a flash of nervousness but I realized that I could either be there with them in real time or second-guess myself in my thoughts. I chose to be there, fully committed to my presentation, and a wonderful thing happened. I was no longer focused on how I was doing. I was able to display passion for my topic, the conviction that what I had to say was important, and the knowledge that my message was significant to my audience.

The looks on their faces were priceless and in that

moment, I got hit with a rush of adrenaline. Even so, I kept going, enthusiastically dropping "knowledge bombs" on them about the history of the Running Man and one of its originators, the legendary MC Hammer. At first, they laughed nervously, as if it was a joke. Then, looks of shock and horror crossed their faces, worried that I might do some sort of cringe-worthy and weird interpretive dance. Undaunted, I forged ahead. As I enlightened them about this important topic, the looks on their faces slowly changed to something resembling disbelief and perhaps a stifled enthusiasm for my go-for-broke presentation.

To help set the mood, I pulled out my phone and played an old-school jam. I invited the interviewers to follow along and participate as I taught the dance steps, but there were no takers. No matter. I continued my presentation in my three-piece suit and tie, capping it off with an epic thirty-second Running Man sequence combined with body rolls, turns, and slides that would have made MC Hammer proud. It was pure fun!

In the midst of it all, the panel of interviewers attempted to keep it serious and remain stone-faced. Nonetheless, I felt free, relaxed and grounded. The weight of conformity and other people's expectations had been lifted off my shoulders and I moved through my fear of looking foolish to being fully self-expressive. Rather than suppressing myself to fit into an idea of what others wanted as I'd done in the past, I invested in the moment, trusted that I would do the right thing, and I had a blast! During the interview that followed, the directors and managers warmed up to me and it felt like I was having a conversation with friends. After confidently dancing in front of them, the simple act of listening, answering questions without pretense and being my most authentic self was like a proverbial "walk in the park."

Needless to say, I got the job. If you feel the impulse to

bust a move, fear not, just dance. You'll have a blast! Fun really is the way to access enlightenment. When I took my attention off of myself and how I was doing, I got out of my head and I had fun – and they're still talking about my dance moves.

7

WHEN DID MY LIFE GET BETTER THAN MY DREAMS?

By Lenore – Yonkers, New York

I'm in sunny Costa Rica galloping on a beautiful horse across an expansive beach. The beach is empty except for me and my friends who are on an immersion adventure that Ariel and Shya lead each year during the winter in New York. The sun is bright and on the dune to my left, palm trees sway in the breeze, heavy with coconuts. To my right, waves sparkle in the sun and there are dolphins frolicking. Yup, frolicking, almost following us, swimming the same direction we're headed. *Wow! How did this happen?*

That experience is a movie-worthy example that highlights the contrast between my life now and my life prior to experiencing transformation. I had been looking and looking for something that would make life complete. By the time I was twelve, I'd already read the Bible five times. But I couldn't shake the feeling there was something more and I couldn't get to it. I kept looking.

Years later, I walked into a meeting that I'd attended before, but that night was different. I'd joined this support group about a year prior and had been hanging out with them for many workshops, including ones where we walked on fire and bent spoons. I'd been looking for consistent well-being, but I wasn't feeling it yet. I'd had some high highs but still hoped the low lows would go

away. Throughout the year the group would get together
and jump up and down to wonderful songs. For a few
weeks, I would feel great. I had workbooks with loads
of notes. I made lists of things to do everyday to have
a great life and usually I could keep the practices, the
sayings and the mood up – for a while. I was hoping
I could keep it up long enough that well-being would
become a habit. It hadn't happened yet, but I was still
hoping.

On this particular night, we were milling around
before the talk and I got to meet some new people, Ariel
and Shya Kane – they seemed chill. They were different.
I couldn't put my finger on what this difference was quite
yet and I was super curious. They were here to talk to us
about their book *Working On Yourself Doesn't Work*. I was
sure that couldn't be true. I was waiting to see what the
trick was and how this would ultimately agree with what
I was already learning.

When the presentation began, they started talking and
I was amazed and a little horrified. They asked evocative
questions such as, "What if you're perfect just the way
you are?" *Noooooooo!* I was thinking. I have so much
work to do. *I have so much more that I want. How can
that be possible?*

I felt antsy while they were speaking, but they had
this beautiful way of interacting. I was intrigued as they
communicated about things too simple for my brain to
comprehend. My brain was set on "complicated" with a
mistrust of "easy." I was trained to believe, "It has to hurt
and/or be hard to be worthwhile." I wasn't the only one
who had internalized this message.

The Kanes' response? "Well, if that's working for you,
keep doing it."

I watched in awe. I felt my world crumbling and a new
one being born. I hoped I was not staring gape-mouthed
at their grace and the respectfulness they displayed with

every single person. Did I mention that they'd met a room full of people that night and they still remembered my name? I was impressed by that. They flowed like dancers as they presented ideas in ways that I'd never heard. My support team buddies were giving them a really hard time. We'd been learning and practicing that we had to work hard and do loads of affirmations and repetitive practices to get to where we wanted to be. Ariel and Shya kept saying, "Maybe not." I looked surreptitiously around at people. We had invited these speakers to present new ideas that the group as a whole now automatically dismissed. I was thinking, *Arrgghh, could we be more arrogant?*

I would have dismissed them, too, if it weren't for the fact that these two people looked so comfortable. They had this something that I'd been looking for. I still couldn't name it but I knew they had it. Ariel and Shya had been together for a really long time. They were obviously a loving couple, working together and enjoying each other, even in this hostile environment. I was shocked at my friends who were being so unkind to our guests.

I stood up to ask a make-peace kind of question. I was stunned by their response. "Lenore," they said, "you really want to make a difference. That's why you're here."

How could they know that? They knew me although they'd just met me moments before. I couldn't believe it. I felt truly seen and heard like I'd only experienced two or three times in my life.

I had to know more. I bought *Working on Yourself Doesn't Work* and read it. I spent every other page being stunned. Could it really be this easy? I might not have given it a second thought except that Ariel and Shya were living in the way I'd been chasing and couldn't hang on to.

I have that ease now. It snuck up on me while I was busy living my life. Now I get a thrill from making dinner with my husband. Did I mention that I'm blissfully married? It's so sweet to see him slice the avocados precisely and arrange the tomatoes just so. He makes it pretty just because I love pretty. Now my sweet side is my most prominent side and I'm super grateful. Wow! When did my life get better than my dreams? I don't know really. Not exactly. But I do recall the night when my life transformed in an instant and it has never been the same since.

8

I DON'T HAVE MUCH TIME LEFT

By Shya – Milford, New Jersey

*I*t was still light outside on a warm August evening when Ariel and I entered a quaint local eatery in the Cape Cod town of Orleans, Massachusetts. The little restaurant was dark with wood booths that had seen plenty of wear. As we walked into the room we were hailed by Captain Bill, who was sitting with his fishing buddies and a group of other captains. He invited us to join them.

We'd known Bill for about five years. He'd grown up on the water in New Jersey and had parlayed his love of the ocean and fishing into becoming a fishing guide. Many times his guests let him fish right along with them so for Bill, this was a dream come true. In fact, he was the person who first introduced us to the Cape Cod area. Generations of his family had gone to this famous spit of land on the southeast corner of Massachusetts. Once he'd gotten to know Ariel and me, he'd recommended that we go there and fish for striped bass.

Going to any new place for boating is often best done with a guide. Even with the regular use of GPS units, there are still underwater obstructions and places that are impassable at low tide, not to mention areas that are hot for fishing and others that aren't. On our first trip to the Cape we shadowed Bill in our boat as he showed us his favorite areas.

That night, everyone ordered bowls of clam or fish chowder – New England style of course – and crusty bread with butter. When the food came, it tasted good after a long day of being out on the boat in the wind, sea and sun. In a companionable silence, the guys and Ariel and I enjoyed our food.

"Shya," Bill said, "I have a confession to make. Do you remember when we first met?"

Of course I did. It had been early spring several years prior. Ariel and I had just gotten our first boat, *Shya's Dream*, and had found a place to moor it on the Jersey shore. The problem was that I had no idea where to fish. As I mentioned, the best way to learn an area is to hire a local fishing guide and have him or her show you where to go. I'd hired Bill. The day had turned out to be windy and sloppy, but I was eager to go so I prevailed upon Bill and we went anyway.

"I hadn't met you before we went out that first time," Bill said, "and we had only spoken by phone. I'd checked the weather and it was going to be a nasty, windy day with the strong possibility of rain. When you called the night before to finalize plans, I suggested that we go another weekend, try another day. You said to me, 'No Bill, let's go. I don't have much time left!' This was before I got to know you, Shya. This was before I learned how immediate you are. I remember spending that entire day with you thinking, 'This is the healthiest terminally ill person I've ever met.'"

I chuckled when he said this. "Yes, Bill." I replied. "Happily I'm healthy but everyone has a terminal illness – it's called life. None of us know how long our lives are going to be. It's so easy to put off doing the things you want, and doing the things that need to be done, but that just isn't my style."

It's been many years since that first day I went fishing with Bill and I still go about my life with urgency, as if this day could be my last.

PART TWO:

FAMILY AND FORGIVENESS

9

LIFE IS IN THE BLINTZES

By Eric – Brooklyn, New York

When my maternal grandmother, Dora, was a child, she came to America from a tiny village in Eastern Europe. One of my fondest memories of her was that she made amazing blintzes, thin crepe-like pancakes filled with savory cheese. When I was a little boy I'd visit her in the Bronx in New York City, and we'd walk together to the store, my small hand in hers, to get fresh ingredients. Then we'd go back to her apartment and I'd watch her make my beloved blintzes. She never followed a recipe. Everything she made was by eye or by heart. The best part of all was eating them. My grandmother was a cheek pincher who loved me with food. And her food, from blintzes to chicken soup to chopped liver, was extraordinary.

By contrast, I hadn't felt as close to my mother. While my dad and I shared jokes and a common interest in music, when I was in my pre-teen years, I decided that my mother was stoic, cold, and unable to connect with me emotionally. We didn't spend much time talking and I didn't enjoy her cooking.

Eventually I decided that I no longer wanted to be associated with the people in my mother's family: Eastern European Jews. Their heritage, religion, language, customs, and even their food, including my formerly beloved blintzes, had become embarrassing to me. I conveniently forgot about the hard work and sacrifices my family had made to give me the life that I was taking for granted. I forgot how my mother had paid for things – my cello lessons, an expensive private college, and financial support she gave me when I was having some significant personal struggles – not to mention unwavering moral support.

Years passed and the gulf between me and my mother widened. When my parents moved to Florida, I never made visiting them a priority although my mom took the time to visit me. When I was cast as a professional actor in plays in Boston and New York City, my mother always came to see my performances. After the shows she would meet me, give me a hug and, before I had a chance to ask what she thought of my performance, she would whisper in my ear, "You were the best one."

When I started to participate in Instantaneous Transformation seminars with Ariel and Shya, I saw that I had preconceived notions of my mother. I didn't see her as she was. I saw her as I *thought* she was. That's not the same thing. My thoughts about her were colored by a filter, put in place by my disgruntled teenage self who'd been insecure and desperate to fit in. Once I saw this important distinction, I was able to truly listen to what Mom had to say and to see things from her perspective. I saw her loving nature and acts, both past and present, because they were no longer at odds with my own very strong point of view. I was suddenly able to remember the hugs as well as the cream cheese and jelly sandwiches with no crusts. I even remembered when I went through my "purple phase" and Mom knitted me a purple sweater. It was well made, but in retrospect it wasn't a great color decision for me. As a result of my new perspective, our relationship became closer and sweeter.

My grandma Dora is long gone. My mother is ninety-one and her health and memory are fading. She's confined to a wheelchair and although her long-term memory is generally good, her short-term memory is nonexistent. She remembers my Dad, but not that he's been dead for twenty years.

I recently went down to Florida to visit her. At first she thought I was a doctor, which was not a total loss. I'm a lawyer and a literary agent, but she had dreamt of my becoming a doctor, and to her I was. She told me she'd enjoyed my comedy show the night before (I was a standup comedian several years ago) although she felt I went on a little too long. Of course there was no show, but she was happy, especially that she'd stayed at my friend Oprah's apartment. I was pleased to learn that I am close friends with Oprah Winfrey.

I wasn't upset with Mom's confusion. As long as she wasn't depressed or scared, I rolled with it, going along with her reality. But she wasn't eating and her nurses and aides were concerned. An additional benefit of my participating in the Kanes' seminars is that I've become very intuitive. More accurately, I've allowed my intuition to override what used to be my denial and doubt.

I knew in my gut that blintzes would reignite my mother's appetite. I asked the medical professionals if there were concerns about fat, salt or any other nutritional caveats. They said my mother needed calories and, at this point, any were good. I went to a deli near my mom's house and on the way home, my car was filled with the familiar aroma of blintzes and matzo ball soup. Images of my grandmother's smile went through my mind. I heard the roar of the crowd at Yankee stadium as we walked through her Bronx neighborhood. Most importantly, I felt the lineage of love that traveled from Dora through my mother to me. Unexpected tears welled up as I drove the Florida roads, far from New York City. I was grateful I could allow myself the pleasure of those tears, the welling of love and affection. When my mother devoured two blintzes and smiled at me, my chest swelled with gratitude. My heritage is rich and full of love and life. In that moment, I rediscovered that life is in the blintzes.

10

A MOMENT IN TIME

By Wendy – Queens, New York

*M*y brother Brian was born a year and a half after I was. My mom told me that when she brought him home from the hospital, I thought he was a gift for me. When we were growing up, Brian seemed to know how to do everything without any help or training. I'd ask him, "How do you know that?" I was amazed and jealous that things seemed to come so easily for him, or so I thought.

Years later when I graduated from college, I found a job in New York City. My brother offered to drive my stuff and me from our home in Rochester, New York to my new apartment in Jersey City, New Jersey. We packed his Suburban to the gills and off we went. We made our way there using a good old-fashioned map since this was before cell phones and Google Maps. We spent the weekend setting up the apartment and took a quick trip into Manhattan to explore the area. The days flew by and the time came for him to head back. We hugged goodbye and off he drove into the horizon. As I watched my brother's truck get smaller and smaller, tears fell down my cheeks.

Time moved on, life happened, and Brian and I grew apart. I held on to my belief that we would be super close again someday, because that's how I thought it should be. That's how I thought life worked. But Brian started using drugs. As his addiction grew stronger, the gulf between us grew wider. He got help, but it was a struggle and he repeatedly slipped back into his old habits. I had a lot of judgments against him, but they had started long before he was using drugs.

Eventually, I discovered a totally new perspective about my brother and my life when a co-worker invited me to one of Ariel and Shya Kane's evening events in New York City. Soon after, I attended a weekend seminar with them and started to look at relationships through a different lens. It wasn't a conscious decision, but my perspective just shifted. As a kid I'd made decisions to not be like my family. I started seeing how I held my family and myself as not good enough. I had ideas about what a "good family" looked like, down to how a good family should celebrate Christmas. In the past, I had sat at home feeling sorry for myself if the celebration was not up to my standards.

Then, one December, I had a spontaneous experience of how my life had transformed. I had flown to Rochester to celebrate Christmas with my family and quickly discovered that no one had made plans for a holiday gathering. Rather than going to that familiar place of feeling sorry for myself, I realized that I could plan something. This was a novel idea and I got excited at the notion of hosting Christmas.

With my sister Holley's permission, I invited everyone to her house on a snowy night in December. I made all of my favorite dishes – cheesy macaroni and cheese, creamy cauliflower mashed potatoes and a big green salad. Holley finished it off with a fresh baked apple pie. My mom brought the frosted buttermilk Christmas cookies that she made every year. Everyone was happy to contribute. *Hmm, maybe my family wasn't such a lost cause after all.*

Earlier in the day my sister and I had bought gifts for everyone, including a chess set that I thought my brother would love. Brian was a pretty good chess player and he loved the game. The doorbell sounded and I greeted my mom and brother at the door. It was as if time stood still. I looked into my brother's eyes and I saw that I had a choice. I could drop my judgments and meet my brother Brian, as if for the first time, or I could hold on to past grievances. In a split second I chose to drop the past. I saw the light flicker in my brother's eyes as I reached out to hug him and I felt the wall between us crumble. Even the sound of his name was sweet and I was excited he was there.

The evening flew by. After dinner we exchanged gifts. I felt sated and happy. I realized the picture in my mind of how Christmas should be celebrated was a child's idea and I preferred the way it had unfolded in reality.

I was scheduled to fly back to New York City on Sunday night and to my surprise, Brian joined my mom and me on the ride to the airport. When we arrived and I found out the flight was delayed, I asked them both to come inside the airport and wait with me. I'd never done that before. I usually couldn't wait to get out of Rochester but this time was different. We sat in Dunkin' Donuts, sipping coffee and eating muffins, and laughing at stupid jokes. It was a lot of fun and the silliness was sweet and intimate. When my flight was ready to depart, we said our goodbyes and I made my way to the gate with a big grin on my face.

A few days into the New Year, I got a call in the middle of the night. My brother Brian had overdosed on heroin and his heart had stopped. He died later that night and I was in shock. I couldn't believe that just a few days earlier we'd had some of the deepest and kindest interactions in years. It was as if I had found my kid brother again only to lose him.

I miss my brother but I'll be forever grateful for the time I got to spend with him that Christmas. I'm thankful that I dropped the past and discovered who Brian really was while he was still alive.

11

COMING HOME

By Valerie – Montclair, New Jersey

*I*t used to be difficult going back to visit family in my home state of California because I fought with my parents, with myself and with my life. A baseline disagreement with my circumstances was not only a way of life, but something I considered distinctive, noble, and almost cool. It seemed to give me an edge on all the complacent people in the world.

With this approach – the best I knew at the time – I landed my first job out of college. I was a California girl living and working in New York City, trying to be successful and discover who I was. I felt utterly lost and filled with anxiety. It was at that point in my life that I met Ariel and Shya and attended my first weekend seminar with them. It blew my mind to discover that I wasn't my thoughts and I didn't need to be hard on myself in order to be successful. Within the space of a few days, I had no trace of the anxiety and internal turmoil that had become so normal over the course of my life. The most incredible part was that I really didn't *do* anything to get there.

Now, more than fifteen years after that first seminar, I continue to learn. One of the biggest keys that has made a difference for me is discovering how to listen without an agenda or preference for the outcome, to truly hear what someone is saying from his or her point of view.

Recently, I went on vacation in California where I visited my family and during a car trip with my dad, my "lessons" continued.

"In some cultures," I heard my dad say, "when people get old and know it's their time, they go up the mountain and never come back."

My body was folded up awkwardly but I was surprisingly comfortable in the back seat of my dad's Prius. I had dozed off at some point during the drive and as I slowly woke up, I peered at the warm golden light shining through the deep green leaves of the rich, red-barked Sequoias. I glanced out the window and I could almost inhale the redwoods and afternoon sunshine that reminded me that I was back in California. I was back home.

My father was driving and Bill, one of his oldest friends, sat beside him in the front seat. They were speaking very matter-of-factly about the process of aging and dying. I eavesdropped on their conversation as they discussed how, in certain cultures, it was generally known that leaving the communal village when it was your time to die was just what you did and everyone accepted it. Hearing these ideas – surrounded by gorgeous mountains, trees and country as we drove up Highway 1 in Mendocino County – it didn't sound so foreign or so bad.

In that moment, something in me felt happy to be alive, happy for my father and Bill, and grateful that they got to live their lives and that I got to live mine with them in it. I saw the man in the driver's seat, my father, as a complete and whole person with a complex and meaningful life, rather than being whittled down to only being my dad. He was simply someone expressing himself, chatting with a friend who was listening to him. I briefly forgot that I was supposed to be worried about him getting older and that I was supposed to have proprietary opinions, thoughts and feelings about him.

The three of us were headed up to one of our favorite places, a chamber music workshop where we play music with about ninety other people for a rigorous and glorious week. I had attended the workshop twice while my dad and Bill had both been going each summer, almost every year, for the past thirty years. Bill plays the piano, Dad has played the clarinet since he was twelve years old and I started on the clarinet when I was thirteen. I treasured this week with my dad. It was a chance for us to do something together that we both loved. I got to speak with him about music, learn from him, eat meals with him, take walks and experience how much people there liked and appreciated him. Hearing his input, his opinions and generally enjoying his company was not something I'd always appreciated. In fact, before I discovered the phenomenon of Instantaneous Transformation, those were all things I had resented and resisted.

As we rode down that sun-dappled road, I recalled a few very funny questions Ariel and Shya had asked me that had made a big difference in how I saw my dad. I began to smile when I thought about them. "Do you realize your parents have friends?" they said. "People who like them?"

I realized that the answer to this question had changed over the years. At first, it was, "Of course they do. But my parents' friends are just like them. They don't get it either!" I felt embarrassed at how narrow my view of my mom and dad had been. The embarrassment melted away and was gently replaced with compassion for them, for who I was then and who I am now.

"Do you care what *my* father eats for breakfast? Do you worry about how much *he* is exercising?" Shya once asked.

No, of course not, I have no opinion on that. Yet, somehow, the inclination to claim the right to an opinion on how *my* parents live their lives was strong. Even stronger was the overwhelming desire to share it with them, which had always proved to be a recipe for disaster and discord. I felt incredibly grateful that, instead of acting on these impulses to automatically criticize my dad for how he lives his life, I now have the ability to see my mechanical thoughts, which then gives me the option to not have to act on them.

Ariel and Shya sometimes define transformation as the ability to transcend your bratty nature. Not to "get rid" of that childish outlook, as it may always be there, but to simply *see* it. And in the seeing of it, it ceases to run your life. There have been so many gifts I've received through discovering transformation. I now live my life as its author rather than its victim. I have discovered that family members can evolve, rather than remain static. I recognize that home is not just a place, but also an experience of feeling at ease within myself. One of my greatest gifts has been discovering how brilliant, loved, admired, strong and fully capable both of my parents are.

In the back seat of the car on that road trip, I felt well in myself. Gazing out the window at the flashes of green, brown and gold, I drifted back to sleep, happy to be "home" amongst friends.

PART THREE:

PARENTING, TEACHING AND TRANSFORMATION

12

BEING WELL-GROUNDED

By Ariel & Shya – Milford, New Jersey

*O*ur friend Amy has come into her own using the technology of Instantaneous Transformation. She was twenty-seven when we first made her acquaintance, but as the years have passed, she and her husband Andy have become firmly rooted in an overall sense of well-being and have become well-grounded in their own personal centers.

When Amy was thirty-eight, she had her first son. Now she and her husband Andy are the proud parents of two boys, Alex, age sixteen, and Aidan, age thirteen. Sometimes she affectionately refers to her family as the "A-Team."

When Alex was five, the couple brought him to a local Taekwondo studio to see if he might enjoy the sport. It turned out to be a hit. The instructor was great and Alex enjoyed the moves, the exercise, and the discipline. He had fun with the whole experience. Taekwondo, like most martial arts, has different colored belts that are awarded for levels of attainment. Practitioners work their way up in hopes of ultimately achieving a black belt. It wasn't too long before Alex was tested and won his very first belt. It was white.

Alex's classes looked like so much fun, Amy and Andy decided to give it a go. It turned out that they loved it, too. When it came time to test for their white belt, young Alex coached them solemnly and oh-so-sweetly. "Don't worry," he said. "You'll be fine. You can do this. Just remember to breathe and have fun."

He was right. They did fine and Amy and Andy have gone on to earn their black belts. In the early years, they sometimes delighted friends with impromptu demonstrations of some of the strength exercises that went along with their Taekwondo training. Amy and Andy would do push-ups with Aidan and Alex on their backs doing push-ups, right along with them.

Like most families, each of their kids has distinctive personalities and differences. One loves doing his homework while the other generally needs encouragement and management to make sure it gets done. One likes to organize his things, the other not so much. Of course there have been typical squabbles between the siblings and times when household rules need to be reinforced. In general though, each boy is well-grounded in himself, achieves good grades, has a whole host of outside activities and interests and is well-liked by friends.

One day when Alex was eight years old, Amy made a discovery. She realized she had underestimated the effect of living a transformational lifestyle. Suddenly she saw how her reality had been organically assimilated by her kids.

It was a sunny Tuesday afternoon when Amy picked Alex up from a play date with his friend Dillon. As they headed home, Alex was sitting in his seat in the back of the car. "Mommy," he suddenly said. "What's grounded?" Amy thought for a moment to compose a response.

"Well, Alex, being grounded is another way of saying 'being centered.' You know, like when you're balanced on your feet in Taekwondo. It's when you're really down-to-earth rather than being distracted by something. Why do you ask?" She added, as she navigated a turn.

"Dillon's mommy is always getting mad at him. She keeps saying, 'Dillon, you're in so much trouble! You're grounded!'"

Amy realized in that moment that being "grounded" was all a matter of context. She smiled as she saw the disparity in the usage of the term. She explained that Dillon's mom meant he didn't get to go anywhere and probably had his video game privileges suspended. When Dillon's mom had said, "grounded," she had meant a strong version of "time out."

Once Amy pulled into her driveway, she sat there for a moment. As Alex got out of the car and headed toward the house, she watched her son open the door and go inside. She realized how fortunate she and Andy were to be parents of these two great kids. When Amy opened her own door and gathered her things, she felt happy that both Alex and Aidan were growing up as well-grounded boys rather than ones who were frequently grounded.

13

AUNT CAILY: A TRIBUTE TO MOTHERS, EVEN THOSE WHO AREN'T

By Ariel – Milford, New Jersey

My Great Aunt Caily was my grandmother's younger sister. My Grandma and Grandpa eventually moved to Oregon to raise their family but Aunt Caily and her husband, Uncle Gil, lived and died in Orange City, Iowa.

Born in the early 1900's, Caily came to adulthood in an era when her childless status labeled her as a lady who *couldn't* have kids, rather than being regarded as a woman who simply *didn't* have kids. I sometimes wonder about the details of her life, things that I will never know. Of course they were never my business anyway.

When I was young, I sometimes confided in Aunt Caily, but like most children, I was mainly concerned for myself. I had little room to be curious about her. I never knew the reason why she and Uncle Gil didn't have a family of their own, but I did know that she was special and they were both very loved. It occurs to me that perhaps she, like many folks, didn't have a clue as to the difference she made. Our paths didn't cross often. It was a long train-ride from Iowa to Oregon (she refused to travel by air) and our family only visited her on occasion. However, there are bright moments that drift through my memory when I think of her.

Diminutive in stature, feisty in nature, Aunt Caily had a high voice and she was quick to laugh. When I was in those difficult teen years, she came to Grandma's house and I recall sitting with her on the couch as she asked me about my day. I'm not sure how it happened, but I confided in her that a lot of kids at school were doing drugs, "speed" to be exact, the 70s version of meth. I found it disturbing and I didn't know how to handle the situation. I don't recall that she gave me advice or that we came up with a plan or solution, but it was a relief to unburden my load to an adult who would simply listen and who wouldn't "freak out" and call the school or take unwanted, embarrassing actions.

I frequently think of my Great Aunt Caily when I'm cleaning up after cooking a meal. She once gave my mother advice that has been passed down as a bit of family wisdom. According to Mom, one time when she was visiting Caily, they had pot roast for dinner. Afterwards, my mom did the dishes and as she was scrubbing the pot that had been used to make the roast, Caily came into the kitchen.

"What are you doing?" Caily asked abruptly, startling my mother.

"The dishes," Mom replied.

"But why are you scrubbing that pot? Don't be silly. Use baking soda."

"Baking soda?"

"Yes, of course. Sprinkle some on the pot and let it soak a bit. It will lift the baked-on grease and leavings."

This was a lesson my mother taught me – a little family legacy from my Great Aunt Caily. Baking soda really does lift the baked-on grease and pan leavings. I rarely have to scrub hard after I use my pots and pans. When Caily gave my mom that nugget of kitchen magic, I'm sure she had no clue that decades after her death, her wisdom would live on in me...and now you.

Most of us underestimate what we have to offer, worrying about what we want to accomplish in our lifetime. We focus on the "big" things, thinking that's what matters, when sometimes it is the little, unexpected things that matter the most.

14

A TRANSFORMATIONAL
TEACHING MOMENT

By Zoe – Manhattan, New York

"*I* feel so retarded!" Jenny said as she entered my classroom one lunch hour.

It hurt to hear that. Jenny is one of my special needs students and clearly she had heard this derogatory term somewhere. Now she was applying it to herself.

Jenny is a bubbly girl with adorable dimples and the kind of laugh that makes everyone else laugh, too. When she was a young child, Jenny was diagnosed with a learning disability and she'd become infamous for evading schoolwork by any means necessary. As her Special Education teacher, I'd spent a lot of the year chasing her down, trying to coax, cajole and force her to finish work she hadn't done. So it came as a surprise when she sought me out during her lunch period.

"I need help with the math homework," she said.

I walked with her to a table and chair, encouraged Jenny to sit and I took the chair next to her. "Take out the work that you're having trouble with and we'll do it together," I said.

I started talking Jenny through the steps of the problem. At first, she was doing fine and required only a few small prompts when she didn't immediately see the answer. Then after a few questions and successful answers we came to a roadblock.

"Ok," I said, "when we subtract seven from five, that gives us...."

I paused, waiting for her to say "negative two." Her face drew a blank. I asked her a few other questions involving negative numbers, hoping to jog her memory, but nothing seemed to work. Then it dawned on me that she'd never learned how to add and subtract using negative numbers.

I thought to myself, *Why didn't I realize this sooner? I should've been more persistent, more attentive. Why didn't she work with me sooner? We could have dealt with this at the beginning of the year.*

I took a breath. Jenny didn't need my judgments or self-recriminations. The "why" didn't matter. The past didn't matter. This was our moment to learn about negative numbers, right now.

I realized that if I held on to those judgmental thoughts, I could be right about what a bad teacher I was, or about what a bad student she was, or even how the school system, her family, and society at large had failed her. Instead, I noticed the thoughts, I didn't give them any weight, and I moved on with the work at hand. I took out some colorful pens and scrap paper, and I drew a number line. I had Jenny put her pen on the five and move it seven spaces to the left until it landed on the negative two.

"Is this making sense?" I asked.

"No," Jenny replied honestly, looking deflated.

I could tell she didn't like feeling stupid. She was judging herself harshly, which was reinforcing her earlier premise that she was "retarded." I tried another tactic. I drew a building. The ground floor was zero, the above ground floors were positive numbers, and the below ground floors were negative numbers. I moved my pen seven floors down on my drawing and showed her how that left us at the "sub basement." Negative two. We talked through a few more problems using the elevator analogy.

"What happens if I start on the third floor and then go down four floors?" I asked.

She used the drawing to find the basement, the negative first floor. But it still didn't compute. I could see she was starting to get it but the information hadn't clicked yet. She looked at me and her face was open and honest. I felt like she had stripped away all her defenses and bared her soul to me. I listened with my eyes, my ears, and my heart to hear what she was thinking: *This is really hard for me, and when I don't understand something I get embarrassed and judge myself.*

Suddenly, I had a creative flash. I looked at Jenny and smiled. She smiled back. At some point during our conversation, a student teacher had joined us and was listening as I went through the different styles of explanations. Jenny turned to her and said, "Listen to this. I can tell this is going to be good."

"Ok Jenny," I began. "I have only five dollars in my bank account. I'm not very good at saving money."

Jenny started cracking up.

"Now I need to buy a…" I paused.

"A Metro Card!" Jenny said.

"Yes exactly. I need to buy a Metro Card for the subway, but it costs ten dollars. I use my credit card, the bank takes out the five dollars that I have, and then takes five more. Now I have negative five dollars in my bank account. And that, Jenny, is how I got an overdraft fee."

She and I were both laughing as we solved other examples using the bank account story – each of us coming up with more and more ridiculous items to purchase.

Fifteen minutes after sitting down with me, Jenny had learned a skill that had baffled her for most of the school year. Now she could complete the rest of her homework with ease. I was so proud of her for sticking with it, for not giving up after the first try, and for allowing me to see what she was struggling with.

When I was with Jenny that day, I didn't judge or blame her or myself. Learning became a collaborative, fun activity. I saw how my ability to listen and be present was contagious. The student teacher was so inspired by watching us together that she volunteered to stay after school to help Jenny finish the rest of her homework.

Since then, I've noticed that when I'm relaxed, I'm easy to be around. Students come to me when they need help and learning happens quickly and painlessly in an environment free of judgment. In the past, when I tried to force this young girl to do her math assignments, I exhausted myself and she avoided me. That day with Jenny during her lunch hour, I found a new way that was fun for us both.

It really was a transformational teaching moment and I've never been the same. On that day, I learned as much from Jenny as she did from me.

15

MEET THE ARTIST

By Andy – Brooklyn, New York

I'm an actor and for the last ten years I've also been teaching acting, primarily to elementary school students. Recently, I was an instructor in a school in New York City's Chinatown. It was a really special program. I was teaching several second grade classes who were all studying New York City landmarks.

The other classroom teachers and I came up with the idea to have each class pick a fairytale and a setting. They would write their own adaptations, inserting the facts they'd learned about the New York City landmarks. It was pretty complex for the second grade but the students did a great job with it. The Gingerbread Man was running through Central Park. The Three Little Pigs' Architectural Firm learned what materials work and don't work to build the Empire State Building. The Three Bear Security Guards stopped the Goldie Locks Picking Bandits from stealing artifacts from the Museum of Natural History. Fun stuff!

Once the plays were written and the students were cast in their roles, we rehearsed. We had three weeks before their parents were invited to come and watch them perform. The students loved seeing their plays come to life and everything was going extremely smoothly. Three weeks flew by in a blink of an eye. Then, on a Monday morning in mid-May, the students came to school, eager to perform. Their parents sat in the audience, their smartphones in the air, recording and taking pictures of the event. The show went great and the kids, the parents, and the school administrators all loved it.

After the performance, each class had a party in their individual classrooms to celebrate their hard work. I prepared myself to go home early since my work was done, but my boss had another idea. "Why don't we visit each classroom to say good-bye and see if the students have any questions?" she said. "Kind of like 'meet the artist.'"

Now, I hadn't said no to an idea from my boss in a number of years. I have become practiced in the art of saying "yes" to my life as it shows up in each moment and operating like whatever happens is my idea. I wasn't about to break my streak now, even though I thought it was going to be a waste of time.

What would they possibly want to know? I thought to myself. *They've been a part of the entire process from beginning to end.*

My boss and I stepped into the first classroom where a party was in full swing. The children were eating cookies, drinking juice, laughing, smiling, playing with one another and having a great time. It was the first time in months they hadn't noticed when I walked into the classroom and I didn't want to disturb their celebration. But I wanted to fully invest in my boss's idea, so I got the kids' attention and announced: "Hey guys! You did an awesome job today and I'm so proud of all of you! Today is my last day with you, so before I go, I wondered if anyone has any questions they'd like to ask?"

One of the boys, Karl, slowly raised his hand. "What's your favorite color?" he asked.

I was taken by surprise. I didn't know what to expect but this really threw me. In that moment, I realized that while the students and I had been together a long time, they didn't know anything about me.

"Green," I answered. The class roared with "Cool!" "Awesome!" and "Me too!" Other hands shot up.

"What's your favorite movie?"

"Star Wars: Return of the Jedi."

"Do you like ice cream?"

"Of course! Who doesn't like ice cream?"

"Cheese pizza or pepperoni pizza?"

"Pepperoni!"

"Are you married?"

"Yes, I am." This was the most taboo question, and it produced a lot of giggles and whispers.

"When you got married, did you...did you...kiss your wife?" a little boy named Jet asked. He could barely ask the question, he was cracking up so much.

"Of course. She's my wife. I kiss her every day," I said. The kids erupted into laughter. The questions and laughter continued in each class I visited. What I experienced was such a gift — that simply being myself is enough. I didn't need to be interesting or think of clever things to say.

Before I left the final classroom, somebody asked, "What's your favorite dessert?" This was a hard one to answer because I've got a pretty strong sweet tooth.

"A chocolate chip cookie," I said.

The child who'd asked the question walked over to the table to a tray of homemade chocolate chip cookies. He put one on a napkin and brought it to me. That was one of the best cookies I've ever had.

16

LISTENING WITH MY EYES
AS WELL AS MY EARS

By Susan – Manhattan, New York

*A*lthough I've been teaching voice and speech to actors at New York University for over twenty-five years, at the start of each semester I used to feel dread in the pit of my stomach. I'd think, *I've forgotten how to teach! I'm not prepared! I don't know the material!* Oddly enough, even with all my experience, I was still afraid I'd be called out as a fraud and an unfit educator. My brain felt fuzzy with fear as I entered the classroom with sweaty palms to see blank eyes staring at me, waiting for me to do or say something "educational."

Will they listen to me? Will they like me? How will they react?

My job is to help actors bring awareness to their habitual ways of speaking, breathing, and moving that inhibit their freedom of expression and their ability to be hired. Some automatically take feedback personally. It can be difficult at times for a young person, fresh out of high school, to realize that they're entering a bigger world where talent alone isn't enough. It doesn't matter how wonderful their acting is, they won't get the role of a person born and raised in Brooklyn if they sound like they come from the Deep South. Before finishing their first semester, most of my students find that my classes provide them greater casting possibilities. By then, they've learned how to speak in a manner that is not defined by where they grew up and the regionalisms they learned in their childhoods.

Before my students came to recognize these benefits, however, I often felt like I was fighting with them to get them to see my point of view. The more I pushed, the more they resisted.

Then I met Ariel and Shya Kane and was introduced to an approach to listening that has transformed my teaching – and my entire life. Since then, I've repeatedly seen that listening is a magical thing that brings me into the present moment. It enables my life to unfold in a natural and brilliant way. Listening is not only a skill set to be honed for teaching purposes; it has been integrated into all aspects of my life, turning it into a rich and rewarding adventure that feeds my ability to inspire my students.

The other day I had a simple yet profound experience through listening. I was walking down a street in Manhattan in an area known as "Hell's Kitchen." This neighborhood got its name in the 1800s, long before gentrification, when it was a dangerous slum. As I crossed 49th Street and 9th Avenue, I heard the sounds of the traffic and I felt the sun on my skin. I didn't realize it at the time but I was being there for my life rather than getting lost in my thoughts. Then, to my delight, right there in midtown I heard the *caw, caw, caw* of a crow. I looked up and saw him take wing as he cried out, his voice rising above the din of traffic and sounds of passersby. Hearing a crow may not sound like something wondrous or monumental, but I've lived in Manhattan for over thirty years and this was the first time I'd heard a crow in the heart of the city. If I'd been lost in my thoughts instead of listening, I would have missed it.

Although I initially attended the Kanes' seminars to look at aspects of my life that I wanted to sort out,

I've discovered the experience could also be considered a master class in acting. Great actors are masters of listening. Great acting happens when performers listen with every fiber of their being, as if they've never heard the words before, though they might have heard them a thousand times. Now, each time I attend an evening or weekend seminar, the Kanes start with the basics: listening to what people have to say. We're encouraged to "listen with our eyes." If we're gazing at the floor or off into space, our attention is more apt to wander. What I've learned and experienced with them has become invaluable in my own classroom.

I now begin each class I teach by talking about listening. I ask my students to listen with their eyes as well as their ears. I'm training them to be attentive in each moment and look directly at whomever is speaking. What I've discovered, and what I am passing on to them, is that when I listen in this way, I have a greater chance of truly hearing what's being said. When my eyes drift, so does my mind. When I use my eyes as part of the listening process, I can hear the speaker's point of view without being distracted by my inner commentary.

I ask my actors to do this in class and the results are amazing. There's a quality of presence in the room that is palpable and sacred. What each person says matters, even if they are uttering a single vowel. The way my students listen trains them to be sensitive, responsive, and aware. It also trains them to hear who and what they encounter in their lives beyond the classroom – their loved ones, their employers, their directors or even a crow flying overhead in Hell's Kitchen.

Recently, our school was being evaluated for accreditation by a panel of three educational experts. They observed me teaching my first-year class and then they interviewed the students privately. Afterwards, my students told me the first thing the panel members said was that in all their years as educators, they had never seen a class so focused and unified in their energy, giving their full attention to whomever was speaking. My students told them that listening with their eyes as well as their ears was part of their training as actors. I am so grateful that I've learned to practice the gift of fully listening, using my eyes, my ears and my presence. It's a gift that I am happy to pass on.

17

A MAGICAL EXAMINATION

By Adelheid – Bielefeld, Germany

*I*t was Monday morning. Holding a cup of coffee, I entered the Chamber of Commerce and Industry in our town of Bielefeld, Germany. I'm the CEO of an advertising agency. I'm also part of an examination committee that organizes oral exams for marketing students after they've taken their written tests.

That morning, three colleagues and I were set to examine apprentices in marketing. This is a task I love and believe to be very valuable for young people, enabling them to have a successful start to their careers. We began by preparing the exam tasks. We gave the students an example of a client's situation and invited them to produce an effective marketing strategy. Then they presented their suggestions to us.

During this process we encountered a student, whom I'll call Jason, who was having problems.

"He used to be a good student, eager to learn and ambitious," my colleague explained, "but his father died unexpectedly a few months ago. He's been despondent ever since. He's lost a lot of weight and his grades have fallen dramatically. The only chance for Jason to pass is if he delivers not only a good oral exam, but an excellent one. In his current state, I don't believe he's able to do that."

"Thank you for explaining the situation to us," another colleague said. "We'll do everything possible to assist him through the exam process."

"Yes," I said. "We'll support him as best we can."

We came up with an exam task for Jason. We planned to ask him to operate as if he were a manager in an advertising agency. His job was to construct a marketing strategy for a client who wants to open a new coffee shop. When the door to the examination room opened, an emaciated young man with trembling hands sat down at the table in front of us. In order to calm him, I asked Jason to begin by introducing himself and invited him to tell us about the topics he covered in his apprenticeship. It didn't help. He stumbled over his words and kept shivering.

"My God," he said in desperation, "I'm not even capable of introducing myself!"

We reassured him that he didn't need to worry because there was enough time for him to prepare and practice his speech in the next room. Jason nodded, though he didn't seem especially reassured. He left, and fifteen minutes later, he returned carrying the notes for his presentation. He sat, glancing nervously at each of us, and I wondered how to put him at ease. Then I remembered what I'd learned in Ariel and Shya's courses about listening. They said if you truly listen to a person, it enables him or her to be self-expressive. I had an idea. I suggested that we perform the exam as if I were his client. My colleagues liked this concept, so we agreed to give it a try.

I turned to Jason and said in a soft, clear voice, "I'd be so glad if somebody could give me good advice regarding effective marketing communications so my new coffee shop will succeed."

I calmly waited for Jason to formulate a response, giving him my full attention. A moment later as he began to speak, I listened, really listened, to his proposals and he really listened to my questions. I looked straight into his eyes and he looked directly into mine. It felt like an invisible thread was connecting us. I felt him relax. I felt him forget his history and his sadness about his father, as he focused solely on answering my questions.

For the duration of the exam, we continued to stay in the here and now. This was a new experience for me, as I'm sure it was for him. In my experience, it's common to make eye contact with another person for only a few seconds, a few minutes at most, and here we were, joined together in this task for at least twenty minutes without thoughts or judgments or fears. It was an intimate and sweet exchange that deeply affected us both. He settled down. He was calm and he stopped shivering. Slowly, his posture shifted and he sat up straight. Only on occasion did Jason glance at his notes, always returning to make eye contact. He answered all of my questions, precisely and clearly applying his extensive knowledge to the fictional scenario. I asked him some additional questions. He thought about them quietly without getting nervous. Then he presented suggestions, some creative and some a little bit outrageous, that made us all chuckle.

As the examination came to a conclusion, I noticed how silent and still the room had become. Usually my colleagues ask questions of the candidate but this time they didn't because they were just listening, too. We were all connected in our listening and attentiveness and the desire for him to succeed. When it was over, we thanked Jason and asked him to wait outside the room while we decided on his grade. He nodded, handed us his notes, stood up, and left the room.

It was very quiet for a few moments. Then excited voices burst out, "That was incredible!"

"Outrageous! Amazing!"

"What was happening here?"

I told my colleagues what I had learned about "true

listening." I explained how I had listened to the candidate with my full presence, not only with my ears but also with my eyes, dropping any thoughts of what I might say while he spoke. At the same time, I conveyed to Jason that I believed he would give me, his fictional client, excellent advice on the marketing strategy for my coffee shop. My colleagues were mesmerized.

We agreed unanimously that he deserved the top grade, which would ameliorate his poor results in the written examination. What had seemed to be a hopeless situation had been completely resolved, as if by magic. *This is Instantaneous Transformation*, I thought.

When we called Jason back into the room to deliver his results, he could barely contain his emotions. Even before he sat down, he began speaking. "I don't have the slightest explanation for what happened here today," he said. "I was so focused on my task, so involved in my dialogue with you. I wasn't anxious for a second. I didn't think about failing and I totally forgot about my sorrow. I've never experienced anything like that. I can hardly believe it."

We told Jason his grade and explained that he had successfully completed his two-year apprenticeship. He was incredulous.

"This was entirely your achievement, Jason," my colleague said. "You knew so many things and you showed us how much you've learned. You made use of your knowledge in a very effective way when you were giving advice to your client."

"Everything was already there," I said. "All your knowledge was inside you. You simply needed to bring it out."

After I handed him his certificate, an extremely happy young man walked out of the room. All of us were deeply touched. I knew I would never forget the magical experience of this particular exam and my discovery of how much could occur, just from truly listening. I'm grateful for learning this life-transforming skill. I suspect that although Jason may not know it, he is grateful as well.

PART FOUR:

BIRTH, DEATH, AND THE PHYSICAL CHALLENGES IN BETWEEN

18

PANIC IS NOT AN OPTION

By Ariel – Milford, New Jersey

*I*t was day two of our bonefishing trip to Christmas Island, a remote atoll in the middle of the Pacific Ocean. Shya and I were with our guide, walking down a shallow stretch of water called a flat. Soon after I had hooked a bonefish that was screaming the line off my reel, Shya and the guide moved away from me down the flat while I fought my fish. It wasn't long before the fish's blistering run broke the tippet, the piece of monofilament that connects the line to the fly. Reeling in, I retrieved my line, minus the fish and fly and as I looked up, Shya and the guide were far away, about to walk out of view. Then it happened – I began to shake.

I had eaten a fish with ciguatera poison several years before this trip and became severely allergic to eating fish and nuts, which reactivate the poison. Now when I eat fish, my breathing becomes impaired. With nuts, I get some breath impairment but primarily a racing heart and full-body tremors. Before I went out on the flat that day, I'd taken electrolytes in pill form. Even though there were no obvious allergens such as fish or nuts listed on the label, clearly there was something in them that hadn't agreed with me.

Fortunately, I'd brought my waterproof pill container with me in my belly pack and I got it out to take an antihistamine before the condition got worse. By the time I opened the bottle, I didn't need to "shake" any out. My left hand was so unsteady, pills spilled out onto my trembling right hand. Incapable of choosing the correct pill since I was shuddering so deeply, I used my tongue. On my first attempt I missed and dabbed up the orange Ibuprofen, which I spit into the sea. Then I got the blue Aleve, which I also discarded. I managed to get the pink Benadryl in my mouth and swallowed it dry. I couldn't begin to open my bottle of water. I spilled out more pills and swallowed a second Benadryl. I figured it was better to be sleepy that day than have no day at all!

I looked up and saw that I was alone. There were miles of flats and no one in sight as Shya and our guide had disappeared behind a distant stand of scrubby trees. By now my legs were shaking so hard, I was having a difficult time standing. *What to do?* Panic was not an option. I knew from past experience that it would take a few minutes for the Benadryl's antihistamine to take effect. I also knew that focusing on my personal earthquake would only heighten the symptoms. I challenged myself to tie on a new fly, shaking and all. I chose a sweet little "gotcha" from my fly box, slowly tied it on, and distracted myself from my physical discomfort by walking down the flat and hunting for Mr. Bonefish. By the time my guide called a boatman to bring our boat around and came back for me, the shaking had largely subsided.

It never occurred to me to panic. Shya was not there. Other help was not there. I was on my own. Yet I was capable – extremely capable. We're all capable but our thoughts about what we can do and the stories we carry around about what we've done in the past can get in the way. These thoughts and stories can cloud the moment so we often look to others, thinking that we can't take care of things ourselves. If I'd had Shya or someone else with me that day, I wouldn't have hesitated to "share the load." But I was reminded once again that being supported by someone doesn't mean collapsing in on myself and abdicating responsibility.

Shya and I are partners and I have many friends and even strangers who would also step up in a time of need. But on that day, I was surrounded on all sides by miles of water and scrubby trees without another human being in sight. Without thinking, I stepped into the reality that panic is not an option. I'm fully capable on my own.

19

SEIZE THE MOMENT, LIFE IS FULL OF SURPRISES

By Eric – Brooklyn, NY

*A*s I raced to the hospital to see my wife Holly, all I could think was, *Please don't die.*

When Holly and I started dating, neither of us thought we would ever get married. We were both in our 50s and had no idea that we would end up in a passionate and enlivening love affair. Now happily married for more than five years, we are on a great adventure together.

This past January, Holly went to California to handle some family business. I was very surprised when she called me from the hospital.

"Hi Honey, I'm in the emergency room. You know those headaches I've been getting? Well, I have a really bad one and now I can't see out of my left eye."

I've heard the expression, "It was like a bucket of ice water poured over my head." But in that moment I actually experienced the sensation. It's an understatement to say I was terrified by the news.

"The doctors say that I have a brain bleed."

A brain bleed – Oh my God!

My mind went into hyper-drive, filling in with largely inaccurate details from television shows and movies.

I immediately thought, *A brain bleed must mean a stroke! Will she be paralyzed? Will she die?*

Reflexively, I panicked. But, even in the midst of

receiving this horrifying news, I knew that panicking wasn't going to help Holly. So I listened. I told her I loved her and I would get there as soon as I could.

What happened next was a whirlwind of all the things that needed to be handled to get me from one coast to the other so I could be with her; schedules, airline tickets, calling friends for support, a hastily packed bag.

Later that day, in the car to the airport, when I was no longer distracted by things that needed to be done, my mind automatically started to run its list of worst-case-scenarios of what was going to happen. But fortunately for me (and for Holly) I've been practicing being here. It has been such a simple practice that I had no idea how well the "muscle" of being present would withstand the stress of potentially losing my beloved wife.

I took a breath and looked out the window. I noticed a light green Prius, a dark grey Mercedes and the clouds in the sky. I watched a motorist's face as he drove past and noticed the street signs.

From time-to-time my eyes would lose focus and I would be seeing the beginnings of a horror movie in my mind, one where I had lost Holly, one where she died before I got there. But whenever that happened, I simply drew my attention outward to see the world outside my window.

It's a six-hour flight from New York to San Francisco. The airline offered "private viewing" services where I could use my iPad to stream a movie they provided. I soon realized that the alternative was torturing myself with a different kind of private viewing – watching my mind's repetitive, increasingly disturbing films about what might happen to Holly and what would happen to me if I lost her. So I put on my headset, fired up my iPad and chose an action film. A comedy was next and I welcomed the distraction.

When I arrived in San Francisco, I was met by Holly's

cousins and immediately rushed to the hospital. As I entered her room in the Neuro Intensive Care Unit, I was shocked to see Holly looking so gravely ill. It seemed to me that she was hooked up to every conceivable medical machine and device possible and I started to cry. We locked eyes and I went to her and hugged her as tightly as I dared. She looked happy to see me and surprisingly calm. Standing by the bed I held her hand. I was so grateful she was still alive, her hand warm in mine.

"Honey, I've gotten back more results." She said. "The bleeding in my brain has been caused by something else. I have a brain tumor."

I did my best to keep the room from spinning and to keep myself there with her. Her hand in mine anchored me as I digested the news that no one wants to hear. I pulled up a chair and sat. We had a brief discussion and decided that, whatever happened, we were going to live as fully as possible in this moment and, despite all temptations, would not travel down a black hole to a tragic future that hadn't happened yet.

It's one thing to make that decision. It's quite another to live it. Luckily, Holly and I had tools. We'd learned skills for being present and honed them over the many years of attending seminars on Instantaneous Transformation. In fact, throughout her month-long stay in the hospital, I was repeatedly surprised that "scary" things were actually delightful moments when seen through a different lens.

For example, after Holly's first brain surgery (she's had three) they brought her back into the Intensive Care Unit where I was with her as the anesthesia wore off. As she awoke, her eyes fluttered open and she looked at me. Then Holly mumbled, "kiss me" in French. Oh how sweet she was. I kissed her face and then she spoke even more French to me.

While Holly is American and English is her first language, she lived in France for a time, and speaks

French fluently. But the nurse nearby didn't realize that Holly was talking to me in a foreign language and thought her speech was badly garbled. I could tell the nurse was alarmed, afraid that this new disability was an unwanted result of the surgery.

"Oh, no, it's not garbled." I said. "It's French!"

I turned back to my wife and did my best to reply in my terrible, broken version of that language.

Suddenly, I was afraid. I thought that the surgery had somehow broken her ability to speak English. As I was smiling at her and kissing her face, I was also frantically trying to figure out how quickly I could learn French so we could communicate.

Then the nurse did something brilliant. She said, "Holly, I don't speak French. Speak English." Holly said, "Okay." And to my great relief, my French studies were put off indefinitely.

During Holly's recovery from each brain surgery, it was crucial that she have as little sensory input as possible. This meant the room she was in needed to be dark and quiet. As I was determined to spend every waking moment with her, that meant I was not provided with any of the usual distractions from my mind's machinations. Television and conversation were not options. Fortunately, I had my laptop computer with me and, as an attorney with my own law firm, I could work remotely.

As Holly slept, I dove into my work. Emails were read and responded to. Legal research was done and briefs were drafted and filed. I was able to serve my clients and give my mind constructive work to do to keep it from going down painful fantasy paths. I was able to respond via text and email in a timely way to all of the wonderful caring friends and family who were, figuratively speaking, there at our side. Of course I'm human and occasionally I would get side tracked and start to despair, but when this happened, I realized that being upset wasn't helpful

– not to me and certainly not to Holly. So it wasn't too difficult to come back to the moment and get back to work.

Our mutual decision to get interested in what was happening around us, especially the people we were meeting, was incredibly valuable. We engaged with everyone we met: doctors, nurses, and cleaning staff. Because it was the Neuro Intensive Care Unit, Holly was frequently examined, questioned, medicated, and having blood drawn. Each interaction was an opportunity to not just exchange meaningless pleasantries but a chance to be with someone and really listen to him or her. Each moment was a chance to operate as if we were exactly where we wanted to be rather than dream of the day when we could get out of there.

As a result, Holly and I could hear the experts tell us how things were without editing in our heads to make it better or worse than it was. This allowed us to make fully informed choices based on facts, not decisions driven by our fears. This was crucial when Holly's surgeon told us that the first surgery, while helpful in removing fluid that was causing pressure on her brain, was not completely successful.

"I was not able to get enough material in the biopsy for the pathology lab. I need to go back in. Without the material, we won't know the genetic makeup of the tumor and won't be able to properly treat it. I understand if you want to go back to New York to have this done."

Holly didn't want to wait. She also intuitively trusted this man.

"You're part of my team. I trust you to go back in and get it done," she said with a smile. And within a week the second surgery resulted in a successful biopsy, and the material was sent to the lab.

As a result of our training in being here, Holly and I actually enjoyed engaging with people. Whether they were changing a bedpan or part of the surgical team, they were all highly qualified professionals and fascinating beings. We got interested in their lives and included them in ours. We didn't let the circumstances of Holly's illness narrowly define us as only a patient and the patient's husband. We were still whole beings with many interests and unlimited possibilities.

After Holly underwent numerous tests, scans and two brain surgeries, she was cleared for travel, and we returned to New York where we met with a new team of doctors. They hoped Holly could start treatment for her tumor right away. Unfortunately, due to complications, she required yet another surgery. They told us we could do it soon or wait a short time. Holly turned to me and said, "Carpe diem, baby." (That's Latin for "seize the day".)

Holly is currently recovering and doing very well. The experts now believe that Holly's tumor is something she can live with over time, a chronic condition rather than a life threatening one. Our relationship remains strong and we remain committed to seizing the day. For fun, we even got matching "carpe diem" tattoos, and have planned several trips together. I'm not certain what will come next but then, none of us are. In this moment, there is love, happiness, and the adventure continues as we seize the moment and encounter our next series of life's surprises.

20

FROLICKING WITH FRITTATAS

By Naz – Worcestershire, England

*R*emember the old parental dictate, *Don't play with your food?* I used to hear that a lot when I was a child. Food, especially at mealtime, was something of a trial for me because I was so fussy, unless it was sugar or chocolate. I became ingenious at avoiding the healthy things I didn't like. I secretly piled food onto my sister's plate when my mother's back was turned and I built mush huts with the evening's offering that would drive my mother wild.

If dessert had been the main meal, it would have been an entirely different matter. I was addicted to anything sweet, from sugar doughnuts to honey-coated cereals that oozed sweetness in every bite. As I grew older, my sugar intake increased. I was one of those children who didn't put on weight and even as a teenager I was pretty slender. I kept on eating the same old things in the same old way with a few variations on a similar theme until I was forty.

Something funny happens to a woman in her forties or fifties. Metabolism or magic, call it what you will, seems to slow down overnight. It's a bit like losing the fairy dust that Tinker Bell scatters to help Wendy and her brothers fly in *Peter Pan*. A woman's body undergoes a shift in gears, running out of steam, slowing down as her hormone levels start to drop. Mine were dropping.

The hormonal "fairy dust" that had helped me keep the weight off seemed to vanish when I turned forty. Almost overnight, the weight began to creep on, slowly at first, then rapidly gathering pace as I entered my mid-forties.

Finally, I decided that enough was enough. I went on a diet, which seemed to do the job. I breathed a sigh of relief after the ordeal of dieting and depriving myself, and I carried on with my life. I managed to stay trim for the first year, but by the second year, the weight began to creep upward again. Before long, I was at my heaviest. For months, I avoided looking in mirrors. I covered up with layers of clothing and baggy tops. Seeing myself was upsetting and the more I got upset, the more I ate.

Eventually, I discovered the Kanes' Three Principles of Instantaneous Transformation, a simple yet potent framework for resetting my body image. Using them as a tool, I found a way of eating that supported my adult health and metabolism rather than being dictated by my childish habits.

In case you aren't familiar with them, let me briefly lay out the Three Principles:

The First Principle of Instantaneous Transformation is: Whatever you resist persists and grows stronger.

The Second Principle is: You can only be exactly as you are in any given moment.

And the Third Principle is: Anything you see and allow to be without judging it completes itself – in an instant.

Here is how they worked for me:

I resisted the fact that I was gaining weight and I was embarrassed by it. I found both the weight and my embarrassment to be upsetting. The more I resisted my "problem" and complained about it to myself (and to my partner, Laurence), the more weight I gained. That was until one weekend, I realized I could stop resisting, stop complaining and simply face reality by taking a good hard look at myself in the mirror. So I literally stared at myself, looking at all the bits I hadn't wanted to look at while giving myself permission to be upset. And it was in that instant of being in the moment I allowed my depressing thoughts about my weight to be exactly as they were. I didn't judge my feelings, either. I looked at the reality of my weight gain and how upset I was by it.

In a flash, I felt the weight of resistance lift off my shoulders – pun intended – and that feeling of helplessness and sadness disappeared. I suddenly felt lighter and better about the situation. The body I was seeing in the mirror was no longer "horrible" or something to be avoided. It just was. I stopped staring hard at myself in the mirror and the face looking back at me was a kind one, filled with compassion and strength. Now that I had seen my body without the filter of critical thoughts, it was easy to own my weight gain and take responsibility for it. In the blink of an eye, I felt free and motivated. I had just experienced the Third Principle of Instantaneous Transformation – *Whatever you allow to be exactly as it is, without judging it, completes itself – in an instant.*

I was excited to discover new ways of eating that would benefit my body and me. I didn't just want to lose weight. I was eager to have a fresh perspective on what to eat and to become aware of what I was eating. I wanted to find something that I could integrate into my life, especially since I could already feel the early onset of menopause. Little did I suspect that Instantaneous Transformation would have such a big impact on my life-long relationship with food. Now that I was clear that I didn't need a "diet" *per se*, I found the perfect plan to support me in moving away from my life-long sugar addiction. It was a low-carb, low-sugar approach based on eating non-processed foods that are high in fat and low in sugar.

The first few days were challenging as my body adjusted to a lack of sugar, carbohydrates and smaller portions. I was following my familiar pattern with dieting, focusing on the outcome rather than letting it be a moment-by-moment experience. It was no surprise, then, that by day four of this new plan, I could feel my initial enthusiasm and motivation wane. Weight loss and renewed health seemed unreachable and too distant for me to grasp – plus I was hungry. By suppertime, my misgivings grew and I began to question my logic in choosing this strategy, which had by now devolved from having a healthy lifestyle into a "diet." I began to berate myself for going on any food plan in the first place.

Before I knew it, I was engulfed in negative thoughts and I was being unkind to myself. I stood at the kitchen counter preparing my dinner of vegetable frittatas, lost in a downward spiral of self-deprecating judgments and those old, upsetting feelings began to creep back in. Mechanically, I chopped the vegetables, getting them ready to add to the seasoned egg mix, all the while thinking of reasons why I should just give up. And then, like a sprinkling of fairy dust, something happened in my internal conversation. It was a soft, kind voice that gently prodded me to refocus my attention on the moment. It was so sweet-sounding, I instantly surrendered to its wishes.

As I looked down at the food I was preparing, I gasped. It was as if I was looking at a different chopping board. Instead of seeing the dull, colorless vegetables I had been chopping as I tried to get the meal preparation over with, they had suddenly come to life. Now I saw a kaleidoscope of brilliant colors made up of all the frittata ingredients: the vibrant ruby-red of peppers glinted in cubes and the earthy green-rimmed zucchinis with their soft, spongy, creamy centers lay invitingly beside the fleshy mushrooms. I was delighted by it. I picked up a glistening, ruby-red pepper, and I began making patterns with my knife as I sliced, diced and carved it into exciting shapes. In that instant, my senses came alive and I could see, smell, touch and feel the uniqueness of each vegetable.

That evening, I had so much fun frolicking with frittatas, my hunger and self-defeating thoughts evaporated. When it came to the taste test, it was simply sublime! I experienced new tastes and textures and my taste buds exploded with the rich sweetness of the peppers, the earthiness of the mushrooms, and the distinctive flavor of the zucchinis, all encased in the soft, fluffy texture of perfectly seasoned egg. At the end of my meal I sat back, satisfied in both body and soul.

Suddenly this challenging "diet" wasn't so challenging after all. In fact, I was having fun with it. Spontaneously the goal-setting and sense of deprivation disappeared and I experienced an entirely new relationship with food, one that was creative, healthy and inspirational.

So, by all means, play with your food. You just may discover a world of culinary delights and possibilities you've never considered before. All you need is a little transformative fairy dust and the practical magic of Instantaneous Transformation.

21

CHILDBIRTH, LABOR, AND DELIVER-EASE

By Pamela – Brooklyn, New York

*I*f you listen to most people, the experiences of being pregnant, having a baby and caring for a newborn are not only exciting but also difficult and painful. These ideas are so ingrained that any suggestion to the contrary is generally met with a strong disagreement. However, my husband Dave and I are living proof that it can be a smooth, easy, enlivening process.

More than three years ago, we welcomed our son Gavin into the world. The labor, delivery and his first days home were surreal and wonderful. It was a miracle that there was a living, breathing, little person in our home who was a piece of us. Those first few weeks came with challenges and we had opinions on how we wanted it all to turn out. But we learned that life is much easier when we don't complain to ourselves about what we can't control. This allows us to enjoy even the sleepless, uncomfortable moments that come along with parenthood. When I say that pregnancy, birth and having a newborn was easy, what I mean is that things didn't always go the way we would have liked, but we handled it all with a sense of ease.

Throughout my pregnancy, I had three strong preferences. First, I didn't want to have labor induced as many people told me what a long, painful process it could be. Second, I did not want to have a C-section. Third, I got along with some of the doctors at my OB/GYN practice better than others and so I wanted one of my favorites to deliver the baby. But of course, we can make plans, we can have preferences, but life doesn't usually show up exactly in line with our pictures. We discovered that when we embraced the way things *were* rather than hanging on to our ideas of how things *should* be, life became easy.

In the early hours of the morning on our son's due date, our doctors found some minor issues and decided that induction was necessary. We didn't know the doctor on call that evening very well. He was not one of our favorites. As we headed to the hospital, Dave and I couldn't help but laugh because the truth was, our preferences were irrelevant. The little guy was on his way whether we liked the circumstances or not and we could get upset or we could choose to act as if everything happening was our idea.

Throughout the labor, we remained present. We didn't get ahead of ourselves, thinking about when it would be over. We'd been living our lives this way, so that attitude carried over during the stresses of this life-altering event. While the doctors and nurses came in and out of the delivery room, giving us updates on the baby and the next steps, we listened and allowed the doctors to lead us. As labor progressed, the baby's heart rate began dropping. For his safety, they wanted me to start pushing and would use forceps to guide him out quickly. This would have been highly upsetting if we let ourselves get lost in the drama of possible negative outcomes, such as: *Will the baby be okay? Is this serious? Will they need to do an emergency C-section?* The list went on and on. But we noticed afterwards that instead of letting our thoughts run wild, we asked questions and then we said, "Okay.

Tell us what to do next."

Less than thirty minutes later, with the guidance of three excellent doctors, Gavin arrived and he was perfect. His heart rate was great and there were no signs of distress. In the end, the doctor who delivered Gavin was a pleasure, no C-section was needed, and inducing him was a great decision.

I spent two nights in the hospital after the delivery and they were sweet. We were enthralled with our baby, and Dave and I widened our focus to get to know the staff that was caring for us so well. One of the beauties of transformation is being of service to others. We created a mutual relationship with every staff member and each was more friendly and informative than the last.

We had been told that when new parents take their baby home, they put him down, look at each other, and say, "Now what?" We quickly discovered that the "Now what?" was simple. Gavin folded seamlessly into our life from the day we took him home. As all new parents discover, life is not what it was a few days prior. We were waking up throughout the night for feedings and we were working from home as much as our new schedule allowed. Rather than victimizing ourselves and complaining about the experience, we knew this was what we chose for ourselves when we decided to have a child.

A year later, Dave and I decided we were ready to expand our family. In short order, I was pregnant once again. Not long after, I called Dave from my doctor's office where I was having a sonogram to learn about the new baby's progress.

"Dave," I said. "I just got to hear the babies' heartbeats."

"Oh wow!" he said. "Wait. Did you just say 'babies' – did you just say heartbeats?"

"Yes." I replied. "We're having twins."

Now as parents of three small children, there are

plenty of opportunities to either step into the moment or get lost in our preferences. Thankfully, we are still practicing the art of being a "yes" to how life shows up and parenthood is an exciting, constantly unfolding, unpredictable adventure.

22

THERE IS NO MAGIC PILL... OR IS THERE?

By Christina – Rutherford, New Jersey

There are some people who can eat sweets, fatty foods, and fried foods in moderation. I am not one of them. I used to go out to eat and see all my friends ordering hamburgers, french fries, ice cream shakes, cake and cookies. It didn't seem to bother them. They looked healthy and happy and obviously enjoyed eating these treats.

For me however, having those foods would inevitably start a downward spiral of eating where I would gain twenty pounds or more. Then it would take weeks, if not months, to come back to reality. Along the way, I would conjure up excuses to go and get more treats from the store. I would secretly plan to pick up sweets on my way home and I'd eat them before I arrived so no one would ever know. Except me, of course. I was embarrassed. I didn't want to admit to anyone, not even myself, that I was binge eating. I was out of control. I never made myself throw up but I'd just keep eating and eating without ever feeling satisfied. The morning after a binge, I'd feel disgusting and disgusted with myself, which just led to more binge eating.

I've struggled with my weight all my life. It certainly got attention from my parents who were distressed by my yo-yoing weight. I tried numerous diets and nutrition systems that claimed weight loss and most of them worked, at least at first. The problem was, time-after-time, I would always gain the weight back again. That makes sense, given the First Principle of Instantaneous Transformation: *What you resist persists and grows stronger.* My weight "problem" was something that I resisted, and so it persisted.

In March 2016, I attended the Kanes' "Step into Your Brilliance" seminar and my relationship to weight transformed. I suddenly saw that I had been thinking, *Weight loss programs just don't work for me* when in truth, I wasn't really doing them. I was saying I was on a diet but then I'd have french fries, pizza, cake, and other sugary or fried treats on the side. I'd been sabotaging what I said I wanted. I was resisting the fact that in order to lose weight, I needed to be aware of the foods I ate and be honest with myself about their impact on my body. I just wanted to take a magic pill and then I wouldn't have to be careful and I could eat whatever I wanted and as much as I wanted. Fortunately, I discovered another way: being truthful.

Weight loss happened when I kept my word with myself and was honest about what I was consuming. It's a relief to be honest, to know that if I want to be healthy, I can choose an apple instead of pizza and a big sugary drink. To my amusement, I've found that I'm even capable of kidding myself into *thinking* I am making a "healthy" choice when I am not. It's entirely possible to eat a honeycrisp apple (one of my favorites) that is three times the size of your average apple without acknowledging that it has a higher sugar content than many others and it's the equivalent of eating three or four pieces of fruit. It's a tricky form of cheating! It's become fun to see how sneaky my mind can be without judging myself for it.

Once I began following a plan without cheating, I

was amazed by how much weight I lost. I was no longer using the excuse that there was something wrong with me that made me unable to lose weight. Following a program helped, but keeping my word with myself was more powerful than any system of eating. Honesty and awareness have now become a lifestyle.

I still get impulses to binge-eat from time-to-time. I occasionally have a sweet that would, in former times, be the trigger for a round of binge eating and hiding from the truth. But now, I have found that there is a magic pill after all. I recommend taking it daily. It's a mix of awareness and honesty without self-reproach and the result is well-being.

23

ALLYSON'S LAST JOURNEY

By Erica – Santa Monica, California

I had the privilege of spending a day with my forty-nine-year-old cousin, Allyson, in hospice in Michigan. She was at the end of her very arduous battle with ovarian cancer and was not allowing just anyone to visit. Her husband, Tom, had called to ask if I would come. She'd told him, "Erica gets it; I would like her to visit."

I was feeling apprehensive at the airport and I called some friends before boarding my flight from California to Michigan. They reminded me that there's no "right" way to do this – to just listen, listen, listen – and that by allowing myself to be myself – whatever that looked like, I would give my cousin and her husband license to be themselves as well.

My time with Allyson was lovely. The effect of just being there with her had a palpable impact on both of us. She needed someone to listen because she wanted to talk openly about dying and Tom couldn't bear it. Over the course of our lives, I'd not been particularly close to her, so perhaps this gave me the distance needed to relax and listen without being overcome by denial and grief. I didn't get lost wishing that things were different than they were. I considered it a gift and a privilege to listen to her. In fact, it felt like Christmas where you just keep receiving gift after gift.

Allyson and I talked about our families. She said that her mother and my father, who are siblings, have some strong similarities. Traditionally I'd had challenges with my dad, but she gave me a new perspective. She pointed out that he had done so much to grow. "I applaud him, however he did it," she said emphatically. She wanted me to be sure to tell my dad that she was proud of him.

When her lunch arrived, Allyson asked me to feed her. While I did, we spoke of simple things like how much cheese the next bite would have. She told me how different meals were at the end of life, from the texture, to the taste, to everything. She said they'd been the most enjoyable meals.

As the afternoon progressed, Allyson told me that she couldn't sit with anyone in her family like we were doing.

"Technically," I said, "I *am* in your family."

She scrunched up her face and then said, "Sometimes it looks like I'm going to cry, but really that's how I laugh." Her body was so diminished it no longer had the capacity to produce laughter.

She told me at one point she was frustrated that it was so hard for her to find the right words to use, and I told her everything was coming across just fine. She said that was because I listen well. I told her I have some great coaches and friends who support me in that.

For some time I sat quietly, listening to her breathing, listening to the silence. Seeing some books on her bedside table, I noticed she had *The Prophet* by Khalil Gibran. I asked her if she wanted me to read anything from it and she said, "Yes, please." From the table of contents, I read out loud some topics and she picked "On Death." When I finished, she simply said, "Again please." When I finished the passage on death again, she wanted the last few lines just one more time. We also read a few others. She enjoyed "Time" very much as well.

Although we only spent an afternoon together, it felt

profound – as if time had distilled down to only intimate
and meaningful moments. The three hours I spent alone
with her I will treasure forever. From the bottom of my
heart I am thankful for having learned the tools to be
there for her as I was. I could sense what a difference I
made for Allyson and Tom and that's really all I wanted
to do in heading to Michigan. When I made that nervous
call from the Los Angeles airport to get support, my
friends told me I was capable. I'm so glad I listened to
them. I'm so glad they were right.

PART FIVE:

DATING, RELATING, AND FINDING THE ONE

24

OPENING THE DOOR TO DATING

By Cheryl – Hong Kong

I'm sitting in my favorite local café having poached eggs, mashed avocado on toast and an iced latte. I'm ravenous after an intense hot Vinyasa yoga class, still wearing sweaty yoga gear, and am of course sans makeup. The lovely proprietors are accustomed to me visiting every weekend in this manner on the way home from my class. The café is cozy with five small tables, so it's not uncommon for the staff to ask people if they would be okay sharing a table.

"Of course," I say when they ask me that Sunday morning as they offer the spare seat across from me to a nice-looking gentleman. In that moment, I see that I have a choice. I can be overly self-conscious about how I look after a sweaty workout and avoid interaction by reading whatever is on my mobile device. Or I can put all those doubts aside, look up, smile, and say good morning. I chose the latter and for the next hour, I had a fun time getting to know a man who had recently moved to Hong Kong.

This scenario could have been out of a novel or a television program, something I might daydream would one day happen to me. However, this chance breakfast "date" actually did happen. Lately I'm finding that similar interactions occur more and more often when

I'm in the current moment and not lost in my thoughts.

It wasn't always like this. Several years ago, when I first moved to Hong Kong after living in Tokyo for ten years, I had fallen into a common mindset around dating. *There are no men to date and there are no good men* were just two of my internal complaints, fueled by the fears already existing in my mind.

But I soon became bored with those limited beliefs – let's face it, that mindset did not lead to dating. So I began reading various self-help and relationship books and doing a lot of "work on myself" to understand and change my perspective. When I found out that a relationship coach was based in the office directly above the art gallery I owned, I contacted her. Among the various resources she recommended were multiple references to Ariel and Shya Kane and their positive influence. Since I'm a believer in "signs," this piqued my curiosity. I searched online for more information about them and ordered their book *Working on Yourself Doesn't Work*. Upon finishing the book, I enjoyed the best night's sleep I'd ever had. Until then, I'd been a person who rehashed everything: past, present and future – while lying, or rather tossing and turning, in bed waiting for sleep to come amidst the tornado of swirling thoughts. To have such a night without any thoughts, just sleep, was absolutely wonderful and somewhat incomprehensible. If simply reading their book could have such an impact, I had to meet this couple in person.

A few months later I flew to Hamburg, Germany, for one of the Kanes' weekend seminars. When I completed the course, it was as though layers of stress and worry had dissolved. I felt light and free. The seminar, much like reading that first book, opened the door to a new way of operating across all areas of my life, including dating.

I've learned that I have a choice. I can hold on to my

mindset and keep my eyes closed to dating, or I can be open to the idea that there are plenty of dateable men. In their courses, I have listened to the Kanes list populations of cities, states, and countries, highlighting the vast numbers of people all around us that are available. I've learned that it's not about dating to find "the one." It's about discovering who's in front of me right now and getting to know that person.

I still have moments where I get lost in my thoughts or look at dating with a serious nature, but now I can choose to stay present. I have become a lot more at ease and, best of all, I don't have to "work on myself." I smile more often at men and I'm open to whatever happens next, even if it's simply a smile back. I've been meeting more men, too, whether it's while picking avocados in the supermarket, during a chat on a tram ride, or messaging through an online dating site. As I stay in the moment and trust myself, I *see* the available men around me and it seems like there are opportunities everywhere. I don't know what lies ahead or whom I'll meet, but I'm glad I've learned how to open the door to dating. I'm excited to see what happens next.

25

ONE DAY MY PRINCE WILL COME – SO WHY ISN'T HE HERE YET?!

By Katie – Chicago, Illinois

*W*hen I was a little girl, I grew up believing in fairytales. I believed that one day, like all beautiful princesses, I would find my prince and live Happily Ever After. But by the time I reached eighteen and still hadn't been kissed, I started to worry.

My first kiss came during the latter part of my freshman year of college. My older sister attended the same school I did and I would tag along with her and her friends. One of her friends was a charming senior named David. I was immediately smitten. He walked me to my car the first evening we met and we kissed in the parking lot. David became my boyfriend and I expected we'd fall deeply in love and live Happily Ever After. I was looking for my prince and he, being male, eligible and showing an interest in me, fit the bill. For the next month David was all I could think about. So it came as something of a shock when he showed up at my door and said, "We have to talk."

"We've lost the spark, Katie," David said. "I'm sorry, there's nothing else for me to say."

I sobbed. For days. It wasn't supposed to happen this way. Once I'd recovered, I picked myself up again and started looking for that prince. I dated a few more guys during college, but every relationship fizzled out within a few months.

When I graduated with a degree in architecture, I moved to Washington D.C. I was bright-eyed and bushy-tailed, ready and eager to begin my career and meet my prince. The trouble was, I had no idea where to find him. Of my three co-workers, only one was male and he was around my age. His name was John and I found him to be exceedingly annoying. Anyway, he was already married. I met a few more guys through friends and at bars, but I rarely got asked out on dates. Still, I waited. And waited. I felt like a loser.

Eventually, I decided to take love into my own hands. I joined both a matchmaking service and an online dating service and I met Damon. We had a fabulous first date and for the following month, I made him my One-and-Only. After we split up, I met Nick and he became my new One-and-Only. After three weeks, that was over, too. The same thing happened with Steve and then John. True love, it seemed, was more elusive than the fairytales had led me to believe. For some reason though, most of my friends had already found their fairytale ending. I wondered what was wrong with me. I asked myself this question over and over and each time I did, I ended up feeling miserable. I'd been heartbroken at the end of every relationship and it seemed as though the love I longed for would never find me. There had to be a solution.

I turned to the self-help section of my local Barnes & Noble bookstore and I came out armed with four books containing exact instructions on how to find The One. I desperately hoped that these books would solve my plight. I diligently applied all their techniques: visualization, prayer, meditation and journal entries. But to my great disappointment, nothing worked. When I think about it, it was odd that none of these books actually instructed me to get out there and date.

Finally, I found a book whose author lauded her coaches, Ariel and Shya Kane. She talked about the transformational effect the Kanes had on her life and love-life after she read their book *Working On Yourself Doesn't Work*. She had also attended their seminars and I was excited. Could it be true? Could the same incredible results happen for me? I returned to my trusty Barnes & Noble to pick up my own copy of *Working on Yourself Doesn't Work*. The cashier ordered one for me and promised delivery by the end of the week. In fact, she was so intrigued by the title she ordered a copy for herself.

Soon I started listening to Ariel and Shya's internet radio show, *Being Here,* and a few years later, I attended my first seminar in New York City. Since then I've attended many of their courses in New York and Costa Rica. It's been a little over a decade since I first read *Working on Yourself Doesn't Work* and my life has become nothing short of magical. My career as an architect and designer has expanded in ways I never could have imagined. I've tripled my salary. The relationships I have with my friends and family have moved from being contentious, sarcastic and competitive to fun, loving, and supportive. I've come to appreciate the love my parents have always had for me and I treasure them as dear friends and trusted advisors.

What happened with my prince? I took the advice of my good friends and coaches, Ariel and Shya, and began dating for fun instead of trying to find The One. With my sister's help, I created an online profile and got busy meeting people. I dated more than one guy at a time. I dated and dated and dated. There were times when I felt like giving up, but I kept going. And I kept being kind to myself. I no longer worried what was wrong with me. I no longer indulged in negative thoughts because I hadn't found him yet. I just had fun. And, if it wasn't fun, I moved on to the next guy.

Then I met Chris. Our first date lasted for six hours

and ended with the promise we'd meet again. Chris wasn't what I'd imagined as the right person for me. He didn't fit my pictures so it was lucky that Ariel and Shya had given me the great idea to date guys who weren't "my type." Otherwise, I might never have gone out with him and now I am happy to say we are married.

Marriage wasn't the fairytale ending I had expected. But then I am no longer a little girl living a fantasy life, and thank goodness for that. Our Happily Ever After is growing and evolving. It takes a commitment to being open and honest and bringing awareness to how we treat each other.

Chris is my best friend and my real-life prince.

26

SOMETHING'S MISSING

By Tanya – Oxford, England

S omething was very different. My ex-husband, Jeremy, was coming to visit our daughter on Friday– there it was clearly marked in my calendar, three days away – and yet I hadn't thought about it, or him, at all.

This wasn't how his visits usually went. Typically, I began preparing myself days beforehand, getting "centered," thinking through all the possible scenarios in which things could go wrong: him being late, cancelling at the last minute, having to leave earlier than he'd previously agreed. I also usually strategized ways to avoid those scenarios or at least minimize the extent to which they would annoy me. No matter how hard I had tried not to, I'd always thought back to the previous times I felt Jeremy had let me down. I was frustrated that years later, I was still in the position of having to "put up with" his unreliability. Invariably, by the time he actually arrived, I was very far from calm.

But this time...nothing. I hadn't thought about him coming at all. Even as I looked at the date in my calendar and drank my cup of Earl Grey tea, I still didn't have any of the usual worries or complaints. I hadn't told my daughter that her dad was coming in case he cancelled, but it was simply a practical matter rather than something I told people through gritted teeth. The experience felt liberating and as I shut the calendar and got on with my day, words Shya had once said, popped into my mind: "When you stop picking on a person in your thoughts, they can transform."

In the past, I'd heard those words and attempted to apply them to my relationship with my ex-husband. But it was always with an agenda. Back then, I would tell myself not to pick on Jeremy in my thoughts, all the while hoping that this would cause him to "transform" and change his behavior.

It makes me smile when I think of it now. I was still trying to manipulate the situation, to manipulate Jeremy into being different. But this time really *was* different. I had just experienced not picking on my ex in my thoughts and I felt really good. Not only did I feel calm and content, but also it didn't really matter what he did next.

Two weeks earlier, I had attended a weekend seminar with Ariel and Shya in Cambridge, England. During that course, I said that I often felt off-center when I was making arrangements with Jeremy. The Kanes pointed out that I wasn't recognizing my part in creating that discomfort.

"You haven't seen the ways you keep those behaviors in place that you say you don't like in your ex-husband."

I felt the truth of that, even though at the time, I didn't know what my part was.

On Thursday morning, the day before Jeremy was due to arrive, I received an email from him saying, "Hi Tanya, I'm sorry but I have to work tomorrow. This was just dropped on me. I'm trying to make some time on Sunday to see her instead."

However, my daughter and I already had plans on Sunday. Now, usually when this kind of thing happened, there would be an exchange of increasingly accusatory emails on both sides. I would blame him as "the villain of the story" for unreasonably expecting us to drop other commitments because his schedule changed. This time, though, I wasn't annoyed. I could feel his disappointment at not being able to see our daughter. I'd never felt that before and it was strangely sweet. I felt no anger or frustration towards him. So, I wrote back to say that I was sorry to hear about his plans changing, that we weren't free on Sunday, but the subsequent Friday would be good. And what he sent in response wasn't the usual defensive tirade but a simple, appreciative note: "Thank you for this... I think the following Friday is good."

When Friday came, the three of us had a relaxing, fun day together at a nearby wildlife park, filled with the sound of our daughter's laughter. It was as though all the past animosity between us no longer mattered.

Later that day, when Jeremy fell asleep in the car as I drove home, I didn't pick on him in my head for "wasting" this precious time with our daughter. In fact, soon they were both asleep and I found myself smiling at how alike they looked. When we dropped Jeremy at the bus station, he looked me in the eye, something he didn't do very often, if at all, and he said, "Thank you, Tanya."

"You're welcome," I said and I meant it. I still can't quite believe it now, as I sit writing this. It's a feeling I never even imagined was possible.

The following Sunday, I hosted a Say YES to Your Life Meetup at my home in Oxford. Our group discussed Instantaneous Transformation, drank tea and ate cakes, and I shared the story of what had happened with my ex-husband. A woman who'd been complaining about the behavior of her ex only moments before, burst out laughing. "Oh my goodness," she said. "I've been judging my ex-husband in my thoughts, too. Wow, I hadn't seen that."

I nodded and smiled, pleased that my experience had inspired her new perspective. Suddenly, I saw that what had once been missing in my relationship with my ex-husband Jeremy was compassion, kindness, listening and being present. And what was missing now was my judgmental nature.

27

A NEW WAY OF SEEING

By Leah – Brooklyn, New York

My life used to be hard. Money was hard to come by, work was a struggle, and my relationships were basically a lost cause. I was always driving myself to do better and to be better, in the hopes that someday in the future, I'd finally "make it" and feel accomplished and satisfied.

The idea that life could be easy, relationships could be harmonious (and lasting) and that happiness didn't require being any different than I was? *Not possible*, I thought. Or at least it wasn't possible for me. I had too many flaws and failings that needed to be overcome. I'd spent my early twenties assessing my strengths, analyzing my weaknesses, and devising strategies for improvement. I knew that if I wanted success, it was going to take hard work, a long time, and lots of effort. In essence, I thought it would take a miracle.

Then, at the age of twenty-six, I packed up all my worldly belongings into two suitcases and moved from Minnesota to New York City in order to pursue a career in acting. About six months later, a new friend invited me to something called Monday Night Alive. It was an evening seminar about "living in the moment." I'd been taking yoga, reading books about meditation and positive psychology, trying to find a way to be less stressed-out and worried. So I went. When I watched the couple who hosted the evening – Ariel and Shya Kane – speak and listen and laugh, I was in awe that his sentences dovetailed seamlessly into hers and vice versa. I watched the other people in the room – a diverse group of all ages, ethnicities, backgrounds and professions – and noticed that they seemed genuinely, weirdly...happy. I didn't know what to make of it. I'd never experienced anything like it. I enjoyed myself but I was confused. My mind was scrambling to understand how this "living in the moment" thing worked. Even so, something ignited in me that night, a tiny flicker of hope, a feeling of connection, a spark of possibility.

Soon enough, though, my mind got back in control and pronounced the whole thing, *Impossible. Everyone knows that life is hard, relationships are hard, and self-improvement takes hard work!*

The Kanes' way of looking at life was completely outside my day-to-day reality, unlike anything I'd experienced before. Since I was unable to assimilate this new information into the existing framework, my mind determined it couldn't possibly be real or true.

Around this time, my new friend also introduced me to a fellow named Andy with whom I fell deeply, passionately, ridiculously in love. Andy had been attending the Kanes' Monday night and weekend seminars for about a year or so, and there was something distinctly different about him and about the way I felt when I was with him. I didn't have to contort myself into a pretzel, trying to be funny or sexy or sophisticated. I could just be myself. My life in general was pretty blurry back then but I was clear about one thing – this new relationship was special and I didn't want to mess it up.

At Andy's suggestion, I read the Kanes' book, *How to Create a Magical Relationship*. It talked about listening – really listening, not agreeing or disagreeing, but hearing another person from his or her point of view. The Kanes also spoke about being kind to yourself and noticing how you operate without judging what you see. This, they said, was enough for old habits to dissolve all on their own. *Hmm.* Intrigued by the book and ready to accept Andy's invitations to attend another in-person event, I signed up for the Kanes' next weekend seminar.

This time I listened – really listened. At first, my mind was buzzing with questions and complaints and confusion, but the more I listened, the more it quieted down. The more I heard the words and experiences of Ariel and Shya and the other participants, the less I heard the chatter in my head. Pretty soon, listening had pulled me out of my worry, stress, and self-doubt and into real time, into the current moment. Something in me began to relax. Suddenly, I could see things more clearly. I'm majorly nearsighted and have worn glasses since I was fourteen, but it felt like my vision had improved. Without the blurry barrier of my thoughts standing between me and the world, everything appeared crisp and vivid. I looked over at Andy and saw how incredibly handsome, sweet and funny he was. Later, when I went to the bathroom during the break, I looked at myself in the mirror and was surprised to see a sweet person looking back at me. Through these new eyes, she didn't seem quite so flawed, after all.

Not long after that, I had a tiny moment of awareness that would profoundly shift my life and my relationship forever. It was the first time I really got what Ariel and Shya meant when they said that transformation happens in an instant.

Andy and I were hanging out in his room one evening. We were having fun, laughing, cuddling, and chatting when all of a sudden he went quiet. His brow rumpled, his sparkly eyes went dull and his energy seemed to withdraw. I'd been in the midst of excitedly saying something, but when I noticed the change in him, I paused.

"Wait a sec," I said, without accusation. "We were laughing and having fun a minute ago, and now...we're not." I really wanted to know what had happened.

He stopped for a moment and took a look. Then said simply, "I started to say something and you cut me off and talked right over me."

As he spoke, I listened without disagreeing or defending myself. I heard him and saw that what he said was true. I had interrupted him and I was completely unaware of it – that is, until the consequences of my behavior were suddenly visible on his crestfallen face and palpable in the cool distance between us.

"You're right." I said. "I had no idea."

What happened in the next moment was even more extraordinary. I didn't pick on myself. I didn't get embarrassed or make myself feel bad or resolve never to do it again. I just saw the simple fact of what had happened: I'd interrupted him. In fact, I had a habit of interrupting, I realized, as well as not listening and driving forward to make my point. I didn't make myself wrong for any of this. I simply saw it and knew that our relationship was way more important than whatever I'd wanted to say.

I looked at him and truly, sincerely apologized. Instantly, his sparkly eyes lit up and the creases vanished from his face. Now we were both feeling good, connected and even more in love than before. I won't go into the details of what happened next, but you can probably guess.

Nine years later, that funny, handsome man is my husband. We have a playful, loving and vibrant partnership that is beyond anything I could have imagined. It's beyond anything I thought was possible. I continue to enjoy and appreciate the transformational skills I've learned – true listening, being kind to myself, and seeing things without judging them.

Life isn't hard anymore. Work is satisfying and rewarding. Money may not grow on trees but I've discovered how capable I am of earning and managing it with ease. And relationships? Let's just say I'm not a lost cause anymore. I am living, breathing proof that miracles are possible.

28

MEETING MR. NICE

By Erica – Santa Monica, California

*T*here he sat across the table from me – yet another first date. With the advent of dating apps for cell phones, technology has led to opportunity, and I was meeting a lot of people. After all, I was really good at dating – I listen, respond, smile, and often really enjoy myself. But part of me felt like I was just going through the motions. I doubted it was possible to meet someone with whom I could share my life through an app. I just knew I had to be dating to even stand a chance. And in this instance, on this date, I found myself thinking, *This is enjoyable, but he isn't "it."* Oh sure, he was handsome and I was having a good time, but he was certainly not "The One." For one thing, he was too nice.

Two nights earlier, I'd been out with a different guy – a tall, good-looking man with smoldering eyes. His attitude suggested that a woman would never be one of his higher priorities. He threw out some compliments but they were probably just to get my attention. And it worked – this was the kind of guy that could hook me. He was smart, made great conversation, and he made me feel like I'd be lucky to catch him. There was a familiar rush of being drawn in quickly, a primal, potent attraction I found hard to resist. Somewhere inside me I knew that a man like this would never truly partner me in life, but I just couldn't help myself.

So there I was, two nights later, making a quick judgment that this guy was too nice. He was open, attentive, and intelligent. My thoughts whispered to me, *I'm not going to feel attracted to this person.* The date was initially set for an hour, but we sat there chatting for three. It wasn't easy to take my eyes off him and it felt good to be with him. But even though I found the conversation enormously pleasant, I still told myself it wasn't scintillating enough to mean anything.

During the following week, I was in contact with both men. Tall, smoldering eyes guy was not always kind, but oh, that feeling of being pulled into the vortex of attraction was strong. Nice, handsome guy was courteous, responsive, unabashedly interested, and actually making plans with me. Smoldering eyes guy couldn't seem to find the time.

I recalled an anecdote I'd heard from Ariel and Shya that described how the best-tasting blackberries off the vine are not the shiny, bright ones. The bright ones that attract your attention may look the best, but they're tart. The sweet and delicious berries lack sheen and often hang out of sight. They are plentiful but they don't dangle off the vine, taunting you with, "Look how good I am." Instead, they hang comfortably in their splendor, available for anyone who is aware of how to spot them.

I'd been through the dating wringer enough at this point in my life to understand that nice, handsome man was the ripened, delicious berry, and tall, smoldering eyes guy was the shiny, tart one. So, I told myself I'd at least go on a second date with the nice guy. It was unlikely to bear any fruit, so to speak, but at least I'd feel like I wasn't giving up on myself. I was concerned all week that I wouldn't be attracted to him, so I headed into date number two believing it would be our last. I would again politely listen, smile, converse, there'd be no real, physical attraction, and I would move on.

When date number two began, I fully engaged. I set aside my preconceived notions that being with a nice man was not all that interesting. I'd learned enough about being present to understand that no matter how compelling, such notions detract from experiencing the moment. And that night, consciously setting aside those prejudices allowed me to experience what it really felt like to be there on the date with him. This may sound natural and logical, but I'd spent my entire life making assumptions about men and acting as if my preconceived ideas were true.

I approached that date as if I were an explorer of each moment. Nothing in the world was more important than the words we spoke. Those words didn't just float around me. They flowed in. I allowed natural sensations to occur without thinking about what they meant or whether I was supposed to have them. In short, I got out of my own way. Before I knew what was happening, I was drawn to him. The apparent façade of niceness turned into a living connection that had its own pulse and energy. I felt happy and safe in this connection and I realized this was what I genuinely wanted.

When he dropped me off at the end of our date, he got out of the car and wrapped his arms around me. I felt warmth and goodness. I also felt attraction the likes of which I'd never experienced. This was not an explosive chemical attraction born out of my mind's twisted yearnings for a guy that would get a rise out of me but never partner with me. This was pure connection. It was only a sliver that night, but it was enough to totally shift my focus. The part of me that had been so attracted to men that made me feel like I didn't measure up was fading – and oh, what freedom followed. All because I had gently set aside my prejudices, giving myself the gift of slowing down and experiencing the moment.

The shifts that occurred for me that evening and in the weeks and months that followed were profound. Ariel and Shya often say that transformation is instantaneous, yet cumulative. While this certainly was an instantaneous shift, it seemed to also be a result of having listened to the Kanes over several years. I'd heard them suggest to several women to date men that don't produce a rush. They encouraged them to spend time with different men and assess how they felt as a result. Despite being single and in my late thirties and early forties, I had thought this advice didn't apply to me. Still, what the Kanes had said to other ladies had caught my attention and prepared me to invest in the moment and not in my preconceived notions and mechanical thoughts.

My blind attraction to men who produced a rush in me resulted in relationships that vacillated between temporary gratification and anxiety. The bonds that formed were marred by discord and a high degree of drama. This was an automatic pattern for me and it could only happen by spending a lot of energy ignoring how I felt in each moment. My relationship with the nice, handsome man has resulted in a sense of satisfaction, wellness, true intimacy, and joy. With each day, our bond grows deeper and a sense of wellness grows along with it. It's fulfilling in a way that I never could have imagined. The magic of the moment, once I stepped into it, produced a splendor for which I will be forever grateful.

29

MY DATING TRAINING RUN

By Corinne – Zurich, Switzerland

I had just turned forty and hadn't been in a real relationship for over eight years. One rainy Sunday afternoon over a cup of hot chocolate, I complained about this to my friend Sonja. A few days later, I received a text from her about a lovely man named Daniel who was single and would like to date.

At first I thought, *No way! I don't need anybody to choose for me. I can do it on my own. Didn't women fight for the right to choose for themselves?*

Then I had a flashback of sitting in an "Art of Relating" seminar offered by Ariel and Shya Kane. They said to one of my friends, "Maybe you're attracted to people who are not a good match for you. How about listening to your friends? They know you and they don't see you as flawed. They see your brilliance. You can only see a little bit of yourself and often you don't even like what you see."

I saw the truth in what the Kanes had said to my friend that day, so perhaps it was true about me as well. I decided I'd give it a try. Five hours after my automatic "no," I wrote back to Sonja and let her know that she could give Daniel my number. She was thrilled and called to suggest that he and I meet in Zurich at a street festival. Sonja figured that a first date wouldn't be as uncomfortable if we were walking around rather than sitting down to dinner, not knowing what to talk about. It sounded great. My understanding was that we would be going out together with a group of friends so I could get to know Daniel casually and not feel intimidated by meeting him one-on-one.

Well, I was mistaken. What Sonja really meant was that Daniel and I would meet on our own and then have our blind date at the Zurich street festival.

Sonja gave me his first and last name and I immediately looked him up on Facebook. When I saw his picture I thought to myself, *Well this will only be training, not the real run.*

In the Kanes' seminars, I'd learned the concept of approaching dating like you would approach a marathon. In order to run a marathon, it's important to train beforehand. In my mind Daniel was not the kind of man I imagined spending a lot of time with. So I took the date with him as a relationship training run.

Daniel sent me a friendly email and we arranged to meet on the day of the street festival. We wrote back and forth and he asked if he should come by train or car from Basel where he lived to Zurich where I lived.

"Come by train," I said, "and if it gets too late, I have a guest bed"– thinking for sure he would catch a return train, since they run virtually all night from Zurich to Basel.

I met Daniel on a cloudy day at the street festival. It started to rain by the time we fancied some dinner, so we went to a restaurant for a nice sit-down meal. As we were seated, I was secretly happy I had chosen a top that showcased my cleavage very attractively because I wanted to see if Daniel was interested in me physically. But, as far as I could tell, he didn't notice what I was presenting or show any intention of being intimate with me. During that dinner I thought, *Definitely a training run!*

The food was delicious. We laughed and talked a

lot and it wasn't uncomfortable at all. When the rain stopped, we went back out to the street party and walked around. It was a lovely evening but pretty soon, it started to rain again. I suggested that we go home to my place, where I was sure that we would only talk. When we got to my flat, we sat in the living room and talked and laughed some more. Eventually it was time to either have him catch a late night train or go to sleep, so I said, "I can put you in my guest bed."

He looked me in the eye and said, "You can put me in any bed."

My brain exploded. I didn't expect that. He hadn't looked at my cleavage or touched me at all. *What?!* For months I'd been complaining to my girlfriends that I didn't have enough intimacy in my life and here I was, being served something I said I wanted on a silver platter. I thought to myself, *When you're hungry it's not important what food you eat. You just want food.* So I ate. To my surprise the "food" was delicious and juicy. I never expected that.

Now some years later I'm happily married to Daniel – this wonderful, yummy man. I'm so happy I didn't go with my automatic "no." What a blessing I didn't refuse "food" that didn't look good at first sight because it was unfamiliar and nothing like all those other empty meals I'd consumed. Saying "yes" to my life is magic and feeds me everything I need and not what I think I need. It's now feeding me for life.

PART SIX:

BEING IN THE MOMENT
AND ACHIEVING YOUR GOALS

30

RELAXATION IN MOTION

By Ariel and Shya – Milford, New Jersey

*P*eople often ask us how to be in the moment and still accomplish their goals. The answer is surprisingly simple if you're paying attention.

For example, the two of us have a "goal" to be healthy and fit. In support of this intention, we sometimes take advantage of a hill in Clinton, New Jersey, a town near our home, which is perfect for walking. On some days, we park by the bridge that spans the south branch of the Raritan River, cross it, and walk down Main Street for two long blocks until we reach the post office. After this warm up, we turn left and head up the hill. The street climbs through the historic district filled with houses that are centuries old. After making a loop through a small neighborhood, we move back down the hill, through town and back to our car. The grade is just steep enough for us to know that we're climbing, yet also perfect for moving at a brisk pace. When we walk this route, we often play the "Relaxation in Motion" game. It's rather organic, not a game with defined rules and regulations – it's something we've done naturally. This way of moving is simply a reflection of how we live life in general, played out upon a specific circumstance. Here's how it works:

Walking happens with a loose and easy stride. We're stepping with alacrity. We move at a brisk pace but we aren't trying to get to the end of the walk or trying to get it over with. We also pay attention to our surroundings and enjoy the view. There are often birds in profusion. Once we saw a flock of vultures standing on the roofline of a house – a captivating sight. We've occasionally startled deer as they grazed on the foliage in someone's garden. In some seasons, the irises are colorful sentinels along the way. Other times, dogwood trees are in full bloom or the maples are blazing red and dropping their leaves. At still other times, we need to dodge the gingko fruit that has fallen to the ground because it emits an amazing stench if you step on it. At those times "stinko-gingko" can be our mantra. We talk. We enjoy each other's company. If either of us takes the walk alone, we enjoy our own company, too.

The game is to take a walk while bringing awareness to our movements without letting stress or forward momentum creep into our bodies and into our stride. It's about moving at a pace without telegraphing a complaint through body language that walking is "exercise," something we *have* to do in order to be better someday. It's a game of moving without reservation yet without giving the impression that we're in a hurry or trying to get somewhere. It's about being a living, breathing, real-time example of relaxation in motion – where with each step we're exactly where and how we want to be.

We've come to appreciate that by catching the knack of being relaxed while in motion it's easy to naturally realize the goal of health and fitness, all while being in the moment.

31

WORRY OR STUDY – CHOOSE ONE

By Jen – Overland Park, Kansas

I have two bachelor's degrees – one in Business Administration and one in Architectural Engineering. I've also taken several graduate-level classes, so, on a smartness and education scale, I score pretty high. But for some reason, when it came to passing my electrical engineering professional licensing exam, my brain seemed to quit working.

As soon as I had earned my Architectural Engineering degree, I immediately found work as an electrical designer with an engineering firm. I quickly advanced, working on increasingly high-profile projects. Within two years of graduating college, I became the lead electrical engineer, designing complicated power and lighting systems. As I continued to take on greater responsibilities, I set my sights on my next major career milestone: passing the Principles and Practices of Engineering Exam in order to earn my Electrical Engineering License.

The "PE Exam" is given twice a year, in April and October. As my four-year work anniversary approached, I decided to take the next exam being offered in the fall. So I began to study. I read through the material and got together frequently with former classmates who were also taking the exam. But during our study dates, I often felt intimidated by my colleagues who seemed a lot smarter than me. After our sessions, I would get lost thinking that I wasn't any good at this at all, that I was lucky I ever passed any of my exams and even luckier that I'd earned my Engineering degree in the first place.

Finally, test day came and I was nervous. My thoughts tormented me: *Did I study enough? Will I fail? What if the test is too hard? Am I smart enough to pass? I tried to reassure myself: You can do this. Just take deep breaths. You've got nothing to worry about. You can do this!*

After taking the exam, I was on top of the world. I just knew I had passed it – no ifs, ands or buts. I was going to be the next electrical engineer in the state of Kansas. I wouldn't be getting the test results until January, so I gave myself a pat on the back and returned to my life without missing a beat.

When January arrived, the results came in the mail. All my study partners had passed but I had failed. I was devastated. I didn't understand. I'd been so sure that I'd passed. I felt embarrassed to tell my boss and colleagues. I compared myself unfavorably to my friends and secretly complained to myself about how unfair it was that they had their licenses and I didn't.

I didn't take the exam again the following April. I couldn't bring myself to study for it. My next chance would be in the fall. But October came and went, and then another April, and yet another October. Whenever I thought about the licensing exam, a voice in my head would argue: *I need to take this test. I need to get my license. But I'm never going to pass.* There were a couple of occasions when I signed up for the exam, paid for it, intended to study, but didn't, so I didn't show up to take it.

Seven and a half long years later, I finally decided I was going to "get serious" about taking that darn exam. I signed up for an online study course that promoted a high pass rate.

Soon the test day arrived. When I sat down to take the exam, I once again gave myself pep talks: *You can do it!* I even prayed: *Dear God, please let me pass.* But when I read the first question, I had no idea what the answer was. I read the next question. Again, I had no idea. I read the next three questions. I didn't know any of the answers and I began to freak out: *Oh my God! I can't do this. I'm not going to pass. I didn't study enough. I'm never going to pass this damn exam!*

I took deep breaths to settle my nerves, containing my "freak out" enough to read through the questions until finally I found one I could solve. I continued to work through the test until I'd answered all the questions. After I handed in my exam, I felt queasy and had no idea if I'd passed. I hoped I had because I really wanted to, I wanted it badly. As I walked out of the exam room, I discussed the test with the fellow who had shared a table with me. I asked him how he thought he did and I confessed that I wasn't sure of my own performance. He shared with me that I'd talked to myself throughout the exam, sighed frequently, and even cursed to myself under my breath. I was shocked. I had no idea I'd done that.

To my great disappointment, once again, I did not pass. Engulfed in my feelings of failure, I resolved that I was never going to get my license because there was no way I was taking that exam again.

Around that time, I had come across a book called *Working on Yourself Doesn't Work* by Ariel and Shya Kane. I read it more quickly than I'd ever read any book before. When I was finished, I started listening to the authors' internet radio show, *Being Here*. Shortly after that, I attended my first weekend seminar where I met the Kanes in person. I became a regular at their courses, traveling from Kansas City to attend their seminars in New York. Each time I returned from one of their events, my life shifted. Things got easier. I felt comfortable in my own skin and for the first time in my life, I was able to actually relax. I also noticed that my steady stream of mental chatter had quieted down.

The next August, after returning home from a weekend seminar on the themes of creativity and intuition, I noticed that I was thinking once again about the exam. *Am I going to take the PE exam in October? No, I'll take it next spring when life is less busy and I have more time to study.*

Then it was as if a bolt of lightning hit me. Suddenly things I'd been hearing during the Kanes' seminars came back to me in a new way. In that moment, I realized that my life wasn't going to be any better or different in April than it was in the current moment. I felt a wave of kindness towards myself and saw that I didn't have to go it alone.

In the next moment, I realized that I genuinely wanted to take the next possible exam. But this time, I intuitively knew I would do it differently. I knew I'd be kind to myself and I'd ask for support. Immediately, I picked up the phone and called Pamela and Dave, a couple I had met in the transformational community. I told them about my "crazy" idea to take my licensing exam in a mere six weeks. I told them all the reasons why I shouldn't take it: I didn't have time to study, work was too busy and so on. They listened. Then Dave shared a great quote from legendary basketball coach Bobby Knight:

"The key is not the will to win, everybody has that. It is the will to prepare to win that is important."

When Dave spoke those words, I was inspired. I saw that my previous study approach had primarily involved ruminating about passing and worrying that I wouldn't. My incessant thinking about whether or not I could or would pass had inhibited my ability to learn the information. Now I realized that by being honest with myself and being kind to myself, my study approach would be far different this time. I would be *preparing* to pass, not just worrying, hoping and praying.

After speaking with Dave and Pam, I hung up the phone and immediately signed up and paid for the exam. Then I gathered all the study materials I'd accumulated over the years, looked at my schedule, and devised a study plan. But, three weeks later, things were not going as I had hoped – work had gotten busier and finding the time to study seemed harder and harder. I was nervous and worried. The road to passing felt insurmountable and once again I found myself strategizing ways to get out of the test.

Then one Saturday morning when I'd virtually given up on myself, my cell phone rang. It was Pamela. She and Dave were cooking from a barbeque kit I'd given them and they were thinking about me. She asked how my studying was going and I started to cry. I couldn't believe the timing of her call.

She listened as I shared with her my fear of failing, of not being able to study, about my frantic desire to get out of taking the exam. Then she reminded me about the Kanes' Second Principle of Instantaneous Transformation: *No two things can occupy the same space at the same time.* In this case, she explained, I was occupying myself with worry about passing the exam instead of actually studying.

Suddenly I saw I had a choice. I could either worry about something that might happen in the future or bring myself back into the current moment. I realized that I could simply study while I was studying and enjoy it, rather than worry about if I was going to pass or fail. Somehow, Pamela knew to call me that day and I'm eternally grateful that she followed her intuition and picked up the phone.

In the final two weeks before the exam, I paced myself.

I scheduled time to solve problems and I solved them. When I wasn't studying, I got engaged in whatever I was doing. When test day came, I was at ease. I woke up before my alarm went off, fully rested and alert. When the exam started, I read the first question. I answered it. I read the second question. I answered that one, too. The next thing I knew I was fifteen questions in and had answered all of them, effortlessly and easily. *YES!* I was doing it! I was taking the exam and it was fun. When I didn't know the answer to a question, I skipped it and came back later. I read each question slowly, really listening to what the words were saying. There was one problem that I had no idea how to solve. However, by slowing down and really looking at it, I was able to figure out a solution. I was on cloud nine.

When I walked out of the exam that day, I felt content. I didn't know if I'd passed or not, but I knew that I'd done my best and that felt great. This was different from any of the previous test-taking experiences. My thoughts were quiet. There was none of the thinking, worrying, wishing, dreaming or panicking. This time I'd done everything I could and I left it all on the table.

On a fateful January evening, I went to my mailbox and found a large envelope from the Kansas State Board. I carried it into the kitchen. It looked different from all those disappointing letters I'd gotten from the State Board in the past. I was grinning as I slit the envelope open and slid out the sheets of paper. On the front page, it announced in black and white that I'd achieved something that for so many years had eluded me. I had passed my Principles and Practices of Engineering Exam.

It may have been cold outside, but I felt toasty warm on the inside as I got out my cell phone and called Pamela and Dave, eager to share the news.

32

THE SEARCH FOR A BETTER ME

By Colleen – Manhattan, New York

I was a dreamer as a child and I believed that all my dreams would come true. Besides wanting to be a famous actress, I wanted to be "enlightened" – like Jesus.

Raised Catholic, my search for enlightenment began at a very early age with a strong foundation in faith. Every Sunday, my family went to church in our small Montana town. My parents would do their best to keep four small children from making too much of a stir in the pew, as we had a hard time sitting still. Back then, the best part of church for us kids was the doughnuts the congregation would eat after mass – I liked the plain doughnuts.

My dad was a cowboy and a signal maintainer on the railroad, and he wasn't home until after dinnertime. I was the youngest, so when my two brothers and my sister were old enough to go to school, I had my mom to myself during the day. She worked part-time and every weekday morning, she took me with her to morning mass. I loved being with my mom, I enjoyed the smell of the church, and I was fascinated by Jesus. What a great guy. I enjoyed reading children's books about the Bible's scriptures and I dreamt about being like Jesus. If I behaved myself during mass, Mom would take me to the Circle K convenience store for a piece of candy. Doughnuts...candy...it must be the Catholic Church's fault that I have such a sweet tooth!

When my parents and the priest noticed my intense interest in the church, I was granted permission to have my first communion earlier than most kids. I also had my confirmation earlier than most teenagers. These early rites of passage were exciting because it felt like I was getting closer to enlightenment sooner than I expected, and faster than all the other kids. From my perspective, Jesus embodied love, wisdom, compassion and kindness. This was what I wanted – to be a better me, as soon as possible.

With love, drama, and a sense of humor, my family laughed hard and cried hard. When my mom and dad weren't working they were making music. Both of them were amazing singers and musicians and they had a country western band that played gigs on the weekends. Country western music filled our home – whether sung by my parents, us kids, or simply playing on the radio. This music defined my reality of relationship: heartbreak, passionate love, challenging life circumstances and the idea that duct tape can fix just about anything except a broken heart. It also included the belief that with hard work, love would prevail. My favorite song back then was Dolly Parton's "Me and Little Andy" about a little girl and her dog. It tells a heartbreaking story of a six-year-old girl whose father is an alcoholic and whose mother ran away. On one cold night, the little girl dies with the dog in her arms while looking for a place to stay. Whenever that song came on the radio, I sang my heart out and was always sobbing by the end.

When I was a teenager, I got involved with a "Children of Alcoholics" program. My parents weren't alcoholics, but alcoholism ran in our family line and I found the meetings fascinating. I studied the mechanics of the Twelve-Step program and used it to try and make myself into a better me all throughout high school.

In college, I studied theater and partied. I experimented with drugs in hopes of expanding my mind. I used marijuana and had a few rendezvous with "magic" mushrooms and LSD. Then I became interested in other avenues of enlightenment, like Buddhism, Native American rituals, and anything else that interested my peers. But I still hadn't attained enlightenment, so I was determined to find another way.

After graduation, I moved to New York City where I went through intense culture shock, crying almost every day. I was struggling to conceal that I was a naïve "hick" and pretending to be a sophisticated New Yorker. It took about six months, but I finally adjusted to city living and after a year, I fell madly in love with being in Manhattan. I managed to get a few acting gigs, but mostly I waited tables and worked at temporary corporate jobs. I continued taking self-help courses and reading books about enlightenment because I knew in my heart that it was possible for everyone, even me. It just had to be. Why would only a few chosen people like Jesus, Buddha, and the Dalai Lama be the only ones to experience well-being throughout their lives? That wouldn't be fair.

Next, I decided that therapy must be the answer and I saw a therapist for about three years, believing it was the best way to make myself a better me. I started digging into my past and found myself feeling angry with my parents and blaming them for my foibles. I had a couple of unfortunate phone conversations with them, grilling them on their choices, letting them know I was screwed up and it was all their fault. Eventually, I would go on to discover that many of my childhood memories were not accurate, that my parents had done the very best they could and had done a great job raising me.

After I quit therapy, I was going through my mail one evening and saw a pamphlet promoting some popular self-help books. The book that caught my eye was called *Working On Yourself Doesn't Work*, by Ariel and Shya Kane. The title made me laugh out loud, so I bought it. It was a great book. I read it quickly, highlighting it with my yellow marker and making copious notes in the margins. Then I put it on the shelf with all the other self-help books I'd devoured. The truth is, I could've stopped my search for enlightenment right then and there with that book since I felt such a sense of well-being when I read it. But I thought, *It can't be that easy*, and I went on compulsively looking for "the next thing, the better thing." I just couldn't stop searching.

Next, I tried meditation. I really liked it but I still didn't like myself. During this time I met the man who would one day become my husband. I was singing in a pop/rock band and we were recording a CD, so we hired a renowned sound engineer named Jay to mix and master it. Jay was sexy, smart, talented and extremely funny – everything I wanted in a man. Once we got together, we had some glorious fights. But that's what I believed love was – just like the country western songs had taught me.

After three years of meditating, I still hadn't found enlightenment so I figured I must have been doing it wrong. In an attempt to do it right, I signed up for a six-week meditation course and my life finally turned a corner. But not, as it turns out, through meditation.

Years before, when I ordered *Working On Yourself Doesn't Work*, I'd ended up on Ariel and Shya's mailing list. As a result I received their bi-annual postcards with the dates of their New York City seminars. For about six years, those cards had ended up in the junk mail pile on my desk. But the weekend before I attended the first session of my meditation course, I received another one of those postcards and this time, something changed: I finally read it. I didn't just glance at the card and set it aside. For the first time, I actually read the words. They asked, "Have you ever wondered what it would be like to truly live in the moment?"

I blurted out, "Hell yeah!"

When I flipped the card over, I saw that there was a seminar that Monday evening. It was only twenty bucks. My meditation class wasn't starting until Tuesday, so Monday night was perfect.

I attended my first Monday seminar with the Kanes on an early summer evening in 2003. It was the most pivotal night of my life. When I got home I went into my husband's recording studio, I sat on the couch and started to cry. Jay was worried and asked me what was wrong. I answered, "I found it. I found what I've been looking for my whole life."

I only attended two of the six meditation classes because they were so serious and everyone was working so hard to be enlightened. On the other hand, Monday evenings with Ariel and Shya were light and fun. My life began transforming without my doing anything to change it. I started to find kindness for myself. I learned to listen, really listen, which completely transformed my relationship with my husband. It was like magic!

Now, Jay and I enjoy being together more than anything. If we get upset, we talk about it and listen to each other. I revel in being responsible for my relationship. If we get out of sync, I no longer look to see what he's doing wrong, I look at myself and see what may be causing discomfort in our relating. When I feel my familiar tendency to start a fight, I find it so much easier to simply drop it, whatever *it* is. I've discovered that, in every situation, I have the choice of either being "right," righteous and unyielding, or being "alive," fully self-expressive, loved, satisfied, happy. I've also come to realize that when I choose the alive route, I fall more deeply in love with Jay and with my life. Originally, I'd been afraid that if I let go of being angry and right, I would become a doormat. But now I have the courage it takes to step up and be honest, which makes it so much easier to communicate rather than blaming Jay when I feel out of sorts.

I've discovered that enlightenment isn't an achievement but a lifestyle. It's a moment-to-moment practical thing that includes discovering that I've lived and continue to live my life perfectly and that my parents raised me brilliantly. Nowadays, my mom and dad are two of my very favorite people.

My dreams have come true. I'm finally perfect just as I am, including my foibles. There is no need to be a "better" me and yet I'm still learning and growing every day. I'm in love with an amazing man, I'm a superstar where I work, I'm writing and recording my own music and I feel happy. I don't cry hard anymore and I laugh a lot. Dolly Parton is still my favorite singer and duct tape can still fix just about anything. Jesus would be proud of this country bumpkin from Montana. I know I am.

33

GRANDMA'S PURSE

By Ariel – Milford, New Jersey

I grew up in Gresham, Oregon. At the time, it was a sleepy farming community where the children had summer jobs picking berries and went for ice cream floats at Rexall Drugstore with the money they earned. Our house was a two-story white structure on the edge of the woods with a separate garage and a little playhouse that was perfect for my sisters, Cathy and Mary, and me.

On the top floor of our house, under the eaves off Cathy's bedroom, was an attic space where my folks stored Christmas decorations, luggage, and things that were out of season. One of the treasures in the attic was my Grandmother's purse.

Ila May Powell, my mother's mother, had died a year before I was born. She was born in 1906 and lived much of her life near Portland, Oregon, until her death in 1957. After she and my Grandpa, Larry Halif Cermack, eloped, she went on to have eight kids. My mom was the eldest.

One day when I was young, my sisters and I were playing in the attic when we came across Grandma's purse. It was black with a single strap and a simple gold clasp at the top. We brought it out to Cathy's bedroom, climbed up on her bed, sat cross-legged facing each other and carefully removed the contents, one piece at a time.

Inside was a comb, a crochet hook, a clean white hanky with tatted lace that Grandma had made herself, a coin purse with a few coins, a pencil, and a small, handwritten, shopping list: Butter, eggs, coffee, milk.

We marveled at the writing. It was wonderful to see something Grandma had held in her hands that she'd actually written. All these years later I remember that list. And I also remember something else. Grandma had things left to do on the day that she died. I've always been touched by that fact. She had a full life. She did many things. And yet apparently she still had things left to be done. That she didn't do them didn't make her life incomplete and she didn't fail in any way. Somehow the fact that she still had a grocery list when she died allows me to be relaxed about my desire to get things finished or over with.

It's so easy during our lives to press to get everything done. Most people feel pressured to complete everything on their list by the end of the day. Many feel that they have failed if there are tasks yet to be accomplished, goals yet to be achieved. But I've come to realize that I am likely to always have a list. It's a component of being alive. So at the end of each day, I can put it away and let myself be. If I'm taking a day off or going on vacation, I can let go of that list. It will still be there when I return. "Finishing" something, completing my list of "to dos," crossing that finish line is not a final destination. It's simply a part of daily living – a part of living my life.

34

JUST WHAT I WANT

By Shea – Brooklyn, New York

A number of years back, I was sitting in one of Ariel and Shya Kane's weekend seminars. The specifics of the conversation escape me, but I remember hearing Shya say, "If you want to know what you really want, look at what you've got."

When I heard this, I immediately disagreed. At that point in time, there were circumstances in my life that I was sure I didn't want, certain areas where I felt unsatisfied, contentious, and inadequate. It seemed unfair for someone to say that I wanted these things, that they were somehow my choice. And yet, during the months that followed that seminar, in spite of my initial disagreement, the idea that I had exactly what I wanted frequently bobbed to the surface of my thoughts.

A part of me knew that the statement was true, regardless of how inconvenient it was for me to admit. But over time, admitting that I had just what I wanted became easier. It allowed me to take responsibility for my actions and suddenly my word to myself had weight. If I was the person who made a choice to eat a sugary late-night doughnut, then I was also the person choosing to go for a brisk run the next day.

When I took ownership of my actions, I stopped being a victim of my own behavior. I saw this clearly one day while I was working as a server in an Irish pub in Brooklyn, New York. At this busy bar and restaurant, I found that I was good at waiting tables. I got to work on time and I got along well with staff and customers alike. Still, on some level, I resented my job.

You see, I'm also an artist, and everyone knows it's a great injustice for a person gifted with creativity to be restricted to the menial, thankless task of serving people french fries and beer. At least, that was the argument in my mind. I remember standing by the big espresso machine one afternoon wiping up coffee grounds, when something I'd heard in the Kanes' seminar popped back into my head, *What if the circumstances of your life persist to the degree that you resist them?*

Though I had been doing my duties at the pub, in that moment it became clear to me that I was still resisting the job. I was operating as though I didn't want what I had, as though it wasn't my choice.

Standing there next to the coffee beans, the afternoon sunlight streaming through the windows, I stopped feeling antagonized by the circumstances of my life. I gave myself permission to go about my job fully, to enjoy myself, and to treat it as my choice, which indeed it was.

For the next several weeks, I engaged in my work as though waiting tables in a bar was exactly where I wanted to be. Whether I was refilling saltshakers, wiping down tables, or reciting the Daily Special to customers, I went about my work like it was my idea. To my surprise, I had fun. I felt satisfied, energized and creative. Ironically, as I went about my life as if it was perfect and I was doing what I wanted, new opportunities began to show up.

Within a month, I found myself in an entirely new and exciting set of circumstances. Following an impulse, I applied for a job at a web company whose software I'd used to make a portfolio for my artwork. After several interviews, I was hired. Getting my new job didn't feel like a hard-won victory or like I had overcome great odds. It felt strangely effortless, like I'd stepped through an already open door.

Nowadays, no matter what I'm doing, I'm going about things with passion and creativity. I'm not waiting for the day when I become recognized as an artist for my life to begin. I already am an artist and I have just what I want.

35

I CAN'T DO THAT!

By Ralf – Cologne, Germany

*I*t was a lovely afternoon in March of 1998 when my boyfriend Arne came home and said, "Did you see the advertisement in the theater magazine? They're doing a new musical in Cologne."

"Yes, I saw it," I said.

"Are you going to audition?"

"No. I can't do that!"

"Why not?" Arne asked.

"I read the description of the roles and I get the feeling that it's not for me."

"It's perfect for you," Arne insisted. "You should apply for it immediately."

Fortunately, I listened to Arne and followed his suggestion and applied. It was the launchpad for a dream come true, even before I knew the dream existed.

Two weeks before at an informational evening led by this American couple, Ariel and Shya Kane, I'd heard about the ideas of "truly listening" and "being in the moment." The seminar had taken place in Hamburg, Germany, where Arne and I were currently living. Our singing teacher, John, had invited us to the evening event. At the time, we'd just graduated from acting school and Arne was working in a big musical production. I was looking for a job and secretly thinking that I would never get one. At the end of the evening with the Kanes, we both felt a lightness, something I'd never experienced before, so we signed up for their weekend seminar that was scheduled for three months later.

By the time the course rolled around, I'd been invited to audition for that new musical at the theater in Cologne. My appointment was scheduled for the Monday immediately following the weekend seminar and I was nervous and conflicted. *I'm not sure I should go to the seminar,* I thought. *Maybe I should stay home and rehearse some more.* I was driving myself crazy, but I remembered feeling light and easy after the introductory evening. I took a leap of faith and went to the weekend course.

During the seminar, I got up and revealed my reservations about being there. I said I was worried that it might have been better for me to stay home and prepare for my upcoming audition in Cologne.

"Do you know your song by heart?" Ariel asked.

"Yes," I answered, without missing a beat.

"Did you learn your lines for your scene?" Ariel said.

"Yes."

"Then forget about the audition during the course of this weekend and instead, fully engage in what is right in front of you," Shya suggested.

What? I shouldn't secretly practice my lines and my song in my head while I'm sitting here? I shouldn't think about what I did wrong in past auditions, or in the past in general? Or worry about whether or not I'll get the part? Just engage in what's happening in the moment? But how is this going to help? It was a strange concept to me.

"If you know your song and you've learned your lines then you've rehearsed enough," Ariel said. "Why not take a break from the future and be here? That's the best possible preparation there is."

"On Monday you can go to your audition and be there

for whatever shows up!" Shya said.

Although the Kanes' suggestions were odd, new, and far outside anything I'd expected them to say, the ideas were relieving. I felt tons of weight lift off my shoulders. When the weekend was over, I felt excited about my life, centered and very grounded.

The next morning, at five o'clock, I took the four-hour train ride to Cologne. Traditionally, I'd have tried to find excuses not to go, but that morning, I felt an inner drive that was totally new. I felt eager to get there and audition.

When the train reached the station, I made my way to the theater, signed in and got a number in the queue of actors who were auditioning that day. As I was waiting my turn, the drive and eagerness I'd been feeling slowly leached away. They were replaced with a host of worries and negative thoughts. I began doubting myself, my ability to sing, my song choices and my talent in general. *I can't do this*, I thought. *I'll never get this job.*

Pretty soon, I was complaining in my head about the director and how "bad" he was, even though I'd never met him.

It wasn't my turn yet so I stepped outside to clear my head and remembered what Ariel and Shya had said during the weekend. "You are not your thoughts. You're not the voice talking to you in your head."

Just then, two actors came out of the theater.

"Are you leaving already?" I asked.

"Yes," one of them said, "we already sang and this director is terrible."

"He really is a jerk," the other one added. "If I were you, I would leave right away without auditioning for him. It's not going to be a nice experience."

When they left, I saw that I had a choice. I could step into the "complaint department," get lost in my thoughts and be right about what a bad person the director was without knowing him. *Everybody knows how these directors are.* Or I could follow my heart, reengage in this moment and step into my brilliance.

I took a deep breath and I resolved to go inside. I was determined to perform to the best of my abilities, meet the director, and be there for whatever showed up.

I was called in, sang, did my scene and was invited to chat with Walter, the director. I found him to be funny, smart, and thoroughly engaging. A half hour flew by and I hadn't even noticed. Walter wasn't anything like what those other disgruntled actors had described. I genuinely liked him right from the start, and I surprised myself by immediately getting the job. In fact, I was hired for a whole year as an understudy for two of the main roles.

I loved my new job and pretty soon, I got an offer to continue working for Walter. After many months of commuting back and forth, Arne and I moved from Hamburg to Cologne and made our home there. Eventually, Arne was hired at the theater also.

Fast-forward fifteen years. In the fall of 2013, Walter, the man who'd been my employer and director for all of those seasons, approached Arne and me. He told us that he and his partner Rolf wanted to sell their theater company so they could retire and asked if we would be interested in buying it.

Wow! Can I do this? Am I ready? I wondered.

Arne and I had been discussing our desire to have a theater of our own and we'd begun looking for possible venues. When this opportunity arose, we were thrilled and quickly entered negotiations. Everything was going well until things got stuck. Walter and Rolf were dragging their feet. After many years of owning a theater company, perhaps the future seemed daunting to them. I'm not sure. What I did know was that negotiations had stalled so Arne and I set up a meeting with them.

"We're wondering if we can find somebody who will

pay us a hundred thousand Euros more than you're willing to pay," Rolf said.

I felt tense, not knowing what to say. I wanted the theater but there was no way we could pay that much money. I felt my panic starting to rise. Then all of a sudden, Arne spoke in a kind but direct way. "Look," he said, "it's likely that if you keep looking, you can find somebody who will pay more. The question is, who do you want to sell your theater to? Ralf and I would be honored to take over your theater and continue your life's work, but it won't make us any happier. We're happy now and we will be afterwards, with or without the theater. We're not going to play the 'maybe-somebody-will-pay-us-more' game. You have to make up your mind."

Walter and Rolf looked at Arne as if a volcano had just erupted. They couldn't believe what they'd heard. Then they looked at me, expecting me to revise or contradict what Arne had said. For a second, I had the impulse to do just that, but I felt the truth of Arne's words. Our truth. We wanted the theater but I knew in my heart that making this deal wouldn't *make* me happy. I was already happy. If this fell through, we'd be perfectly fine rehearsing and playing the upcoming season while we searched different venues for a theater of our own.

I gave Arne a smile, looked at Rolf and Walter and said, "As Arne said."

By the next week, Walter and Rolf had confirmed the price and drafted the contract. A couple of months later, all four of us signed it. That was the day our dream came true.

The thought "I can't do that" is still there sometimes. But instead of the loud, screaming voice it used to be, it has faded to the background. I've learned to engage in what is actually happening in the current moment, and to take care of the people around me.

If I have the thought, "I can't write and direct a show,"

I simply remind myself that I've already written many successful original plays and have directed over twenty successful productions. I catch those thoughts quickly and become amused by the way my mind works, rather than automatically believing them to be true.

Now, we perform night after night in a theater filled to capacity. Performances are sold out months in advance. When the curtain opens, I look out at the audience sitting in our theater, enjoying our show, and feel a rush of gratitude that Arne and I are living the life of our dreams.

Ultimately, I've discovered over and over again – I *can* do that, after all!

36

WAKING UP FROM THE DREAM

By Ariel and Shya – Milford, New Jersey

*B*ack in the mid-eighties, we walked into a health food store and noticed a tarot card reader. She was offering short sessions to the store's clientele for a nominal fee. We were departing within the week for a six-month intensive course at a meditation center in Europe and thought it might be fun to see what she had to say about our imminent trip. We hoped that these six months would produce the self-realization for which we had worked long and hard to achieve. When our turn came, we sat with the tarot reader, expecting a fun, lighthearted reading that would affirm we were on the right path that would bring us the illumination we desired. Contrary to our expectations, however, we were in for a big surprise.

It's shocking how disturbing it can be when someone gives you information that is in opposition to your point of view. There, sitting next to the seven-grain bread and organic beans, this tarot card reader told us what she saw with the best of intentions and we didn't like it. Gazing at the cards in front of her, she said, "I see you're going on a trip."

This sounded like a good beginning. We hadn't given her any information. Then she said, "This trip is not a short vacation but a lengthy stay in a distant land. You'll be traveling over a large body of water so wherever you're going, it's overseas. The cards indicate that this journey is one that is not lightly undertaken but rather it's of a spiritual nature, like a pilgrimage of sorts."

Wow, we thought. *She's really good!* If there had been a hidden camera recording this event, the video would have shown us eagerly listening to catch every pearl of wisdom that this reader had to say. It's funny how we were hoping to prove that the road we were traveling was "perfect" or "right." But the smooth road we were on with this reader was about to take a sharp and bumpy turn. She had created credibility with us by describing the near future events that were part of the script of our lives, but then she said something that sent us into a panic.

We looked at the cards intently, as if to catch some subtle nuance, as this woman solemnly pronounced that as a result of this trip and our experiences, we would become disillusioned.

Oh No! We wanted illumination from this investment of our time and energy, not disillusionment, whatever that meant. It sounded so negative and we wanted our lives to be positive. Here we were, about to invest six months and a lot of money, and we didn't want to be disillusioned as a result. To tell the truth, it's hard to remember what happened next. The idea of being disillusioned by this trip of a lifetime, something we had planned to save us from ourselves and from the domination of life, was very upsetting. We thanked the reader rather stiffly, and left the store, deeply shaken by those few words with which we disagreed.

One week later we were in Europe. Six long months later, we left Europe, disillusioned. On our journey, the two of us discovered that we were not interested in a counterculture way of life, which by its very nature is based in opposition to that which already exists. Rather, we realized that we wanted to live our truth, which is not for or against the so-called Establishment.

When we got back to the States, we thought about what the tarot card reader had said and we broke out the dictionary to look up the word "disillusion." We were surprised by the definition. We'd thought of being disillusioned in terms of what one might find in a thesaurus, i.e., failure, disappointment, falling short of, dashing one's hopes, etc. But in fact, the primary definition of disillusion is "to be free of illusion and false ideas." It means that the illusions under which you have been living dissolves, so you see the truth of the situation as it is, not as you would prefer it to be.

This disillusionment was the beginning of our self-realization. After we returned from Europe, we discovered that nothing was going to save us from ourselves or from the domination of life – for no matter where you go, you bring yourself along. Over the years, as seminar leaders, authors, radio show hosts and individuals living our lives, we have come to realize that the only time life dominates you is when you are not living in the moment. When you are not being here, your hopes for the future create an illusion, a dream of how it will someday be better than it is now.

True freedom happens when the illusion dissolves and you live life directly in each moment – not as you would prefer it, but as it is. In order to live life to our potential, rather than striving to be better, all we need to do is notice without judging how we are being right now...

and now...

and...

ACKNOWLEDGEMENTS

Thank you to all of the contributors who have so graciously allowed their stories to be printed in this book so that others can experience *Being Here... Too*. We appreciate the courage it takes to share your private moments with others.

AFTERWORD

Thank you for reading *Being Here... Too*!

One of the best ways to support this book and its authors is to write an honest review – it's a great way to share the wealth and let others know what's possible.

Why not take a moment and write a review on Amazon or your favorite book review website?

Advance praise for
Arctic Quest

"I was grabbed from the first page. Few young whippersnappers can pull off an adventure this thrilling with such charming and refreshing naiveté and later write about it like an old pro. His masterful story-telling ability riveted me to the book. But by the end I realized I had gained so much insight into the politics of oil exploration in this contended wilderness. I can't wait to see what's next from this new young writer."

—Bernd Heinrich, author of
The New York Times' bestseller,
Ravens in Winter
and *Winter World: The Ingenuity of Animal Survival*

"For most of us, the Arctic exists only as a place of the imagination, a kind of mythic realm of ice-bound ecological purity. Ironically, her destroyers (read: Big Oil) exploit our good-hearted optimism, doing their dirty business at the top of the world under the cover of ignorance. But now they've been outed, thanks to Chad Kister. By foot and raft, Kister traversed the North Slope, down wild rivers and across the caribou plains of ANWR to Gwich'in villages and the belching ruins of Prudhoe Bay. His chronicle of that journey, *Arctic Quest*, cleaves through the myth to reveal a terrain that is much more interesting than our wildest imaginations—and more threatened. This is travel writing in the spirit of Peter Mathiessen. The prose is as crisp as the land it describes and as urgent as the looming threats to its existence."

—Jeffrey St. Clair, Coeditor CounterPunch
author, *Whiteout: the CIA, Drugs and the Press*

"*Arctic Quest* is an account of one young man's willingness to take on Big Business and corporate destructive activities, on his own. It is also a remarkable account of individual survival under conditions of extreme adversity. I highly recommend it to anybody who is interested in the survival of the natural world."

—Farley Mowat

"In case you've heard some Republican congressman explain that the Arctic National Wildlife Refuge is a desolate wasteland, this book will remind you in the most vivid terms of its beauty and transforming power. And it will also serve as a damned good expose of the 'clean' oil development at Prudhoe Bay. Oh, and it's a corking good adventure story to boot."

—Bill McKibben, author
Enough: Staying Human in an Engineered Age

ARCTIC QUEST

ODYSSEY THROUGH A
THREATENED WILDERNESS

Chad Kister

Common Courage Press   Monroe, Maine

Library of Congress Cataloging-in-Publication Data is available
from the publisher on request.

ISBN 1-56751-236-4 paper
ISBN 1-56751-237-2 cloth

Common Courage Press
Box 702
Monroe, ME 04951

(207) 525-0900; fax: (207) 525-3068
orders-info@commoncouragepress.com

See our website for e-versions of this book.
www.commoncouragepress.com

First Printing

Printed in Canada

*This book is dedicated to the Gwich'in people, whose fate depends on the
decision by Congress whether or not to drill on the coastal plain of the
Arctic National Wildlife Refuge. A second dedication goes to Arctic Refuge
activists who are struggling to protect this great ecosystem.*

Contents

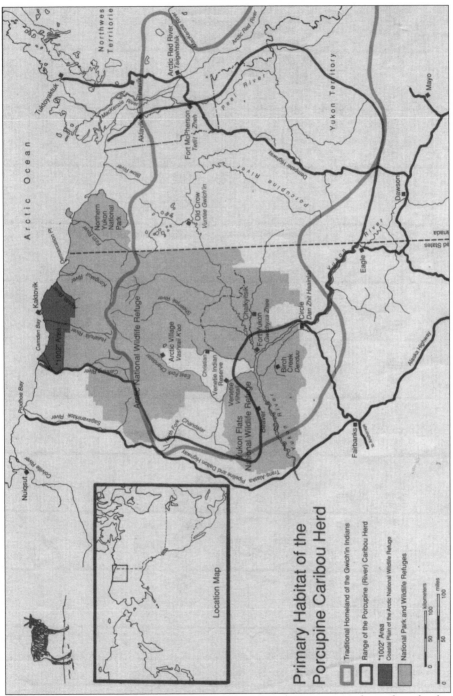

This is a map of the Porcupine Caribou Herd Range, overlapped with the Gwich'in peoples range. The dark area is the coastal plain, where the caribou migrate to calve every spring. It is the calving grounds—the heart of this massive ecosystem—where oil companies want to develop.

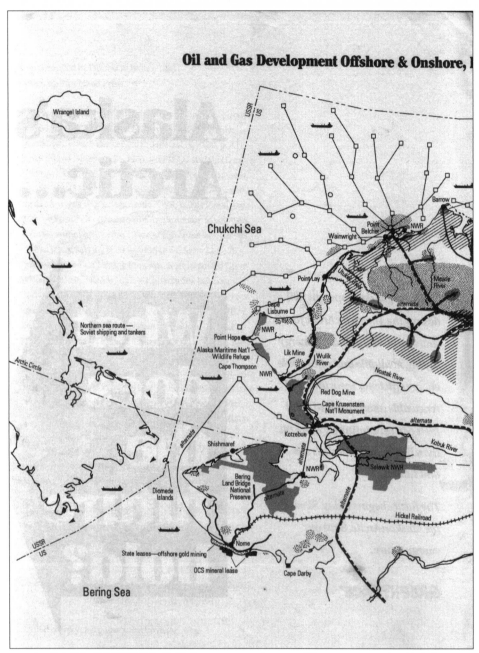

On these two pages: A Greenpeace map showing the proposed development through the north slope of Alaska

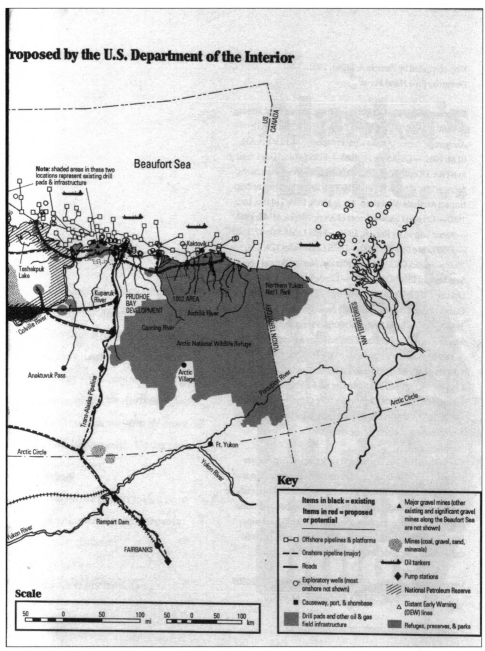

Proposed development in the Arctic Refuge.

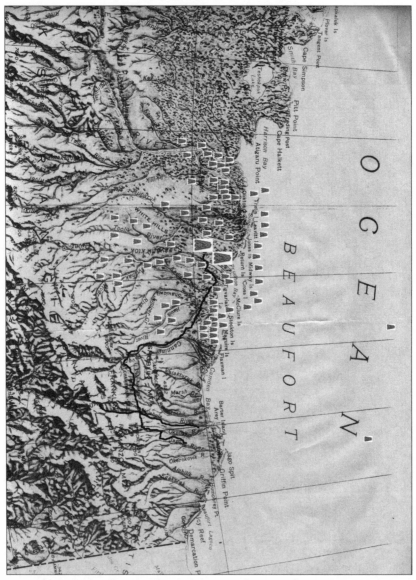

My several hundred mile trek. The dark line on this map shows my route through the Arctic Refuge by foot and raft (not including my many side trips).

Preface

From far south of the Brooks Mountain Range, east into central Alaska and west hundreds of miles into Canada, bands of caribou migrate for a distance exceeding a thousand miles north. Over the glacier-encrusted peaks the caribou climb. They swim across the mighty Porcupine River that gives the herd its name to reach the coastal plain of the Arctic Ocean. On the 1.5-million acre coastal plain, up to 200,000 caribou unite to give birth. North of the 7 to 200 mile wide wetland plain is the Arctic Ocean. To the south are the jagged mountains. This is the land of the caribou, and they have nowhere else to go.

The coastal plain is the heart of the last intact Arctic ecosystem left in America, encompassing more than 100 million acres. The Arctic Refuge is the largest wilderness area in North America, and globally it is the largest wildlife sanctuary in the world. It is a nationally designated wildlife refuge and is one of the few places on earth with all of its original inhabitants still intact. But oil companies and their hired, mostly Republican lawmakers, are trying to develop a massive industrial complex on the coastal plain of this wilderness. What will happen if this development takes place?

*

Lush green tundra of flowering beauty extended to the horizon in the glossy pictures of the Arctic Refuge. Clear water, unscarred mountains, hundreds of thousands of caribou massing together, grizzly, muskox and wolf beckoned me north. I wanted to get away from the stressful college life to see true wilderness. The Arctic Refuge spans from Northeast Alaska into Canada. It has the last remaining caribou herd spared human scar from its wintering grounds to its calving grounds, an area the size of California. The greater ecosystem that the Porcupine Caribou Herd feeds is about the size of Texas, and include the Gwich'in people, who are among the last indigenous peoples living predominately from traditional resources. To the east of the refuge in Canada, corporations developed oil around the Mackenzie River. To the west, a consortium of oil companies called Alyeska developed around Prudhoe Bay and built the 800-mile Trans-Alaskan Pipeline to the port of Valdez. The western 95 percent of Alaska's Arctic coastal plain has been developed for oil, leaving only 5 percent left as wilderness. Now, Alyeska is poised to develop the refuge between these two developments.

To cross the Arctic rivers and lakes, and to get to an island in the Arctic Ocean, I bought a 13-pound vinyl raft and fold-up paddles for $50. Though the trip would last 3 months, with all the weight being taken up by the raft I could only pack about 10 days of food. I packed ultralight fishing gear and a guide to the edible plants of North Alaska: the uncertain food I planned on for the bulk of my summer's diet. I studied Arctic survival techniques, and about the experiences of other explorers of the far north in self-created college honors classes when I was a student at Ohio University.

At 20 years of age, I had about $2,000 saved from 8 1/2 years of delivering newspapers. Most two-week guided trips to the Arctic cost $3,000 at least, not including transportation to Alaska. I called airlines and travel agencies to compare prices. My brother was graduating from the California Institute of Technology in early June, which I would attend and use as a closer departure point than Ohio. I found a $500 round-trip flight from Los Angeles to Fairbanks. I wanted to see Prudhoe Bay first hand, and hike along the corridor they would use to transport oil from the Arctic Refuge to the Trans-Alaskan Pipeline should it be opened. This was one of the environmental movement's front lines.

It was evening when the plane approached Anchorage. Sitting next to me was John, who worked for the Alaska Department of Fish and Game. He was returning from a conference on Salmon ecology.

"I'm in charge of one of the largest Salmon hatcheries in Alaska, at Prince William Sound," he said. "The oil from Exxon's spill had a devastating affect on the sea otter and the birds, and it threatens the future of the Salmon hatchlings." John pointed out the city of Valdez.

"An oil tanker is visible off to the right side in port," the pilot said. The tanker was massive, with several escorting boats along side.

"The escorts are mandatory since the spill. They're Alyeska ships. There's another oil tanker. It's not being escorted. That ship should be escorted."

In Fairbanks, I set up camp at the University of Alaska's campground, and took a 6-mile hike into town to interview Larry Landers, the director of the Northern Alaska Environmental Center.

Landers warned of the ecological nightmare oil development would bring to the Arctic Refuge, as it has to Prudhoe Bay. Development has pushed wildlife into the last fragment of preserved Arctic coast: the Arctic Refuge. "Though ANWR makes up 1/8 of Alaska's North Slope, of the polar bear that den on land, 60 percent den in ANWR. Those denning on land are more productive. Geese and grizzly bears are also sensitive to development there. They are extremely sensitive to oil activity.

"Wolves and industrial development have never been compatible. You're going to have access for hunters where there wasn't before. In the Arctic it is hard to recover when you have an over harvest. The haul road is being increasingly used as a staging area for hunters. They were able to really deplete the wolf population.

"Development in the Arctic Refuge will also facilitate offshore development in the Arctic Ocean. It's their foot in the door. Once you have the infrastructure you jump out. I don't think the majority of people know what oil development would mean and the cultural disruption that would take place. The industry says only elitists can afford to see the Arctic Refuge. Look at the people who go on the raft trips. They are not wealthy people. If you want to see it enough, Americans can afford it."

I smiled. "Yeah, I'm not wealthy and I am going to spend the whole summer here."

"The oil industry is very deceptive. They put out all kinds of propaganda. They have an unlimited pocket. They say their footprint will be the size of the Dallas Airport. But that 2,000 acres is spread out over a large area. It would be a nightmare for that ecosystem."

Larry suggested I talk with Fran Mauer, a biologist in the U.S. Fish and Wildlife Service Arctic National Wildlife Refuge office a few miles away. Fran was in his office.

"I sometimes get paranoid talking here. My superiors open my mail and monitor my calls. My career has stopped. But if I quit giving interviews and speaking out, the tyranny will have won," Mauer said.

"So much emphasis is placed on breaking this issue down into parts in a Newtonian way. Nature is a whole. It cannot be broken apart. How much tundra would be damaged with gravel? How long will those roads last? Those roads will provide access. Development in the North Slope opened that area up and disrupted the wildlife of the central north slope. If we move a center of operations into the Arctic Refuge the pressure will change the whole picture of the place.

"If you came to the refuge expecting a Yellowstone, you're in for a surprise. This is not managed in the same way. This is like Yellowstone was at the time Catlin went in with the intact condition of the ecosystem—except for the roar of aircraft. Our wildlife population is generally intact."

I stopped at the U.S. Geological Survey office and talked with hydrologist Richard Kemnitz. I explained my expedition and route.

"That sure is ambitious."

"Do you think I'll have problems at Prudhoe Bay?"

"The oil industry is leasing the land. You should be allowed to hike on the tundra—it is public land. But the industry has security checkpoints near the fields. I'd suggest flying over that area to see it. Hiking in the coastal plain is extremely difficult. The polygon area is marshy. You should go when the ground is frozen."

I talked with a Native American at a public lands information center.

"How is the hiking along the coastal plain?" I asked.

"This time of year it's awful. Hiking through the tussocks is 4-6 times slower than hiking on a road," she said. With my massive load, this would not be an easy journey. I sorted through my gear again and again. To lighten my load, I mailed a large box of stuff back to my parents.

"You just have a one-way ticket," said the concerned airline attendant. "Yeah, I know. I'm flying out of Kaktovik."

"You're what?" Kaktovik is more than a 100 miles of rugged wilderness from Prudhoe Bay.

"It's fine."

"Let me guess, you probably want a window seat."

"That would be great."

I boarded the plane and sat next to an elder Inupiat woman, heading home to her village of Barrow, our first stop. Her face read of wisdom. Reverence shone in her eyes with the all-knowing yet humble look of a spiritual elder.

"You going to work at Prudhoe?" She asked as the pilot announced the plane's final destination.

"No," I responded. "I'm backpacking through the Arctic National Wildlife Refuge."

"How long are you going to stay?"

"All summer, my plane leaves August 30," I responded.

"What brings you here?"

"I felt a call to come. The land is threatened, and I have to see it," I said.

"This is a place to find yourself," she said. The familiarity of her tone and the confidence in her voice startled me. I wanted to talk more. But she closed her eyes. I pondered, and looked out the window.

I recalled Fran Mauer's prophetic words. "The Arctic Refuge provides the last opportunity for solitude. Those values are very vulnerable to being lost. They are the most precious values and they are the ones to go first. The loss of the feeling of solitude will be noticed immediately with the first invasion of mechanized man."

That is, unless enough people rise up in critical mass to demand that our so-called representatives represent the 3/4 of Americans who want to protect the refuge from drilling. We cannot give up after decades of struggle. If we lose once, the Arctic Refuge will be gone forever. Behind this adventure and my precarious survival is the story of my real journey: how I learned first hand just what is at stake and why we cannot give up the struggle.

Chapter 1

Escape

I plunged down a four-foot waterfall, crashing head-first into its massive wave. I paddled hard to try and pull the boat over it. The water wall pushed the front of the raft up, threatening to flip it back on top of me. I jumped forward to counterbalance it. The boat pivoted nearly vertical before rounding the crest. I crashed down on a second line of waves. I was thrown forward atop my stuff and nearly overboard. I hung on, but the boat was completely swamped. With the added weight of the water, the raft barely responded to my paddling. I was barreling down a flooded Arctic river.

Scooping water out with my cup was useless. Waves poured in faster than I could bail. I searched for an eddy or pool to pull me to shore. I was desperate to leave the rampaging river. But all I saw was white water. A seven-foot wave roared over the raft. I held the paddle in one hand and clung to the raft with the other. It was all I could do to stay onboard; the wave wrestled the paddle from my grip.

I saw the waves forming a "V" just down river—a telltale sign of a submerged boulder. I watched it approach directly ahead, but was helpless without the paddle. The raft caught on to the boulder. The force of the current pulled the back of the boat down. I jumped forward to counterbalance. The boulder raised the raft's front high out of water. I landed on solid rock. The back lowered until water rushed overboard.

The current thrust down the back of the raft, flipping it on top of me. I was submerged in 40-degree water. The deluge swept me toward a line of submerged boulders. I was washed over them and down a five-foot waterfall into the cold water. In shock, I struggled frantically. The current forced me underwater and I gulped frigid water, choking.

*

As the plane circled above Prudhoe Bay, I saw the Trans-Alaska Pipeline zig-zagging to the south into the cloudy horizon. Through clear spots in the fog and low lying clouds I caught glimpses of air strips, parking lots, cranes, construction equipment and gaudy-colored buildings over an expanse of ugly gravel pads. Roads and pipelines spread like a spider web in all directions. The plane bumped to a halt on the gravel runway at Deadhorse. It was early June—spring in the Arctic.

I descended the stairs from the plane to the gravel pad. A cold breeze chilled my bare legs and arms. When I left Fairbanks some hours earlier, the temperature was in the mid 80s. Now, within ten miles of the Arctic Ocean, the little thermometer dangling from my jacket read 35 degrees. Thick overcast skies threatened rain. It was 8 p.m. and the sun was lowering as it circled from the west to the north. The air smelled foul, like midtown New York City during rush hour.

The town of Deadhorse houses the workers, contractors and entertainers for the $25 billion Prudhoe Bay oil complex that produces two million barrels of oil per day and pumps it through the 800-mile Trans-Alaska Pipeline to the port of Valdez. Tankers carry the North Slope crude to West Coast refineries that supply less than one-ninth of America's petroleum demand.

At age 20, I was attempting an expedition everyone said was impossible. The tundra wetlands were virtually impossible to walk through and for the first 70 miles I would be "trespassing" on state-owned land leased by the oil companies. I tried to get oil company permission for the expedition. They refused.

I would have to cross flooded, near freezing rivers and a large channel of the Arctic Ocean. I had only ten days of food for a three-month expedition.

The airport was a one-story building put on stilts to sit above the permafrost, painted with three stripes of gray, dark red and white. Antennas and electrical wires adorned the roof. The Chevy

Broncos parked outside were all tan. I thought they were painted that color until closer inspection revealed sections of dark blue under the coats of mud and dust. The inside waiting room was dark and smoky, with benches, pay phones and candy machines.

I called Arctic Village, a Native American settlement, to ask if I could visit and attend a conference being held there in honor of the Gwich'in people's struggle against oil development on the calving grounds of the Porcupine Caribou herd. I would first hike through the land being considered for development.

"Arctic Village," said a warm, pleasant voice.

"I would like to visit Arctic Village and attend the International Indigenous Peoples Treaty Conference," I said.

"You are welcome."

"How much does it cost?" I asked.

"Pay as you are able," Lincoln Tritt said. "You won't be turned away. It starts in seven weeks but you can visit anytime."

The soothing voice was in stark contrast to the threatening nature of the oil industry when I'd asked about visiting Prudhoe Bay. Big oil representatives told me to visit their Anchorage offices. They said I could not see Prudhoe Bay except by tour. "You can't just wander around," they had said. Now, here I was, wandering around and looking very conspicuous.

I strapped together my massive backpack. It was 90 pounds with all I would need for the summer: five pounds of rice, two dozen oatmeal packets, instant coffee, peanut butter, three pounds of mashed potato mix, a pound of powdered milk, a pound of noodles, spices, cooking oil for fish I hoped to catch, fishing equipment, a four by seven foot one-person raft and paddle, a wool sweater, gore-tex pants and jacket, two changes of socks and underwear, two t-shirts, a compass, two canteens, iodine tablets to purify water, a one-person tent, a sleeping bag, journals, pens, maps for the entire Arctic Refuge, a guide to native edible plants of Alaska, the book *Arctic Dreams* by Barry Lopez, a guide to Arctic birds, a stove, two 32-ounce fuel canisters, wax-dipped blue-tip matches, lighters, a one-quart aluminum pot and plate (for frying fish), needle-nosed pliers, duct tape, a

Jansport frame pack, a pack cover, a film canister of Bacardi 151 rum, needles and thread, information about visiting native villages and phone numbers, insect repellant, clothes line, biodegradable soap, and a high-tech altitude and barometer-reading watch.

With the unwieldy pack, I stumbled sideways through the narrow door and down the steps of the terminal. Thick, puffy gray clouds enshrouded the sky. The sun illuminated the northern horizon. To the east, tall fences and buildings blocked the way. I walked west to the nearest road, then followed it north. The dusty gravel road ran between long reservoirs of oily, filthy water. Roads crossed every few hundred yards. Storage silos, towers, antennas, buildings, trucks, giant cranes, piles of junk, barrels and high fences were laid out haphazardly. The industrial zone was dusty, dirty, bleak and massive. I wanted to leave as fast as I could, before I was apprehended by the big oil police.

I arrived at an "authorized personnel only" sign, warning of arrest for violation. I looked around for a way out. All I saw were more fences, no escape. I turned around and walked south. Fences blocked passage to the east. I huffed along, trying to look as inconspicuous as I could with a giant pack on my back. Trucks drove by about a few hundred feet away.

The fence-line finally opened into an alley that ran between two buildings. The alley ended at a runway, with tundra beyond. I looked about nervously then hurried across the airstrip. I walked past the end of a hangar onto the open runway. I looked up at men peering down from a watchtower 30 feet away. I was trying to slip away by walking under a watchtower. I hurried across the runway and descended a steep embankment to the tundra. I sank ankle-deep into the wetland, sticking in the soggy muck. I had traveled but 100 feet through the swamp when I heard the crunching sound of a police truck braking to a halt on the rough gravel. I turned to see an officer stepping out, looking at me.

"Come back here. You can't go there," he hollered.

"This is public land. I'm allowed here," I called back.

"You're in a forbidden area, come back here!" the security officer yelled again. His voice was stern, like that of a drill sergeant accustomed to controlling his troops.

"I'm allowed to be here," I yelled back. The command of the powers that be is rarely defied. I continued walking. It was some time before I looked back. As I had gambled, the officer was unwilling to follow me across the wetlands. I expected their security officers would not just ignore me. Forgetting to pace myself for endurance, I rushed away like a caribou from a pack of wolves.

Low-lying clouds rolled in, bringing an icy chill. The sun was traveling ever lower on the northern horizon. I tried in vain to keep my feet dry. But pools of water often extended as far as the eye could see to the left and right.

The coastal plain is a great expanse of wetland, even though it receives an average of only seven inches of precipitation a year. Under the coastal plain is a layer of permafrost, or permanently frozen ground from about 12 inches to some 2,000 feet below the tundra. This forms a barrier that traps water at the surface. The tundra resembles a slow, wide river like the everglades. Water naturally seeps down the gentle slopes toward waterways, forming small channels through the landscape which spill into streams then into rivers that flow into the Arctic Ocean.

Avoiding the deep pools put me too far off course. I began plunging through. The temperature kept falling. My feet became soaked and numb from the cold.

As the late afternoon wore on, I zig-zaged across the wetlands, trying to stay as far as possible from the 65-acre gravel pads and metal buildings that housed oil drilling rigs, roads and buildings that littered the landscape. Styrofoam pipe packaging, orange stakes, yellow wire, plastic bottles, tin cans, gasoline cans, rusty barrels with who-knows-what inside and other waste lay strewn about. Tire tracks marred the fragile tundra. Worse were the roads, which caused massive barriers to terrestrial animals, as I would learn first hand. I heaved myself up the steep gravel embankment of a haul road, slipping with each step on the loose gravel, and scurried across.

A few hundred feet later, I arrived at the west channel of the

Sagavanirktok River, "Sag" for short. It was about 100-yards wide and an opaque, gray, milky color. I rested on the shore, and within minutes felt chilled. I had planned to raft across the monstrous river that night, to further distance myself from "security." My raft was a $40 cheap vinyl boat not at all intended for wilderness travel. I could not afford or carry the heavier-duty models. Still, the weight and bulk were quite burdensome. But now, rafting when I was already freezing seemed dangerous

My map showed a bridge several miles down stream. I thought I saw it through the haze and thick clouds to the north. I began hiking toward it, but I soon realized it was a mirage. The bridge was several miles farther. I came upon a flat gravel area which looked suitable for launching the raft. I began inflating the boat. A biting northwest wind blasted against me. I started to shiver uncontrollably. I had difficulty keeping my eyes open in my exhaustion. This was insane. I gave up on the rafting plan.

The tundra ended in a six-foot embankment to a narrow shoreline of gravel and small, polished rocks. The river had clearly been dredged for rock here, with long scars on the tundra where the heavy machines hauled gravel to the road. Development of the roads, parking lots, buildings, poisonous waste dumps and pipelines of Prudhoe Bay consumed an estimated 60 million cubic yards of gravel, enough to fill 90,000 football fields to a depth of three feet. Years of dredging has disrupted the river ecosystem. Washouts of gravel roads and platforms into rivers block fish migrations that are critical to the entire ecosystem.

The cold numbed my hands. I could not set my tent on the gravel without a major effort. I worked to prop up the half blown-up raft with oar pieces to block the wind and settled for the drafty "shelter." I didn't really sleep, shivering throughout the night and scolding myself for not bringing a ground pad. I had considered the foam pads to be more a comfort than a necessity. But on the icy Arctic ground a foam pad would have provided invaluable insulation. I was nervous about beginning a major expedition when I could barely stay warm enough to survive even when wearing all the clothes I'd brought.

The next morning, the cold Arctic breeze chilled my hands, making them clumsy and painful as I pieced together my stove and set up an aluminum wind shield. While I heated water for oatmeal and coffee, I finished blowing up the 13-pound vinyl raft. I had decided to leave my air pump to save weight, relying on my lungs; I had to take breaks to catch my breath. My duffel bag fit in the front of the boat, with my pack on top, leaving room in the back for me to kneel. I fit the plastic oars together with a piece of dowel rod to make a kayak paddle. I waded into ankle-deep water and climbed aboard.

The scenery was anything but scenic. It was an industrial eyesore of cranes, roads and metal buildings. Planes roared overhead. Cars and trucks kicked up dust on the gravel roads. The more I saw, the more I wanted to go east to the wilderness. I paddled toward the opposite shore. When I got there, I was greeted by more oil drilling platforms, pipelines and roads to the north and south. I rafted another mile or so down river, then stopped on the east shore. I packed my gear, waded through several channels of the river and hauled myself up to the tundra bank.

As I neared a pipeline with a road just beyond, I opened my camera to snap a picture. The advance lever had not been working correctly. I tried to pull it back, but it jammed and would not advance the film. I tinkered with it for several minutes then tried again. SNAP. The lever broke off. The camera was useless. It was a crucial item to document the threatened Arctic land. I sat down in the wet tundra, bewildered, staring at the camera. Tinkering confirmed my initial conclusion: there was no way I could fix it.

Clear skies replaced the dense clouds, creating an entirely different scene. The low evening sun cast a soothing glow on the landscape. The Brooks Mountain Range was barely visible on the southern horizon scores of miles away. To the west, the patchwork of steel, gravel and drill towers were also illuminated. I pondered my options: continue on with a bulky, useless camera; or go back into the city—where I had just fled—and either fix it or buy a new one. I wanted to see more of Prudhoe Bay, but surely they would not allow it. I had already escaped once. Walking back to the oil company's headquarters did not seem wise. But nor did the alternative.

The oil industry used its development at Prudhoe Bay as an example of environmentally sound development. Environmentalists had long criticized it. I wanted to see it for myself. Now I had a perfect opportunity to see it first hand. But I had to have a camera to document it. I would leave my equipment as far as I had taken it, and take only my camera back for repair or replacement. That would leave me more mobile and give me more leverage to refuse being deported.

Chapter 2

Captured in Poison Land

The roar of airplanes and helicopters woke me up. To prepare for the journey, I recorded the compass bearing to each visible drill pad to mark my location for the return trip. I thought it would be easy to find my way back in the open expanse of tundra. I would remember landmarks and walk back the way I had come. It was a three-mile hike to the road leading into Prudhoe Bay. Without my pack, I traveled easy.

Gravel pads used for roads, pipelines and buildings act as a dam, stopping the flow of water behind them in unnatural lakes.

I splashed through knee-deep water formed by the damming affect of a haul road. The water surface had an oily film. I dipped my finger into it and sniffed. Petroleum. I climbed the 6-foot pile of dredged river gravel onto the main haul road.

Large trucks, construction equipment, buses full of workers and pick-up trucks drove by, the occupants giving me curious stares. I choked on their dust and exhaust. I walked past oddly colored toxic dumps with oily scum on top. Roads, pipelines, drill pads and storage facilities were everywhere. Even though it was several miles away, I could see the cranes, buildings, airplanes and smog that was Prudhoe Bay.

During construction of the pipeline in the mid 1970s, government regulators said they were often swamped with so many oil spills that they lost track of them. Each year, hundreds of spills, involving tens of thousands of gallons of toxic compounds, contaminate the fragile North Slope ecosystem. The impact of oil spills in the Arctic is far more severe than in warmer climates. Breakdown of benzene and other oil pollutants is several times slower in the Arctic than in temperate zones. The tundra life belt is also much thinner, more prone to damage and slower to recover. Diesel fuel, the most commonly spilled pollutant, is acutely toxic to plant life. The long-term impact of the industry is becoming clear: spill sites from half a century ago in the 30-million acre National Petroleum Reserve in northwest Alaska have shown little vegetative recovery.

Oil is formed when huge quantities of microorganisms accumulate at the ocean bottom and are sealed beneath the ground in bedrock. Alaska's north slope was an ocean hundreds of millions of years ago. The pacific plate pushed over the North American plate, pushing up the Brooks Mountain Range. The ocean was pushed back, burying vast amounts of prehistoric ocean creatures and plants. These were buried under bedrock, and cooked in the tremendous pressure for a few million years, becoming liquid oil.

It took about 600 million years to form all the oil reserves on Earth. This petroleum stores carbon dioxide from the atmosphere, keeping earth cool enough for life. In the past 100 years we have used up most of the oil in the United States and half the world's supply. When burned, oil produces carbon dioxide and toxic gases. Global carbon dioxide levels today are up 33 percent compared to air trapped in Arctic glaciers a few centuries ago. And, as most people know, the trend of rising levels is accelerating. CO2 levels rose 6 percent from the late 1980s to 2001.

Carbon dioxide is a clear gas that lets sunlight in, but traps in the heat like a pane of glass. The United Nations Intergovernmental Panel on Climate Change issued findings in 2002 that human activities have begun to warm the Earth's climate, with cataclysmic consequences. A consensus of 2,500 of the world's leading scientists concurred with the UN finding. NASA concluded in 1999 that 1998 was by far the warmest year in history. Of more than a hundred years of recorded temperatures and 1,000 years of tree-ring data worldwide, the warmest years to date are 1998, 1997, 1995, 1991 and 1999—in that order, according to the National Center for Atmospheric Research. "What's happened in the last decade is way above what has happened historically," said Dr. Kevin Trimberg, director of atmospheric research for the National Center for Atmospheric Research.

*

Traffic along the haul road was heavy. After several miles on the gravel road, I neared the mighty east branch of the Sagavanirktok river that I'd rafted the day before. The bridge across it was a narrow, one-lane structure with no berm. There did not appear to be room for both cars and pedestrians and it certainly was not intended for foot traffic. The one lane ended on either side with a sheer drop-off to the river, except for beams spaced about every yard that extended out several feet over the river. I made a dash across the bridge, eyeing the road in front of me for traffic and taking frequent glances to the rear. A dozen or so four-foot wide stainless-steel pipes crossed above the river adjacent to the bridge. They gleamed in the mid-day sun, carrying oil from the many wells east of the Sagavanirktok River to the terminal of the Trans-Alaskan Pipeline.

I sighed in relief as I left the bridge and hiked toward what appeared to be the headquarters of Prudhoe. It reminded me of the industrial slums of some east coast cities with its pipes, dirty buildings and storage tanks painted in bright colors. I entered Arco's main headquarters (BP has since bought Arco). The glass door opened into a plush lounge with hardwood furniture and expensive wall hangings and rugs. I approached the main desk.

"Where is the nearest store?" I asked the man behind the desk. He looked startled.

"Prudhoe doesn't have a store," he said. After a long pause he said, "Deadhorse does."

"How do you get to Deadhorse from here?" He looked really suspicious. "There is a shuttle leaving in 15 minutes."

I sat down next to a gentleman wearing a coat and tie. He was in the textiles business and was selling filters for the oil industry's water intake pipes. Not far into our conversation, two security officers rounded the information desk and approached me.

"We would like a word with you," said the head officer. He had black hair and a mustache. He was rather short and radiated a "don't mess with me" demeanor. The other security officer was taller with graying hair and seemed more laid-back.

"We just want to ask you a few questions about how you made it past the checkpoints onto the field," said the head officer.

"I want to catch the bus to Deadhorse."

"No problem," the officer said.

They escorted me, with the head officer in front and the other behind. The head officer looked back after every other step. "Can you hold the bus?" the head officer asked the man at the front desk as we walked past him. There was no need for response. We walked down a dark, narrow hall, turned a corner and walked farther. We entered a small office. The superior officer sat behind the desk. I was seated in a chair in the corner. Papers were strewn on the desk. Maps hung on the walls. The lesser officer stood blocking the door.

"What are you doing here?" the head officer asked in an accusatory tone.

"I'm backpacking from here to the Arctic National Wildlife Refuge," I said. "I was several miles out when my camera broke. I left my stuff out on the tundra and hiked here to see if I could fix my camera or buy a new one."

The head officer looked puzzled by my story. "Do you have permission?"

"I sent letters to BP and Exxon informing them of my trip," I said, not mentioning that they had denied permission. "I also talked to the U.S. Geological Service, the U.S. Fish and Wildlife Service and the Alaska Department of Fish and Game. They said this was public land leased to the oil industry and that I was permitted by law to hike in the tundra."

"You were told wrong," said the man behind the desk. "Who told you that?"

"I don't have the names with me," I said.

"You are in trespass. You can't just hike onto the tundra. You need a permit for that. You can damage it you know."

"The oil industry damages the tundra by building roads and dumping toxic sludge on it. In walking I'm just like a caribou. I hope

I don't need a permit."

"Let me see your ID," he said. I fumbled to remove my Ohio driver's license.

"You will be a problem," he said. "Wait in the lobby."

The other officer, Ron, escorted me back to my seat and remained standing next to me. Ron seemed like a friendly man. "The oil industry is like a tenant. You just can't walk into someone's apartment."

It's a neat analogy, but to compare the oil industry's development on public land to a tenant in an apartment is a stretch of logic. Privacy is important—for an individual. But no corporation is going to suffer from not having enough alone time. More importantly, the oil industry actions threaten public resources and the health of the Arctic ecosystem. While individual workers deserve privacy, the actions of the oil industry must be open to public scrutiny. Still, I decided not to respond.

The words of the head officer echoed in my mind. "You will be a problem... You will be a problem."

Arco was a part of Alyeska, a consortium of oil companies that runs and operates the pipeline. Alyeska uses its immense power to silence critics through covert wiretapping, unwarranted lawsuits and massive public relations campaigns according to the *Wall Street Journal* (November 1, 1991). Alyeska hired the espionage-company Wakenhut to create a phony environmental organization, Ecolit, to spy on oil industry critic Charles Hamel. The Alyeska-funded spy team installed electronic surveillance devices around Hamel's home, business and hotel rooms; reviewed his telephone logs and consumer credit reports; and searched his garbage and his home office. The spy team ran a small remote controlled car with a microphone above the office Hamel was meeting in to listen to private conversations.

In 1991 Representative George Miller, D-California, was sufficiently moved by Hamel's plight to write in a memorandum to members of the House Interior and Insular Affairs Committee, which Miller chaired, that there is "substantial evidence" that Wackenhut may have violated several federal and state laws, including recording telephone conversations without consent, burglarizing Hamel's home, paying for the unauthorized release of telephone records and obtaining computer equipment fraudulently. "There can be no doubt that the goal of this activity was to chill any future efforts to detect and expose violations of environmental safety and laws," Miller concluded.

According to court documents, Wackenhut went so far as to send a female Wakenhut operative, posing as an environmental journalist, to befriend Hamel in an Anchorage Hotel Bar and on an airline flight in March 1990 in order to "compromise him."

Hamel's crime had been to expose environmental violations by British Petroleum, Exxon and Arco. He gave information from industry informants to regulators that included oil spills around Prudhoe Bay, the Trans-Alaskan Pipeline and the port of Valdex, air pollution violations and findings of other North Slope oil fields that showed that drilling in the Arctic National Wildlife Refuge was unnecessary. Hamel's revelations had resulted in fines that cost the companies tens of millions of dollars. Hamel settled a lawsuit against Wakenhut and Alyeska for their espionage for an estimated $5 million.

Alyeska also hired Wakenhut to spy on Rep. Miller himself. There seems no end to Alyeska's abuse of power.

Waiting gave me time to collect my spirit and determination. I would be polite but insist I be permitted to go to the store and continue my journey. I absorbed myself in a newspaper. After a while I was escorted to a different office. The head officer asked me to point to the location of my equipment on a map and my travel plans.

"My equipment is here," I said, pointing to it on the map. "All I want to do is hike east."

The superior officer seemed puzzled. "He just wants to hike east," Ron explained to his confused supervisor. I held back a chuckle at the idiocy of the oil industry official. And these were the people who were supposed to make sure that oil did not spill? No wonder so much did.

"Fine," he said. Motioning to Ron he added, "Take him to the store and out to his stuff." Turning back to me he said, "I'm going to file a report about this in case it should be needed."

I hopped in a pick-up truck with Ron. It was a security vehicle with a shotgun on the dashboard. We drove for several miles past buildings and construction equipment. We passed a lake on the right, and several check points, at which Ron had to stop and call out "42" before they let him pass.

"So how do you like working here?" I asked.

"I've been up here 14 years now. We get two weeks on, working 7 days a week, 12 hours per day, and two weeks off. The best job in the world. Imagine getting two weeks off every month. I live in Anchorage. I've got a cabin in the woods where I go for peace and solitude. I'm a moose hunter. I also hunt caribou. I leave the dall sheep and bear alone because they don't do nothing to me."

"Sorry about your having to drive me here," I said.

"Oh, it's quite all right. It breaks up the monotony of the routine." We pulled up to the general store. The store had a distinctly Arctic character with heavy coats, mittens, gloves, hats, Arctic fishing lures, and skis. I bought a cheap camera and, using the post office connected to the store, mailed the broken one to my parents.

"Why is he accompanying you?" asked the store attendant of Ron.

"I began a hike across the Arctic and my camera broke a short ways out. I walked back in to fix or buy a new one and the oil police apprehended me and are now escorting me," I said.

She chuckled. "Yes, the oil industry is notorious for preventing travelers from passing through. George Meegan left from the southern tip of South America. He had been hiking for seven years to reach the Arctic Ocean and was stopped just 10 miles short," she said. "He had to fly to Anchorage and talk with the oil industry execs before they finally let him pass through. We sell Meegan's book about it, *The Longest Walk.*"

After returning to the truck, Ron pulled out a map, asking me again where my equipment was. I pointed out the location. The drive was long and full of security checkpoints.

A radar speed-checking device was affixed to the dash next to the shotgun. "You check for speeding up here?" I asked, bemused. "Does the oil industry give tickets to itself?"

"They want to insure safety. We start enforcing something when people complain. Then people complain that we're enforcing it and we back off. You can't win. The tickets are all within the industry, but they are taken quite seriously. With three tickets in a year, an employee loses his driving privileges. One foreman lost his driving privileges and they hired someone specially to drive him around. His superiors were not pleased. If it were a regular worker like me, I'd be fired. But rank has its privileges around here."

"What do you think about the proposal to drill in the Arctic National Wildlife Refuge?" I asked.

"One thing you have to remember, both sides lie. They stretch the truth. The oil industry does, but oh those antis," he said with a shudder. "They say the caribou will die. Caribou live fine with people. Caribou often go inside or under buildings and on higher places to avoid mosquitoes. I'm a hunter. I do not want to hurt the caribou," he said, meaning that he wanted to insure there were plenty of animals to hunt in years to come. "I am employed by the oil industry, though, and I have a bias. In all the time I've been here, I can only recall two or three caribou killed by cars. Sea gulls and Arctic foxes are killed a lot."

"This is as close as I can come," Ron said.

I had been so engrossed in conversation that I did not pay close attention to where we were going. The landmarks seemed out of place. I considered telling Ron. But I was tired of being captive. I waved farewell, and waded into the marshy tundra. Freedom. It was a hot day, with gusting winds. I hadn't brought a water bottle. Drill pads were everywhere I looked. I was not sure which ones I had used to mark my spot. I studied the map. I could not place my position! Where was my stuff? Where was I?

I approached a drill pad, hoping for a drink of water. A line of buildings housed the drill tower and pumping station. A gravel pad lifted the buildings six feet from the tundra surface. The structure was several stories high, made of metal. The warehouse size of the buildings made them stand out for miles around. I saw no workers. These were automated stations that comprised a network that fueled cars and machines around the world that polluted the biosphere. I knocked on a metal door. Nobody answered. I seemed like a tiny flea next to the enormous machine.

Around the drill well site were massive rectangular ponds of toxic sludge. According to the Environmental Defense Fund, oil industry operations on the North Slope produce 3,000 cubic yards of drilling waste with toxic metals and additives, 40,000 gallons of liquid oily waste and 300 cubic yards of oil contaminated solid waste and sludge every day. Tourists view the north as a last, pristine wilderness. But beneath the image, about 450 open waste pits poison the central North Slope of Alaska. Scores more are created each year.

The unlined toxic reserve pits leak and overflow, poisoning the surrounding tundra and lakes. U.S. Fish and Wildlife Service studies found higher levels of benzene, toluene, chromium, barium, arsenic, chloride and sulfates as well as a greater turbidity and alkalinity in ponds near reserve pits. This has reduced the population of aquatic life and in some cases completely killed ponds. Many birds eat the lake life that survive. The chromium and other toxins in the fish bioaccumulate (like DDT) in the birds to exponentially greater quantities. When Arctic foxes, wolverines or other creatures eat the birds, the predators consume vastly more toxins and so on up the food chain. Gracing the top of this food chain are the humans eating meat.

The Environmental Protection Agency found that "The causal relationship between benzene exposure and human disorders is clear." Benzene inhibits the renewal of DNA, causes birth defects, hematoxicity, cancer and more. To protect human health, EPA studies show that emissions of benzene should be zero.

Arsenic, another ubiquitous poison, causes "chromosomal abnormalities in the DNA chain" according to the EPA. It inhibits the repair and causes cross-linking of DNA. The toxin causes skin lesions, liver damage, birth defects, vomiting, abdominal pain, diar-rhea and gastro-intestinal damage, throat constriction, intense thirst, cramps in lower limb muscles, restlessness, muscle damage, convulsions, heart attacks, coma, and, as many murder mysteries remind us, death.

Mile after mile I trudged through the tundra. I was still uncer-tain where I was on the map. I was dehydrating, having failed to find clean water at the oil pad. But I did not want to drink the polluted water. The boggy tundra grabbed at my feet with each step. The sky was clear and the sun warm. I slowed my pace and stopped fre-quently. I felt light-headed from the dehydration. Here I was, like the crew of The Mariner, with water, water everywhere but not a drop to drink. Only this water was not salty. It had been pure fresh water for millions of years only to be destroyed in a geological eye blink of just two decades by the oil industry drilling.

Water is so easy to take for granted. It is the blood of all life. We can go without food for several weeks, but water we need almost daily. Here on the coastal plain, water was everywhere. It permeat-ed the tundra: a broad river flowing over the permafrost. Toxins migrate rapidly to poison the coastal plain below drill sites, and enter the Arctic Ocean. These oil industry toxins will be contribut-ing to sickness and death through the vast Arctic food chain for decades to come.

Several hours and many more miles later, I spotted a white speck in the distance. I thought it might be another styrofoam piece, like the many before that I'd wished were my tent. The grayish-white speck grew larger. I eyed it in my binoculars. It was my tent! Reaching my stuff, I dropped to the tundra and grabbed my water bottle. The tundra stream source of the water was among few that did not appear to go near any oil installations on my map, but with 400 oil spills a year, and because many more oil spills go unreported, I was not sure.

Chapter 3

Into the Wilderness

I awakened at 12:30 a.m. The sun was low over the northern horizon. What an incredible place to be at midnight with sunlight 24-hours a day. I was so far north that the sun's rays reached over the North Pole from the Eastern Hemisphere where China was in broad daylight. The fire crackled to a start, warming my numbed hands. Knobs and tussocks—clumps of vegetation on small rises of soil—cast long shadows across the tundra, creating a mystical, serene landscape. The wetland tundra was designed in a patchwork of pentagon-shaped craters, crafted from the freezing and thawing of the permafrost. From atop the small hill where I camped, the tundra design was starkly visible.

It would be scores of miles before I escaped the state-owned lands that have been opened virtually cart blanche to the oil industry. In the central North Slope area, roads, pipelines, dumps, refineries and air strips reached their toxic hands in all directions, encompassing an area of more than 1,000 square miles. In 1998, Arco and BP Exploration announced they would invest another $5 billion to expand the North Slope oil fields and drill more than a thousand new production wells. In November 2002, BP announced it would end its effort to develop in the Arctic Refuge. Still, many shortsighted Republican lawmakers and President George W. Bush have made drilling the refuge a top priority.

Development already sprawled to the east to within a few miles of the Canning River, the border of the 19.5-million-acre Arctic National Wildlife Refuge. But there was still a 15-20 mile wide tunnel of open space between a matrix of development to get to the Arctic Refuge—area proposed to be developed. I would be downstream from toxic waste pits. But once I reached the Canning River,

60 miles away, the water would be pure.

Ahead lay five miles of boggy tundra to the east fork of the Sagavanirktok River, which I would raft down 12 miles before hiking southeast toward the mountains. Hiking across the tundra is exceedingly difficult. I could barely move across it at one mile per hour. Tussocks, pentagon structures and numerous lakes and bogs made backpacking exceedingly exhausting.

Tussocks are miniature hills in the tundra on which cotton grass and other vegetation grows densely. They are shaped like a mushroom, about a foot high and a foot in diameter. The yellowish-green vegetation clumps grow within inches of each other. Between them are valleys of wet muck. I learned the hard way not to step on top of the tussocks; they buckled under my weight and twisted my ankle. Stepping in between made my feet get stuck and wet, slowing progress. I tired after only a few hundred feet of the annoying little knobs.

A heat wave struck shortly after I left. Temperatures rose into the high 60s. With it came mosquitoes, those dreaded creatures of the north. Because the coastal plain is a giant wetland, with millions of lakes and bogs, it is also one of the most prolific mosquito breeding grounds in the world. Despite their nuisance, mosquitoes are crucial to the Arctic ecosystem, forming the main diet of more-than 100 species of migratory birds that raise young on the coastal plain each summer. The swarms of bloodsuckers were no problem when I wore my jacket and pants. But I soon became unbearably hot, and removed them. I coated my arms with insect repellent. It helped, but they were still annoying. I had never seen insects so thick. They created a haze when they swarmed. The only relief came with wind. Mosquitoes retire into the tundra grasses when winds exceed seven miles per hour.

My legs ached from the heavy load and difficult terrain. I sloshed through ankle-deep water and my feet plunged deep into the soft muck around lakes and bogs. My canteens were empty. But I hesitated to fill them: oil slicks lined the shores of lakes and streams. I felt weak and dizzy. I came upon a giant lake, about two miles long and a mile across. The southern shoreline nearest me was a glacier of white ice, with open water beyond. Just a month earlier, in May, these lakes were frozen and snow covered the ground. An oily sheen covered the lake surface. Parched from thirst, I had no choice. I filled my canteens, holding them under water to at least try to avoid the visible petroleum on the surface.

Several hours later I crested a hill overlooking the east channel of the Sagavanirktok River. I entered the river valley like passing through a door. This was the home of the mighty river spirit, which was now roaring in spring flood stage. It was an opaque milky color from all the sediment, like the west channel had been. I had hoped the water would be clear so I could catch fish. I needed to supplement my food or I'd soon run out. At least driftwood was plentiful along the river's edge. I had little trouble building a fire to cook lunch. But I wasn't that hungry. I felt nauseous and had a headache.

I tried fishing. Shortly thereafter, I encountered a herd of about a hundred caribou walking upstream. I saw no small calves. I watched the herd through my binoculars while I advanced slowly toward them. The larger animals appeared to be leading the herd. Tormented by mosquitoes, the shaggy caribou shook themselves and bolted about. The herd plunged into the river and crossed to the east. A "V" shaped wave formed behind the powerful creatures. The river was swift: I was eager to raft it.

The caribou were part of the Central Arctic Herd, numbering about 16,000. Caribou migrate thousands of miles each year. From their wintering grounds south of the Brooks Mountain Range, the herds travel over the mountains to calve on the coastal plain. The plain provides a wide variety of nourishing plants and lichens, allowing the animals to fatten up for the long Arctic winter. But the plain also has mosquitoes and biting flies. Mosquitoes can suck up to a pint of blood from caribou in a single day. Flies lay larvae in the caribou skins that live as parasites until they hatch as adult flies the following season.

To escape the swarms on muggy days, caribou seek higher, windier terrain in the foothills, or cool mosquito-free areas along the shoreline of the Arctic Ocean or in snow fields. When winds or cold weather return to ground mosquitoes in the feeding areas, the herd travels back to find food. Consequently, caribou are constantly moving, traveling an average of 20 miles each day.

Oil development obstructs and hinders this movement. The Central Herd once passed through Prudhoe on a regular basis. Although the oil industry displays pictures of caribou wandering near oil rigs, scientific studies show the main herd now avoids the developed area. A Fish and Wildlife Service study of Milne Point, just west of Prudhoe, found that 17 percent of the Central Herd used that land before the oil field was built. Afterwards, only two percent of the herd frequented the area. More disturbing, pregnant caribou are exceptionally sensitive. Although 17 percent of the herd calved around Milne Point before development, less than 1 percent of the mothers give birth there today. Recent biological studies by the USFWS found that the birth rate for the Central Arctic Herd was 63 calves per 100 cows for caribou in undeveloped areas and only 29 births per 100 for females using developed areas. Another USFWS study found that female caribou weighed an average of 205 pounds in undeveloped regions and 187 pounds in developed areas.

The herd before me was traveling east, as I was, away from the oil development and toward the Arctic Refuge. They climbed up the opposite bank of the river and shook off the water, sending droplets flying. Absent here were wolves that have been killed and chased from Prudhoe Bay. From thousands of years ago until 25 years ago, the wolf lived on the central north slope. The loss of predation has further hurt the health of the caribou herd because wolves harvest the sick and weak, keeping the herd in balance.

Illuminated by warm sun, I pushed my raft into the murky water. The wind was calm and mosquitoes were out in force, swarming by the thousands. The channel entered the greater Sagavanirktok River, more than 100 yards across. Ice sheets extended far out into the river with the current flowing underneath. This aufice occurs when the ice builds up above the rivers, and often stays frozen well into July. The current runs under the ice, creating a hazard for boaters and I paddled hard to avoid it.

Sandpipers ran about on the bank. A swan with her three young glided effortlessly on the water. But the tranquility was often shattered by planes and helicopters taking off and landing to the west. A swoosh-swooshing noise increased in volume and intensity. A white helicopter with red markings approached and hovered several hundred feet above me. Through my binoculars, I saw people taking pictures of me from the hovering aircraft.

While floating down the river, I took periodic breaks from paddling to try a few casts. Deep pools created nice fishing holes. But with the damage to the fish population caused by dredging and other oil industry activity, the dingy water yielded no catch. Tired from awakening so early with only a few hours sleep, and cramped from kneeling in my raft, I landed after only a few miles of rafting. I tried a bit more fishing, but again with no luck. I needed to supplement my meager rations. I had only been able to take about 10 days of food. This was day five. I hoped to travel for a month or more before stopping at the Inupiat village of Kaktovik, more than a hundred miles to the east (and hundreds of miles the way I would travel). It would be three months before my return to Ohio.

With the poor fishing, I tried identifying plants. I had studied the edible plants of the tundra and taken along a field guide. First I found and dug some woolly louseworts. They have small, thick, hairy leaves and a cone of small, lavender-colored flowers. Their roots are long and thick, similar to that of a dandelion. Inupiat once gathered louseworts for their highly caloric and delicious roots. I next located some parry's wallflower, which have flavorful roots similar to horseradish. I also collected small willow leaves.

I boiled the roots until tender. Then I added parry's wallflower leaves, which taste like cabbage, and willow leaves and simmered the stew a while longer. I removed the wallflower roots (they were for flavoring) and ate the tender lousewort roots, greens and broth. The stew was delicious. It was also nutritious. Willow leaves contain ten times the amount of vitamin C per weight as oranges, and they also contain iron, calcium and vitamin A.

I pushed my raft into the river. Water dripped from the kayak-style paddle and pooled under where I kneeled. The Arctic winds chilled my body. The river was braided into many channels as it neared the Arctic Ocean. Channels joined and split the one I rafted. I was on the west channel and needed to go many channels east. The river flowed northeast. I wanted to travel southeast, making the rafting more efficient only because I did not want to unpack, inflate, paddle, deflate, dry and pack my raft at each channel. I chose the right channel each time the river split, to eventually reach the channel farthest east.

A strong west wind pushed me toward the eastern bank. I paddled furiously, often with violent thrashing strokes to keep from being beached. At least the wind kept the mosquitoes at bay. My arms ached as I continuously battled against the wind. Exhausted and cramped, I hopped out into ankle-deep water and pulled the raft to shore. I scouted to the east. A mile away, I found another channel of the mighty Sagavanirktok River. That meant more rafting.

On the way back to the river I came upon a small shack made of packing crates, thick beams like those found on a ship, and hundreds of nails. It was about five and a half feet tall, seven feet long and five wide. Time and weather had worn many holes into it. Sod was packed against the outside walls of the structure for insulation. Pieces of burnt wood were scattered about the floor inside the small shack. A small opening was made in the roof at the southwest corner, apparently for smoke to escape.

A human leg bone and a piece of hip bone lay on the tundra just downstream from the shack. Farther downstream I found a wooden rowboat, with holes running along its port side. I had read many accounts of explorers and whalers whose boats had been frozen in the Arctic Ocean, forcing them to stay through the winter. The human remains were a stark reminder of the dangers of the Arctic, and my own frailty. Seeing the bones startled me. Would I suffer the same fate?

Historic structures here are still unmarred by vandals. Places like these accentuate the timelessness and fragility of the Arctic wilderness, where one's mark is long preserved by the long winters and short summers.

Just beyond the shore I encountered sand dunes shaped in intricate patterns. About 20 feet high, their beauty was captivating. Nature had sculptured them with elegant curves. They were crafted perfectly by the wind, monuments from the Creator in this mysterious land. The beauty was as extreme as the climate.

I pushed out into churning waters. The sun was bright. The sky was clear, except for the gray wisps of low-lying fog and clouds far to the northwest that read of the weather to come. Within an hour clouds covered the sky and a thick blanket of fog rolled over the river. By comparing the map with compass readings of the river's course, I estimated that I was about five miles from the Arctic Ocean. The river turned sharply to the right. I could see only its banks; the fog obscured everything else. Finely carved sand dunes formed the east bank.

The fog soon became so thick that I could not see the far bank. Odd-looking islands jutted from the river, rising with steep cliffs. The scene was eerie and surreal. Wisps of fog spiraled about. Visibility was 50 feet. The river meandered wildly. New channels formed. It seemed that the river had turned around and was flowing in the wrong direction. The land seemed more like a dream than reality. I was in constant awe as I floated through the Arctic delta. With the scene changing every few minutes, the obscured unknown just beyond instilled wonder.

The sky was clear again as I unloaded my raft and pulled it onshore to dry. Feeling exceptionally weary, I decided to sleep on the ground without setting up my tent. A light breeze blew about my head and the low rays of the sun warmed my body. My journey had begun. There was so much wilderness ahead. Birds danced in the midnight sunlight. Their melodies lulled me to sleep and entered my dreams.

Chapter 4

Trouble

"Mmmh," I groaned. Something was interrupting my deep sleep. My body was damp and I was shivering. A monotonous patter droned in my ear. Where was I? This was no warm bed. Alaska. The Arctic. The thought process began to flow. I had slept outside. It was raining. My sleeping bag was wet. I should do something. But sleep felt so good. I just wanted to close my eyes and rest a little more.

"My journals!" I awakened to the shock of the realization. I fumbled with the zipper of my sleeping bag, my heart pounding with a rush of energy. I jumped out barefoot and scampered to the scattered gear about my pack. The sky was dark gray. Rain poured down. I stuffed my dampened journals and books into a zip lock bag, which I sealed tight and wrapped in a trash bag for double protection. Fog obscured visibility to some 100 feet.

I unstrapped the tent clumsily. My hands were already becoming numb in the blustering wind. I spread out the plastic ground pad, unfurled the tent atop it and staked it into place. Now it was time for the dreaded poles. My "Walrus" one-person tent had aluminum poles that are threaded through sleeves and bent in a semi-circle to form a frame. This is nice once set up but is tough to fit into place. The poles and tent never seemed to want to cooperate, always fighting one another. The pole got caught in a sleeve; the tent refused to stretch enough; the pole seemed to grow too long. Meanwhile I tried to play referee. Numbed hands were dead lumps flopping at the end of my arms.

Gusting winds made the tent flap loudly. Freezing rain stung my exposed skin. I shivered. Though I pushed and pulled, my hands could not grip the pole or the tent with any firmness. The cold had sapped them of strength. The wind flushed heat from my wet hands, numbing them more and more. I pushed and heaved at the pole, but my feeble grip failed to reach the eyehole. Rain added more water to my clothes and sleeping bag, and the wind stripped yet more heat from my exposed flesh.

Suddenly I stopped, let go of the pole and tent and cradled my hands in the warmth that radiated from my chest. Pain throbbed in my thawing flesh. With better-working hands, I grabbed the notorious pole and shoved it up the sleeve, then pulled it toward the eyehole. Farther and farther it bent, coming within half an inch. I shoved the pole up the sleeve again. This time it snapped into place. Soon I was in a dampened but still warm sleeping bag, curled in a tight ball.

From my newly sheltered perspective the raindrops sounded enchanting. I read Arctic Dreams, caught up on my journals and studied the map. The rude awakening by frigid rain reminded me of my vulnerability. The rigors and dangers were so real, and the solitude. I relaxed awhile. Loons called upon brighter spirits. Amidst all the feelings, loneliness was not present. Bird songs, unidentified animal sounds and the melodic sound of the river constantly reminded me of the greater world about me. That is what I came here to see. I was happy to leave the city behind for the natural world of wildness and spirit.

It was three hours after the rain stopped before my gear dried out enough for me to pack. That gave me time to forage for a tundra stew. While gathering greens, I came upon a large deep pool of crystal clear water bubbling from the ground. The spring ran into the silt-laden Sagavanirktok River, creating a clear streak for hundreds of feet. I had been searching for just such a spot. In silty water, fish often seek out clear sections. Cast after cast I made, but not a single bite. I crawled toward the pool, casting from 20 feet away so as not to spook the fish. After casting a number of times, I gave up and approached the hole. I gazed at the deep pool where water bubbled from the earth. I knelt to the water's edge to see my reflection. Blue skies had replaced the storm clouds.

I extended my arms into its clear abyss. "It's hot" I exclaimed to the pool, startled by the revelation. I had noticed the water steaming a bit but thought it to be just fog that often blanketed water bodies. I took a long, luxuriant bath, nestled against the tundra walls. What a heavenly treat. I was renewed and refreshed.

About a mile east of the Sagavanirktok River I came to the shore of a much different river. This was a clear-flowing tundra river, with pools separated by channels. It looked like a strand of beads extending far to the north and south. I filled a canteen.

The water was clear, cool and deep. The conditions seemed perfect for fish. I spent 45 minutes casting into the clear holes while searching for a crossing. I didn't find either. I hiked far up and downstream. Not a fish chased my lure. I tried to cross in several spots using an oil industry stake to probe the depth. But the water plunged to well above my chest only a few feet out. I could have swum the stream and been on my way in no time. But despite their double packaged protection, my journals and books were too important to risk. I resorted to my raft, which took another hour to blow up, load, raft, unload, deflate and pack.

Some miles later, I noticed a large brown rise on the horizon—a pingo. These are hills about 40 feet high and 120 feet in diameter, shaped like an upside-down bowl. They are thrust from the plain by the freezing and thawing pressures of the permafrost. Pingos are much darker than the surrounding tundra: brown hills on a golden plain. I climbed atop the mound of frozen earth, and set my pack down for a break. Snow lined the northern side of the hill. I gazed across vast tundra plain. This was the route the oil industry hoped to develop into the Arctic Refuge. This was unprotected public land.

I put on my jacket to keep from being pestered by mosquitoes. Even with the sun falling toward the northern horizon, I was sweaty from lugging the massive pack across the difficult terrain. Thick fog rolled in, bringing freezing temperatures. I arrived at a vast expanse of water. I could not see an opposite shoreline. Waves lapped against the bank.

My route took me within a few miles of the Arctic Ocean. But I should have been traveling away from it. I wondered if I had strayed off course. In the Arctic, magnetic north is far from true north. One must adjust the compass readings accordingly. Did I adjust the wrong way? That would have taken me to the ocean. The shore was tundra carpeted all the way to the water. The sections of the Arctic Ocean I'd seen had beaches, though small because the tide is only a few inches. I tasted the water. It was fresh. I would still have to ford around this lake.

Exhausted, I set my pack down for a rest. An icy chill overcame me. I shivered non-stop. I had committed a cardinal sin of northern travel. I had allowed myself to become wet with sweat. I was too tired to stop, remove clothing and heft the pack back in place again as I should have to avoid sweat build-up. Many a traveler has died in the north from carelessly allowing perspiration to build up. Wetness decreases the insulation of clothing. I set up my tent and called it a day.

I found myself constantly delayed by the cold. Nearly every morning I was awake and ready to go, but found that I could not dress and pack in 40-degree weather with gusting winds. I waited until late morning for warmer temperatures. In the late evening and night, when I wanted to continue travel, I could not rest without being chilled. And, with the load I was carrying, I needed rests at least every hour. If only I had more clothing and a ground pad. But then the load would have been greater.

The grumbling of an empty stomach made me constantly worry about and dream of food. If only I was home in Athens, Ohio, I'd go to my favorite worker-owned organic restaurant, Casa Nueva. I'd order a tofu and veggie enchilada, a spinach salad, red zinger tea, and seven orders of taco chips with melted cheese, extra guacamole, salsa, mushrooms and black olives. My mouth watered.

This was day 7, and I still had not caught any fish. I was eating oatmeal with powdered milk for breakfast and mashed potatoes for lunch and dinner, along with periodic salads and stews of tundra vegetation. I did not mind the kind of food, but I did care about the quantity. I rationed my stores carefully, knowing I was in for a long expedition. Collecting roots and leaves yielded a nutritional supplement but not enough calories. Intensifying this predicament, I was traveling ever farther into the wilderness and away from civilization.

The sun broke through the fog late the next morning and soon the sky was clear. The lake I'd thought an ocean was less than a third of a mile across. Clarity changes perspective. On the day's journey I encountered several more pingos, scores of lakes and hundreds of birds. While walking across the plain, I was startled by a squawking sound very close. A few feet away was a nest woven of grass and stalks. Eight white and brown eggs lay camouflaged by the tundra vegetation. It was a willow ptarmigan, Alaska's state bird. The mother could have simply flown away to protect herself. But she squawked and fluttered her wings, attempting to look injured to draw me away from her children, heroically risking her own life to save them. The mother had a white breast and a brown-white camouflage design on her wings, back and head, similar to the color of her eggs. Though pangs of hunger urged me to take the eggs, I was too moved by the mother, and let them be.

Some time later I spotted three female caribou and two calves. I approached to within a hundred yards. The mothers looked weary, eyeing me often before returning to their tundra meal. The wind was just enough to keep the mosquitoes grounded, allowing these great land travelers to eat in peace.

It was nearing midnight, with the low sun giving a magical evening glow. Suddenly the lower frame of my pack thrust into my thighs. The top frame dug into my shoulders. Something was very wrong. I lowered my pack to the tundra, unbuckled the waist belt and slipped out from the shoulder straps. Turning around, I stared at my pack in horror. The middle section of the frame was bent at a 45-degree angle. I unstrapped the raft and duffel bag. I tried to bend the frame back. After a minor improvement the two metal bars snapped! Here I was, 20 miles from the nearest town, at the beginning of what I had hoped would be an incredible adventure, and my pack was broken, seemingly beyond repair. The breaks were halfway between the shoulder strap and the waist belt. I would not even be able to carry the pack by the shoulder strap, even if I could manage without the hip belt.

Chapter 5

In Quest of Food

In wilderness like this, an explorer's pack is his or her castle—and all that separates you from the fate of people like that corpse I had seen by the river many miles back. My pack had been through a three and seven-week backpacking trip through wilderness in New Mexico, several multi-week trips through northern Ontario, and journeys through West Virginia, Kentucky, Pennsylvania, California, Florida and Ohio. Now it lay in front of me, broken in half.

I stood gazing east, across the golden plain. The tundra was dotted here and there by pure blue lakes that glistened in the sun. The scene was one of utter magnificence, invoking a deep satisfaction in spite of the circumstances. Thoughts of turning back were fended off by the fulfillment of gazing into the Arctic beauty. This was a trip of a lifetime, and I was not going to let a broken backpack end it. I set up my tent and lay in my warm sleeping bag, pondering.

The pack was a red Jansport external frame with plenty of room to strap on gear. I had strapped on a full duffel bag to the top and my raft to the bottom. The weight put strain on the frame, probably more than it was intended to handle. The frame was hollow aluminum. I needed to reattach the broken sections and brace them. The brace would have to be extremely sturdy, because the break occurred at the section under the most stress. I could whittle a caribou bone or antler. But none were nearby. Tent stakes might work. I exited my tent to give it a try.

I found some yellow electrical wire nearby, something I had found too many times to count. It was oil industry waste from seismic survey. The oil industry likes to say it's environmentally friendly, and shows clean, plush offices. But out on the tundra where so few venture it scatters its waste across the land. Long angered by such double standards, today I was pleased to find a discarded coil of wire.

I had eight aluminum tent poles, but only really needed four for the tent. I straightened four using my pot as a brace and my needle-nosed pliers. I wrapped two stakes with duct tape until they just fit into each frame piece. I pushed the broken ends of the frame together with the tent stakes in the middle. It seemed to work. I then wrapped the other two stakes to the frames tightly with wire and duct tape to add support.

The sky was crystal clear that evening. The tundra was colored with yellow, red, orange and violet flowers and all shades of green and brown. Spring was alive with freshness and delicate beauty. The mountains to the south were distinct but distant. Lakes and streams splashed a deep blue across the tundra, adding to the breathtaking midnight panorama. It was cold, and the wind was gusting. But the beauty was too overwhelming to go to sleep.

And, I needed food. The thought of food rarely left my mind, a constant hunger and striving to reach the next river and catch the fish which so far had eluded me. Fishing is always uncertain business. Now my life depended on it.

A thin blue line etched in the tundra was barely perceptible to the eye, but as I recognized it as the Kadleroshilik River, it swept over my mood like a tidal wave. "Fish!" I shouted to the loons. It was 3 a.m. and my legs were weak from the extended journey. I had been ready to quit for two hours. But the urge for food prodded me on. Crystal clear water gurgled through the rolling tundra from its source in the distant white-capped mountains. I stopped by the shore of the stream, gazing to absorb the captivating scene of beauty. My stomach growled anxiously.

Rod and reel put together and my favorite spinner tied on, I searched for a deep pool. I scouted far, enjoying the stream's company. But I could not find any good-looking holes. The water was shallow, averaging less than a foot deep. I found some slower eddies, but my spinner lured no bites. I hiked about a mile upstream, casting into a few promising spots. The vegetation on the riverbank was diverse and colorful. I spun the lure through all the fishy spots where boulders, points and islands blocked the current. But the river seemed too shallow—too small. My efforts did not evoke a bite.

My favorite fishing has always been deep in wilderness areas. In New Mexico, after six weeks of backpacking and working with a group of peers to save a forest from disease, I heard there was excellent trout fishing in a nearby river. I called my mom and said I was staying another week. Because I was 15 years old, I would save the details from her for a few years. I hitchhiked seventy miles with a seventy-pound pack. I carried the pack far up a pristine river valley, making camp at the foot of a high cliff. Nights were spent watching the Persius meteor shower. Days were filled with fishing the clear river, catching three to six trout per day. They were my main food source. At that stage of life, I was in search of freedom, and independence. During this odyssey, I searched for the spirit of the Arctic Refuge, and to see first hand what impact oil development would make. But right now I was in search of food.

Here at this Arctic river I had neither a bite nor a promising fishing hole. Around 4:30 a.m., I finally gave up, and set up my tent on the flat river flood plain. I had struggled and pushed myself to reach this stream in hopes of fish, and now those hopes were dashed. I had no idea where the nearest deep pool was. More rivers lay ahead. But the uncertainty of my situation eroded my confidence. I worried about starving to death. The hunger made me question whether I could continue the journey.

"Throup! - throup! - throup!" A helicopter shattered the morning tranquillity. I looked up at the familiar white helicopter with red markings. The intruder hovered about me some 100 yards up for a while until it finally left.

An hour later, still searching for fish, I heard the clicking of hooves in the distance. About thirty brownish dots appeared far ahead, moving toward me. I approached the small herd of caribou. They drank from a pool a short distance from the river, water dripping from their mouths. Their coats were shaggy as they shed their winter insulation. I found large tufts of hair strewn throughout the tundra, often stuck in dense willow thickets. Being a walker myself,

I marveled at the marathon endurance of the creatures before me. Caribou often go without food for days, especially when they migrate. I watched them from a hideout behind a small embankment.

I followed the caribou's example. Using my guide to Alaska's edible plants, I turned my attention to the diverse flora of the riverbank. The tundra is an intricate ecosystem with scores of different plant species, all miniaturized in the frigid north. Most plants did not grow more than a few inches above the ground. Anything protruding above the snow line in these extremes had to be sturdy to survive 70-degree below-zero temperatures and hundred-mile-per-hour winds. I gathered a sourgrass and pink plume salad and made a stew of woolly lousewort with parry wallflower root broth. Woolly louseworts live to be 8 years old and get as large as a small carrot. When cooked, their roots are tender and quite tasty.

I studied my rations. I had five pounds of rice and two pounds of dried mashed potatoes. My noodles were all eaten. I had a quart of cooking oil (for frying fish). My oatmeal and peanut butter were nearly gone. My instant coffee and powdered milk were exhausted. Calorie-wise, I had a week of food if I rationed it. Travel-wise, I had three to six more weeks before getting to Kaktovik.

Because of how long it took to use the raft, I decided to wade across the small river. The Kadleroshilik River was two feet deep at the deepest point of the crossing. But the extremely swift current and slippery stream bed stones made for a precarious crossing nonetheless. If this is what it's like crossing a little stream without a boat, I couldn't imagine what a larger river would be like.

I set a course directly toward the next river, the Shaviovik, nearly due east. I had been traveling southeast toward the mountains. But fish were more important now. I could hike a bit more south later. The map showed that the Shaviovik River had a more expansive watershed and should be larger than the Kadleroshilik River. It also had less oil activity in its watershed. Hopefully, I would find fish.

Travel was boggy and sticky in spots and bumpy with tussocks in others. I arrived at a small tundra river and filled both canteens. I had not found clear water for miles. I gulped down a full quart and refilled it. While searching for a crossing, I saw an oily sheen on the stream surface. I photographed it. Was that the water I had just drunk? I hadn't found a water source for more than an hour, so I didn't want to dump out the remaining even knowing its contamination. As the evening progressed, I began to sweat profusely. Knowing the dangers of wet clothes in frigid temperatures, I removed my hood, thinking that would cool me off. My head became chilled. The sweating persisted. I felt nauseated and faint-headed. I stopped for the night.

Chapter 6

Feast

That night I had nightmares about dying on the wide open plain from a painful illness. The reality I woke up to was of little comfort. I lay on a giant icebox, huddled in a tight ball with the sleeping bag wrapped tightly around. My body heat was sucked into the Arctic ice, leaving me shivering with chills. I felt nauseous and hungry. My stomach growled for food. I felt trapped inside my bag and tent, suffocating in a wide-open wilderness.

I was lethargic and my muscles ached. Feelings of nausea lingered. Hiking in wet, tundra-soaked boots had chafed my feet. Blisters puffed with pus. I drained them using a fire-sterilized needle and cut moleskin to fit around each blister to relieve pressure on those areas so they could heal. Though still weakened, I continued backpacking. Tussocks ripped at my feet. I sank ankle deep into muck, filling each boot with frigid water. I had blisters on the tops of my feet from the exertion of pulling my feet out of the muck. There was no relief. Blisters on the bottom of my feet burned with pain when I stepped down, while those on the top of my feet stung when I lifted my foot.

The tent stakes bracing my pack bent. I did not have a strong enough splint. The frame jutted into my lower and upper back, causing painful bruises. I walked hunched over, straining my back. Mosquitoes buzzed in dense numbers as the sun rose higher and the wind diminished. Hunger urged me to move. My faith was wavering.

Looking up from my hunched position, I was startled to see a herd of 12 caribou lazily grazing just 50 feet away. Four calves pranced around three yearlings, four older females and one I affectionately called grandma. She seemed to be the leader by virtue of wisdom, like the elders in native villages. I sat down in awe of the glorious creatures so near. They seemed oblivious to my presence, save for grandma. She eyed me uneasily, then returned to grazing. She glanced around at the status of the herd, giving special attention to the playful calves.

The young danced with the joy of being alive. The yearlings and older does seemed timid. Grandma was special. There was an unusual grace in her step, a hint of wisdom that transcended fear and desire. She had gone for long stretches without food in her time. When traveling the thousand miles from their wintering grounds, over the Brooks Mountain Range to the Coastal plain, caribou do not eat, depending on fat reserves. As I stood up, Grandma snorted and they all bolted, stopping some 100 yards away. I bowed to them, then stretched my arms out, palms toward the sky. I wanted to show I meant no harm. They resumed grazing.

It was late in the evening when I glimpsed the thread of blue cutting across the tundra plain in the distance. My telescoping rod was quickly unpacked and extended, the reel attached, the line threaded and a Mepps spinner tied on. I seemed to have arrived at a perfect fishing spot, with a deep pool of clear water just downstream from the convergence of two channels. I spent 20 minutes casting into the perfect-looking pool of the Shaviovik River. The low late-evening sun in the northwest cast my shadow over the river. The Arctic fish, being sight feeders and under constant danger from roving grizzlies, were probably spooked by my shadow. But the river was too deep and the air too cold to cross the river tonight and try from the other side. I hiked downstream in search of an evening fishing spot, where I could cast without alerting the fish.

Just downstream from the pool, a peninsula reached out into the main river, with another pool of still water on its west side. I walked onto the peninsula and cast into the sun. The wind created small waves across the pool. This would help to mask my presence. I thought I saw movement in the choppy surface and cast my spinner just beyond it. Shortly after beginning the retrieve, I felt a strong jolt. The fish fought with powerful surges against my ultra-light rod and six-pound-test line. Just a yard from my feet, the large fish shook the spinner from its mouth and swam to freedom.

I now knew there were fish biting right here, right now. Another fish bit and shook the lure free. I hooked a third one, and landed a three-pound, 18-inch-long burbout. It was dark gray with orange stripes along its dorsal and anal fins. I was not going to let this one get away. I lifted it by its right gill, and carried it back to camp. When I reached my stuff, my hands were numb. I fumbled to start a fire. After thawing my hands, I filleted the fish and put a pot of rice on the fire. When sufficient coals were formed, I pushed the burning sticks to one side and spread hot coals out flat. I cut the fillets in half to fit the 9-inch pan.

I fried the fish, waiting until just the right moment to turn the fillets. Cooking fish right is all a matter of timing. Just when the translucent meat turns an opaque white and flakes easily, it is the most delectable dish on Earth. I savored each bite. I mixed the fish and the remaining oil with my rice, making a quart and a half of food. The juicy fish and tender, flavorful rice captivated my attention. All senses focused on the food as I cradled it on my knee and devoured it bite by bite. A bear could have approached me within 10 feet before I'd have noticed. And even then I'd probably have defended my food.

Chapter 7

Fish

Crouched in the orb of heat around my morning fire, I felt a deep contentment. My stomach was still full from the previous night, a feeling I had not had in more than a week. The sky was overcast, the temperature 35 degrees with brisk winds. This would be a cold day. At least the mosquitoes were gone—they can be a nuisance when fishing. I was camped at a perfect fishing spot. My day's mission was to catch enough fish to stuff myself and carry some with me.

Fish in general prefer slower current with fast current nearby, so they can sit and wait for food to wash by, while not expending much energy. Deep pools with riffles just upstream are ideal. Riffles are shallow stretches that often churn up insects and other edible prey for the grayling, burbout or Arctic char.

The pool was clear. It ran over a rock bed with tundra abutting close to the gravel banks. To the southeast, the Brooks Mountains reached to within 60 miles of the coast, and were visible as gray and black silhouettes against the horizon. On either side, the golden tundra extended for as far as the eye could see in both directions. Here is where oil companies want to construct their massive 21st-century pipeline system with roads and toxic pits on their way into the last undeveloped section of American Arctic coastline, should Congress and the President give permission.

I studied the water carefully, watching for fish feeding on the surface and analyzing the flow of the current. I searched out dozens of potential fish hideouts, behind boulders, points, bars and other obstacles that blocked the current. I crawled on three "legs," using my right arm to hold up my rod and reel. I slowly eased my way toward a small knoll on the edge of the river, careful to avoid any fast motions or thumps that might startle the fish. In small bodies of clear water, stealth is critical to catching fish. I hid behind a small rise in the tundra. I cast and slowed the lure with my fingers on the line just before it hit the water, so it plopped in with little splash. Cast after cast I made, full of confidence and zeal from last night's catch.

A series of large boulders formed a chain of barriers between the deep, still waters of the pool and the swift main channel. The calm water just behind each boulder formed a perfect predator hideout, where fish could wait for food to wash by. I examined the status of my numbing hands, the rod, reel, lure, and pool. I searched for shadows of fish. Spotting one I cast just beyond the fish. The lure landed with barely a ripple. I reeled fast to begin the lure spinning then slowed, feeling the buzz of the spinner with my graphite rod. I slowed the lure as much as I dared, lest it quit spinning. The lure spun right over where I'd seen the shadow.

Swooooosh-Plaaattt! A burbout swooped up and gulped the lure, breaking the surface with its momentum. I set the hook firmly into its flesh. It raced for the boulder—a potential snag that could easily snap the line. I rushed downstream and pulled to the limits of the 6-pound line, just stopping the fish's surge before it reached cover. After that the fish tried a series of runs. I slowed then stopped the surges. Soon the four-pound fish was in my hands.

Strong gales, cloudy skies and temperatures in the mid-40s made uncomfortable fishing conditions. I had to keep one glove off to work the reel. When my bare hand was wet from landing fish or cleaning debris from my lure, it quickly became unbearably cold. But cold made fish storage easier. I warmed my hands over the fire. Fish sizzled in the skillet.

Fish are weathervanes for the health of our aquatic ecosystem. Even here in the furthest extremes of the Earth, the water was tainted. The fish have benzene and other oil industry toxins in their fatty tissues. Back in Ohio I quit eating fish from Ohio waters after learning that 98 percent of those tested by the Environmental Protection Agency were found to contain PCBs. Fish in the Great Lakes and Ohio River are loaded with mercury, lead, dioxins and many other toxins that bioaccumulate, increasing up the food chain.

A sharp cold front further chilled the air. To counter the biting cold, I switched between different activities throughout the afternoon. I caught and cleaned fish and washed dishes until my hands became too numb to function. I then warmed them up by packing my gear while wearing my gloves, writing in my journals near the fire, analyzing and fixing the pack break, tending the fire, cooking fish and boiling water to drink. By learning to cope with the cold, life became easier and more enjoyable.

The tent stake braces on my pack had bent, causing back pains and bruises. I looked for a caribou antler, thinking it would make a sturdy brace. Instead I found a ptarmigan wing bone near camp. It was light, but it seemed sturdy. I wired and taped it to the frame. I packed about 10 pounds of fish fillets. It would be a long way before I reached the next large river, the Canning.

The air temperature hovered around freezing. The evening was the worst possible time to cross. But to wait meant 16-18 hours until late next morning when temperatures would be better. Rafting seemed the safest choice, but the tedious chore of inflating, deflating and drying it in freezing temperatures made the task seem too difficult. Nothing dries well with overcast skies and near-freezing temperatures. The only remaining option was to wade.

I walked about a mile in both directions, searching for a place to cross. I finally chose the first one I'd seen, just above the fishing spot. Wearing tennis shoes to keep my boots dry, I gazed at the crossing spot, building my confidence. I put together my paddle that would be my walking stick. A fierce wind whistled about my hood. The thermometer read 35 degrees. It was 7 p.m. and would be getting colder. I plunged into the icy water.

The first channel was a minor, shallow braid of the river, averaging less than a foot deep. Large rapids lay downstream from the main channel I would next cross. The river was shallow at first, but inched progressively higher on my legs the farther I went. Painful icy chills shocked my body. Halfway through, I couldn't feel my feet. They were like lumps going along with my legs for the ride. My lower legs became numb, shocked by the torrent of 35-degree water sweeping past.

The main channel rose to my thighs when I was half way across, and continued to creep up my body. Footing was less secure. The water reached my waist. The force became nearly overwhelming. I slipped and teetered on the slippery rocks, narrowly regaining my footing. I worried about my journals packed in the lower section of the pack. Finally, the river bottom began to rise. I climbed up the steep bank and stood on dry ground. No time to even sigh relief. I must keep moving.

Chapter 8

Land of Plenty

The cold forced me to travel quickly to generate heat. But the ptarmigan wing bone splint broke, making hiking awkward, painful and exhausting. After an hour of hard travel in order to stay warm, I set my pack on a small knoll and rested. Within minutes I was shivering. I had to keep moving, though my legs and back were sore and in need of rest. I stretched, then heaved up the burdensome load. At least for the first time in more than a week I had enough food. With any more, I wouldn't be able to carry it.

My legs would not go any further. I set my pack down. This startled some nearby caribou, who apparently thought the pack was part of me. After scampering a hundred yards away, they cautiously returned, standing nearby as I set up my tent. I placed my maps, journals and books in the tent, followed by my sleeping bag. Inside I stripped off my wet pants and long underwear.

I was settling into my sleeping bag, when fear of bears overcame me. I'd read how grizzly bears roam the tundra, constantly in search of food. From my reading, bears should not be a problem if basic cautions are taken. One caution is to leave all food smelling items away from one's tent at night. I'd left the fish in my pack next to my tent. I was already drifting toward sleep, and my legs were finally dry, though a long way from being warm. The wind howled outside. I pulled on my wet, cold pants and went back out. I removed the fish from the duffel bag strapped atop the pack, and searched for a hiding place.

In New Mexico bear country, I hoisted smellables high in a tree. Looking around, all I saw was tundra, no trees or high places. How does one hide anything from a bear that regularly digs into the Arctic soil? I knew I wanted the fish at least away from the tent, so

I walked some distance away. I examined the tundra, at one point pulling at a tussock. To my surprise, it plopped effortlessly from the ground, leaving a depression that went all the way to the permafrost: a year-round icebox. I placed the fish in the hole and replaced the tussock. I stacked another tussock on top of it to mark its location and retired to my tent.

Finally, I could rest in peace. I pondered over the maps. I planned to meet a Sierra Club group in three weeks 120 miles away, high in the headwaters of the Jago River. At my current pace I would be well out of rations if I tried to make it directly. I had planned to raft the Hulahula River to Kaktovik to re-supply, then backpack to meet the Sierra Club. That would be some 250 miles of travel in three weeks: virtually impossible across the boggy, mountainous Arctic terrain.

The mountains to the southeast were growing in size with each passing day. At Prudhoe, I could barely see small rises on the distant horizon on the clearest days with binoculars, and I'd wondered if what I saw was haze or clouds. Now they were clearly visible. Their foothills extended to a few miles away. Lakes and bogs forced me to walk a mile out of my way for every mile forward. Arctic loons called from the lakes, while jaegers performed acrobatic stunts before me.

I fried the fish I hid the night before for breakfast. Late in the day, I arrived at the bank of a small channel of the Kavik River. Crystal clear water gurgled over a bed of polished rocks. The normally spongy, bumpy tundra was flat and firm near the river, with a sandier composition. The vegetation was darker and far more diverse than on the open tundra. Small willow bushes about a foot and a half tall challenged the fierce Arctic weather. Willows grow exceedingly slowly in the Arctic. A one-inch thick dwarf willow trunk can be more than two centuries old. I was walking over an ancient forest. I tried to avoid stepping on the amazing trees. To survive the eight-month winter, with negative 70-degree temperatures, 100-mile-per-hour winds and two months without any sunlight is quite a feat.

I set up camp by the river. Its soothing beauty would be refreshing and healing. I so enjoyed the company of the river. I was lulled to sleep by the sound of water rushing to the ocean.

The next morning, temperatures soared into the high 60s. I warmed water over a fire to wash with. I washed my clothes in my teakettle. I dumped the wash water away from the river. I wiped my sleeping bag clean with my bandanna and draped it on willow bushes to air-dry.

While collecting firewood, I found a caribou antler lying on the tundra. I'd been searching for an antler ever since the pack broke. It was sturdy, unlike the ptarmigan wing. I tried whittling it, but could barely chip it. Antler is made out of the same material as hair and fingernails, though denser. It should burn well, I thought. I put the unwanted section on hot coals to burn it off. I poured cold water over the section that I wanted to use as a splint to keep it from becoming hot and brittle. I wired and duct-taped the splint to the pack. Hopefully, this would end my pack troubles and sore back.

The combination of good weather and the beautiful music of the river put me in a cheerful mood as I conducted my chores. I packed my gear and hoisted it into place. The splint held the frame from bending. For the first time in many days I was not hunched over in pain under the load. I could now look at the scenery without straining my neck. Previously, walking hunched over forced me to stare at the ground in front of me. I was paying for a week of abuse with lingering back pains.

My feet were also in poor condition, covered in blisters. I recalled a story I'd read about eating willow bark, which contain the active ingredient of aspirin, salicin. I munched on some willow bark and was impressed with the quick results. It soothed the pain. Travel became pleasant for the first time in a week.

I paused to reassess the awesome scene of ageless willows, the pink cones of woolly louseworts and the broad diversity of tundra flora. I hiked toward the mountains. With food and a fixed pack, this quest was taking a decided turn in the right direction.

Chapter 9

Approaching the Front Line

Still charmed by the gurgle of the clear Kavik River, I followed one of the channels until it curved away from my direction of travel. Then I set out across the open tundra. This would be the last long tundra crossing before reaching the Canning River, which I would follow into the mountains. Though way behind schedule, I still hoped to raft down the Hulahula River, re-supply at Kaktovik and meet a Sierra Club trip in the headwaters of the Jago River in less than three weeks.

The day was so nice. I put my maps away and determined to just travel. I was growing more relaxed as I learned to survive on food harvested from the land and water. I felt increasingly connected with the Arctic ecosystem as I depended on it to provide fish, salads and root stews. The antler splint had fixed my troubling pack. The weather was beautiful. Travel was becoming a joy again.

The more time I spent on the coastal plain, the more I admired its unusual beauty. I could see for miles and miles in all directions. This is a unique wilderness. Unlike dense forests or mountainous regions, here I knew that I was alone.

As fears and anxieties lessened, I began to act differently, with less concern about the oddities of my actions. I would talk, sing aloud and holler for joy when I saw a spectacular sight, caught a fish, or just felt like it. This is the ultimate freedom, a time when one can concentrate on wilderness, and on oneself. The simplicity of wilderness life cleared my mind. Walking was a meditation that was bringing me closer to the divinity of nature.

As I neared the mountains, the tundra turned into small rolling hills and depressions. Ah, this was more like the familiar Appalachian foothills around my Athens, Ohio home. Rivers and stream channels cut deeper into the landscape. The vegetation also changed, with fewer louseworts and more northern lupines and willows. Toward the end of my day's trek, I passed near a foothill with snow at its base.

An oily sheen reflected from the lakes and tundra streams. Even as far east as I had traveled, I was nearing an oil installation. My map showed extensive development 10-15 miles upstream. I found oil industry debris and pollution in the tundra. Airplanes and helicopters roared from the installation, shattering the wilderness setting. Not until I reached the Canning would I be free from the oil industry pollution.

I did not drink nearly as much water as my body required, and I worried about what I did drink. I knew the seriousness of benzene and petrol-chemical poisoning. I had hoped this trip would purify my body of toxins. Thanks to the widespread oil industry pollution, the first leg of the trip did the opposite.

The next day was again clear and sunny. Mountains were growing in size and detail. The gray and black peaks were sharp, mystical and elegant monuments on the landscape. I could not wait to reach them. They still seemed a long way away, like a vague dream. The tundra began to roll more with increasing vertical rises and relief. Though there were higher areas to walk on, keeping my feet dry was still close to impossible. Nearing the end of my day's trek I came to my first large foothill, with snow along its base. It was late in the evening. Oddly, I could see the mountains far before the foothills. The hills blended with the landscape and I came upon them quite by surprise.

The next day, I traveled long and far. I reached a new level of endurance that allowed me to backpack for hours on end, with only short 10-minute rests every other hour or so. The surrounding beauty was drawing out my best qualities. I felt compassionate and happy, free and disciplined. Loons, jaegers and ptarmigan filled the air with acrobatics and song. There was never a dull moment, as long as my mind was open to absorb the delights of my senses, and not locked in worry.

The Arctic and the water that flows over it had supported me and quenched my thirst for two weeks. It was a part of me, and I would fight the pollution. I had seen the nightmare of oil development two weeks earlier. I knew I was integrally connected with the land. The oil industry was not only poisoning the beautiful land under my feet, it was poisoning me. And, they proposed to develop the land on which I was walking.

I came upon another willow ptarmigan protecting her eggs. Instead of flying off for her safety, she stayed by her eggs, then feigned an injury and hobbled away to draw me after her and away from her young. I felt like her, seeking safety for the next generation.

Oil is full of substances toxic to plant and animal life. Once it is pumped from the earth, it enters the thin living biosphere. Leaks and spills occur along every part of the global transportation route, poisoning drinking water. As fossil fuels are burned, they add carbon dioxide and other pollutants to the atmosphere. These pollutants contribute to global warming, acid rain and urban smog. These directly threaten me, and all life on Earth. Here, I experienced the sickness of oil poisoning firsthand. I was forever convinced that we need to work for a future free of fossil fuels. Fuel efficiency, solar, wind, biomass and muscle power with trains, mass transit and bicycling transportation are all viable solutions to our fossil fuel addiction.

Later in the afternoon, after about six miles of travel, I lugged the last few steps over the crest of a hill. A giant lake nearly a mile across was before me. The water was perfectly calm in the breeze-less afternoon. A lone island looked too perfect to be real. The scene looked like an artist's picture of a wonderland. The sky was magnificent, with a line of clouds forming a perfect edge over the lake. A light-blue sky faded even lighter toward the land until it formed a yellowish cream-colored edge above the greenish-brown tundra. Nearby, the bumpy moss formed an orange and green base to the delicate shades of pink and purple flowers.

The foothills to the north end of the lake were graced by two lines of clouds forming a diagonal clash of colors with curved edges. The mountains lay to the south, gazing like parents over this magnificent creation of Mother Earth. Snow lay in the crevices of the mountains. Isolated clouds cuddled the taller peaks. A light rain splashed my pack and my note pad. In minutes the clouds gained a purplish-pink haze, as if showing off their splendor. But, as I looked further, I noticed a rusty barrel on the west shore of the lake. What was in it? What toxins invaded the lake?

I wonder how anyone could view such a beautiful lake and then trash it. People today deal in such magnitude. Metals and plastics don't just decompose and become part of the food chain. It takes centuries for barrels to rust away in the Arctic. As I neared the shore, I found more trash. Four barrels of different colors littered the bank. Hundreds of rusty tin cans were strewn about. I also found tires, the same wire I had used to fix my pack, propane tanks, blue plastic ribbon and other junk.

I rambled up and down the rolling hills, through tussock fields and bogs. As I crested another hill on this glorious day, I came upon yet another splendid lake. This gem was again set in a bowl of tundra hills. Two Arctic loons swam about, occasionally entertaining each other with their enchanting song. The mountains lay beyond, with a magical presence about them. A jaeger glided about, showing off its flying skills with tricky acrobatics and tight turns. Two smaller birds chased one another over the lake.

The day was coming to a close, and I still had no idea how far I was from the Canning. It should be close, I knew, but whether I could make it that day, I did not know. My mouth was parched and my body dehydrated. But every lake had oil on its surface. The tundra extended onward in all directions. I had not encountered a tundra stream in hours. I finally dropped my pack, desperate for water. The nearest lake was half a mile away. I was lightheaded from lack of water by the time I reached it and filled my water bottles. An oily sheen covered much of the lakeshore. I drank the water with uneasiness.

It was the need for clean water that pushed me to reach the shores of the Canning River. I was so angry at the oil industry for polluting the source of my lifeblood—the source of me. Examining my map, I traced the Canning's source high into the mountains in the protected Arctic National Wildlife Refuge wilderness. It would be clean and pure, if I could reach it.

It was after midnight when I saw a long strip of white cutting north to south. I recognized it as aufice and snow found along rivers. I had finally reached the Canning! The borderline to purity was in sight. Should Congress choose to open the Arctic Refuge, a pipeline and road would pass through where I now traversed, and air traffic would be many times worse. Toxic pollution would be spilled in the tundra and the Canning River. The Canning would not stop the development then.

Chapter 10

Border to Paradise

Within sight" does not mean close in the Arctic. With nothing of certain size for comparison, distances are obscure. The map showed a wide valley that fanned out into a delta. But because I was not certain where I was along the river, it was of little help. I hiked on but the little white stripe that marked the border to purity didn't seem to get any closer. What I'd thought was half a mile was actually three or four miles. I hiked through willow thickets, marshes and down steep banks. I descended a steep bluff and found a 100-foot wide patch of snow, many feet thick.

The river valley provided an opening in the foothills. The mountains were in full view. Their folds and designs were illuminated by the midnight sun, which shone from the northern horizon. The dark rain clouds had long gone, replaced by a high cumulus layer that glowed in the low sun. The stark beauty forced me to stop and stare in awe. I was finally in sight of pure water, and nothing could daunt my spirits. Although disheartened by the distance left to travel, I began to admire it. This was a giant valley, 10 miles wide in this lower stretch. The Canning branched into scores of channels spanning more than 15 miles in width where it meets the Arctic Ocean. The river had carved out the valley over tens of thousands of years, creating flat, alluvial terraces, like giant stair steps.

I kept expecting to arrive at the river, which appeared to be only a few hundred yards away. My citified mind was fooled. I was used to neat channelized rivers, like the one they straightened into a ditch in my hometown. It wasn't until I arrived a mile later that I realized the gravel channel itself was several miles wide. I'd never seen anything like it. Before me was a vast meander of wild pure-blue water through dozens of channels of gravel and tundra.

I arrived at a nice fishing spot, with deep blue water at the bank. A 25-foot bluff hugged the bend in the river. The riverbank below it was flat and sandy. It was long after midnight, and my legs and back ached. I was not ready to sleep yet, though. I wanted fish. In about half an hour I caught two nice-sized grayling that I filleted and cooked over a fire. As I sat eating the fish and rice, the early morning sun cast long shadows toward the mountains to the south. The sublime scene enchanted me. The bright tundra and carpeted banks contrasted with the deep blue water that churned melodiously along. The mountains were alluring.

Twenty-five miles of riverside hiking lay ahead. I wasn't sure how I would get through the mountains, but it seemed that if I headed up Eagle Creek and found a pass to the Saddlerochit Valley, famous for caribou migrations, I could then make it to Lakes Schrader and Peters. There I could explore a cabin and research station, then raft down the Hulahula River to Kaktovik to resupply, going right through the heart of a pristine wilderness that is the area of the proposed development on the coastal plain.

The next morning, within 10 minutes of leaving my tent, I caught a grayling for breakfast. Another hour was spent trying to catch another. After cooking the fish, I resumed hiking upriver. The ground was sandy and firm next to the river, making hiking easier than traveling through the marshy plain. Willows grew thick on some of the terraces, at places forming an impassable wall. Other terraces were marshy with tussocks growing too close together to hike through. When I encountered these I would hike up or down a level to try a different terrace.

I slowly began to understand the patterns of the river valley. The terraces joined together and formed high bluffs around the outside bends of the river, where the water dug away at the bluff's base year after year. The inside bends form wide flood plains that stairstep up. I'd never seen an entirely undisturbed river valley. There was nothing to block one's view of all the folds and steps. The riverbed had once been much higher, forming the higher levels many millennia ago. All rivers were once wild, pure and free. It was humbling to realize that I was now at one of the few remaining.

The Canning River forms the border between the Arctic Refuge and the state-owned lands leased to the oil companies that I'd just hiked through. On the west bank, I stood on unprotected ground, open to the whims of oil giants who cared little for the majestic landscape. To them this was a "wasteland," to be exploited for their economic gain. Thankfully, the oil industry had stopped a few miles short of the river, out of sight and mind for now.

I tried several fishing spots with no luck. Storm clouds rolled in, along with a biting north wind. I hiked far. In the evening, the temperature fell rapidly. A thick wall of clouds blanketed the valley. I set my tent up in a deep ravine, where a stream entered the river. There I was protected from the fierce wind. Firewood from dwarf willows that grew along the waterways was plentiful despite the fact that I was well above the "treeline." I fished a two-foot deep pool of slower water by camp. Although I saw grayling chase my lure, none grabbed it.

I opened the tent flap early the next morning on a world turned white. About an inch of snow lay on the ground and the willows; it looked quite different from the night before. I jumped out barefoot, admiring the beauty. I caught two grayling from the pool by my tent. With a full stomach, I crossed the stream that had formed the ravine. I climbed the steep opposite bank covered with thick willows. Gusting winds made resting difficult. I stopped around 8 p.m. in a deep ravine near a good fishing spot, after traveling some seven miles. It was a perfect setting for dinner. I caught four grayling. I ate two for dinner and packed the remainder.

It was about midnight when I left. I loved the hours around midnight, especially after a full dinner of fish. It was like a perpetual sunset. Everything was so elegant, so beautiful! Many miles later, I encountered a narrow ravine with more driftwood than I had seen on the entire trip. It was near three potential fishing holes that I'd try in the morning.

My back ached after two weeks of sleeping on the cold, bumpy tundra and carrying such an enormous load. Sitting around an evening fire, I contemplated how to improve my situation. I considered making an elevated mattress from willow sticks, which for the first time I had plenty of. It would elevate me from the worst of the cold, but would be uncomfortable and could easily tear the tent floor.

Noticing my raft, I pondered. It seemed too big to fit in the tent. But the inner section was a series of tubes, like an air mattress, that inflated separately. I unfurled the raft in my tent and folded the outer tube underneath. I blew up the center section. It filled nearly the entire tent. I lay down in comfort and warmth. I had clean water, fish, firewood and, now, a warm bed: my luxury suite on the Canning River.

Chapter 11

Valley of Life

I slept soundly for the first time in weeks, awaking in warmth and comfort. By using my raft as a ground pad, I was able to lie flat, allowing my muscles to relax and recover from the cramps. I was warm and ready to brave the outside cold.

With sparse firewood in the Arctic, I had become adept at using it efficiently. Dry driftwood is perfect for starting a fire, and there was a giant stack at hand. I made a huge fire. With warm water and a few drops of super-concentrate biodegradable soap I washed thoroughly. The fire kept me cozy warm and quickly dried my skin and hair, a pleasant change from the shock treatment usually delivered by Arctic washing. I fried the two fish I'd caught the previous night and ate them with rice. I never tired of this staple dish I called "wilderness cuisine."

I breathed deeply and stretched, while gazing longingly at the mountains that were so close. I felt unusually refreshed after my sound sleep. The Saddlerochit Mountains formed a long wall from west to east just upstream and across the river. They stood above the blue water cascading over the wide gravel bed. I never tired of the river's melodic roar by my side. Another helicopter approached the drill sites a few miles away. The peace and solitude of the Canning Valley were temporarily lost in the noise. I would have to cross the river and travel further to escape it.

What disturbed me most was not the occasional roar of aircraft. It was my knowledge of what they were doing. The fire was an inferno before me. I watched two-inch thick willow sticks that took many centuries to grow turn to ashes in minutes. Meanwhile, millions of fires burn around the world. The petroleum, coal and other fossil fuels burning in most fires these days require hundreds of millions of years to form, a million times longer than nature took to grow my dwarf willow fire. Fossil fuels such as oil, coal and natural gas are stored carbon. Only if they remain stored—and not burned—do they prevent global climate catastrophe.

Studies of Alaska's permafrost, done by boring holes deep into it to capture history recorded in layers of frozen earth, have shown a temperature rise of 3.6 to 7.2 degrees Fahrenheit over the last 100 years; and 1998 computer modeling predicts temperatures will rise another 9 to 18 degrees in the Arctic over the next 100 years unless major changes are made to greatly reduce fossil fuel use and increase forest preservation. Over that same century, scientists predict that the permafrost will retreat between 500 to 1,200 kilometers north of its present location. Permafrost melting causes subsidence, erosion and the loss of vegetation and wetlands. The permafrost holds water at the surface in wetlands and lakes. This surface water is needed for the vegetation in a land that gets the same amount of rainfall as a desert. Oil pipelines and drilling rigs now firmly perched on the frozen ground could sink, causing yet more toxic spills.

Less than a mile into the day's trek, I came to an excellent-looking fishing hole. It was a deep, large pool with areas of nearly still water close to moving water and eddies. After a few casts I felt the surge of a grayling on my line. In about 20 minutes, I had four fish between one and a half and two pounds. The wind accelerated while I was fishing. It blew from the southeast, and churned the water in the pool. Along the northern shore of the pool, the water began to become silty. Grayling and Arctic char avoid silty water. The fish quit biting. Time to move on.

The day was beautiful, with full sunshine and temperatures in the 50s. Unlike before, when temperatures were good for refrigeration, I'd have to use the creel system to keep the fish fresh. I wrapped them in a wet bandanna and placed them in mosquito netting tied to form a bag, which I then attached to my pack. Evaporation of the water from the bandanna kept the meat cold and fresh. This system is used by trout fishermen. Native Americans used vine-woven creels, and wrapped fish with wet leaves and grass for the cooling evaporation effect.

My pace, slow when compared to my itinerary plans, kept me constantly fretting. This was day 17, and I had planned to be twice as far. Still, the Saddlerochit Mountains ahead of me and to my left grew continuously closer. Walking allows one to enjoy every step of the journey into the mountains. The Canning Valley ridgeline narrowed to about a quarter to half a mile from the river. A tundra flat with willow brush formed the bank. When I could follow animal trails, I sped along. But often the willows grew thick, and I had to push forcefully through. It was aggravating travel. I never knew when it would be easy and when it would be tough. When the ridge approached the river's edge, I had to climb the steep bluff. Atop the bluff, there were often tussocks and marshland.

While wading through a swamp at the top of the ridgeline, I heard the coo of a Pacific loon in a tundra pond just in front of me. Loons are beautiful creatures. Their base body color is a slick gray tone, with thin black lines along the body, and a red patch on the neck. The colors are pastel. Mother and father loon swam with two young. Mother loon thrusted her head underwater and caught a small fish. She lifted it above the lake surface, holding it in her bill, then paddled to feed it to one of her young.

I watched the scene close-up through binoculars, thanking all creation for the experience. Two golden plovers flew about, seeming to court one another on the opposite end of the pond. Neither the loons nor the plovers seemed to notice my presence, though I stood just 50 feet away. I stayed for quite a while, watching them. The sky was blue, making the scene crystal clear and sharp.

I stopped in a ravine to cook the fish I had caught earlier. I found ravines to be nice places to cook, because they slowed the wind and usually had plentiful driftwood for fires. I felt increasingly relaxed and sure of myself. I knew I could survive here, at least in the summer. The temperatures were in the upper 30s when I left the ravine. Along the ridgetop, I enjoyed the scenery on both sides of the river. The Saddlerochit Mountains were directly across the river to my left, captivating my gaze. Foothills extended to my right.

Ahead of me, the Canning meandered through the towering Brooks Range of white-capped peaks.

I hiked down the ridge at about 2 a.m. and saw another excellent fishing area. I was worried about my slow progress and dwindling rations, and with 24-hour sunlight, there was no night in the Arctic summer. A stream entering the Canning formed a deep pool. Though I fished more than an hour, I did not get a bite. I moved on. The landscape was surreal, dimensions were on a grand scale. It invoked a contented feeling of happiness whenever I took the time to look. At 5 a.m. I looked for a good place to camp, finally setting up my tent on a flat sandy area. I did not like camping on sand, because it can be very hazardous to equipment, especially zippers, stoves and fishing reels. I found fresh wolf and caribou tracks just a few feet from my tent. Camping near animal trails increases the danger of encountering a grizzly. But I was too exhausted to move camp.

While wading out to retrieve a snagged lure shortly after noon the next day, I noticed a couple of dots of color across the river. In my binoculars, I saw campers, with two large tents. I saw another yellow dot, probably a raft. They were about two miles away. The river was two miles wide, separating into dozens of channels between gravel bars and islands. I was surprised how far the other side of the river was. Rivers naturally span such distances, but in today's society the Army Corps of Engineers sets the width, and it is not supposed to move, because that would damage or devalue riverside "property." I was not ready to cross the river in the early morning icy chill, though I would like to have met the fellow travelers: the first people I had seen camping on my trek. A long deep channel in the river and a steep embankment made more barriers. I wanted to wade across rather than raft because of the hassle of moving a loaded raft between all of the channels. I would try to find the place where the river was spread out the most to avoid deep water.

I climbed the steep ridge and began hiking along the crest. After less than a mile, I had to descend and climb another crest. I looked for good fishing areas as I hiked. In order to stay within visibility of the river, I tramped through tussocks and dense willow patches. I noticed a stretch with slow current. The river cut into a steep wall about 50 feet high, creating eddies and deep pools. It was 60 degrees with a light breeze. Though getting to the river would be treacherous, I decided to try anyway. With my fishing rod and lure box in one hand, I descended the nearly vertical ridge of loose rocks. I could find few good footholds and caused several small rockslides.

After a few casts, I had a nice grayling on my line. I caught four more. I packed the fillets and began hiking upriver, pleased with my self-sufficiency. It was an artful routine that kept my belly full. But I'd soon be leaving the bountiful river for the mountains.

The hiking terrain became increasingly tough with steeper ridges. It was nearly 11 p.m. and temperatures were dropping. I was nearing Eagle Creek, which I would follow deep into the mountains. I decided to cut diagonally across a wide tundra plain toward Eagle Creek to save distance. That meant crossing the river, a fear I had harbored since I reached the river three days before. Could I get across safely?

Descending a high ridge into a ravine, I reached the shores of the river at what appeared to be a shallow area. I put my tennis shoes on and scanned across the expanse of gravel and water, recognizing that the raft would take too long to pack, unpack and move at each channel. I could see that the river had many channels stretching for quite a distance between gravel bars, but I was wholly unprepared for the reality of its great width, and cold! This would not be easy or comfortable, but delay would only make it worse. I plunged into the icy water. The water was a beautiful clear blue. It was just above freezing and extremely swift. The river bottom consisted of loose, slippery rocks.

I crossed the first channel, which I had thought was the largest, and climbed over the first bar. One after another, I crossed the channels, which were far larger than they had appeared from the bank. I slowly inched along through the powerful current, insuring that each foot found a secure hold before shifting weight to it. This kept my legs in the swift, near freezing water for many minutes in each channel. They soon became numb, and my body began to chill. But more channels kept appearing ahead. I ascended what I thought was the other side after crossing 11 channels, relieved that I'd finally made it. Climbing atop the "bank," I soon realized it was only an island. Another eight channels lay ahead; many as large as the first. I was tired and cold, but did not want to stop until I reached the other side. If I didn't cross now, it would only postpone the cold and wet until morning.

I pressed on. One after another I pushed through the river channels. I ascended a rise up to flat tundra, only to find it was another island with eight more channels to cross. I shook my head in disbelief. I had had to mentally push myself to get through the first series of channels, then the second set, telling myself that if I could just make these, I would be there. Now I had eight more to cross!

By the time I stepped up from the last rushing torrent, I could not feel my feet. My legs were weary, frostbitten, numb. I walked through a bit more gravel then ascended onto the tundra. The foothills of the Sadlerochit rose from the river's edge, towering high above to my left. I hiked upstream looking for a good place to camp with plenty of firewood. I knew I was hypothermic, and I needed a fire fast. I did not travel far before settling for a mediocre site. I was tired, cold and hungry. But I had crossed the river, a perpetual fear that I'd had for all the miles I walked next to it. And, I had reached the mountains. But, wet and cold, making a fire became a matter of survival. Sparse wood and blustering winds made what had been an every day chore into a precarious possibility.

Chapter 12

Crisis of Goals

Firewood had been plentiful—on the other side, the outside bend where wood accumulates. I was on an inside bend of the river now. Spring floods had washed away most of the driftwood. The movement of searching, examining and carrying loads of wood from great distances produced some warmth. But when I stopped to try and light the fire, wind gusts chilled my wet body. I was not expecting it to be this cold.

Strong wind can make starting a fire nearly impossible. Match after match blew out. I contorted my body to shield the wind. But 40-50 mile per hour gusts knew no barrier. They blew around me and extinguished the delicate little flames before they had time to grow. I was really getting cold, and using up scarce matches. I wondered if I would suffer a less romantic fate of the man in Jack London's short story, "To Build a Fire," waiting helplessly as the wind snuffed out the remaining glimmer of my life. I had to do something different. I shaved wood strips from some of the driest wood, and piled them below the thinnest twigs I'd found. I waited for a calmer moment, struck the match on a rock and huddled around the flame, like Secret Service around the President. I held it beneath the tinder, and watched the flame grow. "Yes," I said with a smile. "No!" I mourned moments later, as an unforgiving gust snuffed out the flame. Back to making wood shavings. There is no quitting in the Arctic. Quitting means death.

Fighting back the shivers, I shaved more wood tinder, building a pile three times the size of the previous one. I added more little sticks. The wind was relentless. I lay on my side, propped on my elbow, waiting for some calm. My jacket was unzipped and held as a shelter to block the wind. I lit a fire starter and held it under the tinder. The wooden blue-tip match hand dipped in wax stayed lit through a long wind gust. The wind let up as the wax neared its end. The wood shavings caught flame.

I was motionless. My eyes were fixed on the little flame, my life dependent upon its fragile spark of energy. My heart pounded, all senses focused on the growing yellow flicker. Just as the flame took hold it started to drizzle, and the wind whipped over my head. The fire reached critical mass. The wind only angered it now. The flame responded in a fury, growing from a little candlelight into a roaring blaze. The inferno thawed my numbed legs and arms and saved my life.

I cooked the five fish with rice and feasted. The meat was cooked perfectly. The wood burned rapidly. I sat downwind of the fire. The wind whipped the heat horizontally. My legs were roasting, but my head was freezing. A steady stream of hot coals blew toward me. I flicked them off my pants and jacket, hoping they wouldn't burn holes in the only clothes I had for the entire summer. I retired to the warmth of my tent and raft-pad as soon as I finished eating, leaving the dishes for the morning. I had set my tent up on an animal trail, and worried about bears. But I was too exhausted to find another spot. This was the only flat, brush-free space I found despite my extensive excursions.

The next morning, I stared at my maps on the warmth of the raft cushion. I was concerned about my slow progress. I had hoped to be nearing Kaktovik to replenish my food supply. Instead I was still on the Canning, though at least on the correct side. I was nearly out of food. A cabin and research station on Lake Schrader and Lake Peters offered the possibility of provisions kept in storage for travelers, along with fish from the lakes.

I studied the map, trying to figure out the shortest way to reach the great Arctic lakes. Travel through the mountains means studying the contours. Creeks form valleys and gorges with reasonably flat hiking. Ridgetops are possible but more strenuous and colder and often with cliffs and bluffs. Gentler slopes allowed passage over watersheds. The cabin was on Lake Schrader, two watersheds and 50 miles of mountaineering away. Eagle Creek ran straight toward the cabin, but ended in a high ridge, with two more mountain ridges blocking travel to the cabin. Just before Eagle Creek's end I could take a right at Straight Creek and a left up an unnamed creek. I'd have to climb over a high ridge to reach the Saddlerochit River Valley. I'd follow it for a while, then climb over a second pass to Spawning Creek, which led to the cabin. I hoped to complete this ambitious mountain crossing in three days.

Just five minutes after leaving camp, I arrived at a mystical pool of deep, pure-blue water, bubbling from an underground spring. It was graced by a carpeted tundra bank on three sides and flowed into the river. The water appeared quite deep just a few feet from the edge. The pool looked like the ultimate fishing spot. It was better than a pile of gold to me now.

I analyzed the pool, looking for more fish hideouts. I stalked up the bank far away from the waters edge. I crawled toward the pool, my body held close to the soft, wet tundra. I stopped some 10 feet from the pool's edge, analyzing the water. I examined the casting radius. I checked the lure. I cast. The spinner landed inches from the opposite side. I smiled in approval and pulled the spinner to action. Suspense built. I noticed movement in the depths. My heart thumped. The spinner seemed to slow down. I was connected in consciousness to the pool. A black shadow bolted into view, swooped around and grabbed the lure. "FISH ON!" The grayling jumped three feet in the air. On the next jump, the fish's vigorous thrashings threw the lure from its mouth. The fish was free and the lure landed at my feet.

I caught fish after fish. I focused on every turn of the reel, twitch of the line, move of the spinner, flow of the current, ripple of water and shadow on the pool floor. Any change denoted fish movement. I watched grayling dart from the depths and grab the spinner without hesitation. The hook, the struggle, the aerial acrobatics, the catch, the food...life in action. In all, I caught eight grayling and packed them in my creel.

I'd set ambitious goals for the day: to reach Eagle Creek, some 10 miles upriver, and then travel 12 miles up it. There were two ways to reach Eagle Creek. I could follow the Canning River, or cut diagonally across a plain. Rivers are generally easier travel than the open tundra. But cutting diagonally would save many miles. Frustrated by yet another wall of willows, I decided to try the short cut. I would be following the contour of the foothills, which appeared on the map to be the smart way to travel. But I would soon learn my lesson about Arctic travel.

I reached the base of Mount Copleston, which rose more than 3,000 feet above the river. The mountain's base melted into long fingers in the tundra, gracefully intertwined and fanning into a flat carpet before reaching the dwarf willow shores of the Canning. I climbed the steppes from the river and began the shortcut across the base of Mount Copleston toward Eagle Creek.

The breeze slackened and temperatures rose. My thermometer read 66 degrees. Mosquitoes came out in force. The heat, plus full sun, made backpacking unbearably hot in long pants and a jacket. But I could not remove them because of the mosquitoes. The terrain made for terrible hiking and that continually worsened. Tussocks grabbed at my feet with each step, aggravating my raw blisters. They greatly slowed my pace, making me exhausted. The mosquitoes, of course, were the worst nuisance. I'd take my jacket off for a few minutes to try to cool down only to have 20 tiny needle-mouths plunge into my arms, while thousands of others buzzed about my mouth, nose and ears.

I was frustrated. "Damned mosquitoes," I cursed, swatting at them aimlessly. "AAAHHH," I screamed, venting. But nothing got any better. I simply could not move another foot. I was too hot, exhausted and aggravated to continue. I collapsed on the tundra, slipping out of my shoulder straps. I watched my pack fall down, crashing against a tussock. I was too tired to care.

After a break, I pushed on and reached a ravine. I was worried about my fish being in the heat. A large patch of snow remained on the south side of the ravine. It was evening and I had not eaten since early morning. I fetched a tea kettle of ice and soon had five fish cooling, while I cooked three on my stove with mashed potatoes. They were so good that, for a brief few moments, I forgot about my predicament.

All I wanted to do was lie down and sleep. But I was concerned about my slow progress. Though I had fish now, my other food stores were nearly gone. A light breeze blew from the north against my back. A swarm of mosquitoes used me as a shield from the wind. They hovered around my chest and face. The mosquitoes were so thick I had to breathe through my hand to keep from sucking them in. I could turn around when I rested and face into the wind and the mosquitoes were blown to the back of me. This provided further incentive for me to just stop and rest.

By midnight, the temperature had dropped to 53 degrees, but winds were calm and the mosquitoes were even thicker than before. Most aggravating, though, was the tussocks. They were worse than I had ever seen them. I had to kick my way through. It made for exceedingly slow progress.

My trouble was well-known to Arctic travelers. An Army Arctic Manual reads,

> A particular nuisance in the North is the tussock. These are about the worst at the northern limit of the forest, getting less of a nuisance as you pass from the American mainland out upon the Canadian islands. The formation somewhat resembles a mushroom—it is a knob of earth wholly covered with a grass pad which seems to act as a sort of umbrella against the rain, so that the foundation of earth upon which it rests is less in diameter than the head of the knoll. In between the knolls are cracks of mud. Typically, the knobs are of such size that a man with a good stride will step from the first to the third—stepping over one without touching it.
>
> A perennial unsolved problem is which to do, to try to step upon the center of the tussocks and slip off every second or third time, or whether to step in between them every time, straight down into the mud. Usually the slip downward, when your foot slides off the tussock, is something between 6 and 10 inches—seldom as much as halfway to the knee. It is a considerable jar, particularly when you are carrying a heavy back load.

I considered hiking back to the Canning River and following it to the creek. But I was so far, backtracking seemed a colossal waste of time. Even if it means traveling two or three times farther, it is worth traveling next to running water in the Arctic. But now I was in the middle of this mistake, and it was about as much distance through tussock land to Eagle Creek as it would be to go back to the Canning.

Willows grew thick in ravines that my chosen route required me to cross. I pushed through. They grabbed at my pants. I was surprised my clothing held. I shoved with full force to rip through the brush. This was even more frustrating and tiring than tussocks, but luckily I could see it ahead of time and prepare. I could also usually see the end of it, so I knew it would not last forever. With tussocks, I tried time and time again to identify what they looked like at a distance to avoid them. I did find that cotton grass often grows with either tussocks or spongy marshland, both of which I liked to avoid. But I was in a sea of cotton grass.

I stopped at 2 a.m. at a wretched camping spot, too exhausted to move further. I had hoped to stop near water and had forced myself to reach a ravine outlined by willows, assuming it was a creek. It was a dry streambed. I was out of water and thirsty. I'd be dehydrated in the morning. I also couldn't find any spot to set up my tent in the dense vegetation. I finally stamped down the thick growth and set up my tent. The raft kept me comfortable and warm. It evened out the bumps into luxurious flatness.

I had hoped to be near Kaktovik by this time, about a hundred miles away. I had grossly underestimated the difficulty of the hiking terrain. While planning the trip, I had conditioned myself to carry a 90-pound pack for 15 miles up and down steep hills. With 24-hour sunlight, I figured I could easily travel that far each day, especially when the terrain was flat. But my plans were unrealistic. Walking through tussocks with my giant pack, the harsh weather and the time needed to catch fish, forage, cook, clean, write, set-up camp and sleep took much longer.

Reaching Kaktovik was the only sure way to food. Here I was

hiking into the mountains with only a few days supply of food left. At my current rate, it would take a few weeks to get to Kaktovik and resupply.

Lying back on the raft, I relaxed. The warmth that had overheated me in travel was luxurious now. A light from low in the north sky illuminated the right side of my tent. That's odd, I thought. A thick wall of clouds had blocked the sun some minutes earlier. I hopped out barefoot. I was stunned by the sight. A tumultuous ocean of clouds formed the ceiling of a mystical-looking tunnel. A glow emanated from beneath the clouds far to the northwest. I lay back against a tussock hill. The tundra was a patchwork of tussocks, looking like little mushrooms casting long shadows across the land. White cottongrass tufts sprouted from tussock tops, like fluffy lollipops atop little homes. In the quiet of the night, I could hear the Canning's soothing roar from miles away.

Turning south to the mountains, I saw a rainbow above Eagle Creek valley, where I was headed. It was at the opposite end of the cloud tunnel, on the south side of the storm. The brilliant array of colors demonstrated the beauty of nature's harmony and diversity. My budding reverence buzzed in a heart-tickling delight. I was ready for adventure. Mountains lay ahead. I trusted fish and forage would continue to come as well.

I awoke the next morning, my mouth parched with thirst. My tongue was dry, my throat hoarse. I walked around looking for any tundra pools. Finding none near my camp, I decided to hike on, hoping I would encounter a water source soon, though the next stream that I could see on my map was at least a mile away. With my speed of travel, that would place it at least an hour away. I was too thirsty for that. After only ten minutes, I had to set my pack down, lightheaded from lack of water. My mouth was so dry it stuck together painfully. With my canteen in hand, I wandered around, looking for any sign of water. But there was no stream nearby. I knew my situation was becoming desperate. I kneeled down, examining the tundra. I found a small trickle of water in between some tussocks, in a two-foot depression. It was stained brown with microorganisms swimming about. But I was thirsty. I filtered the water through my cotton T-shirt. It was still colored brown. I added iodine to kill bacteria, waited awhile and drank a small amount.

I was traveling with full muster yet barely moving. Soon my throat was parched again. I feared drinking any more of the uncertain water. After what seemed hours, I heard the babbling sound of a tundra brook. A small stream ran down a steep, rock-lined bed protected on both sides by overhanging willows. The ravine was lined with eight-foot tall willows, rivaling any I'd seen before. I was really traveling south, toward the "treeline." Firewood was plentiful.

I stopped to boil drinking water and cook fish. Fish sizzled on the skillet. A wind whipped up while I was cooking. The fire lit nearby brush. I'd been careless. I jumped up and began stomping it with my boots. The fire spread. I jumped around frantically trying to stomp out the growing blaze. The fire was determined. The vegetation was dry from two days of heat. The wind paused, slowing the fire's spread. I overcame the blaze.

In full sun, the temperature rose to 70 degrees. It was the hottest day yet. A nice breeze kept the mosquitoes away. I frolicked in shorts and a T-shirt. The mountains were close. The Canning roared to the west.

Hoisting up the pack, I pushed through tussock land, at a slower and more sustainable pace. I had considered the difficult conditions a sign of my own weakness. But I now realized that this was the reality of the Arctic, and partly what made it so wondrously unique. The tussock vegetation is brilliantly adapted to soak up a maximum amount of sun while conserving water and heat. I was gaining a deeper respect for the wildlife and native people who managed to live year round in the land I was struggling to survive in during its bountiful summer. The Arctic is extreme, and I was gradually coming to accept it.

I arrived at a forest of alders 20 feet high and six inches in diameter. I was far north of what maps showed to be the tree line. The valley was protected by ridges in three directions that sheltered the trees.

I was startled by barking wolves. Looking around, I noticed numerous fresh wolf tracks leading in all directions. I stalked toward the barking. Visibility was obscured by the dense vegetation. I heard several more alert, pronounced barks. Then they were gone. Wolves are social creatures. They travel great distances following the caribou herds. Their lives depend on and enhance the caribou herd by taking the sicker and weaker animals. Vigorous life is sustained by death, all in a balance evolved over billions of years.

A golden eagle perched in an alder tree some 80 feet away. It wasn't concerned with the wolf commotion, or me. It sat in the tree, staring at me. The raptor seemed interested in taking fresh meat from the wolf pack. Great talons gripped the alder branch. Dark, golden feathers adorned its legs and chest.

The hiking terrain became easier after the trees when I found an animal trail. Then the path ended in a willow thicket. It was impossible to tell when the animal trails would just stop. Knowledge is the key to survival here. Caribou follow trails they have traveled for thousands of years. Native Americans also have an intimate knowledge of the hunting, fishing and travel routes around their villages. I was a newcomer. But I had maps and I was learning. Wolves remember the vast acreage that they roam through cognitive maps. Studies of wolves have shown that they do not need to have traveled a particular path in order to know where they are. They can travel in the direction of a known area even if their route takes them far away from anywhere they have ever been.

I encountered a patch of red, juicy berries growing close to the ground. I identified them in my field guide as a bear berry. Because of its sour taste, natives only gather it when other berry harvests are poor. They puckered my mouth, but I ate them anyway. I needed the nutrition. As I ate more, I began to enjoy them. They were still very sour but I enjoyed the rich aftertaste that stayed in my mouth for some time. Berry gathering also made for a nice rest from the arduous backpacking. They gave me needed vitamin C and provided a substantial amount of food, when I took the time to pick them. Learning each new edible plant added greatly to my confidence. I no longer walked over a foreign land. I saw the tundra as a garden providing all my needs.

I was going to make it. I might have to pucker up and eat bear berries, but I'd survive. I crested a foothill. Eagle Creek glistened in the late evening sun below. I had expended so much energy in traveling the ten miles between the Canning River and Eagle Creek, I had begun to think I might not make it. But here I was at what I would call Rainbow Valley.

Chapter 13

Reverence in Rainbow Temple

A large moose stood in a thicket of willows at the entrance of Rainbow Valley. The creature was giant, standing a full four feet above the willows that reached to its chest. I'd heard that startled moose have been known to charge. I watched the moose in my binoculars. The animal seemed very peaceful. I sat down. The moose wandered off without a sound.

I continued. Willows grabbed at my clothes. I pushed through walls of the dense vegetation. I descended to the gravel creek channel, where travel was easy, though it required frequent crossing of the cold waters. My feet were getting used to being soaked. Soon I entered a glacial-carved valley between two lines of mountain ridges. The dimension was tremendous, and the tranquillity like that of a Buddhist temple. I could see for miles.

Because there were no trees with which to place distances in perspective, I often had no idea how far away a mountain really was without studying the map. Rocks could be of all different sizes, and provided little help. The map showed the valley was five miles wide. Mountains measuring many thousands of feet up appeared at times only a few hundred feet high. I was not used to the scale. I felt as if I was traveling in a dream, with this splendid temple all to myself. Everywhere I turned, more beauty awaited me. It is easy to understand why, for those who make the journey, it is a life-changing event.

On the map I noticed a large lake on the south edge of the valley, about two miles away. It was enticing. Though it was off my intended route, I realized that it might hold fish. I spent half an hour placing my exact position with the map, compass and the mountain ridges. Each ridge was different, with its own unique character, if one spends the time to notice. I placed each valley with the contours of the map. By checking various mountain structures with my compass, I noted that due north from my gear was the third crevice on the second mountain from the Canning River valley. I measured the angle from my position to a creek cutting through the south ridgeline.

The lake was 3/8 of an inch away on my map, meaning two miles as the crow flies. Arctic reality made it 3-4 miles of hiking. I took my fishing gear, camera, journal and canteen. I forged around ponds, marshland and dense brush, arriving at a wall of willows, which blocked my path. I followed a creek channel through the worst of the brush. It took me far out of the way, but the scenery was spectacular. I was nearing the south ridgeline, which was far higher than I'd expected. I took a right up another creek, following it for a while before climbing a high hill overlooking the lake. There it was, looking like a little pond in a setting of tundra and willows.

Monoliths of rock forming the south ridge glowed orange and pink in the midnight sun. Mountains changed to foothills toward the Canning River valley. As I approached, the pond turned into a lake half a mile wide and a mile long. What had seemed a few hundred yards between me and the lake was actually a mile. The air was calm, giving the lake a smooth, reflective surface. The low sun illuminated the mountains with soft orange, red and pink hues that reflected perfectly in the placid clear water of the lake.

I sat to write in my journal. "So this is paradise, heaven," I wrote. A loon called out. A grayling slurped the lake surface. I made cast after cast into the lake. Little grayling followed the lure, but none grabbed it. Looking at the reflection in the water, the brilliant spectacle made me forget about fish. I lay down my rod and sat atop a ridge opposite the mountains. A plane flew about the oil installation 20 miles to the northwest, breaking the trance. I turned to leave.

In the dim light, I came upon a large moose just 25 paces away. The startled moose snorted and lowered her head toward me. I backed quickly away, hardly taking my eyes off her. She snorted again, menacingly. I held out my hands in a gesture of peace, as I retreated and climbed a small hill. Now I could see a calf that had been blocked from view by willows when I had been at the bottom of the hill and first saw the adult. A very concerned mother and calf stared me in the eyes.

The moose is a very sedentary animal, staying in thick willow patches along riverbeds and wetland areas. The cows grow to 1,000 pounds, the bulls up to 1,500 pounds, 10 times my weight. Moose are among the most dangerous Arctic animals. Dense willows often hide them from view until travelers are nearly upon them. Cows with calves will charge in order to protect their young. A mother moose who has just lost a calf to predators will also be aggressive. During the fall rutting season bulls can mistake a person collecting firewood for the sound of a challenging bull, and charge them.

Though quite large, moose are stealthy, silent travelers. They know every path through their valley home. They tend to avoid caribou. Koyukon natives say caribou are noisy and clumsy compared to moose. Caribou are quite different in character. They travel great distances and are more lively. They will run in circles for the sheer fun of it. The moose have a meditative calm about them, having purpose with every step.

Walking back, I found a caribou antler, which I took to splint my pack. I returned to my tent at 4 a.m. and slept. I awakened early. I found another caribou antler. Though one side of my pack was firmly braced, the other was bent. I burned off the ends of the antler around the morning fire. I fastened the caribou antler tightly to the broken frame with wire. I took my time and repaired it securely.

I backpacked just one hour before I began to slow and stagger. The valley was in full sun, temperatures rising into the high 50s. Lack of sleep sapped my energy. I set my pack down and lay on the gravel streambed. I tightened my hood until it left just enough space to breath, pulled my hands into my jacket sleeves and folded the ends down to keep out mosquitoes. I drifted in and out of sleep for an hour and woke with more energy.

I moved quickly up the stream bank. In order to stay on the gravel, I crossed the stream frequently, perpetually soaking my feet.

Rest stops were convenient times to forage for fireweed, an edible green, willow shoots and berries while checking for new plants. I found a plant that appeared to be a bear root, also called Indian root or licorice root. It is similar in appearance to a poisonous plant.

Sitting down on the gravel shore, I pulled the plant from the earth and analyzed it. Its root was a three-foot taproot that started with the thickness of a large carrot and tapered smaller until it was about a quarter inch in diameter. Attached to it were about a dozen rootlets, each six inches to a foot long and between a quarter and a half inch in diameter. This would be a lot of food, if it were edible. The only easily noticeable difference between the plants is that the poisonous species has between 9 and 17 pairs of leaves on each branch and the Bear root has between 9 and 22 pairs. To assess whether it was poisonous, I searched for a branch with more than 17 pairs of leaves. Finding three branches with 18 pairs and one with 21, I knew it must be edible. I packed it and continued upstream.

Further up the valley, I saw some fish in a shallow, narrow pool in a stream channel. A hoary redpoll sat on a willow hanging over the little pool. A member of the finch family, the bird had a pure white body with a red patch on its forehead, a short beak and a black face. It sang with a trill followed by "chit-chit-chit-chit." It was a few yards away. The redpoll jumped into flight, singing "Swee-eet, swee-eet."

I stopped and cast a small spinner in the pool. I watched a grayling chase the lure and grab it. The fish appeared small through the water but when I pulled it out, it was about 17-inches long and weighed two pounds. I soon had another one. Three more fish were grouped together in the pool; I cast the lure past them. The spinner spun just inches from their mouths. Instead of grabbing it, they were startled and avoided it. They were spooked. Time again to move on.

Shortly after I left the pool, drizzle began to speckle the valley. Temperatures—that all-important indicator of my welfare—remained in the 50s. It was warmer where I was now, farther south, and away from the cold air of the Arctic Ocean. The rain enlivened the Arctic land. I had been huddled in my tent during rain spells before. In the warmth, I covered my pack and myself with a poncho and hiked on through it. It was still drizzling when I arrived at another pool of fish. This pool was different, though. It was even smaller and was not connected to the main stream. The fish were stranded when the stream water level dropped after the diminishing spring runoff. They would surely perish. I wondered how long they'd been there, and how much oxygen was left.

I was reminded of a fishing experience on a small stream near Columbus, Ohio, when I was a child. The river had been dammed just upstream, reducing the flow to barely a trickle during the summer. Water was pumped out for lush green suburban lawns and golf courses. Pesticides, fertilizer and soil erosion runoff choked the stream. All that was left was a string of pools with fish competing for food and oxygen. The smallmouth bass were the first to die, followed by sunfish, rock bass, carp and catfish. I had watched in sadness as the bass mouthed the surface, gulping for oxygen as their life slowly waned. Soon they would join scores of their kin that lined the banks. I wanted to stop the pollution and save the fish. But I had felt as helpless as the bass to change the powers that be.

Now the situation occurred naturally, and I wanted to make use of the fish. I had already spooked them by approaching so close. They would not chase lures for some time. Wading into the pool, I first tried to grab the fish. The pool was six feet wide and twenty feet long. I tried using mosquito netting. I grounded one side of the netting to the bottom of the pool with several large rocks. The net floated to the surface, creating a fish trap.

The fish were crowded into the deep section of the pool. They hid behind a willow bush. I pulled out the bush. I used my paddle to chase them from the deep end toward the net. Because it only covered a few feet of the six-foot-wide pool, the grayling managed to swim around it. I tried again and again. The water began to silt. I had trouble locating the fish. The silt also clouded the grayling's view of the net.

I chased the fish out of the deep end with my paddle. The largest fish darted right into the net. I let go of the paddle and leaped over the water, pouncing on the netting like a lynx on a lemming. The mosquito netting gave me a firm grasp on the slippery creature. I pulled the two-pound fish from the water and laid it on the bank. The other two fish took about as long to catch (20 minutes), the second being about a pound and a half and the last one about a pound. Another six-inch fish remained. Maybe there would be enough oxygen for it to survive until the next heavy rains came. The grayling had a shiny coat of scales with subtle markings of rainbow color on a dark gray-brown body.

Firewood was dampened by the rain. I broke off dead limbs from standing willows to acquire drier wood. Though still damp, at least the wood was not soaked through. I whittled off the wet parts. With much effort, the fire came to life, crackling, smoking and snapping. While the fish sizzled over hot coals, storm clouds swept through the valley. I watched sheets of rain cast dark-gray streaks diagonally from the clouds as they moved through the valley.

Looking up from the skillet, I was treated to two brilliant rainbows just up the valley. The mountains to the south glowed in the late evening sun, while the ridge to the north formed a silhouette against the blue sky. Weather in the mountains was always changing and unpredictable. The rainbows approached and were soon on top of me. My situation had changed from tussock hell to rainbow heaven.

I unfurled and inflated the raft, and used it as a cushion propped against a steep hill. I relaxed back in my Arctic easychair, watching the rainbows float down the valley. I felt like their chaperone. I could not imagine a more spectacular sight. Growing beyond temporary rapture dependent upon good circumstances, my heart and mind were opening into a constant state of happiness. A life-changing reverence was awakening in me.

The pool I'd raided was clear now. I saw the little graying I'd left behind, huddling in the deep corner. The fish seemed afraid of my presence. I felt for its companions that I had taken. "More water will be coming, little one," I said. The stream was rising some from the recent rain. I returned the willow bush to give the fish some shelter.

So many people live like that trapped grayling, in their pools of property: their own particular worlds. But the wide world is out there. And, unlike the grayling, we don't have to wait for rain to set us free.

Chapter 14

Into the Mountain Heart

The east-west valley was three miles wide here. The fish pool was on the north side of the valley. The clear creek tasted purely divine. Boiled over a willow fire, the water hinted of willow smoke, without chemicals or impurity. My sweat even smelled of the smoke, a reminder that we are what we drink, as well as what we eat. Here I had some of the purest drink and food, in one of the cleanest valleys in the most pristine mountain chain left in the world. My clothes, body and hair were permeated with wilderness smoke, which mixed with my body's natural odors to form a pleasant, outdoorsy aroma.

I was too charged from the beauty to sleep. I hiked through the night. I was attempting a mountain pass I had no idea existed. My map was little squiggly lines of minute detail. Each quarter inch was more than a mile. Each contour squiggle was 200 vertical feet. That 200 feet could be a gradual slope or a steep cliff. From the looks of the mountains around me, the latter seemed likely. I could not be sure until I encountered it. My plan was to ascend Straight Creek, then take a left at an unnamed creek. Both were steep gorges. The contours cuddled the little blue line tight on the map, indicating possibly cliffs and waterfalls. This would be uncertain terrain. I was nearly out of food. Though fish had been plentiful, they would not be available through this mountain crossing. My hope was in the lakes, cabin and research station still 25 miles away over rough steep mountain terrain.

Straight Creek branched from the south side of the valley. I crossed scores of gravel-lined channels. I hugged the south ridge to make sure I did not miss the creek junction. A waterfall poured from a distant ridge. The northern mountains cast a long shadow over the valley. The south ridge glowed pink and orange in the midnight sun.

The air was still. Music emanated from the gurgling stream with the occasional sound of a gull in the distance.

I came to a fork at the junction of two creeks. I followed the south split. My map indicated that Straight Creek ran for many miles through the wide Rainbow Valley after plummeting from a narrow gorge in the south ridge. The creek appeared to come from a shear cliff wall blocking my path ahead, with no valley entrance in sight. I thought there must be a waterfall, or a tunnel or spring from which the stream came, but I could see no entrance through which to walk. What had seemed from an earlier angle to be one continuous wall was a visual illusion that blended contours together. As I continued up the stream, it turned sharply to reveal a 100-foot wide opening between a gate of two rock monuments. The gorge was steep. The only hiking was through the creek. My boots were already soaked. Shortly after traveling through the gates, I was attacked by a colony of nesting glaucous gulls. They squawked and dived at me menacingly. My bird book said the gulls nest in colonies near the ocean shore. We were far from the ocean, but here they were, guarding a hatchling of newborn. The glaucous gull adult averages 27 inches in length. White with yellow eyes and a yellow bill with a red spot on it, it has pink feet and a light gray patch on the wing tops. Several young gulls stood on the other side of the creek, guarded by adults.

A jaeger flew nearby. Jaegers are known to eat young birds and eggs. The gulls also prey on eggs and young of other birds. Now they were protecting their own young. Some gulls swooped at the jaeger while others continued to nose-dive at me. I hastened to leave them behind. Their loud squawks were amplified in the stillness of the valley as they worked to chase away both me and the jaegers.

Arctic terns, which fly 22,000 miles each year—half way round the world from their other home in the Antarctic—show the same tenacity in defending their young. To protect their young, terns will dive bomb polar bears and humans, not just threatening but actually using their feet to hit intruders on the head.

I traveled up the creek, crossing it regularly when willows

abutted the shore. The water plummeted down the steep valley. The rock bottom was unstable and slippery. As it neared 5 a.m., exhaustion made the crossings too dangerous. I found a flat, sandy area on the west bank of the creek and set up camp.

I woke at noon with balmy 65-degree temperatures and a breeze that kept the mosquitoes at bay—luxurious living conditions. I made a small fire and had mashed potatoes, oatmeal and coffee. I was down to a few servings of mashed potatoes, some rice and a handful of single-serving size oatmeal packages left. I opened the trash bag containing a plastic bottle of vegetable oil to add calories to the potatoes. I found an oily mess. A coal from a recent fire had burned a hole through the bottle. About half had leaked. Yet more food was lost. I poured the remaining oil into my green canteen, deciding the oil was more important than having two water bottles. My hands had become dried, with cracks of broken, bleeding skin from the drying effect of cooking over a fire. So I used the remaining oil in the bag as moisturizer for my skin.

I resumed my travel up Straight Creek. I scanned to my left, looking for a nameless creek valley that would be my passage east. After several miles up Straight Creek, a bend in the valley revealed a gorge cutting through the east ridge. There was only one creek on the map, but several gorges. I followed it to see if it was the right one. The creek seemed too small—a mere trickle—and it seemed to go up too steeply. I identified it on my map to be the gorge just before the one I wanted to travel. I hiked up the ridge toward the next creek. The ridge was far steeper and higher than it first appeared.

I crested the top only to find a bluff, plummeting nearly straight down for 200 feet to the creek floor. I munched on bear berries, pondering what to do. A hang glider would sure be nice now. I walked to the cliff edge and scanned for a way to the bottom. I noticed a ravine cutting into the cliff for part of the descent, lined with willows. The loose rocks looked dangerous. But I did not want to backtrack or waste time mulling over it and decided to press forward.

If I broke a bone here, I would never be found. I wondered if anyone had ever been in this nameless valley. I began down the cliff, following the diagonal line of vegetation. The first 100 feet were difficult, but far easier than what was to come. I held onto a protruding rock about 100 feet up from the cliff bottom and lowered down my body. My right foot rested on another protruding rock. As I slowly increased weight onto the protruding rock, it ripped away from the cliff in slow motion, plummeting to the ground along with scores of other rocks and boulders. I held on with one hand to a willow root, my lifesaver. I dangled, my legs scraping the rocks in search of a foothold.

I half-swung, half-scooted to the right to a deep crack in the cliff wall. There I found a foothold, but the nearest handhold was out of reach from the safety of the willow. I let go of the lifesaving willow, teetered over the foothold, and caught another willow on the other side of the crack. Only 100 feet to go. The side of the crack opposite me had crumbled several feet into the cliff wall. I descended the crumbled section. It was the only place I found any sign of foot and handholds going all the way to the bottom.

I slowly inched my way down, starting small avalanches with each move. My footholds wobbled. About thirty feet from the bottom, I stood on a precarious, wobbling ledge. I'd become so used to such dangerous a setting from 170 feet of descent that I didn't think much of it. Until.... WhoaaAAHHH!!! The rock broke away from the mountainside. Thirty feet above the bottom, I was falling. The rock and I slipped a heart wrenching three feet. I was in for broken bones at best.

What? I was alive? It was an amazing chance of fate that the rock stopped on a bump on a near-vertical cliff, some 27 feet above the rocky bottom. Trembling in fear, I descended foot by foot.

I jumped four feet onto the rock-strewn ground. Never had firm ground felt so good. I scurried away from the danger of falling rocks and lay down. I felt a whole new reverence for the earth underneath. I should have walked back the way I'd come, and followed the creek. I rested awhile, recovering from the crazy escapade.

Upon awakening from a short nap, I began hiking west. Unbeknownst to me, I walked all the way back to Straight Creek before I realized I had gone the wrong direction. I checked my map and sure enough, that's what I'd done. I laughed, shaking my head. Then I retraced my steps, pausing at the site of my treacherous descent. It had only taken me 15 minutes to hike the short distance I'd risked my life over.

The mountains towered above each side of the creek, leaving little hiking room. The chasm narrowed even more. I crossed the raging creek every 100 feet or so as it snaked through the narrow valley. Resting on a large boulder, I was entertained by several gulls. Without young, they were less bothered by my presence.

I slipped on a wet stone and came crashing down under the weight of my pack. I hit my right knee hard on a rock. Pain throbbed through me. I limped to the canyon side, and lay on a small patch of dry bank. I massaged the knee, then napped. When I awoke it ached, but seemed functional. I stretched, then pushed on with a severe limp. The path narrowed. The mountains grew. I shared 10 to 14 feet of flat ground with a raging mountain stream. The sides of the gorge were nearly vertical with loose shale overhanging above. I eyed them nervously, hoping they would stay put through my passing. The floor bottom was strewn with fallen pieces. The steepness of the gorge made the possibility of its blockage likely.

The path narrowed. The gorge steepened quickly and turned into a V shape. I was climbing through shin-deep freezing water rushing down. As I struggled against the current, I was exhausted. There were few dry spots in which to rest. The chasm turned sharply to the south. A steep, tundra-covered ridge rose to the east. I followed the creek. A two-foot thick floor of ice covered the narrow west side of the 8-12 foot wide valley floor. Most of the room was taken up by rampaging water. Steep, black shale walls rose on either side. I named the creek "Mountain Heart Creek."

Turning a bend, I came upon a sheer wall of falling water. The 15-foot waterfall blocked passage. Vertical walls of loose shale made climbing around it impossible. Though my way was blocked, the scene was spectacular. I set my pack down on a ledge, and approached the waterfall. It was powerful, its waters clear and cold.

The roar was deafening. The stark contrast of the white water against the dark-gray and black shale heightened the presence of the waterfall. The falls had a rhythm that resonated through the roar. I stuck my head in the icy waterfall and yelled while it washed my hair.

I backtracked to where the creek had turned, examining the steep ridge that, if my orienteering skills were right, was a pass to the Saddlerochit Valley. I craned my neck to see the top of the ridge. It was a 60-degree slope upward: safe but very tough. My pack was lighter without much food, but still quite a load. I'd traveled fast and far today. I began the strenuous ascent. My legs balked at the incline and the heavy load. I took short steps and heaved upward, starting at a height of 2,100 feet. The summit was 3,300 feet. My wet hair helped keep me cool.

I rounded the top of the ridge, rewarded by an incredible view. Mountains were everywhere. I was on top of a divide between two watersheds. A watershed links land together into a living body with river arteries and veins. Each valley is a part of the greater whole of the watershed. Nowhere is that more clear than when standing atop a ridge between two watersheds. This was my bridge from the rocky steep gorge, with its lichens, moss and sheer rock, to the wide, U-shaped Saddlerochit Valley, with its lush, green floor of tundra, tussocks and willows. The Saddlerochit River meandered through the valley a few miles away. But because of a lack of indicators about scale, the river looked more like it was a little creek just a few hundred yards away.

The crevices and ravines of the mountains form the top of the watershed. It started from where I stood. The water gathered in ravines to form intermittent streams that only flow during wet times. The steepness of the slopes makes the streams lively beings. Smaller streams combine to form larger creeks, like Straight Creek. They combine with larger streams, such as Eagle Creek and then combine to form rivers, like the Canning River, itself flowing into the Arctic Ocean. I'd hiked nearly all of it, save for the "short-cut" between the Canning and Eagle Creek and the lower delta where the Canning reached the ocean.

To the east was the Saddlerochit Valley. The wide, lush valley floor was bordered by high, spectacular mountains with snow in their crevices. I was at the headwaters of the Saddlerochit River. It formed from three creeks that joined together seven miles upriver. Another creek came from a glacier across the valley from where I sat. The pass was on the outside bend of a sharp turn in the wide valley. The valley extended south—upstream—for four miles into what looked like a box canyon (one that dead-ends into a cliff). My map showed that the valley continued. It was but another Arctic illusion, like when I could not see the Straight Creek Valley from Rainbow Valley when it was blocked by two stones that appeared continuous but had a gap between them. The Saddlerochit Valley widened downstream, turning to the north-east-east. It was the only distant opening in a slew of mountains.

A herd of six caribou traveled upstream by the river. I watched them with binoculars. They were fast, and were soon far to my right. The valley is a migration route for the Porcupine Caribou Herd across the Brooks Range. Its wide, lush valley offers a smorgasbord of food. Also frequenting the valley is a remnant of the ice age, the Muskox, with curved horns and hair drooping to the ground.

Gazing back west, down the valley that I just climbed, I could see smaller mountains that grew a luxurious velvety skin of moss and lichens on either side of the narrow ravine I'd climbed. I stood on a bold ridge that marked the boundary between the Canning and Saddlerochit watersheds. It was a dark rocky gray, with white snow pockets in its crevices.

I descended the ridge toward the Saddlerochit River. Here the dimensions were of an even grander scale than Rainbow Valley. I reached the river's riparian buffer of willows. The river itself was half a mile wide in many channels along a gravel base. Rain drizzled with a chilly wind. My stomach growled. The river was shallow and fast without any fishing holes. I stopped near midnight to eat two cups of mashed potatoes and two oatmeal packets cooked over my stove. I was down to barely one day of rations.

On the map, I followed the route of the caribou over the continental divide far to the south. They had many steep passes ahead in their journey to their winter homeland. But few were steeper than the ridge I had just hiked over. Potential routes unfolded before me with the successful ascent of the pass. I was tempted to follow the caribou. But the need for food drew me toward the lakes.

An Arctic warbler sang a joyous song perched in a willow. It was gray-black with fluffy white belly feathers, an orange beak, and a light greenish-yellow stripe over its eyes. The bird sings a "zick-zick-zick trill-lll" soprano. Warblers are active birds, flying from branch to branch in search of insects.

The fact that it was 1 a.m. didn't stop the birds. Despite the late hour, I also traveled on. The river sounded through the wide valley meadow. I gulped down two quarts of willow-scented water and filled my canteen. I hoisted myself up the river's embankment. I encountered two caribou calves and three adults traveling upstream. The calves were but a month old, and they were already walking hundreds of miles. They frolicked in joy, bringing a smile to my face. They are the centerpiece of this ecosystem. They veered to make a wide arc around me, a constant reminder that we often have an impact on nature even when we don't want to. The severity of impact of an oil installation is infinitely greater than my walking through. Yet just by my presence I was altering the caribou path.

These animals led the main herd on their way over the continental divide of the Brooks Range. After my intended visit with Inupiat peoples at Kaktovik, I planned to cross the mountain range to visit Arctic Village, a Native American settlement of Gwich'in people who depend on the migrating caribou for food and clothing.

In a little more than two hours I covered seven miles, cruising fast along the riverbank while searching for fishing spots. I found none, but at this rate even if I had to go hungry I'd make the lakes by tomorrow for certain. I veered right, leaving the Saddlerochit River for a hill pass that divided the Saddlerochit watershed from the Neruokpuk Lakes. Just over the pass, the valley opened into the watershed of Spawning Creek, which flowed past the cabin at the creek's outlet into the lake. It looked like a prime fishing spot.

Travel became rough as I hiked uphill against the contours of the river. I waded through walls of willows, interspersed with tus- socks. My pace was so slow. I was again exhausted, my legs weary and weak. I sat against the base of the hill I still had to climb. Then, after a few minutes, I grudgingly hoisted the monstrous pack in place.

I stopped to rest after climbing a third of the way. Sitting against the steep hill, I looked back for the first time. My eyes opened wide. The valley glistened in the nighttime sun. The great cathedral was bordered by mountains. Up the hill I went. From the hill's crest, I gazed over a vast terrain three times as distant and about seven times as expansive as the Saddlerochit Valley behind me. The sky was clear ahead, over the lakes. A dense wall of clouds had blown into the Saddlerochit Valley. I was leaving the storm for clear skies. Lake Schrader looked like a little pond in the far dis- tance. Beyond it lay the mystical pyramid-shaped Kikiktat Mountain. It was veiled in a thin, swirling fog rising from the lake.

I descended the steep hill, looking for Spawning Creek. All I found was wet, tussock-filled tundra. I was exhausted. Tussocks ripped at my feet. I wanted to reach the cabins, but it was nearing 4 a.m. I didn't want to disturb anyone at that hour. All was so calm. I reached the headwaters of Spawning Creek. Tundra abutted the creek's edge with taller, more luxuriant tussocks and willows. I camped on a flat rise next to the creek.

Chapter 15

Renewal at Lake Trout Cabin

The patter of rain woke me late in the morning and kept me tent-bound for several hours. After I cooked a meager breakfast, all I had left was a few cups of rice, coffee and a bit of lemonade mix: enough for today. I trudged through the tussock-infested valley toward the lake. I crested a hill and saw two cabins on the shore of a massive lake. Lake Schrader was an oasis of pure blue water surrounded by golden tundra sloping up into a wall of mountains. Glaciers gouged the valley tens of thousands of years ago. Sediment pushed by the glaciers formed dams that filled Lakes Schrader and Peters. I'd been traversing the Arctic wilderness for 23 days. I needed a break. Maybe they'd invite me in to stay awhile. That is, if anyone was home. There was no boat docked by the cabins. I cut over to Spawning Creek, where I found animal trails. The creek was large, clear and swift. It deepened into pools that looked good for fishing. I saw three big fish swimming upstream. They looked much larger than grayling.

Soon I arrived at the cabins. Both structures were constructed of plywood with black shingled roofs. They were raised on stilts as all buildings are in the Arctic, to keep the permafrost from melting, and the cabins from sinking. They were situated just 20 feet from the water's edge, on the north shore of the creek as it widened into a bay of the lake. The cabin doors were covered with three-inch nails pointing outward every several inches. They were not to discourage humans, but bears.

I knocked on the door between nails. Nobody answered. The small buildings looked vacated. I knocked again. There was no response. I opened the cabin door. My eyes were used to 24-hour sunlight. I couldn't see anything in the dark inside. "Hello? Hello-o?" Nobody home. After a few moments of squinting, I saw a bunk bed, a stove, shelves...stocked with food! A small note tacked to the wall just inside welcomed all to use the cabin, asking that it be left clean. There was about a week's worth of dry food. There were no packs, clothes or other baggage in either cabin, and the last date on a board of its users was 1986. This was 1991. Suddenly I had what I'd been dreaming of for weeks: rations, sheltered space and fish at my doorstep!

There were no windows except for in the door, making it too dark for my preference. After living outside in 24-hour sunlight, the dimness was dreary. I was hungry from rationing and the long walk. I cooked some spaghetti noodles, and made sauce with tomato paste and half a can of dried parmesan cheese. Lacking the proper spices and ingredients, it was a bland dish, but I was hungry and ate it all— a full quart's worth.

I heated a kettle of water on the stove and washed dishes. I poured another pot of warm water over my head just outside, washing my hair and body with biodegradable soap. I dried with a bandanna. Next I washed my clothes and the bandanna in hot water. The stove helped heat the cabin a little bit. I lay on the mattress in my warm sleeping bag. I dreamed of sailing effortlessly with perfect winds, casting lures to unsuspecting fish. I could use an easier life for awhile.

I extended my telescoping fishing rod, tightening each of the five sections. I threaded the line through the rod guides. I selected my favorite bucktail spinner from the lure box, tying it on with a double-clinch knot. I walked about 30 feet from the cabin door to where Spawning Creek entered the lake. The lake bottom was composed of small rocks and gravel and aquatic vegetation. A 12-foot wide island lay about 50 feet offshore, along a point of shallow rock extending from the land. This appeared to be a perfect fishing area, with a fresh influx of clear, wetland-filtered water and fish headed up stream to feed. I figured I might get a few grayling. On my first cast I was disappointed to find the bay was shallower than I thought. The second cast landed a foot from the opposite shore. I started the spinner turning. A large wake formed 20 feet away...moving straight for my lure! The fish did not hesitate. Wham! "Fish on!" The yank was more than a grayling.

The giant thrashed the surface with its tail, trying to dive away. I played it to shore, easing and giving line during frenzied runs. As the exhausted creature slowed, I exerted the pressure. As I did this, the fish charged again, stripping another 25 feet of line from my reel. This time, though, she'd run out of energy. I slowly gained line, easing her to the shore edge and grabbing her firmly through the gill. She was beautiful and fat: an eight-pound female lake trout. From fishless to fish heaven in two casts.

Lake trout are deep green, with white spots along their side. Their fins are outlined in yellow, the tail with a bit of bright red. Lake trout live only in very deep, super-clean water, requiring temperatures no greater than 50 degrees. They can live to be old and giant. Though they average 6-10 pounds, some that have been caught weighed in at over one hundred pounds. In late summer and winter they dive to great depths. Little is known about their activities in the depths. It is only a brief period in spring and fall that they near the surface. And here I was at one of those rare times 30-feet away from a cabin. I cooked the fish, and feasted.

I tried fishing again. Fog shimmered over the lake. On the third cast I had a seven-pound lake trout on the end of my line. I cleaned the fish. I could easily catch enough fish to live from here. I was building self-reliance and confidence. The fish were my declaration of independence. I considered smoking them to preserve fish for travel. But I could not find enough wood nearby. Willows were noticeably absent near the cabin.

Dark clouds covered the sky. The winds gusted from the east, making rafting unfeasible. With the luxury of a table and chair, I laid out the maps to study my course. I had a considerable amount of travel to do before reaching the Sierra Club group in the headwaters of the Jago River. I had originally wanted to go to Kaktovik first for food. That was out of the question. If I traveled 12 miles per day, I could reach them in the Jago headwaters—without any food. I had arranged for them to have three days of rations for me. I could just spend one or two days with them, and use the rest of the provisions for the journey to Kaktovik. I could also most likely catch fish.

Storm clouds were fierce. Rain made a soothing percusion on the cabin roof. I relaxed and wrote. The rain stopped. I caught another lake trout. I looked up from the catch to a glorious sight. From the dense, gray clouds on the far side of the lake came a brilliant rainbow. It bent toward the middle of the lake. Several miles beyond, dark grayish-purple mountains rose from the far shore of the lake up into clouds, appearing like a wall on the eastern horizon. Both ends of the rainbow were visible, with the tops disappearing into the clouds.

Storm clouds unleashed rain over the far northeast corner of Lake Schrader, where I was headed. It formed a dark wall, obscuring the view beyond. The rainbow curved from just offshore the northern lakeside up over the northern mountains and into the dense, gray clouds. The lake was turquoise in the shallows nearby. It changed shades to the dark-blue of the glacier-gouged depths.

I gazed at the large fish lying in front of me on the tundra. Lake trout were once far more numerous, populating near all deep, large northern lakes. But they have been driven out of most lakes by pollution and over-fishing. Lake trout are slow growing. Like grayling and char, lake trout are highly sensitive to acid rain, industrial pollution, pesticide and fertilizer run-off, sewage and soil erosion.

The Arctic Refuge provides a rare oasis; an oasis that would be lost if oil development occurs.

Chapter 16

Petrol Haze

The storm brought colder temperatures. I wanted heat and light. I'd used up all the candles. There was lots of white gas (stove fuel) in the cabin. But that was too dangerous. I tried making an oil lamp with vegetable oil and rope. It lit well and bright. But the rope was synthetic, and the fumes toxic. I blew it out and ran outside, opening the door. Then I became really cold.

There is a certain independent insanity that can occur when one is by oneself for an extended period of time with no one to provide a mirror to the logic of one's actions. Also, being 20-years old made for a nonchalant fearlessness that needed wise temperament usually only gained from experience. I was soon to meet with more opportunity to develop wisdom.

I knew the white gas wouldn't smoke that much. So I poured some of the super-flammable petroleum into a tin can and placed it on an empty Tang can. I knew this was extremely dangerous, because if it were knocked over, the lit gas would spill over the wood cabin, creating an unstoppable blaze. But I would be careful, I thought. The blaze soon reached three feet high. Woe! What have I started? I watched it nervously. I'd hoped to write by its light, but I was too anxious. The smoke was intense, and soon became bothersome. After about half an hour, the gas burned down. I let it rest a while. That was dangerous. But soon the cold crept in along with the darkness.

I filled the can higher with gas then placed several layers of aluminum foil over it. I made a small hole in the foil, hoping that would regulate the flame. I put the can in an empty gallon gas can with the sides opened as a reflector. This, I thought, would burn slower, safer and with less smoke. This way, the flame would be surrounded on five sides by metal, with only the front opened. I imagined a little flame burning all night, reflecting across the cabin so I could read and write in peace and comfort. I placed the "light" on a shelf attached to the east wall, spilling a little gas on the shelf. I was concerned about the flame being near the wooden wall, which is why I had previously placed it in the center of the cabin. But the can of gas was in a metal structure that should have contained it. I found a large roll of heavy-duty aluminum foil in the other cabin. I tried to unroll some to tape to the wood walls, to protect against an accident. But the foil was stuck together. I could only unroll a few small pieces, which covered only a little wood. The task was too tedious, and I soon gave up on this safety precaution.

The flame started small, barely brighter than a candlelight. "A little more," I said to myself. I widened the hole until the flame was about eight inches high, then went back to my writing. After only a few minutes, I noticed the flames were getting higher. Flaming gas boiled over the small can and lit a line of fire over the wooden shelf where I had spilled gas. I grabbed some foil and tried smothering it. The foil was flimsy and weak. I found a rag and smothered the flame.

I wanted it all to end as a stupid idea. But the can was still burning with ever increasing intensity. It boiled over some more and lit the bottom of the gallon canister. The flames were so high that they engulfed the entire gallon container and reached several feet up, above the few pieces of protective foil I'd taped to the wall. The wooden wall would surely catch fire unless I could control the blaze. But how do you stop burning gas? Water doesn't work. It spreads the flames. I could not take the can outside, first because there was no way to grab the inferno, and second because it would cause more burning gas to spill. The only answer was to try and smother it.

I scouted for other tools. There were barrels outside, but they were too cumbersome. The only tool I had to smother it was aluminum foil. I laboriously separated small pieces of foil and draped them over the container, trying to keep from burning myself. By then the entire can was completely engulfed in flames that reached just two feet shy of the ceiling. Black petrol-toxic smoke filled the cabin. My eyes winced and I took short breaths with my nose held low to the floor and filtered through a bandanna. I still gagged. I could have easily escaped outside. But I would not let the cabin burn down.

Because smoke rises, I crouched low to the floor as my father had always instructed. I meticulously separated pieces of foil, wrapping them piece by piece around the container in an all-out effort to gain control of the flame. While trying to make the foil stay on the container to block the flames, I touched the red-hot can often, which made my skin sizzle. My hands were beginning to show the wounds of battle. In the room now dim with smoke, I found my gloves, enabling me to better place the foil pieces.

I finally covered the entire opening of the can with foil. But the flames continued. The fire disintegrated some of the foil. My eyes burned in the smoke. The door looked awfully tempting. But giving up was not an option. Somebody spent a lot of time and money to construct the cabin that I was enjoying and the thought that I had destroyed it would haunt me forever. I worked to remove more foil from the roll. I used my knife to cut through the foil, and tear off thick sections of many layers. I beat back the flames with multiple layers of aluminum. Piece by piece I added, until there was just one hole left, three inches round with an inferno of flame shooting through. I placed a last small piece over the hole, and the flames died.

I waited outside. I watched the can through the propped-open door. The fire was extinguished. Fresh air never felt so good. The cabin was a dense haze. Smoke bellowed outside. I took long, deep breaths of pure Arctic air. I waited 15 minutes before I carried the foil-wrapped can outside. Smoke still exited the doorway. It would be awhile before I could return.

Fresh air is so easy to take for granted. After time spent in an urban smog zone, down-wind of a polluting industry or inside a smoky building, clean air is realized as a basic necessity for health and a basic right. We all breathe in Earth's common air sink several times a minute, whether caribou, wolf, human, eagle or mosquito.

When it is poisoned, all life suffers.

I have long railed against a consumptive, petroleum-based life style for the damage it causes to human life and the environment. Against this backdrop, it was no small irony, then, to narrowly escape being engulfed by a mixture of these very chemicals and my own stupidity.

Chapter 17

Stowaway

The next morning was gloomy. My head ached and smoke still lingered in the cabin. I took my raft ground pad and sleeping bag outside for some fresh air and slept. Within a couple hours I felt refreshed. Rafting depended on the wind. I inflated my raft, packed my gear and cooked a pancake breakfast. Packing readied me mentally as well as physically for the travel. Just before I was to leave, a late morning rain sent me scrambling to haul my gear back in the cabin. I lay back on the bunk bed.

Growing up, I had canoed on Lake Erie off Kelly's Island, where friends of my parents shared a home. I would stand up in the canoe, balancing with the waves while fishing. I caught rock bass, small-mouth bass and catfish, sharing the meat with my family and friends. Now I wish I'd released them. The EPA asked fishermen not to eat Lake Erie catfish and to limit consumption of all Great Lake fish because of toxins. After learning that, my urge to canoe on Lake Erie ceased, except in a demonstration for clean water. Poisonous water doesn't have a strong appeal.

Strong winds blew northeast, toward the wind-tunnel middle of Lake Schrader. Rafting in the Arctic would not be toxic, but immediate dangers were more intense. Unlike boating expeditions before, here I had no life preserver or wet suit. The water was colder; my boat weaker. The danger was clear: at temperatures of 40 degrees, I would have but a few minutes before hypothermia-induced fatigue and muscle spasms caused drowning.

When the rain stopped, I returned to finishing blowing up my raft. But I had been hit by what I believe to be a unique danger in the annals of rafting. The center section was deflated. Three holes were chewed through the vinyl. A squirrel stood up next to the cabin, looking innocent. He was fat, a cabin scrounger. This most certainly was not in my plans. The patching took about an hour. I finished packing while it dried and cleaned the cabin.

As I started out in my raft, winds bellowed from the south. Rafting to the research station would be tough, if not impossible. The cabin was on the far-west side of Lake Schrader. Lake Peters connects from the southwest of Schrader, then extends in an oval shape for several miles south. The research station was on the southeast side of Peters, many miles from my next destination where the two lakes met.

I paddled furiously against the wind, but fought a losing battle. The raft was not sleek like a canoe, and the choppy seas made paddling tough. It blew in the wrong direction, and out toward the open waters! I turned toward shore. Thankfully the wind was not blowing due east, or I'd be blown out to sea. It blew northeast. I was able to paddle diagonally against the wind. Though I gained slowly toward shore, I drifted fast to the north, away from the cabin and in the wrong direction. I'd have to backtrack. I jumped out into the large rock-strewn shallows and waded to shore. Waves splashed my body. I tied a cord from the front of the raft to the end of my paddle, and pulled the boat along the shore—a tedious mode of travel called lining. My feet and ankles soon became numb from splashing through ankle-deep water. I was worried about the strength of my craft, if a squirrel could munch right through it.

I returned to the cabin, the loser in a battle against the wind. I lay back on the bunk bed praying that the squirrels weren't munching on my boat. I felt defeated. First the fire, then the squirrel, now the wind. A short nap later I felt a little better. I was behind schedule. The wind was blowing as fierce as before. I'd have to leave regardless. I'd try lining, and I could always pack it if I had to. I rafted across the narrow mouth of Spawning Creek, then lined along the shore toward the lake's junction with Lake Peters. The going was rough at first. The wind had shifted to the northwest, pushing the raft against the west shore. I waded in frigid waters to push the raft away from the sharp rocks.

I rounded the lake's southwest corner. Now on the south shore, the wind blew the raft away from shore. Here I could line easily, pulling the raft along while walking on shore, without having to wade. Half a mile before reaching the channel connecting Lake Schrader to Lake Peters, I grounded the raft. I realized I would have to hike to the research station, because rafting would be impossible against the wind. On my map, I could not tell if the lake junction was shallow enough to wade. If I could hike, I would save lining time and hassle by leaving the raft there and hoping winds would change. I also needed a rest, and some fish. Many casts later, a 15-inch grayling darted from the depths to inhale my spinner.

Arriving at the channel connecting the two lakes, I was stopped by an expanse of water about 100 yards wide. While I fished the channel, two backpackers walked along the opposite shore. One wore a pink hiking suit, the other a green jacket, blue all-weather pants and a brown hat. They looked older with white hair. They were the first people I'd seen since seeing rafts far away across the Canning River more than a week earlier. We returned waves and long looks. I tried calling across, but the wind muffled my voice. I wanted to talk to them but they would be far away by the time I lined my raft over and paddled across the channel. I caught another grayling on the way back to the raft. I lined to the junction and paddled across the channel.

After a lunch of fish and noodles from the cabin, I unloaded all but my canteen, some food and a first-aid kit from my pack for the day's journey. It was nearly five miles along the lake to the research station. The shoreline rose steeply toward the mountains far above. A pontoon plane buzzed to a start across the lake, rising to the sky. I hoped that wasn't the researchers. I wanted to interview them and to ask if I could purchase food. It was late on a Friday afternoon.

The research station was a cluster of five structures on a flat lip of Mount Chamberlin's base at the shore of Lake Peters. The buildings ranged from a rickety storage structure to two modern-looking cabins. Mount Chamberlin towered above with a pure-white glacier nestled in its peak, the source of much of the station's research. I knocked, but the buildings were empty. In a trash heap, I found a little aluminum cylinder that might help repair my pack.

The sun was low on the northern horizon by the time I returned to the raft. It was nearing midnight and I was tired and cold. But the air was calm, and, unsure which direction the winds would be blowing in the morning, I could not afford to miss this rare opportunity to raft without wind. I pushed the raft into the deep lake. I paddled east, near the shoreline.

Wind picked up from the north, pushing me toward the south shore. Boulders threatened to gnash my raft. Waves rolled under me. My arms were getting tired. There was no way I could cross the lake against these winds. But I could travel along its southern shore. That was principally the direction I had to travel. The wind increased. A wave splashed over the raft, soaking my lower torso. I shivered from the cold. No more rafting tonight. It was after midnight and I had reached a milestone of a different sort, my 21st birthday.

I pulled along shore and unstrapped my gear. The sun illuminated the clouds in a pink-orange haze. The distant mountains were silhouetted against the brilliantly colored sky. I gazed at the wilderness spectacle. Puffy thick clouds glowing in the midnight sun drifted across the sky. Hues of pink, light blue, yellow and purple painted the world in pastels, reflecting across the choppy sea. Before me was an expanse of some of the cleanest water left in the world.

I'd longed for a refuge like this, a vast wonderland open to my exploration. I'd longed to be a stowaway into uncharted lands, to explore and see the world's wonders. Here I was living it all. All was calm, peaceful. I sat back against a large rock, watching the lake scene. I wished for good winds tomorrow, thinking like a sailor. How long I'd dreamed of sailing through distant lands.

It was July 20, my birthday. I could not have asked for a better birthday, or a better place to spend it. The constant wilderness panorama enlivened my innate respect and love for the Earth. I was saturated in Arctic beauty, leaving me warm and reverent. But fierce rapids lay ahead and a trial of my very will to survive.

Chapter 18

Birthday Voyage

Nightmares of bears haunted me through the early morning hours. I awakened with a vision of a bear ripping through my tent. Startled and fully awake, I smelled peanuts. I had drifted to sleep without even closing the peanut can! That was asking for trouble. I closed the can, but knew I should move it to my food bag. I drifted in and out of sleep for another hour, haunted by more fears, until I finally built enough confidence to brave the cold outside my sleeping bag.

Wearing only long underwear, I moved the can of peanuts to my duffel bag outside the tent. Though it was below freezing, there was no wind. I was warm from resting on the raft cushion. Stillness engulfed the land. Fog rose from the lake in the freezing early morning air. It was 4 a.m., the time Mohandas Gandhi awakened in his Ashram. Today I would not be getting up early, however. I'd fallen asleep only two hours earlier. Now, my dreams were of the sea. The sound of waves lapping against the shore triggered fond memories. I dreamed I was on a boat, sailing the wide seas and encountering great creatures of the depths. Excitement came with every encounter.

Peering out the tent door, I squinted my eyes in the brilliance. The scene was bright in the late morning sun and the lake sparkled under the powerful beams. My first thought was the wind. It would determine if today would be a relaxing sail, a grueling ordeal or a hike. I would be traveling northeast. Mother Earth blessed me with winds from the southwest, almost exactly the direction I needed to go. What a perfect birthday present!

I waded out with the loaded boat and hopped aboard. The momentum of jumping in gave the craft a surge forward. The wind gently pushed me away from shore into the deep blue. My destination was five miles of open water away at the northeastern corner of the lake, which forms the mouth of the Kekiktuk River. The tundra hills and high mountains were sharp and crisp against the blue sky. Puffy white clouds floated by overhead. I cast a giant fishing spoon and released about 100 yards of line. I set the rod down, letting the wind do the work. Trolling through the lake's middle was unlikely to connect with any fish, but then there wasn't much effort either. There is always a possibility when one has a lure in the water.

I could just enjoy being, and let the wind do the work, a rare, welcome rest. Gulls followed my boat. Mount Chamberlin's peak towered above where I had camped. At 9,020 feet, Chamberlin's peak was second highest in the 600-mile Brooks Range. It is one of 144 known glaciers in the Arctic Refuge: remnants of the last ice age that carved and sculpted the land into its present splendor. The mountaintop was shaped like a U, two peaks with the glacier encrusted in between.

Like all Arctic glaciers, Chamberlin's peak is melting fast under the harsh effects of global warming. In Alaska alone, the area covered by glaciers has retreated by 15 percent over the past century. Alaskan glaciers have been reduced in thickness by 10 meters over the last 40 years. During this same period, the glaciers in Antarctica have receded 50 miles. From 1890 to 1990, glacier retreat caused Earth's sea levels to rise 3.5 cm (about $1^{1/2}$ inches). Combined with the expansion of water due to global warming, the world's oceans have risen an average of 18 cm (about 7 inches) over the last century. This is in contrast to the melting of icebergs, and masses of ice over water which make no such contribution. Like melting ice in a glass, the water level does not rise. But glaciers, running off land do cause rising sea levels.

I had been sheltered by the south ridge at my camp and during the beginning of the voyage. I floated into a tunnel of strong winds. The waves doubled in size and the wind ruffled my hair. The raft rolled over the waves, creaking ominously. A wave spilled over the raft's side, chilling my buttocks and legs. I bailed out water with my cup, but my lower half was still sitting in an inch of frigid water. Fierce winds magnified the cold. My fishing rod bowed with the increased speed and resistance. Using a dangling cord, I tied it securely to the raft. Another wave spilled over the side. I had to take action. I had been lying back lazily. I pulled myself into a kneeling position, wedging my feet in the raft's corners. With the kayak paddle, I positioned the raft to face the waves. The front of the raft lifted up and over the waves, instead of crashing into them. With this position, water no longer spilled over the side, yet I traveled quickly. This was travel with clean, renewable wind energy.

I began to reel in the line to check it. My rod jerked forward. I played the fish to the raft and grabbed it firmly by the gills. It was a two-pound fish with a silvery speckle and a rainbow tint. It was beautiful! I had never seen the fish before. I thought it was a speckled trout. The lure hook was gigantic compared to its small mouth. I could put on a smaller lure. Neh. I wanted a big one.

I cast the giant spoon far away and let out a hundred yards of line. Some time later, I noticed the lure was not running right. I reeled it in. As it neared the raft the rod bowed into an ark and the line tugged, hard. I tugged back. The drag whirled. Then the line pulled free. I jigged the lure up and down, trying to evoke another bite. As the spoon neared the surface, a dark shadow as long as the width of my raft gave chase. The lake trout turned sharply. We stared each other in the eyes. The giant looked to be about 70 pounds and more than four feet long. Swoosh, it was gone, free. The treble hook of the lure had been caught around the line, likely the reason I did not hook the trout. Still, I felt blessed by just meeting the giant fish.

As the raft neared the north shore, I began paddling to try and keep it from the rocks. It was getting close. The fishing rod bowed suddenly, snagged in the rocks. I let the line loose, turned the raft around and paddled against the strong wind, trying to raft upwind of the snag and free the lure. For several minutes I paddled furiously but the raft just stood still. I dreaded continuing the exhausting task, but did not want to lose the lure. My arms were spent. I balanced over waves and studied their patterns for the best time to paddle. My posture molded into learned perfection, back straight, muscles straining on the paddle. Foot by foot I gained line. I freed the lure, and cast again. I wanted to hook another lunker fish like the lake trout I had just seen. Moments later...another snag. I repeated the chore, taking some 15 minutes to gain 100 yards against blustering winds. Again I saved the lure.

I cast the spoon yet again, still enchanted by the encounter with the giant lake trout. I snagged vegetation. I paddled hard in an attempt to stay in deep water to reduce snags. The lure stopped again: another snag. The wind whistled across the lake. I thrust the paddle into the water and heaved around, trying to beat the wind. It all happened so quickly. One moment my paddle was intact. Then ...snap! I forced the paddle beyond its capacity, and it broke in two. Being plastic, and of poor design, the end of the kayak paddle sank before I could grab it. "My paddle!" I mourned, watching part of the only one I had descend while helpless to do anything about it. It was my means of propulsion. I was confident that even without the raft as a mode of transport I would survive. But I needed that paddle to complete my quest. Now half of it was eight-feet deep in 40-degree water.

What to do? I used the snag as an anchor, though gingerly with line that broke with 6 pounds of exertion. I pulled the raft ahead of the paddle, then plunged the fishing rod into the depths, trying to pull it up. The rod was too short. The winds increased, threatening to break the line. I marked the spot by studying shoreline features and rocks, then let out line, allowing the wind to blow me to shore. I was flustered.

Safe on dry land, I pondered: the end of the paddle seemed hopelessly lost with 1 to 3 foot waves splashing against the shore. But I had no choice. The paddle piece had fallen 30 feet or so from shore. I made an anchor to use back out by the sunken paddle by tying the raft's cord to an odd-shaped rock which I hoisted into the raft. This way I could try and position myself above the paddle. But how to get the paddle out? I looked at the fishing rod with the lure still snagged in the rocks. I tried to unsnag it from shore, but the line broke. I tied a treble hook a foot up the line, and a one-ounce weight at the line's end, hoping I could wrap the line around the paddle and pull it up.

The winds blew diagonally against the shoreline. I had been blown far east of the paddle. I pushed the raft west along the choppy shoreline, upwind of the paddle. I launched the boat and used the good end of the broken kayak paddle to propel me toward what seemed about an anchor-rope distance upwind of the lost paddle piece. The anchor plummeted to the rocky bottom, the cord streaming from the coil. The boat stopped too far downwind. I tried to fish out the paddle anyway, but could barely even see it in the choppy waters. Pushed far to the east, I landed to shore to try again from upwind of the lost paddle piece.

This time I threw the anchor far upwind, thinking I could move it slowly until the position was perfect. Although the thinking was sound, the anchor became snagged fast in the rocks. The winds made paddling upstream to retrieve it impossible. Anchors in choppy seas can be very dangerous, especially with short anchor lines because they pull the boat down, allowing waves to swamp the boat. Mine was 20 feet long in some 10 feet of water. The anchor pulled down the raft's front. Waves crashed overboard. I paddled hard against the wind to ease the tension. The boat began to roll with the waves enough to keep them from washing overboard. But I could not gain any line. The raft had three inches of water in it from the waves. I was soaked and cold. Finally, the wind slowed. I gained line and pulled the anchor free. I dropped it over again, but wind gusts blew me too far. Once more I landed, had to line the boat upwind, and launched another attempt.

This is my final attempt, I decided. I had memorized the point at which to throw the anchor with several boulder features on shore. I paddled out and dropped the anchor at the designated spot. As the line straightened, there was the paddle fast approaching underneath. The line became taut. The boat jolted to a halt directly above my lost treasure. With my fishing rod, I swung the weight back and forth underwater. The line wrapped around the oar shaft. I pulled the prize up. The line slipped off just as the paddle neared the surface. I plunged my arms into the water, leaning far over the raft's side. Teetering on the brink of disaster, I stretched my arm deep and grabbed the tip of the falling paddle, pulling it back to safety.

Chapter 19

Arctic Companions

I spotted the two campers I had seen the day before setting up a tent about half a mile away at the northeast corner of the lake, where I was headed. The thought of company was enticing. I had not spoken with anyone in 26 days since I last spoke to oil security, and 29 days since I began the expedition. I was wet, cold and exhausted. Paddling was tough with the broken paddle. I was barely able to keep from slamming against the north shore. I tried using the "J" stroke, with an added curve at the end of the stroke to keep the boat straight. But I soon tired. In my exhaustion, I just switched sides every other stroke.

The couple watched my hilarious paddling. From my vantage point, the north shore seemed to go all the way to a corner. I figured the creek mouth would be a little trickle. To my surprise I came upon a wide river mouth. The current pulled me down river. I paddled across the river and landed on the shore. Fifty-three year old Paul Poirier stood at the shore as I neared the bank. He was dressed in blue all-weather pants, a green down jacket and a brown and white wool hat. I stepped over the side of the raft into the foot-deep water and pulled the boat on shore.

"That is an awful awkward way to paddle," he said. "I'm a canoe instructor, let me show you some tips."

While still dripping wet, I handed him my paddle. He showed me the "J" stroke, in which one paddles forward then at the end of the stroke curves outward to correct for the turn.

"Let me see you do it," he said.

Saying nothing, I imitated the stroke that I had used for years.

"Good. I was afraid you were going to go down the river like that," he said.

"I almost did, but not on purpose."

"Come sit down and have some hot cocoa," he said.

We sprawled out on the hilly tundra, next to their tent. Paul lifted a pot of water from his stove and poured it in everyone's cup along with a packet of cocoa.

"I'm an electrician from Wenatchee, Washington," Paul said. "This is my companion, Marie."

"I'm Chad from Athens, Ohio," I said.

"We flew into Lake Peters for a two-week backpacking trip," Paul said. "We're going to Old Woman Creek where it hits the Hulahula River to fly out."

"I'm on my way to the headwaters of the Jago River to meet a Sierra Club group. I'm going to raft down river some then hike over to the Hulahula."

"Do you know why they named it that?" Paul asked.

"No."

"A group of Hawaiian whalers were stranded over winter there. They named it for all its meandering."

"I wonder what the Native American name for it is," I asked. None of us knew.

"Was that you two I waved to at the lake junction yesterday?"

"Yes," Paul said.

"I had just caught two grayling," I said.

"I found they are not very tasty," Paul said.

"Oh, I love them," I said.

"Now Arctic char I find delicious fish," Paul said.

"Where did you start?" Marie asked.

"I hiked here from Prudhoe Bay a month ago."

"Wow, that's a long way," Paul responded.

I described my journey. "What brought you here?" I asked Paul.

"My whole life I've been camping, ever since I was a kid. I like isolation and it's getting harder to find. This will be the center of activity if the oil industry has its way. It will not be the same. There has to be wild places left that aren't altered by man's hand. This is one of the most pristine places left. This is like having Glacier National Park to yourself," Paul said. "I worked on the pipeline in

'74. I've always wanted to come here. I think this is a really important place."

"Indians go into sacred areas by themselves to revitalize," Marie said. "That's what I think, it revitalizes your life. It really gives me a boost in life when I go into wilderness. You never forget. I love the outdoors and the animals."

"What's a shame about this whole thing is the oil under here is only a 288-day supply for the U.S.," Paul said. "That's peanuts to destroy a place like this. Increasing fuel mileage a mile per gallon would save as much oil as there is here. Right now oil development is probably going to happen. I belong to some outdoor groups. I'm putting together a slide presentation. I wanted to see the refuge while it's still in its natural state. There's not much wilderness left; it's sad. Opening ANWR would prolong the usage of the pipeline for a decade or more. The pipe is worn out and crude oil is heavy stuff and an environmental disaster is probable along the pipeline. Despite what they tell you their record is not that good. I've been coming north for 12 years. The drilling area around Prudhoe Bay has spread like a cancer. They get their foot in the door and spread like a cancer."

I began to shake from the cold. I tried to hide it, because I did not want to interrupt such an interesting conversation. I eyed Paul's wet suit booties.

"I bet these look pretty good right now with those soaking feet," Paul said.

I smiled. "Yep. Maybe I should put on some dry socks." I jumped up and rummaged through my pack.

"What are your plans?" Marie asked.

"I'm behind schedule and plan to raft on tonight." An icy chill was blowing in along with gray clouds. I was soaking wet.

"You shouldn't travel like that" Paul said, motioning to my wet clothes. "It's getting late, you can set up your tent next to ours if you'd like.

"Yeah, maybe that would be wise. I'll stay. I have a fish to clean as well. I think it's a speckled trout, but I've never caught one before."

I retrieved it from the stringer.

"That's an Arctic char," Paul said. "A female. The males are a bright red color—much different looking."

"Oh, that's what it is."

"They spawn in the lake," he continued. "The young fish grow for four or five years after hatching until large enough to face the ocean. They then swim down the river to the Arctic Ocean where they grow to about 10 pounds. The senior fish return up the river to the lake to spawn." The lake was the nursery for the char, providing life throughout the Arctic ecosystem. Char are a vital food source for grizzlies, fox, polar bear, walrus, seal, eagles, wolves, and Inupiat peoples.

"That's the best tasting fish I've ever had," Marie said. Paul agreed. "It's redder and juicier than salmon. We cooked ours without oil."

I fried it over my stove. The meat was a juicy red. It cooked to a succulent translucent flakiness.

"This is the best tasting fish I have ever had," I said. "A nice Birthday present."

"It's your Birthday." Marie said. "How old are you?"

"Twenty one."

"You're 21?" Marie asked. "I'd thought you were much older."

"So did I," Paul said.

Paul went to his pack and pulled out a spicy rice freeze-dried dinner package.

"Here, consider this our birthday gift. After being in the wilderness so long, you could probably use some spice," he said.

"Thank you," I said. I cooked the rice right there, savoring its delicacy. Shortly thereafter an icy chill set in. Yawns indicated the end of a long day.

"I plan to leave early," I said.

"Well, we don't get up that early," Paul said, prompting a lengthy farewell. We exchanged addresses. It seemed so sad to be leaving them so soon. But I had much traveling to do if I was to make the Sierra Club meeting in five days.

On the map, my goal began to look more and more impossible. My food supply, refreshed at the cabin four days ago, was becoming low again. As I lay in the tent, the pattering of rain began. Wind whistled through camp. I sat up in my tent eating roasted peanuts. I felt cozy and warm with two more friends. Rain continued through the night, and into the morning. It was late afternoon by the time I exited my tent. More gray clouds threatened more delay. I was stiff from being cooped in the small tent. I wanted to be traveling. But the weather was not conducive to rafting.

I cast my lure across the mouth of the Kekiktuk river that formed at the lake's corner. Ten minutes later, I hooked a big one. I fought the large lake trout to the shallows, easing against its powerful tugs. Just two feet from shore it shook off the hook. The lure flung toward me. I dodged it and jumped into the water. I pounced on the dazed fish in one-foot-deep water, grabbing the slippery creature before it got away. I lifted up a 10 pound, 27-inch male lake trout, with white markings over a greenish body. Beautiful! I put him on a stringer.

Winds whistled through the wide valley, whipping up waves and chilling my body. What had been a small, docile river a few days earlier was now full and roaring. I scouted it. The thought of white water rafting was alluring. Rafting would speed my travel along the first leg of the journey across the north face of the Brooks Range to the Jago River. I thought I might still be able to make the Sierra Club meeting, if I hurried.

Paul exited his tent. We marveled over the lake trout. Marie peeked from the tent. Paul took several pictures of me and the big trout with my camera and his. He had brought a tripod, a large high-tech camera and several lenses.

"That must weigh a lot," I said.

"Yeah, but it's worth it for the pictures," he said. Looking at the river before us, he said "I think it's up two feet."

"It should make rafting easier," I responded, looking down

river.

"And more dangerous," Paul added.

"And more exciting," I said.

"Look up there!" Twelve caribou stood on a ridge to the northeast. They paused and stared at us. I was cooking the lake trout over my stove. My binoculars were foggy. I watched the creatures through Paul's binoculars. "They are the essence of wildness," I said.

I fried the ten pound trout good and crisp, and offered some to Paul.

"I've eaten fish the past three days. I don't think so," he said.

"It's really good."

"Well OK, maybe a bite. Um this is good. I like it crisp." He took a second bite. Shortly thereafter rain broke up the gathering. I went back to my tent and drifted to sleep on my inflated raft.

I awakened to an uncomfortable bumpy bed. The center section of the raft had leaked air out, turning the section from a cushion into flat vinyl. The leak came through one of the holes eaten by the squirrel at the cabin. During a break in the rain, I set about fixing the raft and paddle. I laid the raft out to dry then patched the leaking hole. For the paddle, I used the aluminum tube found in the research station dump as a dowel to hold the two hollow oar pieces together. It fit inside, but was too loose. I increased the width with used matchsticks wrapped with duct tape, until it fit snugly into place. I now had a working raft and paddle.

But rafting depended on good weather. Rain droned on through the night and all the next day, reminding me that precipitation in Alaska had increased by 30 percent from 1968 to 1990, attributed to global warming.

"I think the sky may actually be clearing," Paul said as he lit his stove to heat water for coffee. After being rained in for three days, we were ready to brave anything to leave.

"I'm ready to go."

"Just be careful," he responded. "That's an awful flimsy paddle. One boulder could flip you into that frigid water."

As he had throughout our stay, he warned me to watch out for the river's "pillows."

"They look like innocent ripples in the water, but they are submerged boulders that could easily flip your raft. When the ripples form a 'V' pointing upstream, make sure you get out of the way. If your raft gets hung up, the current will force the back of the raft down, and flip it."

"These waters are cold too," I said. "I do worry about a spill."

As a life-threatening risk, hypothermia was the worst danger of my trip, surpassing starvation, breaking a bone, or the more exotic fears of grizzly and polar bear attacks. I had originally planned to bring a wet suit, but the cost and weight were prohibitive. I had also considered an inflatable life vest, but again due to the weight and cost, chose against the safety precaution.

Rain forced us back into our tents in the late morning. At noon the sun came out. We dried our stuff and packed.

"Look over there!" Marie said. Twelve caribou hesitated at the banks of the flooded river. I watched their hesitation. If the caribou paused, maybe I should too.

They plunged into the swift river downstream of us. Caribou are fantastic swimmers, with wide hooves enabling them to paddle up to six miles per hour. The current swept them down river rapidly. I had not realized how swift the current was. They climbed out, shaking water from their coats.

"That river sure is swift," Paul said. "Be careful."

"I will. Don't worry."

"They have to cross rivers far bigger than that one," Paul said. "Like the Porcupine River that gives them their name."

"Caribou have hollow hair that insulate and give floatation when swimming," I said.

Waving goodbye, Paul and Marie hiked up the steep hillside toward where their bush pilot would pick them up a few days later. With the three-day delay, they were worried about being late. So was I. I felt we were already good friends as we neared the end of our stay together. Nature is the ultimate conversation piece. It is something we all can enjoy, creating common ground for new relationships.

Chapter 20

Disaster

Standing a foot deep in icy water, I leaped into the raft to give it a jump-start. I kneeled and began paddling. The current moved me swiftly through the calm water. My make-shift paddle worked perfectly. I maneuvered around boulders, happy to be moving after being tent-bound. Despite the heavy rains, the water was crystal clear.

When I rounded a bend, however, the current changed. Whitewater extended as far as the eye could see. Directly ahead was a wall of five-foot high waves. Finding an eddy, where the current circled back around a boulder, I glided to shore. I scouted ahead. The waves of the rapids were gigantic. If I could paddle across the river before I hit the line of boulders and wall of waves sixty feet downstream, I could slip through. It would be close, and dangerous. I packed my fishing reel in the duffel bag. Because my gear was so tightly packed and tied to the raft, I left the bag containing my fishing rod, cup and mosquito netting loose in the raft.

I pushed off shore and paddled hard toward the other side. The current pulled me toward the rocks and waves much faster than I anticipated. The waves loomed in front of me. As I approached, I saw a deep hydraulic downstream of the boulders. Hydraulics are formed when current flows over a boulder or waterfall, forcing the water down. This creates a pit just downstream of the obstruction. High walls of waves form below the cavity, creating a trap. Rafts caught in hydraulics are easily flipped. The deadly circulating current sucks those thrown overboard underwater, where they are easily trapped and drowned.

I paddled with full force across the river. I turned to face forward. I made it past the boulders but hit part of the hydraulic wall.

Frigid water crashed over the raft, smacking my body and face. This was the ultimate in excitement and adventure. I raised my paddle in both hands and hollered in joy. I then bailed out water while the raft raced through more waves and white water.

A few minutes later I rounded another bend. My exhilaration turned to panic. A line of boulders formed an even larger waterfall and hydraulic than before. I searched frantically for a way out, but seconds later I heard a loud scraping sound. My raft stopped suddenly on underlying boulders, throwing me forward. The current pushed the boat slowly over the rocks, right toward the middle of the hydraulic! The raft slipped from the hold of the boulders and plunged down the four-foot waterfall, crashing head-first into the massive waves.

I paddled hard to try and pull the boat over the wave. The water wall pushed the front of the raft up, threatening to flip it back on top of me. I jumped forward to counterbalance it, paddling all the while. The boat pivoted nearly vertical before rounding the crest of the wave. I crashed down on a second line of waves and was thrown forward atop my stuff and nearly overboard. I clung on, but the boat was completely swamped. I was barreling down a flooded Arctic river. With the added weight of the water, the raft barely responded to my paddling.

Scooping water out with my cup was useless. Waves poured in faster than I could bail. I searched for an eddy or pool to pull me to shore. I wanted to leave the rampaging river. But all I saw was white water. Wave after wave smacked me in the face. The raft bounced off rocks. A seven-foot wave roared over the raft. It was all I could do to stay onboard; the wave yanked the paddle from my grip.

I saw the waves forming a "V" just down river. Paul had warned me to watch for the subtle signs of submerged boulders. Now I watched it approach directly ahead, but without a paddle, I was helpless. The raft caught on to the boulder. The force of the current pulled the back of the boat down exactly as Paul had forewarned. I jumped forward to counterbalance. The boulder raised the raft's front high out of water. I landed painfully on solid rock. The back of the raft lowered until water rushed overboard.

The back was thrust down by the current, flipping the boat over on top of me. I was underwater. The water force swept me toward a line of submerged boulders that formed another hydraulic. I washed over the boulders and down a five-foot waterfall, plunging deep into the frigid water. I struggled frantically. The cold and fury made it all chaotic. What to do? Which way was up? I thrust forward— whichever way I was facing but it was all a tumultuous blur. Somehow, I came to the surface out of the hydraulic but I was still in danger.

Racing down a flood-stage, 40-degree river, my situation seemed hopeless. Sudden immersion into cold water causes hyperventilation and gasping that reduces breath holding to 15 seconds. Limb strength and coordination deteriorate rapidly. Hypothermia sets in nearly immediately, causing irrational behavior; mental activity becomes disorganized. Chances for surviving more than a few minutes are low.

I flushed through wave after wave and rapid after rapid. I saw my raft upside down in front of me. Then the undertow of a hydraulic pulled me under again. I swam up and found I was next to the raft and that it had flipped upright. The vinyl made gripping the side difficult. Grabbing it, my hands slipped off. A safety rope had come with the raft, but in yet another choice I would barely live to regret, I'd left it at home to reduce weight. I heaved myself up the slippery raft side and made it aboard. Both my pack and duffel bag were halfway out of the boat.

I saw the bag containing my gloves, cup, fishing rod and mosquito netting floating about 20 feet ahead. If only I'd put it in my pack or duffel bag. Just then, my paddle rushed by on my left. I reached for it. But it was just beyond my grasp. While still reaching, the raft hit another wall of waves. Caught by surprise, I scrambled to hold on. I stayed, but the duffel bag containing my sleeping bag and food broke free and now bobbed loose in the water. I needed it to survive the journey to the Inupiat village.

The raft rushed down through rapid after rapid. Despite my

repeated repairs, the bottom compartment was flat. It sunk deep with my weight. Blustering winds stripped heat from my wet skin and clothing. The half of my body above water was colder than my lower half submerged in it. I was numb and hypothermia was setting in. I had to get to shore. But there was no break in the river's fury. "Okay" I repeated to myself, "think rationally. I must survive."

The raft hit another pillow and flipped me out again. I tried to dig my feet into the river bottom to stop the boat so I could pull it to shore. But the force of the current pushed me down river. I hit several rocks, fortunately feet first. In a shallow area I flipped the raft back over and pulled myself aboard. Now, my pack joined the duffel bag in the water. Waves gushed over me.

Rounding another bend, even larger rapids lay ahead. I could do nothing to avoid them. The raft spun around and around, hitting a huge wall of waves with the raft turned backwards. The waves stormed overboard, throwing me to the front (now rear) of the raft. I breathed in the frigid water, choking. "Okay," I reassured myself. "I'm still okay." I might be able to make it to shore by jumping out and swimming, I thought, but I would lose my equipment. I needed the food, sleeping bag, tent—everything. I needed a pool of slow current. But the river provided no break, just endless white water.

Suddenly, I felt a powerful blow to my knees. The raft stopped, throwing me forward. Though numbed by the cold, I felt a throbbing pain from both knees. My raft was designed with three separate air chambers so a hole in one only deflates that section. The bottom chamber provides a crucial barrier to underwater obstacles, especially when kneeling. The constant banging and scraping against boulders had ripped off the patches in the floor section of the raft, opening the holes chewed by the squirrel back at the cabin. The cushion deflated into flimsy vinyl. When I kneeled on the raft, my knees sank deep. Being the lowest part of the raft, submerged boulders had passed under the front of the boat and hit my knees. Had I dislocated or damaged them? No time to think. The current pulled the raft over the boulder and I was once again cascading down the river. I couldn't believe how relentless the rapids were.

Finally I saw a stretch of "slow" current. Slow was relative to the raging river; the current flowed six or seven miles per hour, the slowest I had seen since the lake mouth. I jumped out of the raft just above the stretch and dug my feet in the river bottom. My bashed knees made me wince in excruciating pain. I was shocked and pulled down river. I again planted my feet as firmly as I could on slippery rock. I withstood the pain and this time my feet held.

I tugged the water-filled raft to shore, my knees throbbing. Across the river, my pack slowed in a hydraulic. I jumped back into the river, swam fast and grabbed it, hauling my journals and valuable equipment to dry land. Turning from my pack, I saw my duffel bag racing by near the middle of the river. I dove in after it, the urgency of the situation rising above the pains of my cold, aching body and the deep fear of the river's deadly might.

This being a slower stretch, I was able to swim across the river and grab hold of the blue bag. As I heaved the soaked bag to shore, I watched the raft being pulled back into the river. Next, I re-captured the raft in thigh-deep water. I gave up on the paddle and bag of items. I was just too cold.

I jumped about and ran in place, only now realizing how cold I was. But my damaged knees ached from the movement, and I had to stop. I had no dry clothes. I saw no firewood. The rising water had swept the fuel away. Wind gusts stripped away heat far faster than my body could produce it. I had survived the flooded river; I would not drown. But now I faced a tougher challenge yet: staying warm and staying alive. A cold night approached, along with gray storm clouds. I was delirious and needed shelter immediately. I unzipped the duffel bag with great trouble with my numbed hands. I yanked the sleeping bag out and frantically opened its stuff sack. It was dry!

I stripped off my wet clothes and pulled the dry bag around me. But the tundra underneath was soaked. About a foot down, the soil was permanently frozen, creating a barrier water could not easily penetrate. This made the surface boggy, especially after the recent heavy rains. I jumped awkwardly in my sleeping bag towards my raft, which I could use to block the wind. While jumping after it, a gust of wind blew the boat about 20 feet down shore, landing precarious-ly half in the water and half on land. I crawled out of my sleeping bag and ran naked to save my shelter from being swept away. The raft was pulled into the river moments before I reached it, but I grabbed a cord attached to it and pulled it back.

I suddenly remembered my journals: they must be soaked in my backpack, I thought. Despite my predicament, I had to save them. Holding the raft in one hand, I unzipped the lower half of my pack. Fighting a wind gust that nearly yanked the raft from my hand, I pulled the trash bag containing my books and journals from the pool of water in my pack and placed it atop a rise in the tundra. I hauled the raft against the winds to my sleeping bag. With sleeping bag and raft in both hands, I rushed up the steep hillside, looking for a dry, flat patch of tundra to set up my tent. But everywhere was soaked and too steep. I was becoming delirious from the cold. Finding no place flat enough for my tent, I finally lay down on a slight bulge in the tundra and held my raft on top of me. I was at least protected from the wind. But the wet tundra quickly soaked the bottom half of my sleeping bag, further chilling my body.

Lying under the raft, I was faced with yet another dilemma. To prevent the raft from blowing away I kept the sleeping bag partially unzipped and extended one arm out to hold it down. Heat escaped through this hole and my arm was numb. I could not continue the torture. Hoping the weight of the raft would hold it, I pulled my arm inside and zipped the bag.

Shivering is the body's natural means of creating heat. It also means the body has not yet passed into the severe state of hypother-mia that occurs just before death. But in my predicament, shivering caused the loss of heat because the movements forced hot air out and cold air in, like a bellow. The cold drafts kept me hypothermic. I tucked into a ball, holding my legs to my chest. I contracted my mus-cles as hard as I could, to generate heat without actually moving much, then relaxed them. This I repeated again and again, about one every other second.

The cold was far more extreme than any I had ever experienced. After only 15 minutes, my legs were becoming unbearably cramped. The repeated contractions, combined with the cold from the wet tundra sent bolts of pain through my back, buttocks and legs. This was torture. My only desire was to rest. I stretched out flat and relaxed for a few moments. The desire to let go and fall into eternal sleep was more overwhelming than can be imagined. I was exhausted. Physical stimulus from all parts of my body bombarded my brain, asking only that I stop the seemingly insane contractions that were barely keeping my body temperature high enough to survive.

I heard the whistling sound of a heavy wind gust, and I worried about my raft. It stayed put. Moments later, another gust of wind whipped away my shelter. I exited my sleeping bag and ran after the raft. It stopped just above the shore. I scurried back as the wind pulled on the raft like a sail. This time, I took a cord that was tied to the edge of the raft, pulled it under my sleeping bag and tied it to the drawstring on the bag.

What could possibly make my life so important that I must continue this torture, I thought, as sharp needles of pain throbbed from my cramped back and legs. While adjusting my position, the sleeping bag zipper broke open at my feet, creating a draft that numbed my lower half. I tried to maneuver to keep the bag closed. Soon I could no longer feel my legs. I had to do something. I unzipped the bag to where the zipper had opened then forced it past the break. I used such force I worried it would break permanently. After several minutes, the zipper reached the bottom of the bag and I was able to slowly zip it back up. Whenever it split, I zipped it back down and tried again. The process would have been tedious under any circumstances, yet alone the severe ones I now faced. By the time it was completely zipped, my entire body was numb.

I struggled to warm up. Rain began to patter on the raft. This was not my day. The rain increased in intensity. On I struggled against the Arctic cold, one pitiful body against the massive mass of frozen ice one foot below. I worried about my duffel bag and pack. Because of their extreme weight, being full of water, I had pulled them just barely out of the water. If the river level rose, they would surely be gone, and I would be left without food, tent and equipment. But I was so chilled that to attempt to save them might kill me. I peered out from my raft, looking for the familiar items of security. I could not see any blue or red gear. They might have already slipped away. I might as well give up.

I continued the torture of survival, still uncertain if there was any point to my effort. I contracted then relaxed, squeezed my muscles with all my might, then let go for a brief moment. Again and again I squeezed. The cramps became worse, pounding my head with an intense pain. The desire for sleep threatened death at every moment. The strength of my will determined my fate. I remembered Ohio University Professor John Rudger's warning against hypothermia when I'd discussed my trip with him. "It would be the easiest way to go. Just let go into eternal sleep," he had said of his spill into an icy lake. I could not let go of my life.

But a cold Arctic night lay ahead. It was 7 p.m. Rain drops pattered against the vinyl raft. There was no way I could survive the night under the raft, I thought. Although the sun (now obscured behind rain clouds) never sets in the Arctic summer, it travels lower on the northern horizon and temperatures drop. I could not imagine continuing the present ordeal, let alone with colder temperatures.

Meanwhile, the rain pounded harder. While I struggled against sleep and the death that would accompany it, worries about my equipment increased. I had to check on my equipment. A break in the rain gave me a chance. I exited the bag and ran down to my stuff. A bend in the hill had blocked view of the river shore from my raft shelter. I was relieved to find the familiar, though soaked items. I hauled them up. The action was just in time. The river had risen to cover about half of both items, nearly dragging them away. On the way back, I grabbed my wet clothes.

I spread the soaked clothes on the wet tundra under my sleeping bag. Although soaking, they provided at least some barrier between the frigid tundra and my bag. This helped. But colder evening temperatures worked in the opposite direction. I could not rest from my rigorous contractions. Rain started again. On with the torture. Time seemed to stop. After what seemed like several hours, I would check my watch to find only 15 minutes had passed. I was both mentally and physically drained. The urge for sleep was so great. I pictured my friends, my parents, grandparents and brother. They would be devastated. But to continue the contractions would only prolong my death and increase the pain. Why not just let go?

If only the sun would come out.

If only I was warm again.

If only the cramps would subside.

If only I could keep pushing a little longer.

If only my frostbitten toes and fingers could survive. They had already turned purplish-black to the second joint.

Struck down to my deathbed, perspectives aligned with reality. If I could survive, life would be cherished at every moment. Death sent shock waves of fear and panic through my system. I called out, "Help, help!" I thought I heard a helicopter. But the river's roar deafened all sounds, and created weird combinations that my mind twisted into wishes that never came true. It was all so hopeless. Why not just give up, I kept thinking. Hopelessness and despair grabbed hold like a vice. I stopped the flinching and let my cramped muscles stretch out "just a little while." I drifted toward endless sleep, losing consciousness.

*

I awakened in horror, to a reality of cold terror. My legs were numb. My entire fingers were a dark purple, cold and numb. I was in the furthest reaches of hypothermia before death. I don't know how long I had stopped contracting. I had never felt closer to death. I began the contractions. Blood began pumping. My frostbitten flesh throbbed in pain. I focused on the pain, a calling from my body's survival system. I focused on the land beneath me that needed defended. Having been immersed in such beauty for a month, the scenes of the Arctic were diverse and fantastic; those of the oil industry quite the opposite. The struggle for life called upon my inner strength to endure this night for a life of action to protect this and other threatened lands. I had to survive. I had purpose for living. I had to try and protect this last paradise.

I put my fingers under my armpits. The cold shocked my under-arms, draining heat from my core. But I would not let my fingers die. I flinched. Blood pumping through my veins issued throbs of pain from my frozen flesh. This was my hour of reckoning. My very sur-vival would take a seemingly impossible feat.

It was 8 p.m. I had 12 hours before there was any hope of warmer temperatures. I had no idea if my frostbitten fingers and toes would ever recover. I had no idea if I could ever make it through the night. Exhaustion was so real. Again that dreaded invitation: why not just give up? What if it continued to rain tomorrow? I wanted to say "I love you" to all my relatives, friends, pets, God.

I recalled the conversations with Marie and Paul. "This area is so important for the Porcupine Caribou Herd," Marie said. Paul had said, "Once the oil industry gets their foot in the door, they will expand like crazy just as they did around Prudhoe Bay. This place will be gone forever."

I had a mission to work to save this land. Congress was yet to decide. If concerned citizens do not struggle hard enough, the great Arctic ecosystem will die at the hands of oil companies. Concentrating on the cause recharged my spirit. Rain continued throughout the night. Streams of water flowed down the hillside, chilling my bottom half even more than before. I contracted harder and faster.

The thought of death made life so spectacular, so special in its own sense. Petty fears and worries shifted into perspective. Like every human being, I was a miracle for just being alive. Even if I had to stay up all night torturing myself by squeezing muscles that begged to let go, I would persevere. Even though my fingers and toes seemed surely dead, I had to live. The pains were so real, the cause so intan-gible. Still, I squeezed with the rhythm of my heart, grimacing through the throbbing agony of life.

While my immediate want was an end to the misery, my body's need was the endurance of that pain.

*

The minutes ticked into hours. The rain stopped. It was 10 a.m. Struggling against never-ending sleep all night, I had survived. Every inch of my body ached. Miserable and wretched didn't begin to describe how I felt. Peering out of the soaked sleeping bag from under the raft, I saw the glorious rays of sunlight beaming down through breaks in the clouds. A smile crinkled my frostbitten face.

The sun brought the awakening of faith within. My one wish was granted. I would survive. Wrapped in the sleeping bag, I wearily pulled myself on top of the raft, using it as a barrier from the frigid tundra. The center two compartments were deflated from the disaster, but the outer compartment was taut enough to buffer me from the cold ground like a hammock. As I lay buffered from the Arctic icebox for the first time in 18 hours, caressed by the warm rays of the sun, I prayed that the sharp pain from my fingers and toes meant life.

The sun's rays continued to increase in intensity. Never had I more love and reverence for its life-giving rays. The warmth soothed my body. Even with the pain, I was just happy to be alive.

Chapter 21

Recovery

Insulated from the Arctic icebox by my raft, I was finally warm enough to relax. Frostbitten toes, fingertips and cheeks still pulsated pain. But, now, all was in comparison to the tortuous night prior. The barest of shelter was a most blessed gift. Fresh water to drink, some food. I felt like a king in the comfort of the raft hammock, basking under the late morning sun. I relaxed and stretched my muscles. I massaged my sore thigh, which was cramped from the ordeal. Pain pulsated from my frostbitten fingers. I held them tight against my body and concentrated on the pain, feeling the call for help of my own body. The pain throbbed with each heartbeat. That was the life-giving blood rushing through my arteries with healing sustenance for my damaged flesh.

I looked about at the mountain panorama. How blessed I was to be here, alive. Tired of the confines of the sleeping bag, I put on damp clothes and descended the bank to my stuff. First priority was unquestionably my journals and books. Because I'd pulled them out of the water-soaked pack, the journals were dry. I'd had double-wrapped them, and my care was rewarded. To me they mattered more than anything else, and they were safe. The field guide to edible Alaska plants was still dry. The Alaska field guide to birds was wet, the colored pictures sticking together. And the paperback *Arctic Dreams* book was wet. I set them out to dry.

Opening my pack, I was sickened by the mess. Each compartment was still full of water. I'd assumed the water would drain away. But everything had been soaking for 24 hours. My replacement camera was soaked beyond repair—a full roll of film destroyed. And this after I'd hiked back into Prudhoe Bay to buy it. And the food I was already running low on was now soaked, some ruined. I opened the food bags to dry the noodles, coffee, rice, lemonade mix and pancake mix. All my vitamins and precautionary medicines had wetted together into a mush. Vitamins and medicines for diarrhea and flu all mixed together. All lost. My rod, gloves, cup and paddle were lost down the river. My rod was needed for food. My paddle was crucial to getting to Barter Island. I did not know what I would do. Luckily, my glasses were spared.

Winds chilled my body that, even a day later, had still not dried. I took a hike through nature's loving arms so I could stay warm while my clothes finished drying, and to look for lost gear and Paul and Marie. I hiked upriver on a ridge overlooking the river, thinking my paddle may have gotten hung up on something, and knowing I would be hiking downriver to continue my journey. It was a miracle that I had survived the ferocious rapids that roared below. The massive hydraulics and waves evoked awe and respect. I passed rapid after rapid, each terrifying. Each looked deadly. I was happy just to be alive. Despite my soreness, and the gnawing sense of loss, I was stronger, yet humbled. My determination and will to survive was unquestioned. I felt careful, yet confident and patient in a deeply reverent way I'd never felt before.

I walked all the way back to the lake. I hadn't realized how far I'd been swept through the raging water—some five miles from where I'd spilled. The lake was gloomy today, the sky overcast.

I sat on a ridge overlooking Lake Schrader and our rain camp at the mouth of the Kekiktuk River. Two days ago Paul, Marie and I had marveled at the dozen caribou that swam across the river I'd later rafted. In my binoculars I looked miles across the lake at the cabin where I'd stayed. A boat was anchored in front of it. Someone was there. I wondered if they were catching lake trout. I thought back to all the glorious fish I'd caught there, and my wonderful stay there. It seemed so long ago.

I had hoped to find Paul and Marie. They were about done with their trip, so they might lend me their fishing rod. I walked in a wide semicircle, scouting for the couple. They had been hiking for two days, and there are no definite trails in the Arctic. Kikiktat

Mountain lay in between the lake and the Hulahula River, where Paul and Marie were headed. They could have gone either north or south of it. The north route appeared easier. I thought I remembered Paul saying they were hiking that way. I scouted along the ridge between the Kekiktuk River and Karen Creek. Kikiktat Mountain towered above. It was the same mountain that had appeared like a pyramid from the top of the pass to the lakes 25 miles west.

After many miles, I gave up looking for Paul and Marie. My clothes had nearly dried from the hike. I turned from my wide arc and descended to the Kekiktuk. I began hiking down-river, before I came to a creek inlet I knew I'd not crossed. I'd gone too far, and backtracked upriver. I came upon a stretch of rapids with 7-9 foot high waves and boulders strewn for hundreds of yards. The sight of these rapids had a profound effect on me: I realized that had I not gotten out where I had, I would have been torn to bits and not survived.

I continued upriver. Just 200 yards up, I arrived at my stuff, and the short calm section that I'd utilized to escape. I'd nearly ignored it in hopes of a slower spot farther down. My fate would have been far different had I chosen that. I returned to the deadly stretch, awed by its immense power. Thank God I was alive. Things can be replaced; one's life cannot.

I was hungry and still wet. My stove was wet and inoperable until it dried. Wood was scarce, having been swept away by the flood. I searched and searched for more than an hour, collecting a meager pile over which I cooked some food that had gotten wet.

I collected a pink-plume and willow shoot salad and made a dressing with vinegar, oil and pepper with fresh cranberries and bear berries adding flavor and nutrition. Nothing made me feel healthier than fresh, raw greens and berries. In salvaging stuff, I came upon a lime drink mix that was thoroughly soaked, and a film canister of Bacardi 151 rum I'd forgotten about. I mixed up a drink with rum, lime mix and glacier-fed, tundra-filtered Arctic water. From high on the ridge above camp, I sipped in the Arctic beauty.

Chapter 22

Where Eagles Soar

After a busy morning of drying still-damp gear, burning the losses and packing, I left around noon. Much was still damp, and needless to say, the pack was extra heavy. I would first walk down the Kekiktuk River eight miles to the juncture with Karen Creek. Then I'd hike over a pass to Old Woman Creek and down to the Hulahula. Hiking along the Kekiktuk was out of the way and required hiking across steep terrain. But, by sticking to the river, I maintained hope of finding lost gear—chiefly my paddle.

I still hoped to reach the Sierra Club group and join the trip, even though it was to begin in three days 50 miles away. After that, I would travel to Kaktovik, located on Barter Island in the Arctic Ocean. In order to speed travel down river to the ocean, and for the crossing to the island, I needed a paddle.

Because the paddle was large and brightly colored, if it had snagged in flooded willows, I thought there was a good chance I would spot it. I began to think about how I could make one should the need arise. I could bend a willow branch around like a fish-shape and lash it to a stick. Then I could secure a sturdy plastic food bag around the stretched willow frame. It could work, but finding the paddle would be so much better and easier.

The steep bank made for tough travel, and my feet were severely blistered. Staying within sight of the river became increasingly difficult. The riverbank slope steepened. Thick willows often blocked the view to the river, making the task of looking for my lost equipment nearly impossible. I stopped in a willow thicket for a dinner of soaked noodles, French onion soup mix and dried Parmesan cheese—a delicious spread of salvaged wet items. I layered moleskin around each blister. I was asking a lot out of my feet after their being soaked for nearly a month straight. They were not in good shape.

The Kekiktuk River converged with the Sadlerochit some 10 miles downriver, which then poured into the Arctic Ocean. For hours through the evening I hiked along the river, ascending and descending ridges, wading through willows and hiking along steep, precarious slopes. I meticulously scanned the bank, often tripping in the process. Dense walls of flooded willows on the opposite shore and towering willows all around me blocked my view of much of the river much of the time. The gear could easily have been behind me, or made it all the way to the ocean.

It seemed amazing that this fragile land could withstand the flooded river torrent. The cold and force that had nearly taken my life pounded the shoreline minute after minute, hour upon hour, day after day. Even when flooded over with feet of furious water, willows hold on, protecting the river shoreline. The water remained clear.

With the loose-shale bank of the raging river sloped at a 45 degree angle, each footstep became increasingly precarious and dangerous. One slip down the embankment and I'd be back in the river. The valley deepened into a gorge toward the bottom, and was rounded along its top. When hiking from above, most to all of the river was blocked from view. Sitting atop the ridge, I had to make a decision. I still clung to the hope of finding at least my paddle. It should be hung up somewhere, it's so big and visible. But how much longer and how far out of the way should I go to look for it? It was not worth the risk. I reluctantly gave up the search, accepting the loss as final.

The accident had delayed my already delayed schedule, and I had only three days to reach the headwaters of the Jago River if I were to meet the Sierra Club group. I still could make it, I thought, provided there were no more delays and I managed to find good hiking terrain, both of which were highly uncertain. But somehow it no longer mattered. I was alive. That mattered. Should I be delayed, I could just go to Kaktovik—after I made a paddle.

I climbed over the foothill toward Karen Creek. Tussocks and willows hampered travel as I cut against the Arctic grain, but there was no giving up left in my blood. It had died. I'd been traveling for hours and my blisters sent shocks of pain with each step, but I was not about to give up. Compared to what I'd been through the prior night, this was a welcome stroll, and an ever-beautiful one at that.

Karen Creek runs around the base of the Kikiktat's west side. The creek was small and clear, nothing like the flooded rage of the river. Game trails along its bank made travel easy. The tundra slopes of the Kekiktuk Mountain glowed golden in the evening sun, towering to a height of 5,510 feet, more than 3,500 feet higher than Karen Creek. Its folds and grooves wore a living velvet coat of tundra, moss and lichens. The living body of the earth takes hold all over its varied surface and protects the soil from the powers of water and wind.

Nearing the junction, I took a shortcut through horrendous terrain, to reach a little creek that would take me far up the Kikiktat Mountain toward Old Woman Creek, which flows into the Hulahula River. This unnamed creek was smaller and clearer than Karen. The brook had a narrow line of willows buffering its shore, with ample game trails to follow. I was following the northern face of the mountain. Kikiktat Mountain is shaped like a triangular wedge with the northern and southeastern faces the longest, and the southwest face the most narrow.

By the time I made camp, it was after midnight. I was far up the creek at the base of the mountain. The creek would provide water and firewood for the morning, and a soothing melody to lull me to sleep. This brook had a particularly pleasant song that gurgled and bubbled through a full chorus.

The singing brook charmed my morning mood. I'd awakened at 5:00 a.m., still hoping to reach the Sierra Club group. The quiet stillness of the morning accentuated the stream's chorus. Birds added songs of joyful awakening. The air smelled of diverse floral perfume. Cooking pancakes over a fire, I sat back and enjoyed the charm of the wilderness. It was everywhere in the Arctic Refuge's virgin sea of beauty, ready to greet the open senses. It was an opportunity available to all yet is rarely seen by most.

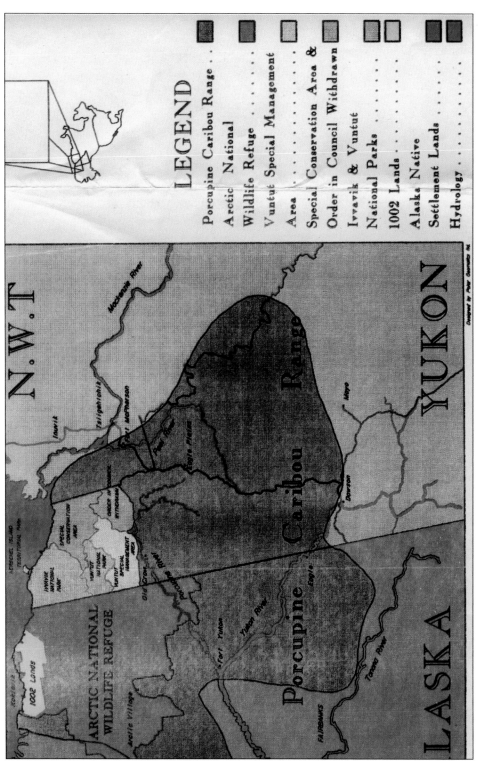

This map shows the Arctic Refuge, and the coastal plain calving grounds (1002 Lands) that is the heart of this massive ecosystem.

Prudhoe Bay was an ugly, polluted mess.

Rafting the Sagavanirktok River with the ever-present cranes and oil industrial blight on the landscape.

This is a herd of caribou staying far away from the oil development.

The summer sun at midnight,. standing at the edge of a vast coastal plain.

The Shaviovik River glistens in the mid-day sun.

Fixing my broken backpack with a caribou antler, wire littered by the oil industry and duct tape.

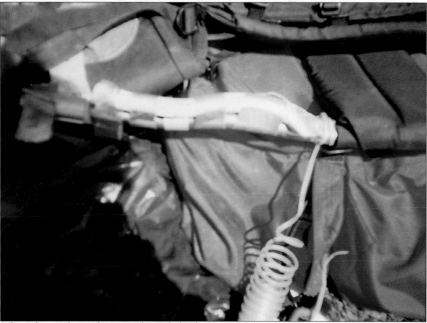

This photo shows how I splinted the broken backpack frame with a caribou antler piece.

I made camp on this sandy spot at the shore of the Canning River.

Mid-July. Snow is still present along the north-facing shoreline of the Canning River.

1.00 A.M. A lake in Rainbow Valley.

This is the cabin Kister stayed in on Lake Scrader. Two lake trout lay in the bottom right corner, and his raft is partially rolled up on the left.

Rafting across Lake Schrader.

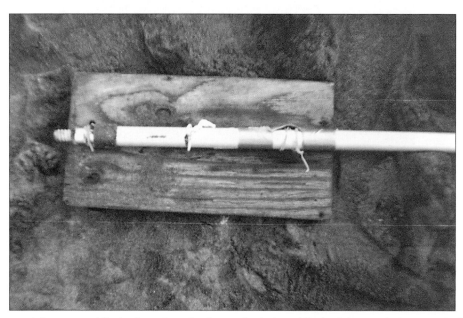

After my paddle broke... I made this makeshift paddle by laboriously burning holes through the wood with hot nails.

The male Arctic Char is darker and has a bright red stripe on its belly, shown here next to the female.

A female Arctic Char lies in front of my pack.

This Arctic vista helped me stay cheery despite my sickness and rpedicament while I pondered whether to hike out.

A grizzly bear advancing too close for comfort.

Bush Pilot Steve Porter stands next to his plane.

Alder trees stand far north of the "tree line," an indication of global warming?

A view of the coastal plain from Steve Porter's bush plane. This is the wilderness that would be developed should oil companies prevail in Congress.

To charm even the most depressed of spirits in the wilderness requires only the focusing of attention on the senses. Nature takes care of the rest. The brook gurgled and chanted through camp, singing her merry song. I looked about, half expecting to find a band of elves playing enchanted flutes and harps. The Kikiktat Mountain rose high above a blanket of fog that shrouded her lower slopes. The mountain curvatures created long shadows in the early morning sun, a mosaic of wondrous beauty ever changing as the sun rounded and rose to the south. Cottony wisps of fog cast a mystical allure over the land. It was as if a giant were resting, with covers wrapped tight around.

The morning hike was easy until the end of singing brook, then challenging with tussocks, steep hills and willows as I trudged over the pass from the Kekiktuk River drainage to the Hulahula water-shed. The thick early-morning fog enveloped the mountain base that I hiked around, limiting visibility and hampering prospects of finding Paul and Marie.

Steep hillsides and tussocks chafed my blisters. I winced with pain at every step, and my muscles ached from the exertion. The pack dug into my back, the brace having been damaged by the flush down Kekiktuk. It was a miracle the frame survived the beating through the river, but the repair was in need of tightening. Fixing it took an hour of tedious re-wrapping and duct taping, but it also pro-vided time to rest. I layered on more moleskin around my blister, but wasn't much help.

The pass was cut by a series of ridgelines and valleys to climb and descend. I wanted to catch up with Paul and Marie. Thick fog shrouded much of the landscape. I stayed along the top ridge, look-ing for my two friends. I'd nearly given up the search in the fog when, cresting a hilltop, I saw Paul and Marie busy packing their gear in a wide valley of a feeder creek to Old Woman Creek. The sight of them brought a joy to my heart. The wilderness was so large and the fog so dense I'd doubted whether I'd see them again. When they saw me, they were equally surprised.

Marie gave me a warm hug, and Paul vigorously shook my

hand, as if we were best friends that had not seen one another in years.

"We were worried about you," Marie said. "A giant grizzly came within 50 yards of camp last night." Looking at Paul, she added "He was setting up the tripod while the bear was coming right toward us," her head shaking with an affectionate smile.

I smiled, imagining the scene. "I bet you got some good pictures."

"I sure did. But I tell you, this time I was really concerned. Last time I met a bear over in Gates of the Arctic, I took pictures until it came to about 100 yards, then I started waving my arms and it bolted away. This bear began to get a bit too close, and he wasn't scared by my waving. That's when I became a little worried. The bear came within 50 yards across the way. I began to think about where the gun was. You didn't see him?" Paul asked.

"No," I responded.

"Good, we were worried."

Changing the subject, Marie said, "You seem different—somehow—than before. I don't know if that's the best word, but you seem different. How have you been?"

"Those were some pretty nasty rapids—we were worried about you," Paul interjected.

"I'll say," I exclaimed. "I lost my paddle while going through rapids. The raft caught a pillow and flipped—just like you warned. I survived—obviously—but I lost my paddle and fishing rod. I was in the water for some time, though, and was freezing throughout the night. It was rough and I'm still a bit shaken."

"We saw those rapids and were worried," Paul repeated. "I stopped and looked from a bluff for anything washing downstream, and I almost walked back up the river to look for you. But we saw you stop, and figured you had decided to hike."

"I wish I had backpacked. I stopped to scout ahead. Then I rafted again. You sure did warn me. I had no idea it was that rough."

"Neither did we," Paul said. "It looked deceptively calm from the lake."

"Are you all right?," Marie asked.

"Yeah. I lost my paddle and fishing rod, but I survived."

Feeling awkward, but knowing it in the interests of my survival, I asked Paul if I could borrow his fishing rod.

"Well, Marie's is more compact." They discussed it a moment and said, "Sure, just mail it back when you get home." I was also low on dry matches, and Paul offered 10 of his.

"Thank you so much," I said. The extremes of the Arctic seem to bring out the best in people, and Paul and Marie were exceptionally kind. I explained further the ordeal I'd been through. Talking about it brought back its horrors, but it ended in my victory of the dark night of my soul. I'd survived, and never had life felt more precious.

"You look shaken up, are you sure you're all right?" Marie asked, trying to find words to heal the ordeal I'd suffered.

"I was more worried about how I'd construct a fishing rod. Thank you so much. I'll take good care of it and mail it back immediately," I said.

"It's the least we could do. Which way are you hiking?" Paul said.

"I was planning to follow Old Woman Creek down, but I haven't studied it much," I said, showing him my map. My map was a 1:250,000 scale that masked unknown pitfalls (like waterfalls). Paul had a 1:60,000 map, showing much more detail. I'd have purchased larger-scale maps, but I would have needed a hundred of them to cover the entire refuge, and I had not wanted to limit my itinerary. We were both headed toward the same place—the Hulahula River—down a steep mountainside five miles to the east.

"That looks awful steep. We're going down the ridge where it slopes gently, then down the river."

I examined his larger-scale map. Old Woman Creek ran through a steep valley. The south ridgetop formed a high window looking over the creek valley as it widened into the Hulahula River valley. The view should be amazing. The one hitch was the ending: a steep drop down several hundred yards. I opted for the view, though it was tempting to hike with Paul and Marie.

"You sure you want to do that?" Paul asked.

I studied Paul's map again to double check that there were no cliffs, just a steep descent. "Yeah, I'll see you down at the river."

The expansive view widened ever more as the valley deepened near the river. To my left, a 400-foot near-vertical cliff dropped off to the roaring Old Woman Creek below. I was startled by a rustling sound just 20 feet away. A Golden Eagle swooped from the cliff side just below and soared over the valley. It was a giant bird-of-prey, with dark golden feathers and a huge white tail. The great bird seemed to fly effortlessly against the gusting wind.

Goldens are the largest eagles, with wingspans of 7-8 feet. They can weigh 11 pounds. Her body was a dark-brown, her head and neck painted golden by God's perfect brush. Feathers covered her legs to her feet, unlike sea eagles whose legs are bare. These are mountain eagles, inhabiting this far northern land year-round. They need feathered feet to insulate them from the Arctic cold. Eagles predominantly eat large rodents and rabbits. They can live to be 80-years old. Younger birds often travel alone during their adolescent years. Before nesting, they are known as mavericks, sometimes killing young caribou or dall sheep by puncturing vital organs with their talons.

The Eagle circled far out into the Hulahula Valley, then back toward the protection of Old Woman Creek Valley. As she approached, we stared each other in the eye. What a life: living in heaven.

I gazed at the eagle for hours while it soared over the valley. She was the symbol of freedom, to be able to fly free over this great land, watching the world from the mountaintops. Like a free young eagle, I was traveling along the top of the world. The whole world was my home.

Chapter 23

Riverside Gathering

The Hulahula River roared through the valley below, an entirely pristine watershed. Her waters were a flooded silty gray from the glacial melt. Her valley was wide and deep. Just upstream, the river flowed through steep chasms. I'd read of many rafting trips down this river, and many fish caught in these waters. But hopes for fish left with my first glimpse of the silty torrent. I would also have to cross the rampaging mass of frigid water.

Old Man Creek emptied into the Hulahula just on the other side of where Old Woman Creek hits the river. Aircraft tire tracks along the flat flood plain were the only indication this was a landing strip from where Paul and Marie were to depart. The tundra river plain was loaded with bear berries and cranberries that I grazed on while scanning for possible places to cross. Old Woman Creek was clear, but small. Maybe I could find a pool. I attached my fishing reel to Marie's rod. But the reel would not turn. Apparently some sand lodged in it during the disaster. I'd fixed many a reel, but it would be tough without proper tools, rags, oil and grease. Paul and Marie approached as I was tinkering.

"That river's not going to be easy to cross," Paul said.

"I know, I've been looking for a good crossing point. My raft has too many holes in it, or I would just raft across.

Noticing my tinkering, Paul asked, "How's your reel working?"

"It doesn't work, I think it got sand in it."

"You can borrow mine," Marie said.

"Are you sure? I could mail it back with the rod as soon as I get home." I gave her mine to reduce weight. Again I felt gratitude inexpressible in words. But all the generosity in the world could not allay my fear of crossing the raging river.

Paul and I scouted the river, looking for a good place to cross. It was a very wide river with swift current, and we found no safe crossing for about a mile in both directions. The sun was low to the west, and temperatures were dropping. Paul and I walked the river, talking about different crossing spots.

"Make sure you have a sturdy stick to help you probe and balance. We'll watch you cross, and we'll have a fire going in case you get in trouble," Paul said. "But the river level is coming down, it would be far safer in the morning."

"You might be right. I'm going to look for a while longer. Thanks for your help." I wanted to travel, and scanned the river again and again. But I had learned my lesson about flooded Arctic rivers, and reluctantly set up camp by an abandoned sled near the riverside. I wondered the history of the sled: it looked likely Inupiat. My feet were sore with blisters, and this would give me time to properly treat them.

With fishing outfit in hand, I stalked up the small clear waters of Old Woman Creek, casting a spinner to small pools ahead. Old Woman Creek's clear waters were in stark contrast to the Hulahula. Her waters were tundra-filtered. The Hulahula's source was far up in the mountain glaciers that churned silt as the mountains were still being shaped. Global warming's melting of the Arctic glaciers increased the amount of silt. The life blanket of lichens, moss, tundra and willows that hold the precious Earth in place to keep Old Woman Creek pure may not be able to adapt to climate change.

I came upon Paul and Marie's camp. They were standing by a fire.

"How's the rod and reel working?" Paul asked.

"Great. I just can't find any fish."

"Yeah that river is too silty and this stream is awful shallow."

"I hope the Okpilak is better, but one thing I do know about fishing is you can't catch anything if you don't have a line in the water."

"So true. Do you want a cup of hot cocoa?"

"Sure."

The fire crackled in the evening light, reflecting on Paul's face. He was calm and happy, clearly enjoying the primordial role of fire tender. Marie too was relaxed and cheerful. No amount of money or technology can replace the inner peace found in journeys through nature's wonderland.

Back in my tent, I studied my maps. To reach the Sierra Club, I would have to cross this river, hike over a 10-mile pass to the Okpilak River, cross it and another 10-mile pass to the Jago, then hike 20 miles up the Jago to the headwaters. It seemed possible, and I could always raft the Jago down to Kaktovik should I encounter trouble or delay (that is, after making a paddle and repairing the raft).

I heard the buzz of a plane in the distance, slowly coming closer. It was 11:50 p.m. The noise got louder and louder and I hurried outside, grabbing my reporter's notebook. A white and blue Cessna landed on the airstrip, bumping to a halt on the tundra runway. I walked over to greet the new arrivals to the wilderness.

The pilot, Joe Firmin of Porcupine Air, exited and immediately started to tinker with the plane. His single passenger, John Haweeli, smiled in a jovial manner, accustomed to respect.

"Welcome to the wilderness," I said, introducing myself as a writer. "What brings you here?"

"I wanted to spend the best years of my life traveling, before I get too old," said 40-year old Haweeli of New York. "I quit my business career three years ago to explore the world. I have been really looking forward to this trip because I have a feeling it won't be like this anymore. This would be a wonderful legacy to leave for the next generation if we are wise enough to do it.

"Have you seen any musk-ox?" he asked.

"No, but I sure hope to."

"I've heard they are common in the Sadlerochit. I'm going to hike there and take day hikes. It was really just an excuse to hike around in the wilderness," he said, "I don't really care if I see any."

"With that attitude you'll have a great time," I said. "You never know what you'll see. It's always beautiful and full of surprises out here."

Joe Firmin has been flying adventurers into and out of the Arctic Refuge for more than 10 years. "It is so spectacular," he said. "It is my home—my backyard."

I asked about the oil controversy.

"Ninety percent of those I take in here are opposed to oil development," the bush pilot said. "I see both sides, but as time goes on I slant towards the opposition. I don't think what we have here should be sacrificed. We should save it."

"We were just talking about that as we flew above," John said. "To trade a wilderness like this for six months' supply of oil is a tragedy. It would be an economic loss for the country. This is the only true remaining Arctic wilderness."

"I agree. I can't believe they want to destroy such an amazing place," I said.

Fog was rolling in, and Joe was hurrying to beat it.

"I don't take it you have any extra food I could buy?" I asked Joe.

"Hm, no. Well let's see...he reached over and pulled out a foil-wrapped something. My mouth watered at the possibilities. "Want some moose lasagna? We've had more than we should eat."

"Sure, I'd love it." He refused payment.

"It'll be quite a treat after freeze-dried food," Joe said.

John added, "Yeah that was good, but we sure did stuff ourselves." Minutes later the Cessna was lifting off, leaving John behind on his camping trip.

I waved good-bye, praying luck be with him.

"Is it O.K. to camp here?" John asked, pointing to a site some hundred yards from my camp.

"Yeah, it would be nice to have some company," I said. A hundred yards is quite close in the Arctic. Paul and Marie were about a mile away but it still felt as though they were in camp.

I heated the lasagna over a rekindled fire. It was luxurious food, well spiced and delicious. What a treat flown right into my camp.

Chapter 24

The Crossing

While I was cooking pancakes early the next morning, John approached from his camp and asked if I could help him choose which route to take. He was traveling to the Sadlerochit River, across hilly tundra.

"Stick to the creeks and ridge tops," I suggested, pointing out different ways to get there. "Be especially careful of the flat, open tundra. It looks like easy travel on a contour map but tussocks are awful. Avoid them if you can. You'll undoubtedly get into them, just push on through them. There's no easy way. Stepping on them is hazardous and stepping in between yanks at your feet and slows travel. Good luck."

"Thanks. Do you think it's possible to go four miles a day with a seventy-pound pack?" he asked.

"That's reasonable," I responded, "but be prepared for weather delays."

"Where did you fly in?" he asked.

"I hiked from Prudhoe Bay a month ago. I'm researching for a book about the Arctic Refuge," I said.

"I'd planned to fly through Prudhoe, but people I consulted said it would make me sick it's so polluted."

"Yeah, it's even worse than could be imagined. They've turned it into a giant toxic dump."

"Have you heard many planes or helicopters?"

"A few, but nothing compared to Prudhoe Bay."

"You should complain to the Fish and Wildlife Service. They're supposed to get a permit to fly over."

After breakfast and packing my gear, Paul and Marie joined John and me at the banks of the river.

"I think this area is the best to cross," I said. "It's the widest so the water should be shallow." The silty water hid the river's depth.

"That also means a lot of wading," Paul said. "Do you have a good staff?"

"Yeah, I found this," I said, showing him a 5-foot, slightly crooked but thick and sturdy willow staff.

The river had not dropped during the night, but I was rested and better prepared for the challenge. Murky water rushed by my feet as I stepped into the torrent with my mammoth pack. I could not see the bottom, and felt carefully with the staff before each step. Slowly I inched onward, leaning against the flood of water. Footing was precarious.

Nightmare scenarios of being flushed down the river flashed in my mind. In the wildreness, trouble was always just one slip away. Each step was a panic to overcome as I felt for firm footing on a riverbed of loose, slippery rock. The water became deeper and deeper. I slipped on a loose rock, falling. I caught myself with the staff. But that feeling of falling unleashed the nightmare fears of my recent disaster. Helpless. Banging against rocks. Choking for air. Though the water was waist deep, fear descended upon me as the water pushed against me—all around and nowhere to go but forward.

I stopped and closed my eyes, emptying my mind of the nagging, troubling fears. I'd survived once. I could do it again. Now I had three companions and a blazing fire to help, should disaster strike. Calm and careful, I worked for complete concentration. Inch by inch. Foot by foot. My staff hit a large boulder that blocked the way. Feeling it with the stick, I found I was near the downstream end of the boulder. I sidestepped around it.

Climbing onto dry land, I raised my stick in the air and hollered in sheer joy. Paul held both hands high and hollered back. I think all four of us were equally relieved. My spirit soared like the eagle. I hollered again, stick raised in the air.

*

About two miles up Old Man Creek, I sat down for a rest. Three mountains rose above an expanse of tundra to the south. I wished my camera was working. I wrote in my journal:

> Jagged peaks with odd curvatures form a sharp line against the blue sky. A few puffy clouds give the sky a slight marbled look, adding delicacy to the picturesque landscape. The near mountains are grayish purplish brown with a tinge of green all perfectly shaded by the many valleys cut deep into the stone over time. I was blessed with a panorama of white-capped mountains, including the mighty Mount Michaelson at 8,855 feet.
>
> The clarity of the Arctic sky magnifies the beauty. The gurgle of the creek adds a melodic grace—wilderness music. Its clear water and rippled surface, with white spots below water-falls and large rocks makes a pleasant hiking companion. Eight-foot high willows form an ancient forest along the creek bank. The willows gradually decrease in size and numbers away from the creek, changing to open tundra, bogs, pentagon structures, tussocks and orange sphagnum moss. I graze on bear berries which grow big and plump on the creek shore. What a joy it is to be alive, and what a place to be living in.

A ridge lay between me and the Okpilak River. The ridge was steepest toward the south, tapering lower to the north. The easiest route would be to cut diagonally north over the lower area. But the view would be nicer from the higher ridge to the south. Though I was nearly out of food, I opted for the higher, scenic route.

Tussocks made for tough hiking. Again they tore at my blistered feet. My pace slowed to a half mile per hour during the roughest sections. The awesome splendor of the Arctic kept my spirit high. I traveled down and up two stream valleys before beginning the steep ascent up the high pass. Up and up I climbed. I hiked for seven hours straight.

Cresting the ridgetop, I was greeted with a sea of glorious wilderness stretching in all directions. To the south was a high wall of white-capped mountains. East, the Okpilak wound its way through the mountains toward the coastal plain and the Arctic Ocean. Foothills rolled to the north before flattening into the golden coastal plain to white specks of pack ice on the Arctic Ocean more than 40 miles in the distance. Not a sign of human disturbance was anywhere to be seen.

I laid out my sleeping bag on the ridge top for a rest before descending to the river. Winds whipped across the highlands. I felt the winds of change among the people. Paul, Marie, John and Joe had all spoken for the land's defense, and against the "progress" of oil development. The past decades have seen a growing environmental movement sweeping the world. Opinions are shifting. People are speaking out in defense of the Earth.

Chapter 25

Flood Weary Along the Okpilak

Was this a dream, I wondered when I awoke at 1 a.m. The low midnight sun reflected off the jumbled mass of ice in the ocean far in the distance and illuminated the golden tundra plain and hills that branched together with deep-blue streams and rivers. Nearer mountains glowed purple, brown, gray and white, casting long shadows on the mountains beyond. The vastness of the wilderness engulfed the senses and humbled the spirit. I felt like I was given the keys to the Kingdom of Heaven, wondering why I was so blessed.

The white-capped Mount Isto, highest peak of the Brooks Range at 9,050 feet, towered to the southeast. Arey Glacier and Okpilak Glacier formed the beginning of the Okpilak River. I examined the watershed of the river I'd soon meet—looking into the land over which the water flowed that I'd soon be drinking. Nothing is more sacred than an untamed river protected from poisons and destruction from mountain headwaters to ocean delta. This was land managed by God, not people. To leave such rare untouched watersheds for the spirit to manage preserves the last few Gardens of Eden left.

But if industry and its political henchmen get their way, the great expanse of coastal plain would be developed into an industrial wasteland like I'd seen at Prudhoe Bay. Development would require seven airstrips, hundreds of miles of roads and pipeline, housing facilities for thousands, scores of drill pads, thousands of toxic dumps, numerous gravel strip mine pits, two ports on the Arctic Ocean and the constant roar of aircraft. Pristine rivers like the Canning, Saddlerochit, Hulahula, Okpilak and Jago would be poisoned and dredged and the tundra polluted with millions of tons of toxic sludge from the wells.

*

I was out of water and miles from the Okpilak's replenishing flow. I descended the steep ridge. I reached the Okpilak some hours later, thirsty but cheerful. Like the Hulahula, it was in flood stage with opaque gray water. The roar was as loud as an airplane engine, but as melodic as a symphony. Once again, my long-hoped for fishing opportunity seemed hopeless, and crossing would be a dangerous challenge. I turned around to see dark ominous storm clouds overtaking the blue skies.

To meet the Sierra Club trip now required crossing the river immediately and hiking full speed all day and all night. To make matters worse, they would be traveling away from me. Maybe they'd go slow at first and I could catch up to them. But my situation seemed hopeless. I had four meager meals left, and a long way to resupply. More rations depended on meeting the Sierra Club folks, catching fish and foraging.

A thick blanket of clouds engulfed the river valley. Drizzle began to dampen the already soggy landscape. Before crossing, I would eat. With the sparsely available driftwood soaked, and wind howling through the willow bushes, a fire was out of the question. Over my stove I cooked pancakes from flour I got from the cabin— near the end of my rations. Being out of syrup, to sweeten the bland cakes I substituted orange drink mix and a little water.

The impending rain would only add more fuel to the river's fury. To make it, I'd have to cross soon. If I slipped and submerged, stormy weather conditions would make drying off difficult. Using a large willow staff as a probe, I eased into the turbulent waters, complete with gear on my back, inching as carefully as I could on loose, slippery rocks I could not see, while a torrent of water worked to take me along for the ride. Large rocks formed precarious obstacles. The flood shoved at my feet and legs while slowly numbing them.

The water became deeper and deeper, inching up past my knees and thighs until I could barely hold my ground against the mighty power of the raging river. I was little more than 10 feet out into a channel that spanned 70 feet. The current chilled my torso. I could not go any deeper, my balance in jeopardy. Prodding with my willow stick revealed that the channel dropped off even deeper ahead. I was already precariously leaning against the flow. Any deeper and I'd be swept away for sure. My legs froze, my heart raced in panic. Any move seemed destined to make me slip. I had to do something.

I tried to turn round. The rock I was standing on slipped and the current swept my legs from under me. Into the raging mass of near freezing water I went! Just downstream fierce rapids lay between giant boulders. Roaring frigid water engulfed me. I swallowed a choke-full of the silty grime. Horrors of the last disaster flashed in my shocked mind. Time slowed to a horrifying series of panic-stricken instants.

I grabbed a slippery protruding boulder and managed to pull myself back to my feet. It had all happened in the blink of an eye. My heart was pounding out of control—I had again been reacquainted with a flood-stage Arctic river. I was still waist-deep. Soaked and shivering I paused for a brief eternity to regain my sanity. Ever so carefully I inched back to the dry land from where I had started, each step threatening another plunge.

Wet from the slip, I was determined not to repeat the trauma I'd barely survived the last time I escaped a river's unforgiving ways. Fortunately, it had all happened so fast that I was not completely soaked. I also had a dry wool sweater wrapped in plastic in my pack. I put it on in a hurry. I had to keep moving to avoid the previous experience of near-death. But which way to go? If I were traveling toward the Sierra Club junction, I should go upriver. If toward Kaktovik, I should go downstream. There was no time to check the map—I was shivering uncontrollably.

With dark gray clouds overtaking the sky, and the raging river an ominous obstacle, I gave up on meeting the Sierra Club folks—and three days of rations. I hiked down river, feeling defeated by the mighty force of the Arctic. Shivering and irritably wet with no hope of warm shelter, my spirit was as gloomy as the sky overhead.

Drizzle began. Fortunately, temperatures were in the upper 50s, unlike the sub-freezing skies of the Kekiktuk disaster. Frustrated, tired and miserably dampened, I set up my tent around noon to warm and rest. Studying my maps in the luxury of a dry sleeping bag, I reaffirmed that there was no chance of reaching the Sierra Club group. All those wonderful plans so perfectly organized—gone, like my paddle down the raging river. Arctic travel is as uncertain as the weather.

I was faced with a major dilemma. My raft was full of holes and I had no paddle. The Inupiat village, Kaktovik, is on an island. With a working raft and paddle, I could float down the river and across the Arctic Ocean to Kaktovik. But the river was in quite a rebellious stage. The other alternative was to backpack to the shore of the Arctic Ocean, and signal the island inhabitants to pick me up. My food supply would run out far before I could reach the Inupiat village. I'd already been rationing myself to two small meals a day. Now I'd have to restrict to eating one. Meanwhile I was traveling farther with fewer rests, which further increased my hunger.

The rain increased. On the map I noticed a large lake near camp. Because of the elongated ridge I'd crossed, I did not know exactly where I was. The lake was on a two-mile wide plateau that extended for 8 miles along the river. Finding it would be tough. But spending any more time in the tent seemed worse. With the rain petering into drizzle, I left with poncho and fishing gear to scout for the lake.

Temperatures dropped to the 30s. Dense fog reduced visibility to barely 100 feet. Freezing drizzle made looking up a wet and cold task. After drying my glasses every few feet I finally gave up and took off the foggy lenses.

I walked west about a mile toward the center of the plateau, then turned south. A few hours later, I gave up and followed the river back, fishing a few slower spots in the murky river. I returned to my tent without fish, but content. The walk had helped me sort out the changing reality of my situation and plans.

I awoke to a bright morning sun radiating on my tent. After two weeks of mostly stormy weather, the sun was a blessing. I jumped out barefoot to gaze south at the majestic peaks glistening in the sun. Sphagnum moss made a carpet for the Gods, cushiony and springy to the step. It grew eight inches high in parts, a cozy mattress I'd enjoyed all night.

The mountains formed sharp outlines in the crisp, clean air. Cloud formations gave them an ever-changing grace. As I head out toward Kaktovik to the north, they will slowly diminish in size and grandeur, until they will be distant specks on the southern horizon. I had grown to love these mountains on the north slope of the Brooks Range: their intricate valleys and folds, the perfect blending of colors and shades—its beauty difficult to capture with words. Snow-covered peaks tower above ridgelines of smaller peaks colored brown, purple and dark gray. Green foothills roll to my feet.

The silty river carries the particles of change. Some valley may be a twentieth inch deeper this year, a mountain groove may be a hundredth inch deeper. The slowness of this change is awesome, as it creates an evolutionary landscape mosaic that fits with a sustainable, ever-lasting ecology. The plants and wildlife can keep up with the pace of this change.

But ever-present in my mind, and always a long topic of conversation with those I meet out here, is the knowledge of what we can do to a place like this. With speeds Mother Earth could not even contemplate matching—or that she has the wisdom to not try—we are altering the carefully evolved land and all life upon it.

Chapter 26

The Bearded One

After rounding a bend in the river, I noticed a dark-brown animal far downstream on an island. As I hiked closer, I noticed a hump on the creature's neck—a grizzly? I approached cautiously. I was several hundred yards up the ridgeline and a channel of raging water lay between me and the creature.

As I neared the animal, I saw its white feet, which had been blocked from view by ground cover. Then I noticed the two curved horns—a musk ox. Musk ox are remnants of the Pleistocene Age that ended 12,000 years ago. They are among a handful of large North American species that survived the ice age. Musk Ox are uniquely adapted to the Arctic, with heavy-set bodies about the size of a large bull and shaggy hair eight times warmer than wool reaching nearly to the ground. This gives them a primordial look, reminding one of the woolly mammoths that once roamed these northern lands. How convenient it must be to carry a heavy coat that sheds in the summer and grows thick in the winter. It's a reminder that our distant relatives came from warm climates. But by wearing the skins of Arctic animals and building insulated shelters, humans perfected skills to survive even the Arctic extremes.

Musk ox are permanent residents of the coastal plain. When threatened, musk ox form tight circles with the young in the inside and their horns pointed outward. While this protected them for hundreds of thousands of years from wolf, polar bear and grizzly bear attacks, it made them easy prey for bullets. The whalers in the 1800s came ashore and slaughtered the herds for meat and hide. The musk-ox's compassionate tendencies to protect fallen loved ones made killing them even easier. Other sailors took young musk ox for zoos—after shooting protective parents and leaving them to rot.

These placid inhabitants of the harsh Arctic climate since long before the Pleistocene era were completely exterminated in Alaska by the end of the 19th century.

In 1969 and 1970, the U.S. Fish and Wildlife Service transplanted musk ox from Greenland to the Arctic Refuge. Protected from hunting, their numbers rose from 40 in 1972 to about 500 today. But their future is not bright. Their original low gene pool from starting the population with 40 animals can cause inbreeding. Added to this, U.S. Fish and Wildlife Service studies warn that oil development would cause "major disruptions" in the musk ox herds. Indeed where the musk ox and I stood would be part of the industrial heart of the oil industry's toxic wasteland, if the refuge were opened.

I perched on a ledge about 100 feet from the musk ox, with a perfect view of this spectacular creature. The musk ox stood in a thick patch of willows on an island about 100 by 200 feet. Motivated by the realization that Musk was an expensive ingredient in perfume, the name "musk" was established in the 17th century in hopes the creature had musk glands, apparently from the musky smell of its urine and droppings. They don't.

Then in 1816, the creature acquired another misnomer, the name "ox." The animal is not at all related to an ox (half sheep, half cow). Its direct descendants are extinct, and its nearest relatives are goats and antelopes. The Inupiat name "Oomingmak," or "bearded one" best fits the shaggy creatures. The bearded one below wandered from one side of the island to the other, stopping periodically to graze on woolly louseworts and willows. There was no thought of leaving now. This would be a good place to eat my one meal for the day.

Although I could see the musk ox fine from my position, I wanted a better look. My binoculars were foggy from being packed with items still wet from the rafting accident. I laboriously opened them using my pocketknife as a screwdriver and laid the pieces out to dry in the sun. The afternoon sun and brisk Arctic winds soon dried them. I reassembled the binoculars for a closer view. The beautiful creature had a knowing walk, seeming to have forethought with every step. At first I'd thought it was trapped on the island by rising waters. But its movements were self-assured. He was not trapped, just foraging.

Once he laid down for a rest. Having just finished eating, I followed his example, though I rarely took my eyes off him. There was an aura about him that charmed each moment of the many hours I spent with him. Watching the bearded one stand up was another wonder. Like the rest of his actions, he exemplified grace and harmony as he lifted his hefty body. In a manner opposite to real ox, first he rose on his forelegs, then, pausing in a stretching motion, he lifted his rear onto four feet.

Snow-capped mountains rose to the south, with large snow-fields down the northern valleys that faced me. The flood-staged river of grayish, silty water let out a constant roar, emphasizing the power of the moment. Usually when encountering wildlife, one or the other creature is frightened. Rarely do the encounters last long. This was a treat. Though low on food, I ignored the urge to push on for the wonder of the creature. Hour after hour I stared through the binoculars, just watching the furry mammoth. I wanted to hug him.

After six hours of reverent observation I decided to move on, but first I approached closer. I slowly descended the ridge toward the riverbank, trying to hide myself behind willow bushes. I felt a conflict between wanting to be nearer the giant and not wanting to disturb him. I stalked closer, eyes glued to his turned head. He was grazing on willows, occasionally lifting his head to stare at me, before returning to his lackadaisical eating. I stopped about 20 feet from the riverbank and 50 feet from the creature. I wanted to approach even closer to the majestic symbol of the extreme Arctic ecosystem. But I was stopped by a deeper sense of respect for him and his right to be left alone in this, his wilderness home.

Mountains reflected off the river, which meandered through steep canyon walls. The peaks of the Brooks Range were a deep purple color, with a rich, velvety texture. The shades of gray from the folds and grooves, valleys and peaks melted into rolling green foothills. The roar of water tumbling toward the ocean added melody to the moment.

The Greenland musk-ox repopulated reasonably quickly after being hunted. But oil development brings poisons that can't just be fixed like other ecological problems. How do you clean cancer-causing benzene from the tundra wetlands? From the Arctic Ocean? The damage of toxic pollution is far deeper than previous ecological crisis.

"Good luck," I said, waving to the creature who felt like a friend after spending these hours together. "I'll be fighting for your homeland. I'll lie in front of the bulldozers if I have to." The paradise I stood upon was in imminent peril. The creature before me had an uncertain future. Much hinged upon the actions of politicians thousands of miles away.

In our "democracy," (a limited democracy, skewed by the interests and values of industries like the oil industry), citizens can make a difference. I'd just participated in a successful recycling campaign at Ohio University. At least we have to try to make a difference, despite the odds. I did not want to let the musk ox down.

Chapter 27

To the Jago

Many miles and hours from the musk ox, I cast my spinner into a small patch of clear water where a stream entered the dingy river. I had stopped several times to check crossing points and try potential fishing spots. My confidence in fishing was at an all-time low. The last thousand or so casts had churned empty water without even a stir. Ignoring the doubt within, I concentrated on the end of my line, guiding my lure around large rocks and snags.

In four inches of water, as the lure neared the shore, I watched a dark shadow dart towards the spinner and inhale it. "Yes!" The nine-inch long grayling would have been nothing a week ago when 10-pound lake trout abounded at my doorstep. Now the half-pound meal was a treasure. Exhausted and cold, I hid the fish in a crevice between two large rocks and piled rocks over the opening to discourage scavengers from stealing my breakfast.

The fish made a perfect morning treat, succulent and juicy. I needed more food. The surest source of food was to reach Kaktovik. But the Inupiat village was on an island in the Arctic Ocean 35 miles away as the raven flies. The village lay equidistant between the Okpilak and Jago river deltas. To reach the shores of the Arctic Ocean on foot would take at least three days with good weather. I then had to cross a channel in the Arctic Ocean to reach the island.

If I could patch my raft and create a paddle, I could raft down either the Okpilak or Jago Rivers. I had to choose between following the Okpilak to Kaktovik or going to the Jago and traveling down it. I wanted to get some food soon. Just seven miles east, between the Okpilak and Jago Rivers, flowed a smaller stream whose entire source was tundra-filtered. It would likely be clear. If I could find a deep pool, my food situation could easily change for the better.

In the information about the refuge that I had with me, the Okpilak was rated as poor for rafting, the Jago as good. The Inupiat Camp Bitty lay on a hill next to the Jago a few miles downstream (north). There may be Inupiat with whom I could buy or trade for food. Two large lakes lay on the far side of the Jago. Streams connected them with the river, giving them the potential of being sanctuaries for hungry fish seeking refuge from the likely flooded, silty river. That would require crossing the Jago, but the fishing could be like Lake Schrader. Maybe the Jago would be clear enough to fish. It had somewhat less of a silt-creating glacial source than the Okpilak.

Still it was an uncertain move, and a potentially deadly detour from the straight route to the security of Kaktovik. Studying the map, it seemed smartest to travel down the Okpilak to Kaktovik—a more direct route. With all the rain, maybe the Okpilak would be safer to raft because it was slightly smaller (judging from the comparison of the size of the two watersheds on the map). Hiking to the Jago would take me east of Kaktovik—out of the way. I would have to backtrack west against the wind—quite difficult by raft.

Also, about 10 miles of hiking lay between the Okpilak and Jago. The quality of the hiking is what matters most in the Arctic. The farthest fingers of foothills now lay between the two rivers. Despite the climbing, they made for far better hiking terrain than the lakes, marsh and bogs just a few miles farther north. I would have to cross here if I were to reach the Jago without being bogged down in tussocks. Though it was out of the way, the abundance of fishing potential to the east kindled my survival spirit. I would cross the river.

After a few hours of hiking downstream on that crisp sunny day, with my eyes glued to the river, I found what appeared to be a crossing spot. Although this was the best-looking point I had found in nearly a dozen miles of river, the water gushed toward the ocean in a raging torrent of deadly might. It would be a dangerous crossing. After the terrifying experience a week earlier and the plunge in this river two days before, I was not eager to risk another disaster.

The afternoon was warm, with sunny skies and light winds.

This brought out the pesky mosquitoes, but would make crossing much safer. While searching for a willow staff, I noticed storm clouds approaching from the southwest. I could not afford to wait. The disaster loomed in my memory. To step into a raging torrent of murky water, blind to unforeseen boulders and drop-offs, is a terrifying experience, like looking down from a 100-foot diving board.

Analyzing the river for the best-looking spot, I finally stepped into the river, using the stick to probe for hidden obstacles and drop-offs. The river raged over boulder fields. I teetered up and down slippery rocks and around obstacles, struggling to hold my balance against the rampaging current. I pushed across the river, and climbed onto dry land.

From a vantage point hundreds of yards above the river, I looked down upon where I crossed. The ferocity of the rapids looked impenetrable. I climbed the thousand-foot foothill that separated the Okpilak and Okpirourak Creek. From a perch at the top of the foothill, I scanned north across miles of tundra to the white pack ice of the Arctic Ocean some 30 miles away.

The Okpilak roared from the west, cutting through the landscape to the ocean. The Okpirourak Creek to the east flowed north for dozens of miles before turning to the east and converging with the Jago. Tundra rolled for as far as the eye could see to the east and west. Threatening storm clouds approached fast over the mountains from the south and west where I'd come.

What is so incredible is the vast expanse of virgin, pristine land. In the era of mass change to the Earth this remnant has survived, to protect an entire ecosystem in its original state. From the foothills of the mountains where I sit, across a rich, tundra plain where millions of birds and hundreds of thousands of caribou breed, to the Arctic Ocean where seals swim playfully about and polar bear stalk in search of a meal. All untouched, open for the traveler to pass through and admire. It fulfills the need to live close to the Earth that nurtures our soul. Here, stress is replaced by reverence.

*

I descended the hill toward the Okpirourak Creek. In the wilderness one sees so clearly the essence of nature's design. Everywhere on Earth, valleys cradle streams, rivers and lakes with vegetation to hold the soil in place and purify the water. Valleys have wood for cooking and warmth and water for cleaning, cooking and drinking. Mountains and hilltops tend to be dry, wind-swept, expansive and mind opening.

Reaching the lower valley flatlands, the travel became rough with tenacious tussocks and willow thickets. Bear berries and cranberries were plentiful. I trudged through, grazing constantly. Many miles later, I heard the gurgle of the Okpirourak Creek. I pushed through thick willow brush to the stream bank. I was overjoyed to find a clear-flowing creek like I'd predicted.

Dozens of casts throughout many miles of creek came back without a bite. Unless I found a deep pool, my chances for finding fish were slim. I considered following this creek until it met the Jago. But I wanted to check out camp Bitty and the lakes. I was uncertain if the creek contained any fish and had hoped to raft the Jago. Rain began to pelt the landscape. The temperature dropped to the 40s. My hands became too numb to fish.

I cooked my last meal: stuffing mix. With rations depleted, survival now hinged on my ability to find food. Even my most optimistic predictions put me three days from Kaktovik. I'd already been rationing for more than a week and was quite hungry. Before, when I ran out of food at day number 22, I had a cabin that turned out to be stocked with provisions and a large lake just ahead on the map to provide hope. Now hope was distant.

I headed for the Jago. Just in case I saw a plane or helicopter, I had empty food bags ready in my pockets, which I could use to signal that I was out of food. But this was some of the most remote wilderness in the world. Chances of a rescue seemed akin to chances of finding a grocery store.

It was now late evening, and the rain made travel uncomfortable. Tussocks and marsh grabbed my feet, protesting travel across them. My aching legs begged for rest, but I strained on, heaving through the sticky wetland. I was relieved to hit another foothill. Tussocks are worse than climbing steep hills. I hoped the Jago was clear. I crested the last hill before the river. Below was a hot-chocolate colored, flood-stage torrent of water. Exhausted and soaked from the freezing downpour, I set up camp near the river and retired to my warm, dry sleeping bag.

Chapter 28

Rescue

It rained through the night and into the morning. With food my central concern, I wanted to leave early to check Camp Bitty, a temporary hunting outpost for the Inupiat at Kaktovik. Hopefully, it had some food. Rafting down the river or trying to cross it to reach lakes on the other side would be suicidal in its flooded state, at least from my present location. Once out on the coastal plain, however, I might be able to safely raft to Kaktovik. As I lay in my tent, lulled by the monotonous patter against the nylon walls, I planned how I would make a paddle.

I could bend a green willow stalk and tie the ends together. This could be lashed to the sturdiest, straightest branch I could find. I had some very sturdy plastic bags that the freeze-dried food I got from the cabin came in, which could be fitted around the willow frame and tied into place. Duct tape would come in handy for adding the finishing touches.

I worried that the rain would continue for many days, like it had at Lake Schrader. I could not afford to wait. Out here, you can't just open a door to a heated house. I was dependent upon the insulation of clothing and my sleeping bag. As I lay in my sleeping bag, staring at the ceiling of my tent, I was left with a decision: to stay and risk starvation or leave and risk freezing. What a choice!

Humans can go for quite some time without eating, but not when burning thousands of calories from intense backpacking. My stomach growled and complained. My body was weak. I was noticeably thinner. It was more than a number of miles and a channel of Arctic Ocean to Kaktovik, but relative to where I'd been I was quite close.

My weakened condition made challenging the elements riskier.

When I survived the river disaster a week earlier, soaked and naked on the tundra icebox, I was able to rest for several days and gorge on fresh fish. Now my stomach growled continuously. I feared my otherwise hardened stamina might give.

As the rain subsided into drizzle, I decided I could not wait for clear weather. I would have to keep as dry as possible, but I must travel to Kaktovik. I packed, strapped my pack cover on and hoisted the huge load in place. Rain added several pounds to my load. The easy hiking along game trails was flooded, leaving a terrain of dense willow brush and boggy muskegs. Hour upon hour I hiked down the Jago, traveling a mile east or west for every mile north as I zig-zagged around impassable willow thickets and bogs.

I stopped periodically to graze on lowbush cranberries, blueberries, willow shoots, young willow leaves and pink plumes. I often stopped to pluck wooly lousewort roots from the soaked tundra. These required about 30 minutes of cooking so they did not provide immediate satisfaction, but they would make a meager dinner should the rain and wind slow enough to make a fire. I felt conflicting urges between stopping and gathering edible plants and traveling as fast as possible to Kaktovik.

By 8 p.m., I reached the base of the foothill upon which Camp Bitty lay. A thick blanket of clouds obscured all but the very bottom of the hill. I stopped to set up my tent for a rest. The rain ceased while I put together my tent, but the sky was an ominous gray. My raft was soaked. I unfolded it to dry before retiring to my tent. Should the weather clear, I could patch it. Hour upon hour of exposure had dampened everything. My wet sleeping bag afforded little protection from the Arctic chill. Shivering with my sleeping bag drawn tightly around, I stared at my maps, contemplating again and again how long it would take to reach Kaktovik.

The swoosh-swoosh sound of a helicopter stirred me from deep thought. I jumped out of the tent in socks and long underwear, waving my arms frantically. The helicopter was flying down the river under the low-lying clouds. By the time I got out, it was directly toward the river, some 150 feet from me, and flying quickly away.

Thick clouds and rain obscured the view. I waved my arms frantically and jumped up and down.

Suddenly, the University of Alaska helicopter turned around and flew toward me, landing about 30 feet away. A deep feeling of relief overwhelmed me. The helicopter was loaded with three people including the pilot, and had solar panels and scientific equipment attached to it. One of the scientists hopped out and asked what was wrong. Yelling over the roar, I asked, "Do you have any food?"

"We can send a Fish and Wildlife Service helicopter to drop some off," the researcher said.

"That would be great," I responded.

After some discussion in the helicopter, graduate student Carol Peters came out and asked how long it would take me to pack up. "Twenty or twenty five minutes," I said, realizing that my stuff was rather sprawled out. "Hurry up, we're going to Kaktovik," she said. "We'll take you."

"Thank you so much. I'll hurry"

I rushed to put on my pants, jacket and boots, take down my tent, stuff my sleeping bag, pack my gear and fold up my raft. Carol helped to load gear and we were done in five minutes. The crew had to unpack my gear and put it in various spots around the helicopter to fit it all in. They were not sure if they had enough fuel to make it back, and were worried about the extra weight. I crammed in the back, and thanked them profusely.

"Sorry, we don't have a headset for you," Carol said.

"That's O.K.," I yelled over the roaring sound of the engine, still overwhelmed with glee. It was probably for the better of us all—I was giddy and would have been overly talkative.

Carol started digging through her bags for juice containers, an apple, crackers and other food items, which I quickly devoured. We lifted off, and flew down river. The co-pilot was looking at the map and communicating with the pilot. Low-lying clouds forced us to fly just 10 to 30 feet above the rolling tundra. I was captivated by the experience, both out of fear and exhilaration. We were flying fast through a narrow slit of clear air that rolled with the landscape. We passed a lone grizzly, who turned to stare at us, seeming angered at the noisy beast that disturbed his solitude.

We stopped at a fuel cache farther down river. The two pilots carried a fuel barrel over and hand pumped it through a hose into the aircraft's tank. I wanted to help but realized I'd be more of a nuisance. After many more miles of flying low over the tundra the clouds lifted and the Arctic Ocean, full of white ice chunks, appeared on the horizon. We flew toward two huge radio dishes visible tens of miles away as giant black ears. They are part of the Distant Early Warning System established in the cold war on Barter Island after World War II to monitor the then-Soviet Union.

We flew over a short expanse of ocean to the east side of the island. The ocean was full of white chunks of pack ice moving with the current and wind in a mass of little islands, making it abundantly clear that even if I had made a paddle and repaired the holes, rafting would have been very dangerous. We landed by a large Air Force hangar. As was often the case, a group was camped next to it for protection from the wind, waiting to be flown into the refuge for a backpacking trip.

"Do you want to stay in the hotel or camp?" the pilot asked.

I was beyond any sense of ideological loyalty to the outdoors; a hotel room sure would have been nice at this point. But I did not have the money. "I'll camp," I said.

After unloading my gear, I again thanked the crew profusely. I offered to pay for the ride, but the pilot responded, "We're just glad you're alive."

I started to run around the back of the helicopter to get to the other side. One of the scientists grabbed me firmly and saved me from running into the rear propeller that was spinning so fast it was invisible.

"Always go around the front of a helicopter," he said.

I pondered the irony of surviving in the wilderness for more than a month, only to nearly die in the closest semblance of civilization by running into the blades of the helicopter that had rescued me.

I thanked the scientists profusely again.

I'd been so worried about how I'd make it to this wind-swept Arctic island of security and food. Here I was. I said farewell to the helicopter crew and introduced myself to the group of six adventurers camped by the hangar waiting to be flown into the refuge for a backpacking trip. They had overheard my conversation with the helicopter pilot, and asked about my situation. I described my trip and food situation.

Paul Banyas, the group's guide, gave me a bag of backpacking bars, granola bars, seeds and nuts. Other members of the group also gave me much food. Kaktovik's general store was closed until the morning, and I was extremely hungry. I devoured more than a dozen of the high-energy, calorie-laden packages, until I was pleasantly stuffed. I began to set up my tent, and two members of the group took over, saying I should just rest. Banyas encouraged me to sleep in the heated bathroom, a modern structure built by the native corporation for the airport.

Just an hour earlier I'd been shivering on cold tussocks. Now I lay on a ground pad (provided by one of the group members) in a heated building with a full stomach.

"Let me pay for all I've eaten. These backpacking bars are expensive," I said.

"Don't worry about it, I might be in your situation some day. We help each other out up here."

"Thank you so much. I still can't believe this is all real. This isn't a dream is it?" I asked, half seriously.

I was giddy from the unexpected changes. I was well past the point where safety is so easily taken for granted. When threatened, bare necessities become luxuries. Food, shelter and warmth, what more could a person ask for? All was thanks to the kindness of these new friends. The Arctic extremes can bring out the best in people. Everyone here is concerned about surviving in some of the harshest conditions on Earth. Only by working together and helping those in need can the people of the far north overcome the awesome challenges just to stay alive.

Looking out over the Arctic Ocean and its floating mass of pack ice, I wondered what would have happened if I had not met the helicopter. Crossing the ocean from the mainland to the island sure would have been dangerous with pack ice floating rapidly by and in such a flimsy, damaged raft. I emptied a pocketful of wooly lousewort roots into a bag. They would make a nice organic Arctic stew. Banyas had given me the entire bag of high-energy food. I ate another bar.

My sleeping bag was still quite damp, as were most of my clothes, tent and raft. But I was warm, cozy and relaxed in the over-heated building. I had no set plans now. I wanted to explore this island and its native inhabitants. But that would wait until morning. I enjoyed the newfound luxury and slept a sound, restorative sleep.

Chapter 29

Arctic Transformations

Barter Island's main landmass is three miles long and three wide with long narrow peninsulas reaching miles to the east and west. Our camp was located at the start of the east peninsula, Pipsuk Point, which extends miles out from the northeast corner of the island. The gravel airstrip runs along the point. Beyond the ugly airstrip, the strip of land goes east, then curves to the south with shallow channels and a series of smaller islands. The Air Force hangar was a large three-story high building of perforated aluminum. Two miles to the west were the two giant black dishes I'd seen earlier. They stood more than 100 feet high and could be seen for more than a dozen miles.

Our camp was 50 feet from the shore of the Arctic Ocean. The endless expanse of slurry-blue water with giant chunks of white ice slowly floating by was tantalizing. Some 1,200 miles away was the North Pole. Another thousand or so miles beyond lay the northern shore of Scandinavia. The Arctic Ocean's abundance of fish and sea mammals has supported the Inupiat people, the bowhead and beluga whales, walrus, ringed and bearded seal, polar bear, arctic fox, whitefish, Arctic char, clams and krill for thousands of years.

In the small building, I could stand up and stretch in warmth. I took my first shower in seven weeks, leaving me refreshed and cheerful. It was 5 a.m. Everyone was asleep, but I was full of energy. I noticed for the first time how grimy my clothes were. My pants and jacket were stained a dark sooty black from kneeling by so many fires. The pants were ripped badly at the groin and right leg bottom. The tossing and turning down the Kekiktuk River had ripped the seams. I didn't care about it in the wilderness. But it was the only pair of pants I had, and I was self-conscious about it here. With the sewing kit I'd brought, I stitched the rips. The warm washroom made a great recovery area to dry and repair my stuff. What a change from a day ago!

One by one, members of the backpacking group awoke. Each person was eager to learn of my quest. I told of the pack breaking, showing them my improvised splint, of nearly slipping to my death descending the ridge atop Straight Creek, of encounters with fish, caribou, moose, musk ox and golden eagle, and of the rafting accident.

The group's guide, Paul Banyas, was among the first to awaken. He worked for an environmental consulting company contracted by the oil industry to study the ecological impacts around Prudhoe Bay. Working around Prudhoe Bay and Deadhorse, Banyas has seen many changes as the Arctic Refuge issue soared into constant front-page controversy. In the mid 80s, before the major publicity, Deadhorse looked far worse, he said. Trash was everywhere. Rusting barrels, styrofoam chunks, cups, and every conceivable form of litter was strewn across the tundra. As people began to visit the area more, to determine whether the Arctic Refuge should be opened, the oil industry began to clean up the visible litter. Meanwhile, the less visible toxic pits remain, leaching into the tundra waterways and Arctic Ocean.

Lutz Zugler, a world traveler, awoke soon after. He's traveled throughout New Zealand, the jungle of South America, Australia, the United States and Europe. In Europe, he could not find a place to escape the hectic city life. "Even in the Alps, I go out trying to get some recreation, but I can't get away from people. Not everyone wants to get away, lots of people love big cities. For me, it is necessary to get away and see some nature. Almost everywhere you look it's been damaged by people," he said.

Bored with his work at Volkswagen in Germany, he came to the Arctic in search of adventure, excitement and wildlife. "There used to be bears in Germany. Now you can only see them in zoos. Since we're driving cars, use oil to heat homes and make produce, we are dependent on oil. We could have done something already to replace oil with other resources, but as long as there is no major shortage, the governments won't think about giving money for research into alternative fuels."

Another group member, Paul Henderson moved to Alaska for the expansive, open lands, expecting to find a state of nature lovers. "I thought everybody would be like that. But I saw some really strange attitudes and opinions about conservation." Paul, who works at an Air Force base near Fairbanks, read Debbie Miller's book *Midnight Wilderness*. He wrote a letter to the *Fairbanks News Minor*, pleading for the preservation of the Arctic Refuge.

"I caught a lot of flak from my coworkers," he said. "One guy I work with thinks it would be progress if man put a tin can in the middle of the 1002 lands (the coastal plain of the Arctic National Wildlife Refuge), because it would show man conquered nature. Some people think anything man does is progress. It's bizarre. We need to preserve this area for future generations. I want to show my children in 20 or 25 years the Arctic wilderness as I saw it.

"It is frustrating. It's nothing more than green money. The Congressional delegation has been bought out by the oil industry. The things they say, I wonder how they can look at themselves in the mirror every morning."

"That's one of the main reasons I chose this trip," Henderson said. "We backpack right through the 1002 area. Some people say, too much land has been set aside. Some say energy is everything. People say we need resources wherever we can get them. I say that is bullshit. It is not a matter of need, it's a matter of greed."

Henderson visited the Northern Alaska Environmental Council (NAEC) after reading a column by NAEC president Peter Lankas in the local paper. There he received studies and fliers about the Arctic Refuge issue. Paul copied three classic videos about the Arctic Refuge issue, a National Geographic documentary, an Audubon special and a 15-minute NAEC video and sent them to relatives. "In the videos, I saw the immense herds of caribou going to calve and the wilderness, so untouched, so pristine, so pure. It just really grabbed me and choked me up. Wow, this place is something special. To me, in this day and age, it didn't seem possible that there was an area that huge without human development. I think that is something that needs to be preserved."

The group was more than a day behind "schedule." The bush pilot for the group, Steve Porter, was waiting for calmer skies. Here, the weather determines when flights can be made and a laid-back attitude and flexibility are a prerequisite to Arctic travel. The group worked to make the best of the situation, spending the time building friendship among themselves in the secure environment of the island, before the upcoming wilderness expedition.

I joined Banyas in a hike to town. "The Inupiat, are wonderful people," he said. "They are so aware of this land and ocean and the life in it."

The airstrip was two miles from the center of Kaktovik. Boats in various conditions, new and old were docked haphazardly on the inland side of the island. Walking into the village for food, my first impressions were negative. The town looked cluttered. The houses were built on stilts and were quite small. Most had long entranceways to reduce heat loss. Four-wheelers, snow machines, gasoline cans, rusty barrels, pieces of perforated aluminum, and other junk lay strewn about.

Closer inspection led me to a respect for these people who were trying to balance their traditional way of life with modern conveniences. The community was alive in action. Inupiat were busy fixing homes, 4-wheelers, snowmobiles and boats, leaving for fishing and hunting expeditions, carving up fish, tanning hides, tending packs of barking dogs, fishing along the coast and riding about in four-wheelers. Though cluttered, the permafrost prevented digging landfills. While modern cities may look cleaner, a tour to any landfill shows that they are merely better at hiding the waste.

We stopped at a house on the main road in town, with a long entranceway. I stayed in the entrance while Banyas went inside to call Steve and get some provisions.

Walking again, I asked, "How do you think development would affect the Porcupine caribou herd?"

"Caribou need to get to the coast where it is less buggy and back to the open tundra to feed," he said. "Pipes and roads hinder their travel. Caribou are most sensitive when they are calving. That's why they congregate: for protection in numbers. The proposed development would be on the most sensitive area for the herd."

"Do many others share that view?" I asked.

"Nine out of ten of my co-workers are against developing ANWR, but they can't be too vocal about that. Someone has to do these studies. It may as well be people who will do them right."

The store was surprisingly well stocked, but, not surprisingly, prices were two- to three-times those back home. This pays for the cost of flying the food in, and makes non-subsistence life difficult. I bought $70 worth of groceries—two grocery sacks full. It was 5 a.m. eastern time—too early to call my Mom.

While walking back, a conscientious Inupiat gave me a lift on a four-wheeler. Before I could thank him, he was gone—speeding out towards the island's end to fish.

I watched a boat loaded with people approaching from the south toward my camp. Inupiat Elder Isaak Aukluk slowly steered the fishing boat to shore. It was packed with people, and pulled a fully loaded raft behind it. Aukluk had picked up a group of 12 rafters who had just reached the delta of the Hulahula River as it entered the Arctic Ocean. I was finishing my third meal in two hours. The group had just completed a 10-day trip down the Hulahula River, with several day hikes into the mountains. They set up camp next to me. Their faces read of elation and exhaustion. Although strangers before the trip, they had become best of friends and were laughing and joking with one another as if they had grown up together.

"As I was entering the tundra plain, a Golden Eagle flew right over my head and glided away," said Stanford graduate Patrick Mrotek. "I was thinking about the spirit of the land. The eagle was a symbol of that spirit. I think as a culture and as a nation we have become estranged from the land and the places from which we live. The land is alive. It has its own spirit, although different than the one we're used to. We're integrally connected, but we've forgotten this.

"I found the land to have many mystical moods. It could be

windy and foggy one moment and clear, calm and sublime the next. The importance of having a place like this is for wilderness. It is a different perspective than seeing things as resources. I felt a call to come to this place. I think the outer wilderness touches a deeper inner place that is difficult to reach in other settings."

Growing up in Montgomery Alabama in the 1950s and 60s, Mrotek joined in the struggle for civil rights. "Many people at that time believed that civil rights would not be won for the blacks in the area. I learned from my exposure to that, that sometimes one must do the right thing, even though it may seem like a lost cause."

Mrotek organized a group in San Francisco, where he now resides, to write letters for the Arctic Refuge. "This area deserves wilderness recognition. To squander the wilderness for some short-term gain would be a tragedy. I plan to speak about the area as someone who has seen it."

Linda McLellan, an artist from Ponchatovla, Louisiana, and her father, Bob McLellan from Three Rivers Michigan said the rafting journey helped them grow closer as family. "It was a great trip... unbelievable and fantastic," said Bob. "Every time you move around a few feet it's different. It is so beautiful. The wildflowers are so small, so delicate with such vivid colors—too beautiful to believe."

"Every day was a new thrill," Linda said. "The country was so big I don't know where to start. It is the most beautiful place I have ever seen. I was really impressed with the tundra—the wildflowers were incredibly beautiful. I hate to leave. The most memorable experience was sitting on a mountain ridge at midnight and seeing mountains and mountains as far as the eye could see."

She added, "The rapids were fun—it gives you a different dimension living on the water."

Linda told of watching an eagle chase a duck, encounters with dall sheep and caribou and a pair of foxes that barked at her.

"What do you think about opening the coastal plain to oil development?"

"I think it's horrible that they're thinking about that," Linda emphasized. "The lichens grow a quarter inch a year. We saw six to eight inch tall lichens. You can't replace that. We need those lichen. It fits into the system. It's disgusting what they want to do. People keep taking more and more. They have no respect for what's here. Once we destroy nature we're going to pay for it."

"To realize the vastness of God's creation opens the mind," Bob McLellin said. Linda added, "wilderness opened me to a lot of soul searching. You almost can't help it—the big sky and open land. It makes you feel important just being here. It gives you all this space to sort out stuff."

Thirty-seven-year-old Jeff Decales brought along a kite, which he flew in the midnight sun. "The Arctic Refuge is not replaceable," he emphasized. "You can't quantify it. It is one of the equations in the quality of life that can't be quantified. And they want to ruin it for oil."

Ellen Anderson, 62, and her husband, Bob Anderson, 67 said they both had life-changing experiences on their Arctic journey.

Ellen said, "We had such a wonderful experience—just a perfect delight, just a joy. Down the line we will see oil as a precious resource we just burned away. I climbed onto a ridge and looked down upon a vast oasis of tundra. You just can't comprehend the size of it and the humility it instills. We're just a small speck—it puts you in perspective with the whole world and our insignificance. Those are the times that touch the soul. I'm revising my goals because of it. The bleakness and barren openness gives it fullness. It's a paradox."

There was a deep respect and humility evident in the interactions of the group. Each was patient as others spoke. Each wished the vacation could last forever. Maybe, someday, we can restore the vitality of nature's splendor all over the world, as it once was. With large, expansive wilderness near everyone's home, we wouldn't have to fly half way around the world. For now, I felt like the luckiest, wealthiest person in the world. I still had another month here.

"We're going to hike out to the end of the point—do you want to come?" asked Fairbanks elementary school teacher John Schaver, one of the guides of the rafting group.

"Sure," I responded. The group had just returned from dinner with Isaac Aukluk. It was August 1. The sun was to set tonight. This was the perfect place to watch it, across a northern ocean. There was an unusual calm to the air. The sky was clear and sharp.

As we walked out, we were all awed by the scene. We were on the northernmost tip of the world. A vast ocean of pack ice lay still and calm to the north. The sun circled from west to north, diving ever lower until it skimmed across the horizon, illuminating the pack ice in enchanting reds, oranges and yellows. This would be the fourth day the sun set, but the first day the sky was not cloudy.

Huge racks of baleen from bowhead whales lay strewn about the rocky coast. Bowhead whales are among the least known of the sea mammal specie, though they were nearly wiped off the earth by American and European whalers in the 1800s. Two-thirds of their fifty-foot-long bodies is made up by the whale's head. Baleen corsets—much like combs—filter out krill and other small crustaceans from the Arctic Ocean. The whale has long been hunted in sustainable numbers by the Inupiat people. Now, whaling is limited by international agreement. But the hunt has been questioned by environmental groups since the Bowhead is listed as an endangered specie, its survival uncertain.

The sun was in perpetual setting as it skimmed along the icy horizon. Dancing orange borealis lights illuminated the northern skyline as we returned. The complex array of light was shaded and patterned like an intricately laced quilt. Hours passed. The group returned to camp and retired to their tents. I was pleased to hear such a unanimous view of development from fellow travelers. But what of those who lived in the region over the long term, I wondered? I could not leave the boreal wonders. I grabbed my fishing rod and cast lackadaisically into the calm waters.

Along the jagged pack ice in the ocean, the sun reflected in a glorious array of color. It descended ever lower until it was but a sliver of a crescent against the Arctic horizon.

Over the night hours, the sun rose: first a crescent, then a half. To the south, white mountains shone in the distance across the vast coastal plain, illuminated by the rising sun.

Chapter 30

Inupiat: Native Whalers of the Far North

It was early August, and I had now been in the Arctic wilderness for for a month and a half. I had originally planned to reach Kaktovik two weeks earlier, by mid July at the latest. This is what I'd told my parents, showing them a rough map of my proposed itinerary. On July 22, I'd given a letter to Paul and Marie to mail home, but figured it would not have reached there yet (it can take weeks for mail from bush Alaska to leave). I was prepared for some concerned parents. I dialed the familiar numbers and waited for the answer. "Hello," came the expectant voice from my mom.

"Hi Mom."

"CHADDD!!!!!!!" she screamed into my ear, with a panicked tone I'd never heard. "Are you all right?"

"Yeah I'm fine. I'm in Kaktovik. It just took a little longer than I thought to get here. I sent a letter out with some people I met but there was no way to contact you. I guess you haven't gotten the letter yet."

"No. We were going to call in the rescue teams, but we didn't know where you'd be or what to do. Thank God..."

I described my journey, leaving the exciting parts for later. She repeated the words "thank God you're alive" at least a dozen times. I smiled to myself. If only she knew, not really comprehending what it meant to have a child—even an adult one at that—take such risks.

"I'll write a longer letter from Arctic Village."

"You're out of the wilderness for good, right?"

"I might visit Prince William Sound, I'm not sure. I'll let you know."

"Oh, I hope not. Well, definitely let us know."

"Will do." I walked back to camp.

Some hours later, an elder Inupiat woman approached on a four-wheel drive off-road vehicle—the standard transportation in Kaktovik. She waved hello as she passed my camp, stopping at the shore of the Arctic Ocean. Removing a fishing rod from her vehicle, she cast a pink pixie fishing lure far into the Arctic Sea. The pack ice had moved several hundred yards offshore, permitting easy fishing. I turned off my stove, grabbed my fishing gear and joined her at the ocean shore.

"How's the fishing been?" I asked.

"It's best in the morning and afternoon, when the sun reflects off the pixie," 70-year-old Perry Auklet explained. "The Arctic char swarm around Kaktovik in mid-July. We fish the beaches. Early August (now) is the lull period. In another week or two, whitefish will swarm. We'll net 'em by the thousands." There was a jovial charm about Perry that made you smile with her. Her wrinkled face and deep brown eyes read of wisdom.

Perry was dressed in a down jacket and pants. "Is that what you wear in winter?" I asked.

"Oh no. I'd turn into ice—like that," she said with a smile, pointing to a slab of pack ice floating by in the ocean. "White-man's clothes are worthless when wet. We live on the water's edge. We use 'em in the summer. It keeps our parkas fresh for winter. I make parkas from caribou skin, with the fur inside. They take much work to maintain but there's nothing like 'em. White explorers who came quickly bought our parkas to keep 'em warm. I'll be riding full speed across the frozen ice in negative 40 or 50 degree weather and I'll have to flip my hood off to keep from sweating. We know how to stay warm."

"What do you think about the proposed development of the Arctic Refuge over there," I asked, pointing south to the coastal plain. Her face changed immediately. She displayed a look of serious concern—a shocking change from the jovial humor.

"The white man can get money from the ground," she said. "We can't do that. We need some oil to heat and live with, but nothing like the white man. We are a friendly, close-knit people. When we get a whale, we share it with other villages who need it. We share it among our people. Oil brings greed and alcohol. I've seen it before. We need the sea for food. A spill—like that Exxon disaster..." She shuddered in alarm, recalling the Exxon Valdez spill.

Oil development would poison her and her descendants. The bowhead whale, seal, Arctic char, white fish and walrus are sensitive to crude oil. Being at the top of the food chain, toxins bioaccumulate in these predators, that then toxify the Inupiat who eat them. Unlike Valdez, the Arctic Ocean has very low tides—only a few inches here at Barter Island. Oil pollutants like benzene and toluene persist for decades in the Arctic and concentrate in fish and sea mammals eaten by Inupiat and travelers like myself.

Bowheads are highly prized by the Inupiat both for the 20,000 pounds of meat each of them posses that feeds whole villages and as part of their stories and songs. A threat to the whale is a threat to the Inupiat people. The Bowhead is now among the most endangered of all whales. Yet the Inupiat continue to kill many bowhead whales every year.

About 60 million years ago, shortly after the dinosaurs became extinct, land mammals ventured into the water. As they evolved over time, their front legs became flippers. Hairy skin changed to a thick blanket of blubber, nostrils moved to the top of their head, legs connected and broadened into flukes and they grew to enormous sizes and live for a long time—likely hundreds of years. Whales evolved into two groups: toothed whales, with 65 species; and baleen whales, with about 100 species.

Bowhead whales have 325 to 360 plates of baleen that filter small crustaceans from the Arctic waters. The huge baleen walls of bristled slats act as a strainer, collecting the plankton and releasing the water. Mature bowheads measure 50 feet in length and weigh in at 65 tons.

Bowheads spend the fierce winters in the Bering Sea south and west of St. Lawrence Island, where the warm Japanese trade winds prevent the formation of solid ice. In March and April, the whales begin their northward migration around Point Hope, Cape Lisburne and Point Barrow, following the breaking ice toward their summer range in the eastern Beaufort Sea off Canada. They feed upon the abundant krill. Krill are tiny crustaceans that eat phytoplankton, a plant that feeds on the nutrient-rich ocean salts. The whale has a reinforced upper head used to break through ice up to a foot thick to breathe.

After exterminating the most easily accessible whale populations in temperate waters, whalers moved to the Arctic in force in the 1800s. Bowheads were prized for the large yield of oil their blubber produced (70 to 90 barrels), and the baleen was used for corsets and household brushes. By 1991, more than 80 percent of the original population of Bowheads were wiped out by whalers, according to the International Whaling Commission which estimated the original population at 20,000. Inupiat say many times more whales once roamed the sea. Today, about 3,900 bowhead are thought to remain. Scientists are not sure if that is enough to sustain the species. They say oil industry noise and pollution at Prudhoe Bay and the Mackenzie Delta interferes with the migration.

Now listed as an endangered species, bowheads are protected against commercial exploitation. Under federal law, the Inupiat are permitted to take .55 percent of the estimated population, but average about 30 whales per year. While this certainly adversely affects the whales, policy makers hope that the small percentage will still allow for an overall recovery of the species, if its habitat is not further disturbed by oil development.

The whale is far more than food, blubber and hide to the Inupiat. It is an integral part of their spiritual upbringing. It is in their songs and stories. A successful hunt is an occasion for celebration. The whale brings the community together and it is a vivid reminder of the bounty of nature. In the Inupiat society it is a time of generosity and thanks. Ten villages currently hunt the bowhead whales as they migrate past. Eight participate in the spring hunt and three in the fall, with the Point Barrow Community taking whales in both seasons.

Twenty-five-year-old Lonnie Solomon is a whaler. Having grown up in Kaktovik, Solomon said his village is isolated, and he likes it that way. "We hunt whales in August." After the ice has receded from the coastal waters, ten boats leave to search for Bowheads. When one is spotted, they near the whale in their gasoline-powered boats and subdue it using explosive-tipped harpoons. Using this technology, the whales are killed and taken back to the village within a few hours. "Then the whole village comes out," Lonnie said with excitement. "We give to everyone. The captain of the boat that is successful gets half, and half is shared among the village. We also always give to other villages in need."

Despite extensive studies of the Bowhead whale as a result of its being listed as endangered, little is known about this giant sea traveler. Whales have large, complex brains comparable to that of primates. They have developed a communication and navigation system using high-pitched songs. Sound waves echo off structures and are sensed by the whale, providing a vast radar picture of the sea. These sounds can be heard hundreds of miles away and are used to communicate among the herds.

Now, oil development threatens the mighty whales of the north. Bowheads depend upon sounds for guidance and communication. But oil development brings seismic testing—sonic booms of 210 decibels, levels unheard of in the Arctic Ocean. Boat traffic, air traffic, drilling and general operations create more noise pollution which override the natural sounds that bowheads need to sense and communicate. Sound travels five times faster in water than through air. Sound is the primary sense Bowheads use to explore and live in their vast marine environment. Bowheads are known to dive from the noise of low-flying airplanes and from loud boats. Assertions about the impact of oil development on the whale are no longer speculative. Scientific studies revealed that oil industry development off Canada caused a marked decline in the bowhead whale use of that area.

Everyone I spoke with agreed that nearly all Inupiat people strongly oppose oil development and seismic activities in the Arctic Ocean.

Beyond noise pollution, and whaling, oil pollution is the biggest threat to the bowhead whale today. Every year oil is pumped from the Mackenzie Delta and Prudhoe Bay, more toxic pollution is released into the tundra and ocean. The entire food chain is being poisoned. Oil development in the Arctic raises the very real threat of a major spill. A Valdez-size oil spill in the fragile Arctic Ocean would be virtually impossible to clean. Should a blowout occur under the ice, it would not be possible to stop. The prospect of oil development leaves the fate of the bowhead whale, the Inupiat and the Arctic marine ecosystem highly uncertain.

Chapter 31

Locals Express Concern of an Uncertain Future

Rafting guide John Schaver suggested I talk with Isaak Aukluk, the Inupiat elder who had transported the group to the island. The crew of 12 had eaten a traditional dinner at Aukluk's house. I asked a middle-aged man walking about if he knew where his house was. He said of course he did, that everyone knew everyone there, and he pointed to Aukluk's house. I knocked on his door. His house was sturdily built with numerous sleds and some boat pieces neatly stored outside. Isaac welcomed me inside the darkened room. The house was small, cozy and adorned with all kinds of carvings and other art objects.

As important as hunting skills in the far northern extremes are the tight ties and congenial harmony that keep the society intact. Entire families, grandparents included, live tightly packed together, sharing the precious warmth through the long Arctic winter. Families lived together without need or desire for private space. Inupiat parents once slept in the same beds with their children and played with them continually. Inupiat babies rarely cry. But much has changed, and new problems now face these once happy people.

"The oil companies came in and we have all kinds of traffic. We can't hunt anymore with all the traffic," Aukluk said. "I was born here in 1922. I've been walking out to the Brooks Range hunting since I was a little one. The Porcupine Herd comes and breeds but there was not that many this year with all the traffic. The white man changed our life. The kids don't speak our language anymore. We lost our language, but we haven't lost our culture. We're still eating Inupiat food—ducks, caribou, fish, whale, seal.

"They have to be honest to this village. After they get their oil they're going to be gone. We'll still be here. But the caribou? If they start to do work here, nobody knows. I have no answers for that. I'm 69-years old. We've got six children and they're all up here. I have feeling for the caribou, ducks and geese. They're scared by all this traffic. It's hard to believe us, but caribou are scared.

"It's the oil spill—that is a real concern. Prudhoe has many spills. If they blow up over here, this area drains right into the ocean. Who knows. Oil companies say they'll work carefully. But Valdez is real to our people. We're subsistence hunters. Oil spills are real bad for the birds and wildlife. We see the pictures. Valdez is real to these people."

Barter Island is the ideal location for the Inupiat village, being located between the fertile waters of the Jago and Okpilak deltas. Kaktovik means "seining place" in their native language, Inupiaq. The people rely on subsistence hunting and fishing for 90 percent of their diet.

Fundamental to the traditional Inupiat way of life is the three main spirits: air, sea and moon. In the open Arctic expanse, blizzards can bring wind chills of -150 degrees that cause frostbite to exposed flesh in seconds and can kill in minutes. In this context, keeping in balance and harmony with the air spirit is deemed extremely important. The sea is the provider of nearly all the Inupiat food and much of their clothing. Moving and crashing pack ice and frigid temperatures make the sea a dangerous place should the spirits be angered by broken taboos. But it is also a bountiful source of life if its limits are respected, something the invading power structure isn't concerned with. The moon is an important light source—particularly during the two months without sunlight in the winter. The moon cycle is considered integral to the land animal spirits, such as caribou. Inupiat depend on caribou for food and for warm winter parkas.

Keeping in balance with these spirits means following the culture evolved over millennia and passed down through stories and songs. This culture is one of the most complex of native societies. What makes it thrive is that each person is a participant. Children grow up practicing stories of their own. They play string games that are said to connect them directly to the spirit world. Elders tell tales through the cold, dark winter months to keep their oral tradition alive.

The Inupiat live on coastal areas of the Arctic Ocean. From Greenland across polar North America, along the Siberian coast, and with their relatives, the Yupik and Aleuts along the Aleutian chain of islands of south Alaska, the Inuit and Inupiat people stretch across the furthest expanse of any cultural and linguistic group in the world. They spread quickly around 2,000 B.C. and have developed different sub-groups. The Inupiat live in northern Alaska, with the Inuit extending from Canada to Greenland.

Inupiat have refined their knowledge and survival techniques in the harsh Arctic environment for thousands of years. Their language and culture revolve around the Arctic world. Words have qualifiers added onto them that give different meanings. One verb can have 600 meanings depending on the qualifiers. This precision allows Inupiat to describe the exact position of a seal on the ice with one word.

Inupiat rituals, beliefs, taboos and ceremonies discourage over-hunting and instill a respect for all living creatures. They promote a harmony between earth and people, in an interconnected web. Integral to the spirit world are the creatures and phenomena the Inupiat deal with every day. The seal, walrus, caribou, Arctic char, whitefish, beluga whale and bowhead whale each have a soul. The paradox of living is that a soul must be killed to sustain the Inupiat. It is in seeing the transcendent spirit world that the Inupiat can make sense of this.

Integral in the balance of life are predators who consume other animals. It is the sacred hunt that solves this paradox. Stories tell how animals willingly give themselves to the Inupiat to be taken, with the understanding that their souls will be returned to the spirit world for rebirth through proper ritual and respect. The belief creates a sense of empathy toward these fellow souls that makes this subsistence hunting far more humane than white America's "sport" hunting massacres of whole herds of seal, walrus, whale and musk ox. It is those massacres, and not the hunts by native peoples that have caused the current ecological crisis that has so harmed those closest to the Earth.

When Alaska was established as a state in 1959, Inupiat children were sent to far away cities for school. Children were punished for speaking their traditional language and rewarded for speaking English. The effect was a loss of much of a culture spanning millennia before Christianity. The American Indian Movement of the early 1970s served as a catalyst for Inupiat pride. There was a resurgence in relearning the traditional way and a questioning of what the white man's true motives were. Now, in many villages, Inupiat learn their traditional language alongside English. Those living along the Arctic Coast still practice subsistence hunting and many retain spirit world beliefs in addition to considering themselves Christians.

Traders first brought the wonders of industrialized society to the far northern lands in return for Arctic furs. Steel knives, pots and pans and bright jewelry were the first to come. Alcohol followed. Firearms made subsistence hunting easier. But it wasn't until thousands of dollars came from government jobs through the Alaska Native Claims Settlement Act of 1971, that transportation changed from the traditional dog sled, paddled canoe and walking to snowmobiles, outboard motors and all-terrain vehicles. Housing also changed from the traditional homes dug into the permafrost and abandoned each year to permanent wooden structures built on stilts to keep the permafrost from melting.

These changes have created a reliance on money that keeps the Inupiat dependent on the economic system in a land without private employment. Shipping materials from the lower 48 often costs as much as the actual material. The wooden homes on stilts shift with the unsteady permafrost and doors rarely shut right. The houses are often drafty, requiring vast amounts of fuel oil to burn, which itself must be flown in at great cost. While dog teams no longer need to be fed 200 pounds of fish per week, gasoline is expensive.

Snowmobiles and four-wheelers break down. Each costs $6,000 or more.

Only a few people in most villages are steadily employed, and most of them are not happy about being confined inside every day, away from their hunting life. The Bureau of Indian Affairs hires some as teachers while some work for the village council. Some furs are traded and Inupiat carvings are sold, but rarely is enough made for fuel alone. Many receive government welfare and food stamps, while others work seasonally to provide money. The Inupiat chose to incorporate under the billion-dollar settlement that paved the way for the Trans Alaskan Pipeline. Money from the settlement and from leases with oil companies on Inupiat land financed the community center, fire station, health center and more. But that money is nearly gone. And they have created an infrastructure based on petroleum and continual maintenance, both of which require enormous amounts of money. Still, the Inupiat oppose drilling in the Arctic Ocean, despite the fact that they would make money from it.

The 224 residents live in a grid of gravel roads and small wood houses. The town was strewn with sleds, dogs tied up at stakes, snowmobiles, nets and old boats of various sizes and degree of decay. Once, there was no garbage because everything was made from material that would burn cleanly, decompose or be eaten. Now rusty barrels, automobiles, snow machines, four wheelers and other junk dot the landscape. They are destined to clutter the island for centuries unless removed and recycled.

The last 20 years has brought much change to the island. The Trans-Alaskan Pipeline was stalled by the fact that the Territory of Alaska had been purchased from Russians who had no treaties with the native landowners for nearly the entire area. In return for 90 percent of Alaska taken from the native people, Congress passed the Alaska Native Claims Settlement Act in 1971, which provided $1 billion to Alaskan Natives. The Natives were left with 40 million acres, which were divided among the various nations and villages. In order to tap the enormous amount of money, villages were required to become corporations. Societies once ruled by the wisdom of councils of elders turned into for-profit businesses run like other corporations.

The North Slope Borough belongs to the Inupiat Corporation. It is larger than the state of Utah with a population of 6,000. Corporate leaders leased much of its land to oil industries, over the objections of many elders and those thinking about future generations. The corporation has received millions of dollars from oil industry activity, making Kaktovik one of the wealthiest local governments in the country, while jeopardizing its future with toxified lands and pollutants that invariably end up in the Arctic Ocean.

Kaktovik Inupiat Corporation owns 92,000 acres of the coastal plain across from the island—land potentially rich with oil. The corporation stands to make millions of dollars in royalties should the Arctic Refuge be opened to oil development—without having to do any work. Kaktovik's Inupiat Corporation Vice President is Herman Aishanna. He is also Mayor of Kaktovik. I met Aishanna in a small office in the community building after the village meeting. After the village representatives left, Aishanna sat back in his chair, sipping a mug of coffee and like so many, smoking a cigarette.

"We originally built our homes on the point that is now the landing strip. The U.S. government decided it would be a good place for an airport and forced the villagers to move," he said, shaking his head in displeasure. In 1964, the Air Force asked the villagers to move again for more military development. "This is how we have been treated." All the controversy over the Arctic Refuge brought Congressional delegations, the Governor and journalists to meet with Aishanna over the previous two years, taking much of the mayor's time away from subsistence living. "We catered to the Governor. But the summer is the only time you can work outside on sleds and things without 100-mile-an-hour winds blowing in your face," he said. "But I guess this is my job. When did you fly in?"

"I walked from Prudhoe Bay," I said. "I made it to the Jago, then was lifted by a helicopter the last part."

"You're the first one I've heard do that. You walked? Over the plain? What about the tussocks?" He asked.

"They were tough, but I got used to them."

"Did you see any caribou?"

"Yes, I saw a herd traveling up the Saddlerochit," I said.

"They must have been with the Central Arctic Herd," he said. From my research, they were likely with the Porcupine herd, but I did not question his comment.

"What about oil development?" I asked.

"We just feel that if there is going to be oil development, we want no damage done to subsistence resources. We are not necessarily against it, but we know it will happen no matter how much we protest. We want access to our hunting grounds and we want a say in how it is developed. Especially we want a say in the boat docks that are directly in the path of the migrating whale we hunt in the fall. Opening ANWR would provide good employment and more of a tax base that could be used for education, village services and health care," he added.

"When I first came here in 1958 there were a hundred people and they still used dog sleds. Through the North Slope Borough and through federal agencies we built all the houses, the new school, fire station, health clinic building, and all are maintained by the North Slope Borough. But everyone is talking about the oil declining and the money is declining."

"With all the changes, is the Inupiat culture still alive?" I asked.

"The children no longer speak our native language. But the culture survives, through subsistence hunting," he said. "But all you visitors and especially the Fish and Wildlife Service are scaring the game. I doubt if 20 caribou have been harvested this year. That makes us boiling mad. When the caribou come the Fish and Wildlife Service want to be the first to see them. They spook the herd. One time I was invited to get on board an aircraft to take pictures of snow geese. I couldn't believe it. I felt sorry for those poor birds."

I nodded in understanding. "As you said, current plans are for the two ports that would block whale migration, and the oil industry also hopes to develop more in the Arctic Ocean around here as they have near Prudhoe. Would you favor the development and all the money it would bring, even if it risked the bowhead whale?"

He leaned back in his chair. "No amount of money is worth taking away our whale. Let me show you a map." We walked down the hall of the community building, where he showed me several maps of the village. "This is where the whales migrate, right through this channel between Barter Island and the mainland. Ports would block that. I should make a documentary of the Bowhead whale. Then maybe people would care more. I've seen them feed just 50 yards off shore. Don't let them build the ports. Inupiat know the importance of protecting the Bowhead whale more than anyone."

I met 21-year-old Sharon Thompson in Kaktovik's Laundromat, while I unsuccessfully tried to clean the soot from my jacket and pants (from cooking and warming myself over so many fires). Thompson, who grew up on the island, said she, like most in the community, is opposed to oil development in the Arctic Refuge.

"The people going to the meetings are interested in the economy," she said. "The people who don't want it are not the movers and shakers of the village. There are a lot of people who are against it. It is beautiful up here. We are lucky to live here. Living in a peaceful place is far more important than a big paycheck. I worked at Prudhoe. It's ugly and so industrialized. It is so beautiful here—like no place I've seen. I've taken it for granted but I realize it may be gone."

Like most of the villagers I spoke to, Thompson fears that oil development will bring the crime and a general lack of concern for the fragile land that is so rampant in Prudhoe Bay and Deadhorse. "I like the closeness of the community. If someone needs help, everyone will help. If your house burns down, you know you have a place to stay and a sense of security. If ANWR is opened, it will be overrun and we'll lose the closeness."

While in the Kaktovik store buying food, I met a college student, Aaron, who was working as a cashier. While a student at Washington State University, Aaron roomed with the son of Mark Simms, an Inupiat who runs a food store in Kaktovik. Aaron was invited to Barter Island, and he decided to spend the summer in

Kaktovik working at Simms' store. He welcomed the opportunity to visit another part of the country It had long been his dream to see Alaska, and he recalled the cabin fever and boredom he felt while forced indoors in cities.

The Simms' adopted Aaron for the summer and took him on several fishing trips. "I love watching the ice floes and the brilliant evening sky," Aaron said. He also joined an extended inland expedition to hunt caribou. He was successful in both, with nets full of fish and four caribou shot during the hunting trip. He said the Fish and Wildlife Service is hated by the Inupiat because they interfere with hunting. On one hunt they followed caribou for five hours only to have them scared away by a Fish and Wildlife Service plane. The hunters were so mad. "They shot at the plane," Aaron said.

Aaron knew everyone who came in on a first-name basis, sparking conversation with them. He informed them that the plane with the government checks would not come today. But residents don't go hungry, even if their pay is slim or late. The Simms store runs on credit, and most who came in added their purchases to their credit. "There is a sense of community on the island," Aaron said.

Chapter 32

Steve Porter

Now it was time to figure out how to get to Arctic Village for the upcoming International Indigenous Peoples Treaty Council. Commuter flights from Fairbanks were reasonably priced and frequent. But there were no direct flights from Kaktovik to Arctic Village. I'd have to fly to Fairbanks then backtrack to Arctic Village—for about $450—ouch! How was I going to get to Arctic Village? While camped with the backpacking group that had waited two days to go into the refuge, the skies finally cleared, and their pilot, Steve Porter, landed on the gravel strip in a white and blue single-prop Cessna, the standard plane of the bush. Giant all-rubber tires showed that this was no ordinary plane, it was designed to land on some of the roughest "runways" in the world. Trying to find the most opportune time to butt in, I said "I'm looking for a flight to Arctic Village. I'm on an extremely tight budget, though."

"The going rate is $360 per hour and that's a two-hour flight."

My jaw dropped—$720. That was more than I'd paid to fly to Alaska.

"But, I'm going there to pick up another crew in a few days," he said. "I'll take you for half that—$360."

As a student, I was not in a good financial situation and that was an enormous sum of money. But in the dangerous flying conditions of the Arctic—and for a one-passenger flight—I knew that was a good rate.

"I'll call around a bit first. How can I reach you?"

He gave me his card. "That's the best deal you'll find," he said.

"I'll probably take it then," I said. "I'll call around today and let you know." Steve's price was indeed the best. I called him back. "I want to take the flight," I said.

"I'll meet you at the hangar camp sometime today."

"Great," I said.

Steve arrived on his four-wheeler, and began tinkering with the plane. While he refueled the tank, I asked "What's it like being a bush pilot?"

"It's the tundra that keeps you going," he said. "It's so beautiful." Steve's four-passenger Cessna held fuel in each wing, requiring him to fill both tanks.

"Isn't that an odd place for fuel," I asked.

"No. Spreading the weight out gives it stability," he said. "If it were centralized and you got in a tail spin, you couldn't get out." I felt hypocritical using so much petroleum to travel. But, I reasoned, he was making this flight anyway.

There was something very alluring about flying in such a small plane. I handed Steve my gear, which he carefully tied in place in the rear of the plane. Bad weather had already delayed us many hours, and light fog wisped about Barter Island.

"I don't know if the weather's clear enough or not, but we'll give her a try," he said. Seeing the concerned look on my face, he said, "Don't worry, we'll just turn back if it's too cloudy—I'm just not sure how it is over the mountains."

Flying due south about 1,500 feet up, the tundra was a web of pentagons splashed with lakes of various shades and hues of blue. Tundra streams meandered through the golden coastal plain, connecting pools of water like beads of blue strung together with dark green thread. Mile upon mile of tundra plain rolled into the horizon on all sides. Bogs of reddish sphagnum moss appeared near lakes, which I was all too familiar with from my journey across the plain. Though they appeared mucky, the water flowing through was clear, though hiking through them is tough. It was from my recent experience on the ground that made the view from above so much more interesting.

We hit a wall of clouds and Steve banked the plane in a tight turn, flying close to the tundra down the Jago River. Passing Camp Bitty, I recalled my predicament a week earlier, and my gratitude for being rescued. The river was now turquoise and clear, radiating its clean beauty to the world. What a change from the flooded torrent several days prior. Channels braided wider and wider through the gravel riverbed as we traveled farther north onto the plain. We were directly over what the oil industry hopes will be their new industrial home.

Across the Jago River with its wide, braided channels of gravel, we saw no scars at all. The river meandered through the golden tundra carpet with no signs of human interference. We were flying only a few hundred feet up. To my left, I gazed across miles of coastal plain to the pack ice and blue open water in the Arctic Ocean. Out my window to the right, I looked south across the rolling foothills, building up to the majestic giant mountains with gray, steep slopes and white caps where the snow never melts. We passed a stream and I followed its watershed from high up where it fanned into little channels to the delta where it entered the Ocean. All was as free as through time.

One creek snaked back and forth almost in circles, traveling at least three miles back and forth for every mile to the ocean. Clouds obscured the higher mountains beyond the foothills, but there appeared to be a clear space below them, which Steve hoped would connect to the other side of the mountains. As we approach the Kongakut, which flows within 12 miles of the Canadian Border, the coastal plain shrank. From more than 200 miles wide west of Prudhoe, the tundra plain narrows into a 7-mile funnel at the Canadian border.

The Kongakut cuts a deep, wide valley through the mountains, then spreads through a two-mile wide gravel basin before reaching the ocean. We turned sharply to the south, following the Kongakut. As the plane banked for the turn, I looked straight down from my window at the river. The clean-flowing, wild watershed was magical and enchanting. In the Arctic, sparse ground cover permitted a view of the entire river as it cascaded toward the ocean. Steve descended to within a few hundred feet above the light blue, translucent water.

The river turned to the east and the foothills grew into ridges. Clouds closed down until we were flying about 150 feet above the ground. The clouds formed a wall directly in our path.

"I've seen enough," Steve said. "We can't go over the top or underneath it. We'll fly back to Barter Island and see what tomorrow brings." I was thrilled—we would fly over the coastal plain again.

Seeing my fascination, Steve said, "It's really not flat at all. That is one of the beauties of the Arctic. It is such an expanse of open space—it's like mirages all the time. People think it's flat but it's rolling. You can see it by flying 200 feet above the ground—here, I'll show you," and we descended far closer than 200 feet. "If they put pipelines and road out here, it is going to mess up your perspective," he emphasized.

It is so incredible here. All I can see is untouched wilderness.

Ascending, Steve said "We're 300 feet above the ground and you can't see Barter Island. Usually you can see it from here. Maybe it's fogged in or something." I wondered if we would be camping out in the wilderness tonight—something bush pilots often do when airports were obscured by clouds or fog. I longed to be in the wilderness again. Cotton grass dotted the tundra. Steve descended to between 10 and 20 feet above the rolling tundra. Trying to act relaxed as I gripped a hand hold tightly, I looked Steve in the eye as he turned to say, "The Arctic cotton is just like snow," before turning his eyes back and pulling up to avoid hitting a hill. We rushed by at 130 miles per hour, flowing up and down with the tundra, as if we were hovering. The tundra rushed by below, moving slower toward the horizon. Lakes and streams whizzed by.

At the Jago River, we encountered a caribou and a calf trotting southwest—the last of the great herd that had massed here 180,000 strong six weeks earlier. They stopped and stared at us. Moments later, we came upon a herd of about 60 musk ox just east of the Jago River. They immediately formed a giant circle facing outward and stared up at us.

Steve circled around with wings nearly perpendicular to the ground, giving me a direct view of the huge primordial giants from my window, before flattening out and flying just to the right of them for my viewing pleasure. They were exciting to see, but nothing compared to encounters on the ground. While I gazed at the caribou and musk ox,

Steve looked in the other direction at the dark layer of fog just above the ocean. "We're probably going to be fogged in here," he said.

Approaching Barter Island, we crossed a narrow channel of the Beaufort Sea to the eastern end of the island. Steve swerved to miss a duck before turning and setting down to a bumpy landing on the gravel runway. I was not looking forward to setting up my tent again on the bleak, wind-swept island. With a storm approaching, Steve said, "You can stay at my house." He tied up the plane and we rode his 4-wheeler to the Kaktovik house he shares with other pilots.

I'd stopped by the house with Paul Banyas on the way into Kaktovik some days before. It had a large porch for changing into and out of winter gear and as a buffer to keep the cold gusts from directly chilling the interior. Unlike Inupiat homes which tend to have one large room that all share, it was divided between three different rooms with an upstairs where he keeps navigation and communication equipment. Steve lit the oil stove and worked on business accounting. I perused his library of Arctic books and magazines.

The next morning brought fog. Steve called for weather reports. Weather reports in these remote regions depend on whoever is bravest to go first and see what it's like. Seeing a helicopter land, Steve took out his radio, went upstairs and dialed some numbers. He asked for a pilot report of the coastal plain. "250 foot ceiling, light drizzle and snow flurries," the voice said over the radio. "I don't know how much icing you can take, there's a lot."

"It looks like we won't be flying for a few hours," he said. "Icing," he sighed with a shudder. "It's very insidious. Weather is a big obstacle. Most of the accidents caused by the weather are deadly. Most caused by mechanical error or pilot error are survivable." Icing is caused when ice builds up on the wings of the plane. Wings are shaped with a curved upper section and a flat lower side. The flow of air over the top creates an upward lift that is interfered with when ice forms on the wing tips. This can suddenly destroy the lift, making planes plummet to the ground.

Steve started flying 10 years earlier when he was 23 in Salmon, Idaho. While studying geology in school, he became interested in gold mining. "I dropped out of school, looked up an old timer and we worked for a summer. We were quite successful and I used the money from mining gold to buy an airplane. I came here and started flying for gold miners—there was more money in that. Eventually I got enough hours to get my commercial license."

Not only has Steve flown across most of Alaska, he has explored deep into the remotest wilderness areas on foot and kayak as well. He floated down the Cobuck River in a kayak for a 25-day trip in 1985. He's climbed Mount McKinley twice, at age 21 and 22, along with Mount Santon and Mount Renan. "I spent a lot of time in the mountains. You have to do it when you are young. I knew it was not going to last forever. You probably wouldn't believe it, but your energy levels start running down when you get older."

Steve also backpacked throughout the Arctic Refuge on a regular basis. "Since I moved to Alaska, it's been one long adventure." Now he has a wife and a 5-year-old child. Steve said he would probably make a lot of money should they drill in the Arctic Refuge in the short run. But the devastation caused by the oil industries would keep people from coming in the future.

"This is the last chunk of frontier. We haven't learned anything in the last 250 years with manifest destiny. We want to put pipelines on it, why? Because there aren't any there yet. They try and feed all this stuff to the American people that they are concerned about the beauty of Alaska. They only care about money. They say they care about the beauty because they want to placate their enemy: those who care about the earth. They just want to rape, pillage and plunder."

Steve chastised the U.S. Fish and Wildlife Service for shelving critical studies about the Arctic Refuge ecosystem because they would show oil development to be devastating.

"All knowledge about the refuge will be shelved by the government. The caribou is something everyone knows. It is the symbol of the Arctic. By the time they figure out the herd is decreasing it will be too late.

"We know that there is no way we can have a flawless jewel if we start hammering on it. It will crack. ANWR is fragile. We know that. It doesn't take a scientist to know that. It is a flawless gem. The worst fate for ANWR is there is a hell of a lot of oil under it. They'll find more and more ways to produce marginal fields, and it becomes something you can't stop. It is a real shame they want to mess around with ANWR. It's pretty sad."

After some pause, he said, "I only know three other people who have attempted expeditions like yours—two that made it. The past few years have brought more and more backpackers and rafters to the Arctic. I think there is more interest in it today than there was in the 60s, individually and collectively. But the temperature of the argument seems to have cooled down. You don't have any John Muir's this time. You don't have a Bob Marshall out there. There are probably more people who know ANWR intimately, definitely. But they are not professional writers or photographers."

Fog rolled in under the low ceiling. "It might clear this afternoon," he said. Giving up on finding weather reports, Steve launched into a series of stories about his bush pilot experiences. He worried that the crew in Arctic Village, his original reason for making the trip, would be upset at the delay, but emphasized that there was nothing he could do.

"It takes such a physical and mental toll. It is not a job, it is like being at war, and the attrition rate is about the same. There have been four (bush plane accidents in Alaska) so far this year. I can't count the number since I've been in it. It is dangerous. Most of them died with no money in the bank. One of the contributing factors is money. They are concerned about it and are pushing it too hard. Every year and a half that country is going to eat up an airplane. One little mishap and it's a total loss. We're insured to a million dollars, but a million bucks is nothing. There isn't any reason for pushing the weather or pushing the schedule. You hurt someone and that's it. There is no schedule. You try and get the work done and those who hired the pilots are still pissed.

"Low ceilings of visibility in the Arctic are very common. You have to plan for contingencies. We often get lulled into thinking things will go our way. Then we look for someone to blame. There is no blame in the Arctic. There is just the Arctic. If you don't have knowledge and flexibility in the Arctic you are going to break. Mentally and physically break.

"People don't realize there are the four constraints: time, weather, space and energy. They figure out the three, then the weather is bad—you are supposed to control that. I've had people who were delayed say 'I hope someone leaves you stranded in the wilderness for a week.' I say 'I've been stranded for longer than that.' In a survival situation there is a certain amount of luck, but anyone trying to blame someone is wrong. You put yourself in the situation, you get out of it. You put the blame where you want, but the Arctic has no conscience. The Inupiat know that."

Steve flew for the fishing industry across Prince William Sound every day for two years. It required two hours flying 140-miles-per-hour to travel from one end to the other. "It is so immense, so intricate. With the 9-10 feet tides you have to re-learn it at different parts of the tide. If you've only seen one tide, it looks like you've never seen it before at another tide. There is often a low 200-foot fog. On clear days I climbed to several thousand feet and learned the crags.

"Prince William Sound used to be a lot like ANWR in that it was a pristine, untouched ecosystem," he said. "That place was amazing. It was incredibly prolific. It was really one of our only resources like that in the world. It had many species, diverse sea otter habitat and was the fish breeding grounds for the world. You've got the largest pink salmon runs in the world.

"The oil industry had sold us about how they were an Earth friendly industry. They sure had us fooled. It was just a matter of time before she hit the rocks," Steve said with a shudder. He had seen the oily mess Exxon left. "You can't have both wilderness and development, especially in an untouched ecosystem like this. It is as primordial as it was, because they can't come across that border on the Canning," he said, referring to the river that marks the borderline between lands leased to the oil companies and the Arctic National Wildlife Refuge.

"I'm thinking of kayaking or hiking through Prince William

Sound after my stay at Arctic Village," I said. Steve, an expert kayaker, discouraged kayaking unless I had a good sea kayak. "I would really prefer to raft the Hulahula," I said. It had been a gnawing urge ever since listening to the crew of twelve that completed the journey a few days earlier.

After thinking for a moment, Steve said he was flying to Grasser's strip in a little more than a week, and could offer me the same reduced rate as he gave me to fly to Arctic Village. I could raft from Grasser's to Kaktovik where Steve could fly me to Deadhorse. "Yeah, I'll do that," I said, jumping at the opportunity. That's what I'd really wanted, but I'd figured it to be cost prohibitive.

"Rafting should give you a chance to see the land without all the strenuous work of backpacking," Steve said. "It gets cold, but it will let you see the Arctic's autumn and winter."

"I really want to spend more time in the Arctic wilderness." I realized I did not have enough food for a two-week trip. "Let me run to the store and stock up on food—do I have time?"

"Hurry, the fog is lifting, but you should have time."

With a limited budget, I studied the high prices in the small store. I bought 20 pounds of rice, a large container of oatmeal, brown sugar, coffee, sweet and sour sauce and powdered milk. I did not want to go hungry this trip. Rafting allowed me to take more than I could carry. I returned laden with food.

"It will be a few minutes yet for the fog to lift," Steve said. Encouraging my decision to raft the Hulahula, he said, the only way anything will happen to save ANWR is if people see it. "It will become personal when they see how beautiful it is. It is the last crown jewel though, and it is the last chunk of the last bit of frontier left. But our expansion west won't stop. We can't keep our hands off it. We can't stop. It is so ingrained in us to keep going."

"We have the last bastion of true Inupiat culture right here. Their culture is intact. That's the beauty of it. The scary thing is, you can't preclude what's going to happen to this place. You've been to Deadhorse and Prudhoe Bay. Can you imagine taking an overlay of that and putting it here. It just won't work."

Chapter 33

Over the Mountains

After examining the clouds some more, and conversing with other pilots, Steve said, "Let's give 'er another try." I loaded my gear and food on the four-wheeler and we sped back to Steve's single-prop Cesna. As we lifted from the runway under the cloudy sky, Barter Island decreased in size. Soon we were engulfed in an expanse of icebergs extending about a mile north before turning into a solid sheet of ice. The Inupiat were waiting for the distant ice to break up for the fall whaling.

We turned south and climbed into the clouds. All was white until we rose above the low-lying clouds. Some 20 minutes later, I saw the Hulahula through holes in the clouds. The foothills grew in size until they formed beautiful, towering mountains between which were willow-lined valleys and cascading creeks. The Sadlerochit River was to the west. Beyond it was white-capped Mount Chamberlin, with its giant glacier in a high valley. Lake Schrader and Peters appeared like little kidneys from 9,600 feet up, with a deep greenish-blue color in the middle depths and turquoise near the shoreline. The tundra was like a carpet rising steeply from the blue lakes, into mountains.

As we passed over Mount Chamberlin, I saw many waterfalls in the unnamed valleys and creeks of the Brooks Range. We followed along the Hulahula, which forms a wide, "U" shaped valley, rising steeply at the side into high rock precipices and ridges. The river was a beautiful turquoise color that divided into numerous channels.

We are now flying above the highest peak at 10,200 feet. Huge glaciers and snow patches rest in the crevices of the grand peaks and ridges. The mountains are dark gray with almost black rock in places. Along the lower slopes, lichens and mosses form carpets of greens, oranges, reds and many other colors.

"It's a pretty impressive sight isn't it," Steve said. I nodded, not wanting to take my eyes from the awesome scenery to acknowledge his statement. We descended where the East and West Poluck creeks enter the Hulahula River, landing on Grassers' strip where Steve refueled from his fuel cache. Grassers is an old-time hunter who built the gravel runway to operate a hunting base camp. This is where I would be dropped off to raft the Hulahula after my stay with the natives at Arctic Village. We were in the heart of the Brooks Range. I was excited about the rafting trip I'd start here a week later. But first it was time to meet the Gwich'in at Arctic Village.

A sheer wall of rock towered above some hundred feet to either side as we flew slowly through the winding pass. We were engulfed in rock. Thick clouds blanketed the canyon just above, leaving only a few hundred feet for Steve to maneuver through in his single-engine plane. The turquoise clear-blue waters of the Hulahula gushed north down the steep valley toward the Arctic Ocean, smashing into boulders and plummeting down waterfalls on the way. We were traveling up the headwaters of the Hulahula River, as it meandered through the continental divide of the Brooks Mountain Range. The plane began to shake violently from air turbulence through the mountains. I gripped the hand loop tightly, remembering Steve's comments about all the bush planes that crash each year. Looking over, I studied the pilot's face. Despite the turbulence, he was calm.

Passing over the divide, the mountains widened into a fertile valley of tundra and muskegs. The water, now flowing south, formed the Chandalar River. Many dozens of miles down the valley, the river began to snake to an absurd degree. It flowed about three miles east or west for every mile south. About another hundred miles downstream, the water would enter the great Yukon River. Spruce began to appear, first as isolated, stunted trees, and after a while as thin forests with lakes splashed here and there. This was the northern limit of the tree line.

"See that?" Steve asked. I could barely make out a gray strip. Not until we were almost directly above did I see the small houses and the two main roads of Arctic Village. The small community blended into the wilderness, seeming an integral part of the landscape. In the miles of bogs and spruce stands, the log houses appeared insignificant. Bumping along the gravel runway, Steve pulled up to the hangar and revved the prop to clean any debris from the blades before turning off the engine.

Several other backpackers, waiting to be taken into the wilderness by Steve, helped me unload my gear. There were seven in their group and they were tight-knit, having traveled together for years. They didn't seem to mind a bit that Steve had been so delayed. "Have you eaten yet?" a gruff man of about 40 asked us. "No," I responded and he motioned us to a large pot full of stew.

Chapter 34

Caribou People

Holding the caribou leg in my hands, I pulled the tough meat from the bone with my teeth.

"Do you like it?" Arctic Village elder Lincoln Tritt asked.

"It's excellent," I emphasized between chews of the juicy flesh.

Tritt smiled. The Gwich'in elder joked about the amount of food I was eating. I told him of how I had gone hungry in the wilderness and about my journey.

"Why didn't you make a snare and catch small game?" he asked.

"I don't know how, but I should have studied it. I did eat roots, berries and salads. I mainly ate fish I caught, but often the rivers were flooded or damaged by oil industry activity, and I could not get a bite."

"Well, you survived. That's all that mattered."

Tritt, a writer about the Gwich'in people and a part-time teacher in Fairbanks, immediately interested me. After eating, I joined him on a mound outside the dining area.

"All villagers take part in the hunts and the preparation of the caribou. That makes everybody equally important. Everybody is needed," he said. "This creates a feeling of reciprocity and kinship. The community is tied together in our daily activities. Only through cooperation can we successfully collect food, firewood and clothing.

"Since it is such a close-knit community there is no need to lie," Tritt said. "Everything is geared to the unity of the people. That is why the singing and dancing is so important. You won't find upper class or lower class in our culture. Everybody has the same things so there is no need to steal. Police are absent because they stand out. They are a threat to the unit.

"You have been out in the woods. Paper money won't do you

any good there. Politicians talk themselves out of things. Out in the woods, if you get in trouble, you can talk and talk and talk and it won't get you out of anything. Experience and knowledge, not money and material wealth, are the true measures of success here in the wilderness."

To teach their children the basic skills needed to participate in the community, parents and elders encourage the youth to observe the natural world and use their senses. Gwich'in children attend school provided by the government, but they are also taught the native ways by their parents and elders. Such socialization is taken very seriously in the village, Lincoln Tritt explained as we sat in a thicket of cotton grass.

"Our people consider children very pure. Their minds are blank. They absorb information. The parents watch themselves around their children," he said. "We learn a lot from the environment. More than from the schools. All of our knowledge is out there in the woods. Our kitchen, our workplace, our storehouse, our school are all out there in the woods. You don't realize freedom until you get educated. I'm sitting on top of the world. I've been educated in both worlds."

The Gwich'in people have been living off the northern land in Alaska for tens of thousands of years, making them one of the oldest cultures still intact today. Gwich'in means "caribou people," and it aptly fits. The Porcupine Caribou Herd feeds, clothes and forms the spiritual basis for them. It is through the integration of the deep environmental ethic of native spirituality in everyday life that they have remained in harmony with the land and animals. The caribou upon which they depend are revered as brothers and sisters with souls and spirits of their own. The Gwich'in respect the limits of their environment to keep in balance, enabling them to survive for tens of millennium.

Arctic Village is the northernmost of the 17 Gwich'in villages, located 150 miles south-southeast of Kaktovik, and 125 miles north of the Arctic Circle on the south slope of the Brooks Range. They built their village by a little stream that flows into the East Fork of the Chandalar River. The stream connects a strand of giant lakes, including the mighty Big John Lake, which is larger than Lake Schrader. Fish are abundant in the stream as they migrate to and from the lakes. Houses are clustered. Their small wooden design fits right into the environment. Being off the grid, the village constructed a shower and laundromat facility and a community solar-powered freezer for storing food in the summer. The solar panels turn to face the sun through the day.

Many Gwich'in had come to the International Indigenous Peoples Treaty Council from the neighboring Gwich'in village of Venetie, Arctic Village's nearest neighbor about a hundred miles away. One of them, Gary Simple works for thirty days a year as a fire-fighter, earning $5,000. He uses this money to support his family, for gasoline and maintenance of his four-wheeler and his snow machine. "We get by," he said. "We don't go joy riding, we use them to hunt and fish." His mother makes bead jewelry which she sells to tourists in Fairbanks. Other villagers earn money by trapping. Villagers in both Venetie and Arctic village also fish along the Chandalar River. Simple said he fishes right in front of his village. He once owned a boat, but traded it with another villager for an off-road vehicle. "We have that kind of relationship in the village," he said. "Nobody tries to cheat anyone."

In addition to the direct environmental damages to the Gwich'in people, Simple said development would destroy the culture by enticing many of the villagers into oil industry jobs for the money. Doing so would divide the village in two and greatly increase the alcoholism and suicide rates, he said. "We see oil as a threat not only to the caribou but to socialization."

The building of the Trans Alaskan Pipeline in the early '70s caused a serious disruption in both Venetie and Arctic Village that nearly destroyed the villages. "We finally are a community again," Simple said triumphantly. "In the pipeline years, we lost it. Now we got it back. More people are at meetings. Back in the pipeline years, nobody cared. They had so much." With their income coming from a foreign source, many Gwich'in felt like most in America, independent of the health of the wildlife, and some shot animals just for the fun of it. "Now they are going to disrupt it again. This time," he said prophetically, "our people will die."

I sat outside my tent, writing, when two young children approached.

Six-year old Rockie John picked up a straight stick lying near my tent. He threw it into a mound of soil nearby and it stuck. "You can sharpen it and catch fish," he said.

"Do you fish?" I asked five-year-old Lemmatth, who was accompanying his brother.

He nodded his head shyly.

"Have you caught any fish?"

"Yeah."

"How many?"

He opened and closed his hands over and over and over.

"We catch all kinds of fish," Rockie said.

"Let me show you how to catch fish," Rocky said as he threw the spear again. It stuck deep into the mound.

"Good job!" I said.

Rockie pointed to my water bottle, "Coffee?" he asked

"No, it's water. Do you want some?"

"Yep."

I opened it and handed it to him. They each drank a good bit.

"Stay longer. You can hunt caribou," Rockie said. A raven swooped by and they dropped their spears. "Sacred bird," Rockie said and they ran after it, hiding behind small spruce trees to keep from scaring it.

Later, one preschool-aged girl was asked how late she was allowed to stay out. "I've got to get home early tonight—by 4 a.m.," she said. Although to an outsider, Gwich'in parents may seem negligent, with the 24-hour sunlight provided by the Arctic sun, this seems only logical. Tritt said they are allowing their children to learn by natural curiosity. Here there are no highways or busy roads. Despite this freedom—or perhaps because of it—the youth were remarkably well disciplined. The children were often present during the conference workshops and ceremonies. Although usually polite, when a child began to be disruptive, one look or word from an adult would quickly quiet him or her.

Villagers need little money, since they make much of their clothing from caribou skins and cook and heat their homes principally with wood. But electricity costs 78 cents a kilowatt and they, like the Inupiat, use money to buy guns and ammunition, 4-wheelers, snow machines and, gasoline to fuel them. This money is earned from trapping, government jobs in the village and fire fighting during the summer. But this seasonal work takes people away from the village for extended periods and is not dependable.

In an attempt to create a sustainable village-based economy Arctic Village Council made a circle of buildings representing the daily life of the village. The tribal government is advertising the model community as a tourist attraction. They are also considering building a fishing lodge on Old John Lake, which lies about 10 miles east of the village. The lake is renowned for its giant lake trout. All development goes through the council of elders, which considers very carefully the long-term impacts of each activity. This is far different from the corporate boardroom's bottom-line decision-making based solely on profit.

Lincoln Tritt said, "In my studies, I have found that today's society is based on the exact principles that the Gwich'in society was set up to prevent, namely greed, ego and power. All these are very destructive to the idea of unity, which is essential to the continuity of life on this planet. Our people see themselves as part of nature and are nurtured by it. For this reason they have developed a deep-rooted respect for it, much like a person respects their parents for giving them life."

Chapter 35

The Gwich'in Struggle

Wе were already working to get international protection for the Porcupine Caribou Herd when the oil companies proposed drilling in the refuge," said Arctic Village leader Sarah James before the gathering of native nations in the village's community hall. "Then, the elders met and said that the nation was threatened. When something threatens the nation, we must gather. The last one was 150 years ago. Gatherings are done to make a stand or take a direction. From June 5-11, 1988 we called the Gwich'in Nation together. This community hall was built in 30 days. The elders got together. We left it to the elders as was done a long time ago. We used a talking cane. We allowed only a native broadcast station to record it. We made a resolution to protect the caribou, and formed the Gwich'in Steering Committee with elected representatives."

The resolution states, "Now, therefore be it resolved that the United States Congress and President recognize the rights of our Gwich'in people to continue to live our way of life by prohibiting development in the calving and post-calving grounds of the Porcupine Caribou Herd. Be it further resolved that the 1002 area of the Arctic National Wildlife Refuge be made Wilderness to achieve this end. Passed unanimously this 10th day of June, 1988 by the chiefs and people of the Gwich'in Nation in Arctic Village, Alaska."

Sarah James was elected spokesperson for the Gwich'in Steering Committee. A heavy-set woman with bushy hair, Sarah is the godmother of Arctic Village, and the Gwich'in. She speaks in a loud voice and has a natural humor. When it comes to the fate of her people, she is all eloquence, and determination. She has traveled the world and nation, speaking in defense of her people, and of the caribou upon which they depend.

"For years now Congress has ignored my people on this issue," she said. "Maybe people think Indians are not important enough to consider when making energy decisions. Every summer people come up week after week to visit Prudhoe Bay and the oil companies. They fly over the Refuge and go to Kaktovik, but never stop in Arctic Village. They say transportation is too complicated, but they fly right over our village. Even when they are in Kaktovik they are only allowed to talk to the people who support development. We cannot understand this. It is my people, the Gwich'in people of northeast Alaska and northwest Canada whose future is threatened by this development.

"This is not just an environmental issue, it is about the survival of an ancient culture that depends on the caribou. It is about our basic tribal and human right to continue our way of life. The Gwich'in are Caribou people. For thousands of years we have lived with the caribou right where we are today. We're talking about an Indian nation that still lives on the land and depends on the herd. In my village about 75 percent of our protein comes from the caribou. It's not just what we eat; it is who we are. Caribou are our life. It is in our stories and songs and the whole way we see the world. People don't understand what is at stake. The Porcupine herd is 200,000 caribou strong and migrates across two countries. It helps feed 15 Indian communities.

"It's not just the caribou, though, it's the whole ecosystem that we're concerned about. It's about all the animals and plants, ducks and geese and other birds, and fish too. We still have clean air and clean water. We believe we have something to teach the world about living with the land. It's our responsibility to keep this land pure and pass it on to our children and grandchildren and so on for generations yet to come, both Indian and non-Indian.

"The oil companies try to say that development would not hurt the caribou, but they are not telling the truth. Our people know that. The elders say the birthplace can never be disturbed. Even during hard times it was always protected by our people's ways.

"Finally the caribou biologists are also finding out about that.

Now we see that the Central Arctic Herd around Prudhoe Bay is failing. Dead caribou have been found all around there, especially near Nuitsuk. Last winter all the villages that hunted those caribou saw skinny animals where the bone marrow is all red and runny when it should be white and firm. They are also having trouble with their calving with many cows aborting their young in the winter. After almost 20 years pregnant cows and cows with calves still avoid the haul road.

"Before, they told us they could take oil out safely from Valdez; that if anything did happen they were ready to clean it. You should ask the native people of Prince William Sound who don't have anything to eat and have to buy store food now.

"If our country could go back and do it over again, would you vote to allow them to kill off the great buffalo herds, and destroy the Indian peoples that depended on those buffalo? I don't think so, but Dances With Wolves isn't just history. This is exactly what the Gwich'in could face if development goes forward and the caribou were hurt.

"We are a caribou people. We live with the Porcupine herd. It is so important to us. It is the way we live, the way we believe. The system works here—the whole ecosystem. The migratory birds come here. We are not just doing it for the caribou. We breathe the same air. We are not just saving ourselves, we are saving the world."

The International Indian Treaty Council I then attended was held in Arctic Village in support of the Gwich'in struggle. The community hall was packed with native leaders from all over the world. In the middle stood three Gwich'in elders around a large, birch-framed drum. They were situated above a smudge bowl on which a Raven feather lay.

They began pounding the drum with three gray mallets. Boom. Boom. Boom. The rhythm reverberated through the room, uniting us in the rhythm like the beating of a common heart. The room was transformed from the barren wooden structure into a temple enlivened with great spiritual power.

The Gwich'in elder began with a high-pitched call. The faces of the drummers and singers reflected the seriousness of this gathering of Earth peoples. This was a movement to save cultures that have survived tens of millennia, but which are now on the brink of extinction.

Giddian James was chief of the 1.8 million acre Venetie Indian Reserve that includes Arctic Village and the village of Venetie to the south. He pleaded to those gathered in the community hall to help the Gwich'in struggle for survival.

"If the Gwich'in people let the development happen, the clear water will be gone. The land will be poisoned. This problem is not just Gwich'in, it is all over the world. A few individuals will make a lot of money by destroying the land and water. They care less about the future. We must make our point known to the outside. They threaten to destroy the air, water and land.

"They take us to school and they don't want us to speak our native language—they punish us if we do. They don't want us to eat wild game or wear our native clothes. They tell us not to wear our hair long. We held our head down in white man's country. Now we hold our head high. They took us out, but somehow we came back. We got a message from the Great Spirit."

*

Arctic Village residents danced around a giant rack of caribou antlers in the village community hall, performing the sacred caribou dance. Conference participants formed a large circle around the exterior.

Adorned in clothes made from the hide of their beloved animal, they danced chaotically at first, with little organization. Slowly they began to follow the oldest dancer. This represented the caribou's unorganized pattern in the morning until a leader emerges. Slowly, the dancers began to form a circle, and ended by coming together in the center and sitting down, imitating how a herd of caribou sleeps close together for protection in the evening. They wore moccasins adorned with colorful beads and caribou skin jackets decorated with beads and feathers. Sarah James led 14 young dancers ranging in age from three to twenty. The older dancers lifted their feet in impressive synchronism while the pre-school-aged children simply walked.

Three middle-aged villagers held a drum flat between them with one hand, using their other hand to drum in synchronicity with a gray mallet. They chanted a heart-felt song so powerful I found myself swaying with the beat, spellbound. We were all swaying together as one, united in the great struggle for our Mother Earth.

While helping to prepare food for the conference, I talked with Lillian Garnett. Three caribou heads hung over a fire, roasting. Garnett was born in 1941 in Fort Yukon, a Gwich'in village about 100 miles south, because Arctic Village did not have a hospital. Garnett said she was required by law to go to school in Fort Yukon, forcing her to stay away from her village. "I had to learn the white man's way," she said. "But they never said why. They said you have to get away from the Indian way." After graduating from high school, she moved to Cleveland, Ohio where she worked for ten years.

"When I came back in '71, everything was changed. They said 'Indian power.' There were a lot of programs for the Indian people—I couldn't believe it. More Indian people were going to college." Garnett now teaches the Gwich'in language at the University of Alaska at Fairbanks. "A lot of kids want to learn why they were never taught. The native language is alive here now. A lot of people know and use the language."

"What do you think about oil development here?" I asked.

She had been breaking apart frozen caribou meat while answering my earlier questions. Now she stopped and turned to look me in the eye. "I think they are going to really hurt us and our subsistence lifestyle. They are going to ruin it and take it away. The elders say the caribou were fatter 50 years ago, but the oil industry bothers them too much in their migration. They are going to ruin our water. They are going to ruin everything."

*

While hanging around native rights' activists, I was invited to visit a little gathering at Edward Sam's house on the east side of the village. Inside, the house was small as all the dwellings were, to best utilize the precious heat in this frigid land. There were only three rooms: an entranceway/kitchen, a larger living area, and a very small bedroom. A large stove made of a metal barrel stood out in the living room, surrounded by chairs and a bench. Venetie Chief Earnest Eric, Arctic Village Gwich'in Edward Sam, native rights activist AJ Ruloon, University of Alaska student Geoff Butler and I sat around the room.

"The oil is important to the Gwich'in people right where it is. When they take it out, it kills the animals. It kills the plants. It kills the people. It is important for the plants to grow and the animals to live that it just be there," said Eric. "For heat, we don't cut down trees. We use already fallen trees. In the Gold Rush days the people came and didn't respect the land or the people. Many people came in unprepared and we saved their necks many times. They wouldn't be here if it weren't for the Indian people. Now they still have no respect.

"Villagers use four wheelers, snow machines, outboard motors on boats and an oil generator to produce electricity, but it is nothing compared to American motorists driving their car to work every day. Gas costs three times more here, which discourages over-use. I still use dogs to trap and travel," Eric said. "We use the dead salmon that we find for dog food. We are a clean people here. This is the last frontier in the world that is still clean. I kiss the water because it is pure. And look what they want to do with it."

The next day, Arctic Village Chief Giddian James spoke to the conference: "What I came to realize a long time ago was our people were healthy. The land you see out here, my people walked that land and my people were healthy. They walk from here to Sheenjeck and beyond. Not too many people can do that today. I remember how we traveled this land when I was a boy. When I was six-years old I remember walking. Today people want to fly, people want to ride four wheelers, people want to ride snow machines. That is the difference today.

"As a Gwich'in people we keep our land clean. There is a lot of contamination going on around the world. When native people occupied the land, the air was clean. The water here—the lakes, the streams are clean. You can drink from it. That was the case 200 years ago all across North America. They sacrifice the land. The land is no longer clean. It's time for the other side to sacrifice. People do not need three cars. They do not need to run around the block in their cars. It's as simple as that. My people we know, let's sacrifice and quit mis-using what is available to us."

*

The following day, I went for a long hike to a high ridge far in the distance that Lincoln Tritt had pointed out as the place the Gwich'in go to search for caribou. My map showed it as Camp Look. I saw Ernest Eric, whom I had hung out with the night before, driving a load of people in a pickup and we exchanged waves. About a mile from the village, I was startled by two squawking ravens. The raven is a sacred bird. Villagers are forbidden to shoot them, because, as scavengers, they clean Mother Earth. They are honored with the raven dance and they are characters in many Gwich'in stories. The raven is sacred to both the Inupiat and the Gwich'in, two completely different cultures, as well as tribal peoples throughout the northern hemisphere, particularly in the far north. The ravens seemed to have magic in their watchful eyes. They flew about me, curious of the newcomer to their lands. I bowed to them, to show respect, then grazed on plump blueberries that grew in abundance around the village.

About five miles later, the gravel hunting road turned into a dirt path and rose steeply. I climbed above the spruce tree line to a glorious view of mountains, lakes and the meandering Chandalar River. Atop the ridge, I could see for tens of miles across the river valley. The village was a small speck in a valley of lakes, bogs and forest. Here was a culture that had lived sustainably from what the land provided, without leaving more than a speck on the landscape, for tens of thousands of years. Here was a land alive with the spirit and music of the birds, caribou, moose, bear, wolf and tribal peoples.

The conference ended in ceremony. "I have been taught a ritual. But I have not felt ready to perform it, until now," said Gwich'in Jonathan Solomon. He lit a smoldering dish of sage before the packed community hall, blowing and fanning it with a Raven feather until it was smoking. "This is the breath of the spirit. From it and through it we will be united in the common boat we all share." He walked around the large circle of participants, stopping at each one and fanning the sacred smoke toward them. The native peoples pulled the smoke toward them. When it came to me, I did the same, enjoying the herb's fragrance. Returning to the center, he explained the four raven feathers adorned on caribou antlers. "This is to the North, to the Great Spirit. This for the East represents birth. This to the South, growth. And this, the West, death, the passage to a new world."

All the indigenous people are connected. I see it now in this room. But the oil companies are sucking the blood from Mother Earth. They are sucking our very existence for we are a part of the ecosystem. We know we cannot exist without the 1002 lands of the Arctic National Wildlife Refuge. And we are taking action. We no longer despair. We are too busy to despair.

"The trees and ecology are on the way back to the top agenda, so we are on the way back to freedom and spirituality. Let us defend our Sacred Mother the Earth," the elder rallied to a global uproar of joyous agreement.

Chapter 36

Autumn Raft Quest

My mind was full of new awareness, new insight. From the Gwich'in, I felt a deeper attachment to the Arctic wilderness. Their stories told of heroic journeys and vision quests across valleys, streams, gorges, mountains, glaciers, lakes and rivers, each with a name and a history. Each, a sacred entity, respected for its timeless spirit.

Water is the blood of Mother Earth, trickling and gushing wild and pure through her valleys. Her tundra, grasslands and forests are her skin. Fire from the native campfires and from religious candles lit all over the world symbolizes her spirit. We are her caretakers and spiritual voice. But recently we have violated our trust, and instead of responding to her gifts of life, beauty and health with love we have poisoned her blood, befouled, paved and clear-cut her body, polluted her air and blasphemed her soul.

During the last few days of my stay at Arctic Village, my excitement at returning to the coastal plain bubbled into ecstasy, and I devoted much time to preparations. I would need a paddle to replace the one lost during the flush down Kekiktuk River. Arctic Village elders said paddles were in short supply. Searching through Arctic Village's small dump just north of the village, I found an aluminum pole, a broom handle and two boards about 10 inches wide and a little more than a foot long. These should work nicely, I thought, as I envisioned the finished paddles.

I would need to attach a board to the pole in a very sturdy manner. The Gwich'in talked of how they make pipes by slowly burning holes with iron rods heated on a fire, I collected some nails. I could heat them in a fire, and burn holes through the wood. I had plenty of wire saved for fixing my pack, which I could use to attach the pole to the wood. Thus, I was not only saving money, I was re-using good material from a dump instead of purchasing a new paddle from virgin material.

I was very low on patching material. The Arctic Village general store did not have any vinyl patches, but they did have some rubber patching material, which I purchased, though I was not sure if it would work. I gave my credit card to Steve to buy me a camera and a flannel shirt and I also bought an Arctic Village embroidered jacket, both for a souvenir and for added warmth for the cold weather of fall. I mailed home the journals I had filled along with other assorted items that I would not need, and went to the community dining area to bid farewell.

Trimble Gilbert and several other Gwich'in stood about talking. "I am leaving," I said, handing each of the Gwich'in a Daredevil fishing spoon as a small gift.

"Lake trout love these," Trimble said.

"So do northern pike," I said.

Lincoln Tritt said, "Thanks. Good luck rafting. Remember, there are two schools. Learn from nature's school here."

"Thanks again for the wonderful hospitality."

We lifted off the gravel strip, rising above the expanse of wilderness. Arctic Village was soon a speck, blending into the boreal landscape. We flew back as we had come, over the spruce forests which gradually thinned before turning to willow brush in the mountains. The Chandalar changed from an expansive river near Arctic Village to a raging stream crashing down from the mountain heights. The Chandalar-Hulahula Pass forms a large "S" through the Brooks Range continental divide. We descended into the deep valley at the headwaters of the Hulahula, between great walls of granite and shale. The plane bounced to a halt on the "runway."

We were surrounded by some of the highest peaks of the Brooks Range. To my east towered the Romanzof Mountains, with 8,000-foot white-capped peaks. White peaks dotted the jagged southern landscape of the continental divide I had just flown over. The Canning River started 12 miles to the southwest, first cascading south from high, glaciated peaks before rounding a wide bend westward and finally north toward the ocean. The Hulahula began some 15 miles almost due east, flowing west and south before turning to the north about 8 miles upriver from Grassers' strip.

I had not had time to make the paddle prior to leaving. Over a fire of abundant driftwood, I began the task of heating nails in the hottest coals, then pressing the tip against the wood piece with needle nosed pliers. The wood smoked, indenting a bit farther with each application. With six nails, I was able to rotate so I would always have a red-hot nail, making the job faster. For several hours I continued the chore. Mosquitoes were a nuisance in the 56-degree heat wave. Steve had predicted their numbers would diminish with the frost that had hit Kaktovik. It must not have hit here yet. By 11 p.m., with only two of the six holes finished, rain forced me into my tent.

I worked on the paddle and patched my raft throughout the early morning hours. The task took far longer than I'd thought. With proper tools I could have drilled the holes in no time. But when you're a hundred miles from the nearest store, complaining does little good, as Lincoln Tritt had said. Bit by bit I burned through the holes. Next I secured the wood to the aluminum pole with wire wrapped around and around, and duct tape to keep it from slipping. It was not the best of paddles, but it would do.

Rain kept me tent-bound throughout the afternoon, affording time to relax, read, write and think. There is nothing more soothing than the roar of a river combined with the rhythmic pattering of raindrops on the tent wall. Scores of miles from the nearest permanent resident, there was no roar of engines, no racket of machinery: only the sounds of the wild.

During another dry period, I set to repairing the raft. I was nearly out of vinyl cement, and I found that a small tube of superglue that I was relying on was dried out, useless. The three large holes chewed by the squirrel at the cabin a month ago leaked air despite hours spent trying to patch them. They were in the center air chamber. I worried whether I could travel without the center support of the raft. The two outer sections held the most air and would support me, but the center section normally supports the most weight and keeps the boat from sagging. My gear would be lower and wetter. Also, what if one of the other air chambers, or even both were punctured? With the temperatures plummeting as winter drew closer, this would be a dangerous adventure. I still had no wet suit or life jacket, and I would need to raft the Arctic Ocean channel to Barter Island.

I used the last of the vinyl cement in patching the center compartment. Blowing it up, I found that it still leaked. The rubber patches were not working on my vinyl raft. The noxious fumes from the cement gave me a painful headache. I stood up, staring at the raft. My raft was full of holes and I was already out of patching supplies. Enthusiasm leaked like the air from my raft.

I noticed holes in food bags that had been stored under the boat. A mischievous squirrel sat 10 yards from camp. "Aaaa!" This trip was doomed from the start. I patched up the bags with duct tape and moved the food to my tent, hoping bears wouldn't get any ideas.

Two hunters flew in, the plane buzzing right by my tent. The hunters stayed in Grassers' camp on the opposite side of the runway, a half-mile away. I walked over to visit them and see if they had super glue. The main tent was a large wooden semicircle-shaped frame around which was stretched white plastic. I knocked on the door and two men called "come in." The inside was comfortable, with a table and bench seats, and shelves stocked with canned and dried food. There were two middle-aged men, one a guide and the other the hunter. The guide was from a small village in southern Alaska. Like most Alaskans I had met, he had strong opinions about everything. He lamented about excessive government regulation on hunting, saying, "The Soviet Union just failed because of the same thing and the US is approaching it more and more every day." Neither had glue, but they offered me a beer and a seat.

"The government is dividing the people by blaming some groups and playing favoritism. The hunters, natives and environmentalists all share the same land. The government wants to divide and weaken," the hunter said.

Rain delayed my departure another day. Dark gray clouds loomed above and wind howled through the valley when I finally left shortly after noon on the third day of the trip. My gear was loaded on the front of the raft, atop two boards and a broomstick brought as back-up paddle material. They served to keep the gear above the puddle that invariably formed in the sagging middle. Cans, jars and well-sealed bags went first in my duffel bag, which was wrapped in a trash bag. My pack rod and dry foods wrapped in several trash bags were on top. Both were strapped to the raft. I tied my pack cover over the whole pile of equipment.

Previously I had kneeled in my raft, in order to afford the lowest center of gravity. But kneeling pushed my knees deep into the water, making them the lowest part of the raft and prone to slamming into rocks, as had occurred during the disaster a month ago. I found a new position that was quite comfortable, by sitting on the rear of the raft with my feet wedged into the sides and leaning forward. Falling out was also easier though.

My gear in place, I pushed out into the rain-charged river, hoping my makeshift paddle and patches held. The wind pushed upriver and to the east, requiring constant corrective paddling. The gusts made the task of avoiding boulders and fierce rapids challenging. I scouted the upcoming rapids from overlooking bluffs, planning my route. I reveled in the adventure and thrill of the river. Nothing compares to the exhilaration of plunging down waterfalls and charging through walls of waves, completely drenching the body with water as pure as the high, jagged peaks. Most Arctic rafters take along wet suits that keep the body warm even when wet. Most rafters also use bags that are waterproof. My loose-plastic-wrapped food and other gear were doomed to get wet. But I was on a limited budget.

The slower stretches required constant and full-force paddling to keep from beaching with the 30-40 mile per hour winds—so much for the easy way of travel. Unaccustomed to the paddling, my arms tired quickly. The makeshift paddle was awkward and cumbersome, but its wide surface afforded much power when I used it right.

The constant splashing of freezing water combined with the cold winds chilled my body. Despite the exercise from paddling and wearing all the clothes I had, my hands and feet became numb and useless. The winds increased, blowing me into boulders and the shore. Maneuvering a raft through rapids is difficulty enough with no wind. I was paddling full force just to keep from being blown to shore, affording little strength to avoid obstacles. Drizzle turned to rain, and after only a few miles travel, I carried the raft to high ground, calling it a day.

I had nearly two weeks left to reach Kaktovik, which was 80 miles down river and a bit east. That seemed plenty of time, and I loved the mountains. Hopefully the weather would improve. Just a few calm days and I could really travel.

Compared to the fancy outfitters with watertight bags and hundred-pound rubber rafts, my gear was pitiful. My food had already become dampened in spite of all the plastic wrappings. Paul had shown me a dry bag he had brought for his camera equipment. They are high-tech bags that are absolutely waterproof. They are also quite costly. My raft was cheap and already the center section was damaged beyond repair. But having lugged the 13-pound mass of vinyl across hundreds of miles of the most rugged terrain in the world, I could not imagine having taken a heavier raft. My fate and my craft's seemed intricately intertwined. Still, the scenery overcame all worries.

A golden eagle soared above. A wolf prowled high on a ridgetop. The caribou had gone south to their wintering grounds. The northern wind brought with it a new chill, a new excitement to the valley. Willows turned a soothing yellow, low bush cranberries and bear berries a fiery red. The change was slow, occurring first on north-facing hillsides in brilliant patches of red, yellow and purple. The willows about my feet were still green with hints of yellow on the lower leaves. Experiencing the change of seasons brought a feeling of belonging to a place like a home.

This is Paradise, Eden.

Chapter 37

Sharing the Hunt

My eyes opened to drizzle against my tent and the whistling of strong northern winds. It would be another cold day. My fingers numbed as I worked to find dry wood and start a fire in the heavy wind. The fruits of my labor soon warmed my hands as fire danced from the earth, spouting heat in the land of cold. A hearty pancake breakfast, with fresh brewed coffee left me feeling ready for the world. Soon I was battling the rapids in my little vinyl raft.

About an hour into my day's journey, I encountered the fiercest rapids yet, though nothing compared to what was yet to come. Scores of three to five foot diameter boulders lay strewn randomly through the 100-yard stretch of white caps. The river funneled through two boulders, leaving only five feet for my four-foot wide raft to fit through. Just upstream of the narrow route lay a boulder blocking the path. I would have to maneuver into place in the 10 feet of roaring current between the boulder and funnel and turn to fit through the two boulders. If I made that I would plummet several feet down then hit a four-foot wall of waves headfirst.

I would need much momentum to surmount the wave. And if I made it, the river plunged through 30 more yards of boulders before slamming against a jagged shale cliff and turning 90 degrees to the right. With the momentum from the rapids, turning that quickly would be quite a challenge. Portaging or lining my raft was out of the question because the shoreline ended abruptly in a steep cliff with the river raging against it.

Pushing away from the security of dry land, I paddled with powerful strokes that sent water broiling. Passing the boulders, I hit several large waves, which spilled over the raft. The added weight made steering and maneuvering impossible. My half-sunken craft was married to the current. Together we awaited our common fate.

A partially submerged boulder lay directly ahead. The front of my raft scraped onto it, jarring me to a halt. I flew onto my stuff. The raft and I were on top of the boulder. The current pulled the stern (back) down, filling the boat with water. The raft would soon flip. I jumped into the three-foot deep raging river and heaved the raft off the rock and guided it slowly through the maze of boulders to shore.

I untied and removed the gear, dumped the water out and tied my stuff back in place. I wanted to hike around the rapids, but scaling the cliff was out of the question. I sat down on a rock, staring at the rapids. I hadn't even hit the hard part. I was soon wet and shivering from the cold. I couldn't get much more wet. I might as well go for it.

Back in the water I went. I headed straight for the funnel. I maneuvered around the largest waves that lay downstream of large boulders, trying to avoid spilling water into the raft. I paddled hard to gain momentum as the raft neared the left side of the boulder that blocked the direct trajectory. Passing the boulder, I hit its wake, throwing me off balance momentarily. With a powerful sweeping stroke on the port side, I turned sharply starboard. Three hard "J" strokes powered the raft a few feet diagonally towards the funnel and a sweeping ark stroke turned the raft to face the funnel. The vinyl hit the left boulder, but I was far enough that it scraped off rather than stopping and flipping.

The raft crashed through the wave. Water was everywhere, nearly sweeping me along with it. Stunned by the sudden drenching, I opened my eyes to another dozen or so boulders placed to block passage. I tried with all my muscles to avoid the obstacles. But, with my craft bloated with water, invariably I hit every one in my path. The vinyl scraped menacingly across the boulders before sliding off with much help from the paddle.

Passing the boulders, the raft now headed straight for the wall of shale that rounded the bend like a guardrail around a hairpin turn. Only this guardrail was jagged and sharp. I paddled furiously to try and follow the river's sharp bend, but the momentum barreled the raft toward the rocks. I crouched on my stuff and thrust the paddle ahead of the raft to try and keep it from slamming the shale. I thrust forward with my paddle in front against the wall to try to protect the raft. I slipped and banged my forehead hard on rock. But I saved the raft. Blood trickled down my face. Stopping downstream, I wrung out my blood and water-soaked flannel shirt in the blustering winds and 40-degree temperature, happy to be downstream of the fierce rapids. I blotted the bleeding inch-long gash in my head with a wet bandanna.

Next came another set of rapids of equivalent challenge, then two more. Then, I scouted another set of rapids. They were the worse yet, forming one long stretch of white water for a hundred yards. Cresting a ridgetop to afford a better vantage point, I noticed two men on the opposite bank outside a large framed tent.

We exchanged waves. The roar of the river and the distance prevented any verbal communication. It was about 3 p.m., and I had hoped to go farther. But the drizzle, heavy winds and impossible-looking rapids just below, in addition to soaked clothes, a cut head and the opportunity to meet new people prompted a change of plans. I paddled across the river just before the rapids. With my equipment secure on high ground, I walked to their tent. It was the same kind of structure that the hunters at Grassers' had, looking like a small greenhouse but with white plastic. "Hello, is anyone there?" I asked.

"It depends," was the answer.

This should be interesting, I thought.

Two men came out.

"I'm rafting down the river but was stopped by the fierce rapids. I'll be staying nearby and thought I'd say hi."

"Come on inside," said the middle-aged hunting guide, Don.

The tent cabin was cozy warm and full of cooking gear, food and chairs. Don introduced me to Jim Block, who had paid thousands of dollars to shoot dall sheep, sitting on the far side of the tent, and Eric Wear, a hunting guide from a neighboring camp who I had met outside. Don motioned for me to sit down.

"Want a cup of hot coffee?" Don asked.

"Yeah, thanks."

I was thoroughly dampened but the tent was well heated. The hot liquid warmed me.

"Where are you from?" Don asked.

"Athens, Ohio," I said. "It is the more scenic, hilly part of Ohio."

Don was a hunting guide from Anchorage. He said, "You can fly for two hours and not see a building. There are not many places like it in the world."

"I've come to study what impact oil development would have on the Arctic Refuge," I said.

Jim, on vacation from Minnesota, said, "The problem with the oil industry is increased access. The haul roads bring more and more hunters and poachers."

"They'd have a hard time stopping it," said Eric, a guide from a neighboring camp. "They'll put a road right through here and it will end the sheep hunting."

Don said that he favored oil development, and that he was tired of outsiders telling Alaskans what to do. "The caribou do fine with oil development, Prudhoe Bay has proven it," he said. "You've got millions of acres of tundra out there. A few drill rigs aren't going to hurt."

I disagreed, telling how scientific studies showed that caribou tend to avoid development; and that the Gwich'in people had said the caribou in the Central Arctic Herd that went through the Prudhoe Bay development were sicker than the Porcupine Caribou Herd.

Upon mentioning the Gwich'in, Don bemoaned the giving of special hunting and fishing rights to Native Americans, and called the mentality of Inupiat as "like kindergartners."

The rain pattering the tent walls made the outside world inhospitably cold, creating a feeling of relaxed contentment among the company, a perfect setting for deep, animated talk.

"Want a beer?" Don asked.

"Sure."

"The problem here in the Arctic," Jim said, "is the environment is so fragile. It is not 100 but 500 years before it will recover. If I had my choice, I would have things just the way they are. It makes me mad that the oil industry is going to make a lot of money out of our national wild lands."

Eric had driven the haul road five times, visited Prudhoe Bay eight times and had been in Alaska during the pipeline years. "I remember them saying 'it won't happen.' The environmentalists fought it hard then. But when the millions of dollars were there it went right through the system."

We heard the sound of feet rustling outside. "Get a camera," came an exhausted voice. We exited to see two men slumped over with packs. They apparently shared the same cooking tent. Zeke, the guide, had a mustache and a rustic, hardy look. He had tied a set of sheep horns on his pack. Ralph, the hunter, was a shaven, charismatic middle-aged man, and the two together formed the best comedy act this side of the Arctic Circle.

Eric left for his camp, and the two men entered the tent. Noticing there were not enough seats for five, I made a motion to leave. "You don't have to go," Don said, and a seat was improvised from a cooler. We all opened another beer.

"Oh are my knees locked up," Ralph said. "It's his fault," he said, glaring at Zeke.

"Couldn't keep up could ya?" Zeke smiled back.

"All I saw was your heels," Ralph replied. "He wouldn't let me pass him. I fooled him though. I cut around a bluff and Zeke went up and over to try and beat me—he just couldn't stand following. He hit the bluff and had to come all the way back. I couldn't stop laughing."

Yesterday, the two had spotted a herd of sheep and watched them for hours. With wild herds, only the older sheep are legal to kill, so Zeke eyed the herd in his scope and told Ralph which one to shoot by ranking them.

"There were three lined up," Ralph said. "Zeke says 'the one on the left is number one, then number three, then number two.' Then another sheep came into view, and he'd say 'No! That one is number one, this is number two and there, there is number three.' Then another one would come. He'd say 'No that one's number one to the left. That one's three there's two.' I was about ready to give Zeke the gun."

"One sheep was clearly the leader," Zeke said.

"It stood for more than an hour while the others laid," Ralph added. "When one of the others tried to stand, he'd look over and they'd lie right back down. Just one glance. They weren't gonna mess with him."

"Some of 'em butt horns—quite a sight!" he said, with a reflective glance. "Finally I got a good sight on him and shot several rounds."

From watching it in his scope, Zeke thought Ralph had wounded the creature in the knee, and Ralph ran full speed up the steep slope to follow it.

"Meanwhile Zeke just took his good old time," Ralph chided.

"I was prepared to get another sheep," Zeke said, "but Ralph ran ahead."

It took the two an hour to reach the dead sheep, and they were surprised to see two fellow sheep standing by, mourning their fallen leader. "Those two sheep stood by him till the end," Ralph said.

Zeke pulled the meat from his backpack, and unwrapped the sheep's testicles and liver. "These are a delicacy."

Don sautéed them. Then potatoes and beans were placed on the stove. "Are you hungry?" Don asked me.

I responded with a nod and was handed a full plate of food. I waited to watch Zeke bite the juicy balls before digging in. Sure enough, the testicles were succulent and juicy. I couldn't help but shift in my chair as I ate, though.

"They're the best part," Zeke said, smiling. "There used to be herds of 40 to 50 sheep just a few years ago. Now they're smaller and less of them. You can tell how old they are by counting the rings on the horn." He showed me the impressive horns of the ram just shot, counting 12 rings. "He was 12 years old. They live for more than 30 years."

"How does hunting affect them?" I asked.

"It's nothing compared to the wolves. There used to be dozens of rams this size in herds three or four times the size today," he said, lamenting the change. He had written a book about hunting in Alaska, he said, but would not give me his last name.

Don showed the skull of a wolf in a bucket in the tent. "We shot that yesterday. They're killing off the sheep."

"Wolves have always been here. They help to keep the balance," I said.

"They're sheep killers," Zeke said.

I felt like saying "So are you," but with a mouth full of mutton, I didn't.

"I hope to leave early so I best be getting to bed. Thanks again for dinner and the beers." I said.

"Stop on by for breakfast if you'd like," Zeke said.

"I just might, thanks again."

I was up early, broke camp, cooked, ate and packed. As I was readying to leave, a plane landed nearby and taxied close to the hunter's camp. Realizing I had not asked about superglue, which I sorely needed to patch the center air chamber, I joined the crowd that had gathered around the plane.

"I need super glue or vinyl repairing glue to patch my raft. Do any of you have some I could buy or trade for?"

"No, sorry" came the five replies.

"Do you want breakfast?" Don asked.

"No thanks, I already ate and need to be going," I said, waving good-bye "Thank you again for the hospitality."

"It's the way of the North," Zeke said.

Clearing skies and a wind on my back made for perfect rafting conditions. I maneuvered through series of rapids, around sharp bends and back and forth around boulders with precision. The ride was exhilarating and challenging. Long stretches of shallow riffles where the river stretched wide forced me to line my raft and wade through the frigid water.

I saw a plane land just downstream. It looked like Steve's. I rafted down, parked and waded several channels to greet him. Steve flew in a man named Mark and his son for a hunting trip. By coincidence, I had met Mark at the Deadhorse airport. He owned Mark-Air, the airline I flew in on and I had talked to him in the airport at Deadhorse.

"What a small world. Remember meeting in the airport?"

"Yes, you have a beard now," he said. "We were all wondering how you did. Have you had pleasant travels?"

"Yes, this has been a very exciting and enlightening journey," I said.

"It's a small group of people in a giant wilderness," Steve said. "You haven't gone all that far," he said.

"I was rained in at Grasser's."

"You still have a week and a half. That should be enough time," he said, referring to when he was to fly out looking for me if I did not arrive at Kaktovik.

"My raft has some holes. Do either of you happen to have any superglue?" I asked.

Again, no one had any.

"Are you going to be able to make it with the raft?" Steve asked.

"I think so. Only one of three air chambers is damaged. But I'd best be going. These are perfect rafting conditions."

We waved good-bye. A golden eagle soared slowly by just 100 feet up, peering down at me. I noticed white specks on the ridgeline to the east. I beached the raft. Through binoculars, I watched a small herd of sheep walk dexterously across the steep heights of loose rocks and hundred yard drop-offs. Such amazing creatures sheep are—able to move effortlessly across such dangerous terrain without a hint of fear. I felt closer to them now, having learned of the threat to their population, and, ironically, tasted of their flesh. I felt they were a part of me and I would work to protect them. For starters, we need to reduce hunting quotas and increase enforcement of dall sheep and wolf poaching laws. It is hunters and development, not wolves that threaten the dall sheep.

Chapter 38

Earth Connection

Mount Michaelson, with a white cap on steep, contoured slopes of gray, stood behind closer slopes of green tundra and grayish-tan colored rock. Patches of bright crimson and yellow signified the changing season. The clarity of the Arctic sky made distant mountains seem close enough to touch, sharp in contrast, intricate with detail and overwhelmingly sublime.

The tundra was turning more crimson and yellow every day. The mountainsides were a patchwork of brilliant colors, glowing in the pure-blue Arctic sky. Just a mile down from where I'd met Steve, the river turned around an S-shaped bend of riffles and rapids, ending in a deep pool. A high cliff wall with a dark-gray, jagged surface rose vertically from the depths on the west shore, while the east bank was a flat beach. The river was deep and turquoise blue for about 150 feet, perfect for Arctic char to pause and rest on their journey upriver to spawn. Deep holes of slow water are usually loaded with fish.

The spinner plopped a few inches from the rock wall on the opposite side of the 60-foot wide pool. The lure vibrated as I slowly reeled it through the depths. The spinning spoon looks like the flashing light of sun on a frantically swimming minnow. When it was just a few feet from shore, a silver streak darted from the depths, turned and bit the lure, all within a rod length from my feet. With only a four-pound strand of monofilament separating us, I gave to the strong runs and took back line when the fish tired. The female char tired after some time. I waded in and grabbed the beautiful fish by the gill. Her skin was bright silver with a bluish lateral line, speckled with salmon-colored spots.

I put her on a stringer and cast repeatedly to the same spot.

After the tenth or so cast, I reeled the lure diagonally with the current. As I readied to pull it from the water and cast again, the lure suddenly stopped. I set the hook. My rod bent like a U. The water boiled in anticipation. The male char surged three feet out of the water. He was in the prime of his life, in the last struggle of his life. He was bright red with a hooked jaw and pure white lines on his fins. His belly was a bright red, his back a darker greenish gray. The fish was huge: more than two feet long and at least eight pounds—twice the strength of my fishing line. I would not be able to pull the fish vertically, but with enough line and patience, I could tire the fish and then pull him to shore.

The char charged across the river, stripping line from my reel. He jumped clear of the surface again. The fish shook above the turquoise-clear water. The hook held on by a tiny piece of the char's mouth. Using the advantage of the current, the fish charged downstream. I followed until we neared riffles and rocks that could snap my line. With my line nearing breaking point, the fish tired just before reaching the rocks.

We were in a stand off for several minutes. Slowly I gained line. The mighty Arctic char surged, stripping the line from my reel that I had just recaptured. I finessed each thrash by giving with my rod, yet keeping a light tension to prevent his throwing the hook. Then he stopped thrashing and stayed motionless against my tugging.

He surged once more, gaining barely an arm's length of line. He tired and I pulled him nearer to me. I waded down the steep shore until knee deep in the river. Just a few feet from my reach, he regained strength and jolted for the depths, stripping line from my reel. This time he became really tired. I pulled him within reach. Painted with colors as pure and brilliant as nature creates, the Arctic char was fresh, alive with power.

I pulled hot coals from deep in the fire and spread them flat. I cooked the fish until perfectly juicy and tender, when it just flaked with my spatula. "Thank you fish for your life and spirit. Please give me strength and endurance for the journey ahead. May your rivers, oceans and lakes forever be wild and pure." With driftwood set on two columns of flat rocks built up like bricks, I made a bench to sit on and a rack for the remaining fillets. The abundant driftwood afforded a large fire, which danced about in the evening sun like spirits reaching from the Earth. I feasted late into the night on the succulent flesh, roe and rice.

Chapter 39

Wolf: Spirit of the Wild

Sun broke through the clouds early the next morning. Gusting northwest winds and frigid temperatures promised a cold day for this, day 75 of the expedition. A series of shallow stretches required extensive lining, heaving and a short portage to carry gear on foot around impossible rapids. The winds blew the raft against the right shoreline. My paddling was no match when the winds whipped strong, pushing the raft to an abrupt halt against the shore. I would wait for the strongest gales to subside, while resting my arms, before pushing back into the river and paddling against the wind.

This made for strenuous, stressful travel. In an effort to save time I would try to either make quick scouts or none at all, when I could spot a route from my lower point of reference. Boulder fields presented seemingly impossible challenges, with fast current and innumerable obstacles. They were often strewn in stair-step fashion, requiring speedy maneuvers. But I usually managed to scrape by boulders without being stopped. I had less luck avoiding walls of waves that filled the raft and numbed my feet.

The mountains shone in the bright sun. The willows, with leaves now turning in the fall, formed a golden carpet that padded the valley floor. Foothills were painted a bright crimson from the changing leaves of lowbush cranberries and bear berries. A rainbow extended from one end of the valley to the other, in front of a great, unnamed mountain.

After a series of particularly rough rapids that sent waves over my raft, I narrowly made it to shallow water before hitting an impossible boulder field and rapids. I stared at the torrent of white caps for an hour, searching for possibilities. I finally decided to make a 150-yard portage over a narrow, boulder-strewn beach overgrown with willows. There was no possible route for my raft through the rapids, even counting on great luck and numerous bounces and scrapes.

The mighty Mount Michaelson had just come into full view to the east, with its pure-white cap shining brightly. The tundra was aglow in the bright afternoon sun, with scattered patches of brilliant red and yellow glowing on the mountainsides, dotted with white or gray boulders here and there. The river danced among boulders with white waves and turquoise brilliance. A small ridge of gold and brilliant red stood out before the soothing, gray mountain behind it, shaded now by the falling western sun.

Only a few hundred feet from the portage, I encountered another impassable spot. The shoreline ended abruptly in a steep ridge on the west shore, making portaging difficult. I paddled across to scout the other side. My intuition told me to portage as I looked down upon the river's fury. But my concern over the excessive delays said go for it. I had to get to Kaktovik or Steve would come out looking for me, at my great expense. I compromised, carrying my pack with me when I scouted the rapids and depositing it and my camera safely at the other end of the rapids.

The lighter raft with less damageable gear gave me added mobility and courage. But the rapids were the fiercest I'd encountered since the Kekiktuk. They required tricky maneuvers this way and that around boulders, through funnels, over small waterfalls and the subsequent hydraulics and walls of waves, and finally around a steep bend; all hoping I'd keep the raft from getting too waterlogged, so I could paddle to avoid slamming into the shale wall.

I had to pass a boulder, dart to the opposite side to avoid a line of boulders, turn and fit through a funnel. I narrowly missed the first boulder. Rounding it, I paddled hard to avoid the line of boulders just downstream. I didn't make it. I slammed head on into a boulder just 10 feet upstream of the funnel, stopping the boat to a jarring halt. Water welled up behind the raft, pushing down the stern. Water rushed overboard.

I jumped out the port side into the fierce current. Much of the river was funneled through the narrow section in which I stood thigh deep. The force was unbearable. Realizing I was in the main channel, I rolled over the raft to the starboard side and lowered myself into shallower water. The current made heaving the raft back off the boulder impossible. By using the current to help push, I lifted the side of the raft and it scraped over the boulder and headed straight toward the funnel.

Once off the boulder, I played tug of war with the boat. I had assumed that once off the rock, I would be able to easily pull it to shore. Heave as I did, I was slowly losing ground. The raft was so full of water that it was submerged, catching the powerful current like a parachute. The funnel formed a two-foot waterfall and a massive wall of waves. I could make it to safety easily if I let go of the raft, but the boat would likely be flipped and churned.

With the momentum from plunging down the waterfall plus a decided push from paddling I might just make it over the waves, I realized. It was either that, or leave my raft and food to the mercy of the unforgiving rapids. I leaped onto the raft, sending it moving. I managed to get in a few strokes and a sweeping turn to miss the right boulder of the river's narrow gate. The plummet down the fall was exhilarating. The raft hit the water wall with unstoppable momentum. Water crashed over me. I hollered for joy, and bailed out enough water to maneuver around the sharp bend.

The sun dipped lower in the western sky, falling below the high ridgeline that rose steeply from the shore. This was a narrow chasm apparently missed by the wide-carving glacier. Without the warmth of the sun's rays, I quickly chilled. My hands were nearly inoperable when I clumsily pulled the raft onto the west beach. My fingers stung from the cold and my clothes were soaked. Rafting had left me chilled. I set up my tent and prepared to call it a night. But it was so early. I did not want to stop. Looking across the river, Mount Michaelson glowed in the evening light. Above me to the west, on my side of the river, a ridge reached up several thousand feet.

I climbed the steep ridge west of camp, higher and higher. Warm blood soon thawed my feet and hands. First they throbbed in pain with each beat of my heart. I'd faced frostbite before, and knew the pain to be a part of recovery. Soon my extremities were warm for the first time since the morning fire. Cresting the ridgetop that formed the base of Kikiktat Mountain, I was greeted by the sun, still high above the western horizon. The sun cast a shadow across the river valley and against the base of the opposite ridge, moving slowly south and up as the sun traveled north and lower on the horizon.

Firelight flickered above the rock-strewn beach in the low evening sun, long blocked in this valley bottom by the western ridges. Mount Michaelson and Tugak Peak glistened across the valley. I noticed some fresh, large wolf tracks. These wise hunters, weathervane of the Arctic's health, had walked through my camp while I was hiking. Following the tracks down the beach, I came upon some firm dog-like droppings full of caribou hair. The center of the pile was still warm despite the 30-degree temperature, indicating that they were nearby or their dung would have cooled in the whipping Arctic wind.

I took a few deep breaths, preparing myself for the call. I had learned it from a Gwich'in in Arctic Village. It begins in the soul, he instructed, and flows from the heart. Starting with an "Ah" the pitch escalates in a glorious howl, full of passion and force. After a brief, high-pitched howl, it tapers off into an extended wail of emotion.

From the high western ridge I had recently descended, came a howl as wild as the river, followed a split second later by a second high-pitched call, both tapering in harmony to a long, gloriously wail. The calls were longer, more pure than mine. I envisioned two wolves on the ridge top, with heads thrown back. We connected as two of the most intelligent mammal species, one calling the Arctic home, the other a visitor. The connection between me, and a species my culture has long persecuted, was for me powerful proof of my soul's long belief: that these are special creatures to be respected, loved and above all protected.

Among mammals, wolves once had a geographical range surpassed only by humans. That was until humans intervened. Now they have been slaughtered from all but 3 percent of their range. There are only a few places left where wolves live free. In a nation founded on conquering nature, wolves have long been the front runner in U.S. government extermination efforts. The U.S. government paid bounties to exterminate these loving animals from the lower 48 states. Now they survive in only a few areas.

In the mid 1990s, Alaska Governor Walter Hickel passed and implemented a wolf annihilation program that is devastating the wolf packs in the Yukon flat region that forms the southern range of the Porcupine Caribou Herd, and this great Arctic ecosystem. Hickel said, "Nature can't just be let to run its course. It must be managed." Nature did a pretty good job for the first three and a half billion years. It's Hickel's slaughter management style that causes problems.

In 1991, U. S. Fish and Wildlife Service Arctic National Wildlife Refuge Biologist Fran Mauer said, "Wolves in the coastal plain are vulnerable to being hunted out. The federally-funded wolf control program really hurt the population. Hunters try to keep the population in a pit, and they can't get out. We've noticed a marked decline in the wolf population with the recent increase in sheep hunting." Dall sheep numbers, too, are in marked decline because of hunting, Mauer said. If, as my earlier companions claimed, dall sheep were falling prey to wolf and not the hunter, sheep numbers should be increasing as the number of wolf decline. The fact that they, too, are declining in tandem with their predators indicates it is human hunting that is taking the toll.

Throughout fairy tales and stories, the wolf has been characterized as evil, vicious and mean. The analogy of wolves and men in western society dates back to Greek philosophy. Following the ancient proverb "Man is a wolf to man," Thucydides rationalized Athenian enslavement of Melos islanders. His reasoning: their naval empire was stronger, and therefore it was entitled to do as it wished.

This is a complete misunderstanding of wolves—if we were in fact like wolves to other humans, we would live cooperatively, without war and in harmony with our environment. Wolves are able to hunt larger animals by working together as a team. They live in packs ranging in size from about 10 to 20. Their territories stay generally the same from year to year and are well marked by scent posts of urine. The pack is one of the most complex and developed forms of social organization in the animal kingdom. "Parents, pups, grand-parents, uncles, aunts, cousins—many generations of the same fam-ily—all live together in a remarkably amiable, efficient manner," wrote Dale Brown in *Wild Alaska*, 1972.

Packs are organized with the wisest and strongest animal as the leader. Wolves form strong emotional ties within the pack, and work together in amazing unison during hunts. They follow regular sched-ules, often assembling in late afternoon or early evening, with much tail wagging and frisking, happy to see one another. Despite stereo-types of a ferocious, independent, selfish animal caring only about meat, wolf biologist Dr. Gordon Haber found that "food brought back from a successful hunt is always ignored temporarily while the entire pack engages in an intense round of nose-rubbing, face lick-ing, hugging of one another with paws, romping, whining, crying and generally ebullient displays of play and affection."

Koyukon natives a few hundred miles west and south share "a strong sense of shared communality, a kind of shared identity," with the wolves, anthropologist Richard Nelson found. "This remarkable and elegant animal is also given great spiritual power in the Koyukon world. One elder said he does not like killing wolves because 'They're too smart, too much like people.'"

In the spellbinding moments of silence that followed my com-munion with the wolves above, I stood still, in awe. To howl with a wolf connects us to our wild roots. Brilliant sunset colors shown above the western ridge, extending like rays of hope into the black-ened valley.

Wolves once roamed all of the lower 48 states, keeping the ecosystems in balance, culling the deer and smaller animals. Today, newspapers are filled with stories about how many animals, lacking natural predators, are overpopulating, causing car accidents when crossing roads among other problems. While wolves take the weak and sick, human hunters tend to take the strongest. Our actions, altering the balance of weak and strong in the opposite direction from what the wolves do, can have a devastating impact on animal populations.

With wolves having been extirpated from 97 percent of their former range, the greater Arctic Refuge ecosystem is a critical refuge for them. To have the Governor of Alaska promoting the massacre of these wolves in one of the largest refuges they have in the United States is ecological insanity.

Chapter 40

Sandstorm

The morning sun illuminated the white-capped Mount Michaelson that towered to the east. I felt as confident as the wolves. Rafting conditions were perfect, with no wind. I hustled to eat a quick breakfast, pack my gear and push off into the river before the wind decided to change.

Shortly after leaving, a frigid northern wind whipped up, slowing my progress downstream and pushing me against the shoreline. Gusts made maneuvering impossible. I hit two boulders broadside. The raft filled with water. I jumped into frigid water and heaved the raft free.

With the thermometer hovering around freezing and the addition of a considerable wind, every splash of water was a dreaded, lingering chill. Shallow riffles required me to jump out into the Arctic waters and line the raft—soon numbing my feet. Paddling kept my upper body warm; the cold winds chilled my wet legs. At least when I splashed through the water I was moving them. Warm blood refreshed my numbed, cramped body. When less active, the blood slows and limbs can easily frostbite. My feet were nearly always numb through the rafting trip. I could only hope my toes were still alive.

The winds gusted stronger and stronger. I propped my raft up on my paddle as a temporary shelter against the wind and ate lunch. What had started as a perfect day turned into nightmarish rafting weather. I had serious doubts about making it to Kaktovik, because I knew the weather would only worsen. Wind gusts sent sand flying, pelting my skin. Clouds of sand whipped up by the blustering winds could be seen for miles upstream, looking like low-lying fog or mist. I watched the clouds approach as I scurried to protect my gear, but I soon found it hopeless. Sand is notorious for clogging and breaking zippers, fishing equipment and stoves.

Setting up my tent in the gusting wind and sandstorm, it blew several hundred yards away, requiring a lengthy chase. It evokes comical images and memories today but at the time this chase was in the midst of utter frustration. I tied the rear of the tent to a huge rock with clothes line, and laboriously tied each corner to big rocks. The storm was furious, pelting any exposed skin with sand. Try as I might to keep it from my tent, by angling the door away from the wind and covering it with a rain fly, a lot got in. While trying to zip up my sleeping bag, which already had a somewhat dysfunctional zipper, it suddenly stopped and jammed. I could not free it. Patiently, I picked at it with a needle for more than an hour, but it would not budge.

Sand also broke the zipper on the main compartment of my pack, a zipper that had withstood seven years of heavy wear and tear in some of the remotest regions of North America. After hours trying to repair it, I gave up. I punched holes along each side of the zipper and laced it together with clothesline. Now my pack required laborious lacing that did not provide the rain resistance and ease of the zipper. Small items had to be moved so they would not fall out. And the gear I needed most crucially to function properly was stuck open.

I lay in my tent, frustrated by the long delay and the sudden failure of these two critical pieces of equipment. I was way behind schedule. Getting to Kaktovik in time to avoid a search for me by Steve was becoming tougher with each delay. And the weather would only get worse. Steve had told me of one August when 20 inches of snow fell in the Hulahula Valley in a fierce blizzard. It was now August 25. I watched the barometer slowly plummet on my high-tech watch. I felt and watched the temperature drop as well: falling below freezing, then to 25, then 20. I wanted to do something but there was nothing to do as long as the wind was whipping torrents. And with the colder weather, rafting would be too cold.

Drifting into a light sleep, I dreamed I was climbing a mountain. I awoke with my mind on hiking. More than anything, I wanted to leave my tent. I knew I had to be traveling if I hoped to reach Kaktovik, but the weather prevented rafting. The wind was not going to die down soon. I climbed the mountainside behind camp. My legs had been cramped from sitting on the raft and lying in the tent. Up and up I went. Hiking without a pack was easy.

I looked down over the wide river valley below, and the waves of sand blowing across the gravel plain. Rafting was out of the question. But why not hike out? It made sense—I could hike in drizzle and heavy winds, and I could quit worrying if the patches would hold. But this was a rafting trip. I loved the challenge of the rapids. Besides I had too much food to carry. Rafting afforded easy travel when the weather was nice. But with hiking, at least I would be doing something to progress toward the Inupiat village, and to safety. I thought back to the thrill of the rapids and those first two relatively easy days, when the wind somewhat cooperated.

I admired the unique beauty of the sandstorms that danced along the river valley. From high atop the west ridge I watched blasts of sand sweeping up the valley. The sand clouds swirled around boulders and obstacles: spinning about with fantastic spiral whirlwinds on either side of boulders before joining back together beyond the obstacle.

See the purpose of the wind. It sees obstacles as opportunity for creative, exciting action. It whirls around them, dancing. Then it unites together again as a mighty force. I was like a sandstorm. Hit with obstacles I was whirled about and delayed, but I stayed on course. Seen over time, such challenges are exciting opportunities, creating a dazzling interplay of life. We are but sweeping storms of sand. Sometimes moving in great valiant force. Sometimes lying still. Always influenced by the greater forces about us, whether we see them or not.

It was late evening before the winds died down. I returned from my hike. Plummeting temperatures and fog chilled my body. I wanted to raft farther. Temperatures fell into the teens, then to the single digits. I shivered in my half-opened sleeping bag. Rafting would surely bring death from hypothermia. Again I fought back concerns over the delay, drifting to sleep with a troubled mind.

At seven the next morning, I peered out of my tent to see fog and low clouds threatening another stormy day. Bundled in all the clothes I had brought, I blew up the raft tight and shoved off into the river. The rapids were as fierce as ever. But so was my determination. One after another I challenged the white caps and boulder fields. Long stretches of shallow riffles required wading in the frigid water.

Several hours into the morning's journey, the clouds began to lift, rapidly changing the scene from the white fog of introspection into the spectacular clarity of exploration. I saw a plane circle and land about a half-mile down river. Reaching the single-prop Cessna and the lone man that walked about lazily, I eased the raft into an eddy and pulled up on the beach. It was a man I had met in Arctic Village named Don. He was waiting for the fog to lift to pick up a camera crew at Sunset Ridge.

They were working on a documentary about the Arctic Refuge. He had heard of my earlier adventures in conversations around the community eating area.

"You said you ate edible plants. Could you show me some?"

"Sure," I said. I plucked off some young willow shoots and leaves that had not turned color yet, and shared them, along with some bear berries and pink plume leaves. "Willow leaves are loaded with vitamin C. They have ten times the vitamin C per weight as oranges. I don't see any here, but you can also eat wooly louseworts, parry's wallflower and bear root."

"Aren't you worried about traveling alone, with bears and all?" he asked.

"No. Bears and people have coexisted for millennia," I said. "I am having some problems with my raft, though. Do you happen to have any super glue?"

"No I'm afraid not."

"I think I'll be fine. The fall is so beautiful here."

"Those are bright colors. That sounded like some adventure you were on. I heard you talk about it at Arctic Village."

"Yeah, it was some trip. This rafting expedition has been quite adventurous as well. That was some gathering too," I said, referring to the Gwich'in gathering.

"They are the nicest people."

"God help their struggle," I said.

The clearing sky revealed the mighty Mount Chamberlin with its white cap and glacier to the southwest.

"Could you take a picture of me?" I asked. I posed in my raft with Chamberlin's heights in the background. I had seen the other side of Chamberlin's face while rafting across Lake Schrader. Past and present were intertwining with each encounter. I bid him farewell and pushed off into the river.

Chapter 41

Patches

I stopped for lunch at a particularly aesthetic spot on a narrow beach just before the river snaked between high walls of rock. Higher light-gray mountains towered in the distance above the darker, vegetated slopes. Just to be in such a place uplifted the spirits. The next set of rapids presented numerous challenges. I contemplated the route over Ramen noodles, crackers and tea.

I maneuvered around rocks and through a funnel. Waves poured over the raft, making it unresponsive. The river turned sharply to the left, blocked by a high cliff wall of jagged shale. I paddled furiously to try and slow the raft as I hurled from the rapid's momentum head on into the cliff. The paddling seemed to do no good. The raft was submerged too deep, and was headed straight for the wall of jagged protrusions. A deep whirlpool formed just in front of the wall. Just before slamming into it, I leaped over my equipment and shoving my paddle like a jouster into the wall with my feet wedged against the raft's sides. But the momentum was too great. The raft slammed into a sharp protrusion. I watched the shale rip a three-inch gash in the thin vinyl in a loud, tearing sound. "Ahhhh!!!"

The forced turn in the river formed a deep pool and a giant whirlpool that I was now caught in. The water was turquoise and deep like the earlier fishing hole. Air bellowed out of the raft as I paddled with all strength to reach shore. But the rain-logged and quickly deflating raft resisted movement out of the whirlpool. My seat sagged. I nearly fell out. I jumped into the wet center and renewed my determined thrusts of the paddle.

Slowly the raft moved. But the deadly swirl of water sucked back. The raft began to bend. I had little time. All force, all concentration was on the paddle. Ever so slowly, seeming like eons in the super intensity of the moment, the raft inched towards shore. Water began to pour over the edges of the sagging craft. I jumped out into four-foot deep water and waded my tattered boat to shore.

I stood, staring at the gash for some time. "This is the last thing I need. Now how am I going to make it?" I considered abandoning it and hiking out. But that felt like quitting. I set to the task of repairing the rip. After unpacking my gear, I turned the raft over, so the section with the gash faced up, to dry in the sun. I marveled at the spectacle of mountains and the raging, wild river that cut its course through the steep valley.

I patched the rip with a rubber patch, reinforcing it with duct tape. I knew it would easily rip off and would probably leak as the other rubber patches had. But it was all I had. I hoped care and good luck might keep it in place. Several strong blows into the raft and I knew it was a failed patch. Air whistled through the hole.

But it didn't leak that bad. And I had to get moving. Unsure of the raft's safety, I turned my attention to the river. Just downstream, it snaked around several more tight corners of jagged shale below fierce, uncompromising rapids. This was the chasm of the Hulahula's fiercest waters. With the raft blown up and my gear stowed, I waded into ankle-deep water. I hoped to make it through the rapids before it deflated too much.

The patch held through two rapids. I had to blow it up before each and during a stop in the middle of the second. But the third set looked especially rough. It was a narrow chute steeper than anywhere I had yet seen. The water was funneled through the center, forming a long chain of waves from the sheer speed of the descent. Keeping a dry raft would be impossible. Just below the chute was a short boulder field requiring tricky maneuvering. With a water-logged boat, I had doubts I could make it.

I stood high above the west ridge overlooking the river and contemplated the best route. If only I could stop to empty the water from my raft after the waves and before the boulder field. If I paddled backward to slow the pace during the plunge through the chute,

I could utilize the last wave to slow my raft enough to make the maneuvers, even with a waterlogged boat. As long as the raft did not become completely full, I had a reasonable chance of making it. Below the boulder field, the river turned sharply, with a jagged-cliff wall threatening another puncture.

The river was fast. I paddled backward, slowing the raft just enough to flow over the first wave instead of barreling through. But the momentum from crashing down the other side sent the front of my raft deep into the next wave. Water crashed overboard. Subsequent waves filled the raft full—nearly sweeping me out several times. The constant crashing and flood of water over the raft made paddling impossible. It was all I could do to stay on board. I was powerless to alter its course.

Crashing through the last wave of the chute, I regained my balance and thrust my paddle into the swift current, paddling with all my might to slow the raft before it slammed into the boulders. With a diagonal pulling stroke, I both slowed the waterlogged boat and pulled it away from a giant boulder directly in its course. The front of my raft hit the rock, stopping it in a shudder. The fast current spun the rear of the raft around with the boulder as an axis, affording me time to quickly bail water out.

I had counted on the raft staying on the pivot through the turn. But just halfway through the turn, it slipped off, sending me cascading sideways into a large wave below. The wave over-topped the boat, nearly washing me away. It succeeded in taking perhaps the most precious thing after my life: my paddle. Just twenty feet away the river turned 90 degrees, stopped by a vertical, jagged and sharp cliff wall.

Now I was paddleless to face its wrath.

I yanked the broom handle from under my equipment and quickly analyzed the rapids just ahead. The sagging bottom of the boat hit a submerged boulder, slowing me briefly. Scraping off, the cascading river resumed its strength, hurling the raft head on into the wall. I jumped belly-first onto my equipment and thrust the broom handle forward like a jouster with a lance. The wooden pole hit the rock hard, and I braced against it, my feet wedged in the rear of the raft and both arms thrusting with all strength against the momentum of the boat and water. The raft stopped one-foot clear of the jagged cliff. The current pulled me backwards through some more rapids. Finally I reached an eddy. By poling the raft with the broomstick, I reached shore.

I pulled the raft to high ground and ran downstream after the paddle. The river current was swift, but so was I. I hurtled boulders and charged through willow thickets, slowly gaining on the paddle, which was clear on the other side of the river. Just ahead the beach ended in a steep cliff. The paddle caught in an eddy, and I gained a 100-foot lead before I plunged into the river. Deeper and deeper I waded, passing my waist and nearing my chest. The current made footing precarious and the chance of being swept into the rapids below increased with each step. The paddle slipped from the small whirlpool and continued downstream in a trajectory about 10 feet past my reach. I half swum, half jumped in great leaps, just catching a corner of a blade with my outstretched hand. I pulled it to safety.

I emptied water from the raft and re-inflated it. Soaking wet but wild with enthusiasm, I plunged into the rapids I had scouted on the way back from retrieving the paddle. Giant waves nearly filled the raft with water. In the brief stretch between rapids, I cupped it out as fast as I could, hoping to avoid the lengthy delay required to stop and empty it. But I had to stop after the next stretch of rapids. The air bellowed through the loose patch and my raft had deflated to a dangerous level.

It was around 7 p.m., and I made a large fire to warm up, dry off and cook dinner: four cups of brown rice with curry and powdered milk, my staple. Nearby, huge crashing waves were created in an awesome display of power and beauty. It was a vivid manifestation of the wild spirit of the mountains. Rafting it had been so exciting and exhilarating—at first. But the patches weren't holding.

I scouted the rapids, plotting a potential route while sipping hot tea. They looked difficult. I considered portaging. But that was time consuming and cumbersome, particularly with the steep, boulder-strewn shoreline lined with dense thickets of willows. The waves were huge. It was an exhilarating ride and I went through the white water without a hitch. The next set of rapids were impassable, with a line of boulders extending all the way across, without room for a boat to fit through. By the time I finished the portage it was 11:30 p.m., and the sky was brilliant in sunset. I realized I had lost my gloves, apparently at the spot I had stopped at for lunch. High ridges abutted the river. I was exhausted and the sun had long set below a ridge to the north. It would soon fall below the horizon.

I set up my tent and pondered the thought of an evening hike to rescue my gloves. But the fast diminishing light and the realization of just how exhausted and cold I was convinced me to call it a night, and forget the gloves. I hated the thought of losing them. Gripping the aluminum paddle in the morning would be cold with bare hands. But a hike in the morning would take too much time. I was already behind schedule.

I stretched out in my sleeping bag. I knew my situation was becoming precarious. I had six days to reach Kaktovik. I then had to fly to Fairbanks, for which I did not yet have a ticket, then catch my plane at Fairbanks, with a connecting flight in Los Angeles back to Ohio. Both tickets were non-refundable and non-changeable.

My raft was in pitiful shape, with numerous holes and poor patches. Without vinyl cement or superglue, patches just pealed off. There had to be a solution. Duct tape had not worked—it came off faster than the rubber patches. Blowing it up before rapids was becoming a time-consuming chore as the patches worsened. The only solution seemed to be to abandon it and hike out.

I wanted to raft, because of its excitement and, I thought, its speed. I was nearing the airstrip where Old Man and Old Woman Creeks converge into the river, where I had camped and crossed six weeks earlier. Hunters would likely use the spot, and they might have superglue. I had put so much into that raft, carrying it for hundreds of miles and spending hours patching it up. I couldn't leave it now. I was captain of the little vessel. I had pride in my raft even if it was now full of holes.

Besides, Barter Island was 40 miles of boggy tundra away, and across a channel of water. If I left my raft, I would be stuck at the channel. I could try and wave down an Inupiat to take me across the short channel to Kaktovik. But it was an uncertainty. Giving up the raft was giving up. Admitting defeat. I'd already failed to make it last time when I was rescued by helicopter from starvation. I didn't want to be defeated this time.

I spent the next morning patching my raft—or at least trying to. But I could not keep the rubber patches affixed. With the raft leaking badly, I plunged through the crazy rapids below my camp and around a tight bend. Waves poured over the bow drenching me and nearly washing me overboard. I held on, teeth bared and eyes winced from the force of the water slapping my face. My hands clinched the ropes that bound my gear in place. As I opened my eyes, I saw a new landscape before me. I had rounded the last bend of the mountains. The valley opened up just ahead: the golden plain lay ahead.

The patch was worse than ever. I used the last of the patching material. I tried to seal it with duct tape, spending several hours in frustrating attempts. I would blow up the raft full and push out, paddling hard. Soon water would spill over the sag where I sat. I tried to position myself over the center of the raft but it was extremely awkward. Wherever I stood or kneeled, the raft sagged, making my feet or knees prone to hitting submerged boulders.

The raft began leaking so fast that stopping and blowing it up took too long. I tried blowing it up while barreling down the river. Then I hit rapids, but the raft was still deflating. I kept blowing it up, even while I was rampaging through. The air spout was on the starboard rear of the raft, forcing me to kneel backwards to blow it up. Rafting was challenging enough watching where I was going but backwards it was a recipe for disaster. I made it through the first rapids by bouncing off boulders.

I hit a boulder head-on while I was stooped over blowing the raft up. One moment I was in the raft, the next I was rolling over my stuff then splash, I landed back first into the water. Now I was completely soaked. In spite of my shivering, I was not going to stop. I had to make it.

Blowing the raft full, I launched into fierce rapids. I maneuvered through, avoiding the boulders and survivng the waves. The river turned slightly to the left, with a high wall of rock as a backboard. The raft began to sag from the loss of air, distracting my attention from the needed turn. I nearly fell off backward from the quickening sag and water spilled overboard. I jumped in the center, awkwardly positioning myself to keep water from spilling over the sides. This delayed paddling needed to follow the river's sharp turn.

As could be expected I slammed into the wall with great force, though cushioned somewhat by the semi-deflated air chamber. Unsure if I'd ripped more holes, I felt powerless as the current pulled the raft slowly into the eddies of whirling water, and I was stuck again. Meanwhile air continued to leak. Now stuck in the middle of another whirlpool with a deflating raft, I paddled furiously. The raft grudgingly pulled out of the swirling pit. Air whistled from the main chamber. I jumped out and waded the deflating raft to the shore.

I was becoming weary from the increasing series of dangerous situations. I noticed an abandoned Inupiat fishing camp just down river on the other side. I blew up the raft again and lined it for the hundred yards to the camp. It was cluttered with rope, wooden sleds, crates and platforms. The site looked messy. It would be nice if they kept it cleaner, but in the greater picture it was a minor blemish compared to Prudhoe Bay's nightmare. Besides, it might have something I could use.

Having enjoyed playing with fire while camping as a youngster, I recalled burning nylon rope, and watching the balls of flaming, toxic plastic drip down in brilliant drops of bright yellow, trailed by black smoke. Building a small fire, I dripped melted balls of nylon around the failing patch. I was worried it would melt through the vinyl, causing even more problems. But I was desperate, willing to try anything.

It worked, I thought as the black plastic splattered perfectly half on the patch and half on the raft. Slowly and tediously I splattered nylon around the patch. But when I began to blow the air chamber up, the splatterings flaked off like wax, and air whistled out.

Repacking my gear, and blowing up the raft, I pushed out into the riffles. Every 30 seconds or so required more blowing, and soon I was blowing nearly constantly. I slammed into boulder after boulder. I didn't care anymore, and just let the raft pull itself off the rocks. My kneeling legs sank deep into the water, making them the lowest point. Then came rapids. I tried to blow up the sagging chamber between waves in the middle of one stretch and was nearly thrown over board. My knees slammed into a submerged boulder. They throbbed in excruciating pain. But the raft was still barreling downstream, and deflating.

Not knowing if my knees were functional, but realizing I had no choice, I jumped out of the raft into the swift current and pulled the raft to a halt. Finding that my knees were operational, though quite painful, I lined the raft for a while. Lining might just be the solution, I pondered while splashing through foot-deep water, over slippery rocks and around boulders.

Without my weight, the raft could go for about 10 minutes before needing to be inflated. It was nearing 11 p.m., and the sun had set behind the western ridge. It was then I noticed where I was. Old Woman Creek cut through the northeastern base of Kikiktat Mountain to the west, and Old Man Creek cascaded from the heights of Mount Michaelson to my right.

I stopped on a large island covered with willows about a half-mile up river from where I'd camped about a month earlier while waiting to cross the river. Noticing a flat spot surrounded by willows to block the wind, I shored up the raft, calling it a day. I tossed and turned in my drafty, half-zipped sleeping bag on the cold, bumpy ground. Cold winds were sweeping from the north. My watch showed the barometer dropping. A storm was coming.

Chapter 42

Rotting

I was on the raft, charging through rapids, in control. All was easy and luxurious. I slammed into a rock wall. My paddle fell out of the boat. Suddenly I was trapped in a whirlpool. Helpless. I couldn't move. Down and down I went with no end in sight.

I awakened from the nightmare without much hope. My right side was numb from the scant insulation buffering it from the frozen ground underneath. Drafts of icy air flushed heat from the half-opened sleeping bag, sending shivers through my body. I drifted back to sleep.

Having finally found a warm enough position around 4 to permit some sleep, I awoke at 7:30 a.m. I was determined to get on the river early and make at least 10 miles by lunch. Just 10 minutes later, as I readied to leave the tent, the pattering started. This was a land that receives only 4-7 inches of rain a year. Why all the rain! And why now, when I had a precious five days to reach Kaktovik? At least I had enough food.

I considered backpacking. But now that I was out of the mountains, the rapids should be gentler. Maybe I could line the raft. One problem with backpacking is I had taken more clothing and more food, because weight had not been a concern when floating down the river. I wasn't sure I had the stamina for even more weight than before. Water had seeped into the raft from the holes, and it would be a heavy load.

The constant patter of freezing rain, blustering winds and frigid temperature would make any activity outside dangerously cold. I was already bundled in all my clothes, wrapped in my sleeping bag and sheltered from the wind and rain by the tent, but was still shivering. If I could start walking, I would warm up. But I couldn't just leave my raft.

So the vicious circles of thought went, over and over, around and around: to hike or not to hike. And meanwhile I lay in my sleeping bag, doing nothing. The rain continued. I pulled my map out for the dozenth time. I had 30 miles to go. But the weather presented seemingly insurmountable challenges to travel. The rain died down around noon. Low gray clouds extended in all directions, threatening more rain.

I knew I had to do something. I considered lining the raft, but it was so cold. If only I could fix the outer air chamber. I inspected the large rip in the raft. I had only one more rubber patch large enough to cover the gash from the shale wall. Thoroughly dried and wiped clean with a bandanna, I roughed the area around the rip with a small metal scraper to increase the adhesiveness. Not having the vinyl cement I needed, I applied rubber cement, and pressed on the patch. The patch was cut with rounded edges to reduce the tendency of corners to peel off, patted into place then pressed to eliminate air bubbles.

I went for a walk while it dried. The valley was colored various shades of gold, from the golden-yellow willows to the brownish-gold tundra covering the lower slopes of Kikiktat Mountain, and the foothills of Mount Michaelson across the river. The mountains were a darker gray, casting a dark outline on the horizon. The tricks of depth played upon the mind, with nothing to place mountains in perspective. Old Woman Creek cut a deep valley through the long, flat-topped ridge to the west.

Returning from my hike around 2 p.m., the sky still threatening rain, I kneeled down, drew a deep breath and began puffing up the big, outer air chamber. "RRRIIIIPPPPP," came the awful sound. A full inch of the patch tore from the vinyl, tearing with it my one hope. Stunned by the final blow, I lifted my head from the hole, letting the air I'd just blown in blow back in my face.

Rain began shortly thereafter. I huddled in my tent. I felt powerless, unable to fix my one vehicle to safety. The raft for me was the exciting and exhilarating way to travel. It allowed me to enjoy the wilderness without the rigor of backpacking, and with all the excitement of the rapids. Now it was beyond repair because of a gash. With rain pattering upon the tent, I did not know how I would get to safety. I could line my raft. I was searching for a way in which I would not have to carry the massive load and be stuck at the Arctic Ocean. But I couldn't line the raft until the weather improved.

My stomach felt bloated, cramped and sick. I had diarrhea, and was quite uncomfortable. I held it in, hoping the freezing rain would cease. Finally I couldn't bear it anymore. I was already shivering. Another trip into the cold dampened and chilled me more. And so I lay, sick and trapped for two days, only exiting during brief breaks in the weather.

The one thing I could do was eat, and I did have plenty of food. I knew I should eat less or even fast to cure diarrhea. But that required discipline. Eating was one of the few pleasures left. But the more I ate, the worse I felt. On and on the rain pelted the tent. On the third day, I was becoming ready to brave anything. Wind whistled and the thermometer fell. Temperatures dropped below freezing.

Then, the rain turned to snow.

Opening my duffel bag from under the protection of the upside-down raft, I felt the last inkling of hope drop from my heart. Through the "water tight" clear bags, my once-white rice was now speckled with brown decomposing rice. The rice was ruined. All three bags—15 pounds of rice was gone. At least I knew what had caused the diarrhea. But I was counting on that food.

Chapter 43

Awakening

The white slopes of Kikiktat caught my eye, glistening in the afternoon sun that peaked through a mostly cloudy sky. I fought off the urge to retire to my tent. Hikes for me have always been the best way to sort out problems, and I was in quite a predicament now. Taking a journal, binoculars and camera, and bundling up with all the clothes I had brought, I set out to climb the mountain I'd long admired.

Wading across several channels of the river, I was engulfed in golden willows, partially covered in snow. It was a glorious sight—a marbled green, yellow and white carpeted valley. Surrounded by such beauty, my worries were soon forgotten. Reaching the foothills, I methodically climbed up the steep hillside, with short, rhythmic steps. Looking over the valley from just a few hundred yards up, I soaked in the awesome panorama before me.

Upward I marched, higher and higher. I took a roundabout way, following a small stream that cut through the mountain. By carefully perusing the contour map, I insured I was taking the most gradual-sloping route so as to climb to the highest point possible with the slippery ice and snow cover. The sparse willows turned to tundra, gradually thinning into moss and lichen. The stream turned into a narrow ravine before branching out and up slopes too steep to climb with the covering of ice and snow.

Wanting a better view of the river, I climbed out of the ravine—ever so carefully with the two-inch layer of snow. Following the contour, plus a bit up, I neared a sharp bend, nearly slipping several times. The snow-coated slopes were extremely steep. Rounding the bend, I encountered a huge rock ledge extending out over a cliff.

Standing on the end of the rock perch, I looked over the beautiful landscape. I had a full view of the expansive Hulahula Valley. The river was emphasized with the snow cover, appearing as a magical-blue vein through a valley of white. It is amazing how a layer of snow can completely change the look of a place. I followed the river up to where it disappeared around bluffs abutting the river. A steep jagged wall forming the backdrop of the river was among the scant land that was not white. The wall had a patchy appearance, white only in places where jagged pieces of shale protruded.

I had waited for three days when I could have been hiking. I didn't want to think that those days were wasted. Rafting was the ultimate in excitement, adventure and thrill. It was the easy way down the rivers.

It was like the lifeboat of material affluence, a false security. But material rots, rips and breaks. Consumer culture's relation to the automobile was like mine to the raft. We live in a self-constructed petrol auto infrastructure full of holes and sinking fast. Try as we might to patch it, it is doomed. Cars are the easy, comfortable way to travel. Just turn the key, press a pedal and steer. Millions of years of fossil fuels and trillions of dollars invested in roads, highways, automobiles, oil extraction, refining, pipelines and trucks do the rest. Once we have tasted of the easy way, it is difficult to think of another way. Ultimately, we must change. Oil and clean air are finite. The more we invest in an oil society, the more we take from our children. When oil runs out, what will be left? What about air pollution? Global warming? This Arctic Refuge?

The biting cold of the approaching winter made me decide to hike, not raft. There was no more question about it if I wanted to survive.

Chapter 44

Grizzly

Walking, I was made acutely aware of my weakened condition. My legs were weak because I had not backpacked in several weeks and I still had diarrhea. I had heard from trusted friends that fasting helps the digestive tract and can cure diarrhea. With the diarrhea, most of what I was eating wasn't being absorbed by my body anyway. So I decided to trust my friends back home. Besides, it would save food for later. Being nearly out of food anyway, I skipped breakfast and decided to skip lunch as well. I wasn't sure how it would affect backpacking.

It felt warm and good to finally be hiking. It was nice not having to blow my raft up while crashing through rapids and slamming into boulders. The blustering winds no longer swept me against the rocks. I no longer cursed the cold or the wind. I waded across Old Man Creek. On the other side of the Hulahula River was the confluence of Old Woman Creek into the river.

The snow-covered Sadlerochit Mountains shone in the afternoon sun, sculpted into a natural masterpiece. The tundra was painted red, yellow, orange and green, so much more colorful than a month ago. Rounding a crest in a small hill high above the river, I looked up to see a female wolf standing erect just 60 feet from me. She was large, some 100 pounds or so with a whitish gray coat and brown markings on her face. The hair on her back stood erect, making her look giant. Her eyes fixed on mine. She darted into her den. Bones of caribou, dall sheep and smaller creatures were strewn about.

Dens are kept clean of fecal matter and animal remains. The soft underfur of the mother's coat lines the chambers, creating a warm, cozy environment for the young. Newborn pups stay in the den for two or three weeks. When the pups are old enough to travel with the adults, the pack leaves the denning area, and the young stay in nursery areas with an adult baby-sitter. In our civilization we have yet to provide affordable child care while parents work jobs away from home. But it was long after the denning period, so this wolf was apparently just using the den to hide from me.

Finding a hiding spot behind some willow bushes, I stopped to rest and watch the den, hoping to see the wolf again. After nearly half an hour, she cautiously stuck her head out of the hole, sniffing the air. She looked right at me despite my being 200 yards away and, I thought, well camouflaged. I watched her through my binoculars as she looked me in the eye. Her eyes glowed yellow, with a narrow, horizontal slit. Gazing with another in the eyes transcends differences. It narrows the gap between species and connects whole worlds of understanding. The communal gaze ended. She scurried back into the den. It is no wonder she was scared. My species has long persecuted hers. Maybe one day our relationship will change, and the human powers that be will once again respect these great creatures.

The wolf was a symbol that this land was still alive. The truest treasure is life, and nowhere is life more evolved and in balance than in a complete working ecosystem. The lower 48 states have few working ecosystems left. The ecologist Aldo Leopold has pointed out that, for the ecosystem to work, all the parts must be present. Wolf and bear keep the system in balance, and alive with their enchanting howls and spirit. Without them, life is imbalanced.

I hiked between the river and a steep ridge, on a gradually sloping plain. Heavy cloud cover and fog limited visibility. Rounding a bend, I noticed a big brown splotch several hundred yards down river and approaching. My binoculars confirmed my fear: a grizzly! He was downwind, and couldn't smell me, making for a dangerous situation as this is how bears are startled, and sometimes attack.

Bears are afraid of people and will avoid us whenever possible, if they sense us before being startled. Bears have poor eyesight to begin with, and in foggy conditions will rely primarily on scent with their ultra-sensory olfactory glands, aided by their hearing. But this giant grizzly was ambling up the river with the wind, so he could not smell me. I wanted to alert it to my presence as far away as possible to avoid startling it. So I called out constantly and waved my arms. But, oblivious, on he came. Fortunately, I had read a lot about bears, having been warned so many times about them. I knew that an Alaskan was 50 times more likely to be killed by lightning than by a bear, and that bears are quite afraid of people. It is when grizzlies are surprised, food is left in a tent or when mother bears are protecting cubs that they are dangerous.

Bears spend six to seven months hibernating, without eating any food. While hibernating, mother grizzlies give birth in January or February to a cub weighing 8 to 10 ounces. Over the next several years, the cub grows more than 2000 times its original size to attain weights exceeding 1,500 pounds. It is this immensity in size that intimidated me. Full-grown males weigh three times as much as a lion and stand nine feet high. That's about 55% taller than me!

Onward the bear came. I walked toward the ridge, increasing the distance between our closest trajectories. The wind was blustering from the northeast. If the bear would continue straight down the river, and not toward me, I would be able to get up wind of it.

The closer he came, the bigger he was. Without anything of known dimensions nearby, it was difficult to judge just how big the bear was, until he neared. I held my breath as he came within 50 yards, then stopped, between me and the river. He stared at me. The number one rule in avoiding bear attacks is not to panic, not to run away and not to show fear. Fear casts one in the role of prey, which one may soon become. Above all one should try to get upwind so bears are not startled

I drew deep breaths, trying to act clearly. I pulled out my camera and snapped several pictures. I began waving my arms and shouting "hey ya hey," a chant that a Gwich'in elder had taught me to scare off bears. The grizzly stood up on two feet, far taller than me. It was an awesome sight. Bears stand up to better sense the adversary before deciding on either an attack or a retreat. Bears perceive our reactions, and make decisions accordingly about whether to attack. Hoping to get directly upwind of him, I moved slowly—somewhat toward the bear. He descended to all fours and began approaching. My heart beat faster.

The first time I'd seen a bear in the wild was in New Mexico during a backpacking trip through remote wilderness. I was 13 and we stumbled into camp, exhausted from 10 miles of steep hiking to the base camp of Mount Baldy. We walked into what was to be our camp to find a mother black bear standing on two feet in front of a tree, with one cub perched 15 feet up and another in a notch some 30 feet high. I snapped several pictures while our leader yelled for us to leave. As we stared each other in the eyes I'd felt her determination as she stood in defense of her young. Black bears are about half the size of grizzlies. That time, I made it to safety, living another day to make an encounter with the far larger version.

Closer the grizzly came. Closer I walked to get upwind. The wind was blowing steadily upriver. I still had a long way to go to get up wind. I began to doubt my plan. My trajectory actually brought me somewhat toward the bear, in order to get upwind at the nearest possible point. Maybe he'd think I was attacking and charge? Would he be frightened from my smell even if I made it upwind? Books and research are one thing. This was real life. The bear glistened a pure golden color, with a staunch, muscular body. I was awed by its size and strength. Its dish-shaped head and snout looked like a teddy bear, seemingly out of place on such a giant creature.

He looked annoyed by my presence. I couldn't blame him. More and more people had been using the Hulahula, which is also a favorite bear corridor. This grizzly had little more than a month to prepare for a 6-7 month fast. He needed fat to survive. I hoped I wasn't in his meal plan.

My heart began to race toward panic as we neared each other. Testing the wind with a wet finger, I sensed I was nearing upwind of him. But he was still approaching. I snapped more pictures, not knowing if I would live to pay for the developing. I waved my arms and hollered out. But he was not frightened. Why should he be? At

6 to 10 times my weight, with the ability to break the neck of a caribou with one swat of his forearms and 6-inch claws, he had nothing to fear.

The gap between us narrowed to within 50 feet. Bears are amazingly fast and agile, with a 20-25 mile per hour gallop and the ability to charge up precipitous slopes and down near vertical inclines. If he attacked, I would defend myself. I felt a welling of courage within. I planned how I'd swing my pack around and use it as a shield. I'd unstrap the paddle and thrust it at his tender nose and eyes, just like I'd read of others doing who had survived. But above all I wanted to avoid a tangle. I continued to move toward the river in an effort to get upwind.

Suddenly he stood up high with his nose twitching. I admired his muscular figure and beauty. I would have loved to hug him if I could communicate my peaceful intentions. He'd apparently caught my scent. Having not washed in two weeks, I wondered what had taken him so long. He descended to all fours and ran away from me. In a few seconds he covered what took me near half an hour to walk, disappearing over a far hill.

Bears fear people and need a home like the Arctic Refuge where most of us are visitors. Grizzlies crossed the Bering land bridge along with the first American people and spread throughout the continent. Like the wolves, they have been exterminated from more than 90 percent of their range, with scattered populations in the lower 48 states and larger areas in Canada and Alaska. Bears are particularly sensitive in the Arctic, where they grow until between 6 and 12 years of age before rearing young. Cubs stay with their mothers for up to five years. Grizzly bear populations in Prudhoe Bay have been greatly reduced. This is one of their last refuges.

As evening approached, my stomach was growling and my mind turned to food. I had fasted for a full day, and my diarrhea had disappeared. I felt pure, clean in mind and body. My thinking was more lively and creative. My senses were keener and my enthusiasm greater in spite of the hunger.

The bear is the king of fasting. Imagine not eating for six or seven months. It made my daylong fast insignificant. The bear spirit is worshipped by many native nations because of its healing powers. Many plants that bears consume are used by native people. The bear is regarded by the Koyokun people of north Alaska as being so powerful that every word spoken about them is carefully chosen. Bears represent fearlessness, healing powers and calmness.

I began retracing the bear's route. Gouges fully three-feet deep were torn from the tundra, where Old Griz dug for squirrels and squirrel caches. Smaller gouges here and there indicated places he'd dug for roots. Bushes stripped of berries and half-eaten plants marked the bulk of Griz's diet. He'd eaten fireweed, pink plumes, willow, parry's wallflower and wooly lousewort—all staples in my stews and salads. To the Sioux, the bear spirit represents the knowledge of medicinal herbs. Black Elk was said to have received bear-like powers from a vision. He could discern more than 200 different herbs.

I stopped at an area particularly rich in wooly louseworts to collect roots and petals. Throughout the evening I collected bear root, parry's wallflower roots and leaves, sourdock, bear berries, lowbush cranberries, pink plumes, cottongrass roots, sourgrass and lousewort roots. Before a roaring fire I washed, scrubbed and chopped the roots into chunks. With a kettle of some of the purest water on earth, I boiled the roots then added the greens. I added the berries and the sourdock later. They are loaded with vitamin C that can be destroyed with too much cooking. The ingredients blended well together. The roots were tender and succulent; the broth excellent in flavor.

The next day I awakened to a world of wonder. The Sadlerochit Mountains were sparkling white from an overnight snowfall. The morning sun made them glow in holy light. My tent door was faced toward them, and I was greeted with quite a morning spectacle. The turquoise river wound its way through a golden plain colored with splashes of brilliant red and yellow.

I caught an eight-pound male Arctic char. I ate about half of him for breakfast and took the remainder with me. Unlike before, I packed all of the fish except the intestines, as well as the fillets, as

I'd learned from the Gwich'in, to make an evening soup. I did not want to waste any of the wild creature I had caught.

Things were different now than when I came, and it wasn't just the season. I lounged in the tundra without looking first for any strange bugs or creatures. I felt at home in this Arctic land. No longer did I fear the roaming grizzlies after encountering one peaceably. The mountains were my pictures. The river was my kitchen plumbing. The tundra was my garden, carpet, restroom and bed. Earth's natural cycles kept it clean with showering rains.

Chapter 45

At Stake

As I walked down toward the ocean, feeder streams converged with the river. More and more caribou tracks came from the different valleys, combining into one large path that I followed. The tussocks and willows were beaten down, making travel far easier. Always the paths converged on the plain. The caribou gather together by the hundreds of thousands every June. They live cooperatively: a unified specie that congregate year after year.

I waltzed through green-yellow willows and fiery red lowbush cranberries and bear berry. My steps were light and easy, my attitude cheery as I continued hiking through nature in her finest splendor. Walking atop the crest of a ridge above the river, I scanned across miles of rich, colorful tundra. The pure Hulahula River cut a winding course from the distant snow-covered mountains, meandering through a sea of life.

Farther on, I noticed three orange stakes in the tundra. They were somewhat obscured by willow growth. I wasn't sure what they were. I felt a swelling of rage at my hypothesis. One had a mirror attached to its base for easy location by air. Yanking one from the tundra, my fears were proven right. The word "seismic" was written on its side in black ink. This was the site of seismic testing to find if and how much oil was underneath. Seismic testing involves the use of heavy explosives that damage the tundra, disturb wildlife and leave scars. But they pale in comparison to the massive destruction and toxic waste should the oil development proceed.

I lowered my pack to the ground and sat down, still staring at the stakes. All was so clean, so pure here. The river ran free and the landscape was open for miles. Caribou tracks and antlers reminded me of their recent presence. I felt a pain from the innards of my soul, a wrenching of the gut, like the feeling when loved ones are in jeopardy, but we feel powerless to help. I loved this land. It was a deep relationship born from hour upon hour of interconnection. To drill for oil here would poison the heart of this vast ecosystem the size of Texas. It would poison my spirit forever. I now knew far deeper the pains John Muir must have felt during his struggle to save the Hetch Hetchy valley in Yosemite from being flooded. He lost. At stake now is the furthest frontier of North America: the last Arctic Refuge.

To a big corporation, land was a commodity, a line item on a ledger. But to any lover of life it is the fabric upon which our species and the life of the entire planet depends. And this is among the most sacred of places, the core heart of a massive ecosystem upon which hundreds of thousands of caribou, 160 species of birds, thousands of musk ox, wolves, bear, fox, hundreds of other species, 17 Gwich'in villages and the people of Kaktovik depend. What greater sin could there be than to poison and befoul a place like this?

It was 10:30 by the time I stopped again. The sun was setting in a fiery display of red, pink, yellow and orange, marbled in the distant wisps of clouds. I stopped at a sharp curve in the river, where driftwood was piled high. The temperature had fallen well below freezing, making rests cold. Arctic winds chilled my sweat-dampened clothes. I made a fire and cooked the remaining fish. I ate some and left a little for breakfast piled under rocks hundreds of yards from camp for bear protection.

I felt a need to act in defense of the Arctic Refuge. In the glory—and terror—of the last several weeks, I had shut the oil threat from my mind. It is always easier to shut out the bad, and wish it away. The stakes shocked me back to reality. The impending oil development threatened a deep part of me. I had grown attached to this paradise of pure wildness. I would defend this wilderness—a warrior of the Earth called to duty.

Chapter 46

Change

Some miles into the next day's trek, a helicopter passed nearby. The large machine turned, approached slowly and landed 30 feet away. It was a U.S. Fish and Wildlife Service aircraft with three scientists and much equipment.

One young, clean-shaven blonde-hair man approached. Over the roar of the helicopter he yelled, "Are you all right?"

"I'm fine," I said.

"Are you with Steve Porter?"

"Yeah, he's my pilot. I'm a bit late."

"There's a search out for you. Where are you headed?"

"Kaktovik," I responded.

"You can't make it there," he said, shaking his head sternly.

"I figured I could flag someone and get a ride across the channel," I said.

"You can't make it from here," he repeated.

"My raft got lots of holes in it, so I am walking."

"You can't make it," he interrupted. "We're fully loaded or we'd take you. There is an airstrip several miles downstream. Do you have enough food?"

"I have plenty. I'm fine," I said.

"We'll notify Steve of your location," he said.

"Are you sure you're O.K.?"

"Oh yeah, I'm fine. Sorry if I caused any hassles."

"No problem, we're just glad you're alright."

"Did you see any grizzlies?" he asked.

"Yeah, one a few dozen miles upriver," I said.

"We saw five giant grizzlies feeding just upriver," he said. "We're just glad you're all right."

I didn't bother with my ritual request for superglue; my rafting was over.

The evening was spent in calm enjoyment, gathering roots for a stew. I had difficulty finding green leaves because most had changed color, losing nutrition and flavor. But the roots were rich with nutrients stored for the long winter ahead, making a fine Arctic soup with the char head, liver and heart creating rich, flavorful broth. Thousands upon thousands of snow geese flew in great flocks overhead, darkening the sky with their graceful beauty. As I had, they spent their summers in the constant sunlight of this Arctic paradise, then head for southern latitudes. The Arctic is a crucial breeding ground and flyway for the great flocks of migratory birds that connect our world in a global web of life.

The Arctic Refuge coastal plain is the route of a million king eiders, half a million oldsquaws and 300,000 snow geese. Bird watchers in Europe, Asia, Antarctica, South America, Africa and all over North America enjoy the songs of birds that give birth and rear their young on the Arctic's coast of life. They are the weathervane of our planet's health, and they are pointing to a very dismal future. International bird counts show that 70 to 90 percent of the number of migrating birds that existed two centuries ago are gone: their habitat destroyed and polluted. Every year more disappear. Extinction is the direction we are headed.

The next day, I heard the buzz of a plane in the distance, and saw it approaching. I threw sphagnum moss and yellow grass on my campfire for a smoke signal, and waved my arms. I saw the white and blue markings and knew it was Steve. As he approached I waved my arms, and he turned to circle. After a full circle, he flew some 30 feet above the ground and dropped a brown paper bag with an orange ribbon tied around its top.

I ran to grab and open it. It was full of candy and a sandwich. A note tied to it read "Can't land here with Cessna. Could bring tundra jumper. Signal: Two arms stretched up: hike to landing strip 6 miles downstream—by orange stakes. One arm up: I'll return with tundra jumper. Lie down: send emergency help." The tundra was boggy, with no firm area to land. I raised two arms. Moments later, the plane tipped back and forth: the universal signal for acknowledging with an aircraft. Good, more time in the wilderness, I thought.

On down the river I hiked. I was saddened that I would soon be leaving. This summer was a time of solidifying a deep well of faith needed for a lifetime of service for Mother Earth in the uncharted wilderness of tomorrow. It was an experience that radically changed my life. Change was in the air. Millions of birds were already leaving their Arctic refuge, including many birds born just this summer.

I saw orange stakes across the river after hiking more than an hour down river. I did not think I had gone 6 miles as the plane flies, but I'd probably actually hiked that much with bends in the river and obstacles. I waded across the river and waited. I ate the sandwich and candy Steve had dropped. Steve flew by and circled awhile, then dropped another note taped to an orange ribbon. It read, "Wrong place, 2 miles down river, other side. Raise two hands if O.K."

I raised two arms. Steve tilted his wings back and forth. I hoisted the pack and plunged into the river. I entered the delta of the Hulahula River just a few miles from the Arctic Ocean. Great flocks of geese squawked overhead. A snowy owl swooped by in front of me, glistening like the mountains in all-white plumage. The owl was ready for winter, a permanent resident of the Arctic land.

I reached Steve's waiting plane.

"Are you all right?" Steve asked. "Have you eaten enough?"

"Oh yeah, I'm fine. Thanks for the dinner drop."

Steve tied my gear in place. The plane bounced over the tundra "runway" slowly gaining speed. The wings pulled us up. The river cascaded down its gravel bed as wild and free as ever. The tundra was an uninterrupted wilderness of colorful beauty all the way to the mountains.

As I was saved that glorious autumn day, my exhilaration was tempered by the knowledge that the last Arctic Refuge is in jeopardy. Though the size and scale of the effort was daunting, I vowed to join the fight for its preservation. The final chapter of its fate has yet to be written.

Acknowledgments

Special thanks to my family: my mother, Joanna Kister, who helped in so many ways to make this trip possible, to my father, Robert Kister for his optimistic enthusiasm and support, my brother Scott and my grandparents, Carl and Bernice Hunsinger. It is they who helped me survive the dark night of my soul when freezing on the tundra through my deep attachment to life when it was so nearly taken away from me.

I want to give my thanks and praise to my high school journalism teacher, Sarah Ortman, for all of her courage to stand up to the principal and all of those who tried to censor me. It is through Mrs. Ortman's enthusiastic instructing that I learned the power and joy of writing.

Thanks to the many people who read and edited the book: Lola Lafey, Art Gish, my mother and grandmother, Jason and Jessie MacLeod, Patricia Westfall and many more. Special thanks to those who let me house sit to afford me the time to write: Patricia Westfall and Keith McPencow.

Thanks to all those who allowed me to interview them, not knowing if their words would ever find their way to print. Thanks to Ralph Izard, Richard Edgar, Ted Bernard, Chris Crews, Kevin Sanders, Dru Evarts, Ann Bonner, Tom O'Grady and the countless others who have helped me along the way.

Above all, thanks to the many environmental organizations and concerned citizens who have acted in defense of this great Arctic Refuge, and all of those who will take action, before it is too late.

About the Author

Chad Kister was born in Columbus, Ohio. He spent much time on his grandparents farm in rural Ohio where he learned to fish and gained a deep appreciation for nature from his staunchly environmental grandmother, Bernice Hunsinger. While earning the rank of Eagle Scout, he learned much about wilderness survival. Kister's love for writing flourished in high school where he wrote hundreds of articles, earning him National High School Journalist of the year and a full scholarship to college. At Ohio University, Kister joined the environmental movement that won numerous victories, as well as some defeats. Kister graduated with a journalism degree with honors from the Honors Tutorial College. Kister is currently working on his Master's Degree in Environmental Studies at Ohio University.

After the 700-mile journey through the Arctic Refuge in 1991 that is the subject of this book, Kister lobbied the U.S. government to do more at the Earth Summit with a week-long fast in front of the White House, and went on a speaking tour about the environment throughout Japan in 1993. He returned to the Arctic in 1993 to climb Misty Mountain. Kister organized numerous political walks from 70 to 849 miles long, and is now the coordinator of Dysart Defenders, a group working to save one of the last ancient forests in Ohio. He is also the coordinator of the Arctic Refuge Defense Campaign and has personally lobbied senators and representatives with his first-hand experiences of the Arctic National Wildlife Refuge and thousands of petition signatures. In addition to working politically to protect the environment, Kister strives to minimize his impact on the Earth by walking, bicycling and using mass transit when possible and growing much of his own food.

Color photos and maps of the journey are at www.arcticrefuge.org where a CD with high quality maps of the entire Arctic Refuge and hundreds of photos can be ordered.

He can be reached at www.chadkister.com or www.arcticrefuge.org